INDIAN WOMEN
WORK AND DEVELOPMENT

INDIAN WOMEN
WORK AND DEVELOPMENT

Volume Three

DR. ANITA ARYA

GYAN

GYAN PUBLISHING HOUSE
New Delhi-110002

INDIAN WOMEN
WORK AND DEVELOPMENT
[*Women Study, Sociology*]

ISBN: 81-212-0626-X (Set)
ISBN: 81-212-0691-X

Published in 2000 in India by
Gyan Publishing House
5, Ansari Road
New Delhi 110 002

Laser Typeset at Alphabet, Delhi
Printed at Mehra Offset Press, New Delhi.

Contents

Foreword

I feel great pleasure and honour, while penning down this Foreword for Dr. Anita Arya's first book. I am further happy that this book is on women's studies, which must be the natural forte of a female social activist and a popular leader, which she certainly is.

For years, I have watched Anita Arya growing into a good leader, concerned with basic and vital social issues. She has come a long way from an humble party worker to her present status as Member of Parliament. In between she represented her people in the civic body and rose to become the first citizen of Delhi, as its Mayor. Since her entry in public life, she has never looked back.

It gave me an immense pleasure when I went through her lengthy work: INDIAN WOMEN spread over three volumes. The one thousand or so pages exposed me to a new world, which the women's world is. The way she has treated the subject and handled the material available is really remarkable. What pains she must have taken in collecting material and laying hands upon the original sources over the years, is another story. No doubt, she must be praised for her meritorious work.

Anita Arya, while preparing this book has worked in a large spectrum, which shows her clear understanding of the issues involved and her prowess to overcome the resisting factors whatsoever these were.

The peculiar speciality with Dr. Anita Arya is that she speaks politely, negotiates gently, debates strongly, concludes wisely and acts firmly.

Over a decade or so, I have seen her participating in meetings arguing the matters and making her points assertively. I have always marked her concern for the Indian women. She has her own ideas — based on observations and findings of course — on problems and perspectives, in regard to Indian women, a result of which is the present study.

Here, I take liberty to say that this book by Dr. Anita Arya is a different book on the subject, as it has the support of the experiences of a grassroot worker, practically involved in social activities and mixed up with masses. In this manner, this book has earned a status of a first hand study.

I believe — and quite strongly — that the scholars and readers will find the book thought provoking and eye opening and this is a fact which guarantees her success as an able editor and a good authoress.

As far as I know this gentle lady, known as Dr. Anita Arya, I can say without any fear of contradiction that she will rise steadily in life and career, scaling new heights year after year and achievement after achievement.

I wish her all success and look forward to her vital role as a parliamentarian during the next millennium.

Jagmohan

Preface

Women's world is a world in itself. Similarly, Women studies, as a branch of knowledge has become vast like an ocean. I am proud of being a student of this vital discipline, which has a large room for contribution and work. This effort of mine is a small step in the same direction.

Over thousand of years, our society has changed, a new civilization has replaced the old ones, people have developed culturally, economically and socially but an unfortunate section of the society in the East in general and in our country in particular is still living under the same circumstances, that is women. Their lot is same and they—barring a few fortunate ones—are either shackled, chained and bonded or they are bound to live under the dominance of the men, as ever. Ironically, that's true, in spite of the guarantee of the constitution, protecting laws and all the sincere efforts of various governments over the years. In fact, we cannot change the lot of a community or the whole social system altogether, in one go. Social change has to come from within and it takes its own time.

Throughout my two-decade involvement with women's problems and issues and my search for remedies for them, I have always found it challenging to work in these areas. As a grassroot worker and a down to earth social activist, since my student days, I have felt debted to do some thing for this happless group. I have done only a bit so far but I determine to do a lot in the years to come, in and outside Parliament. I have no illusions and realise that the path is ardous thorny and long enough. However, we have to assert and strive.

As my first humble contribution to women's studies, I am presenting this book of mine. Honestly, I was a bit confused when Gyan Publishing House urged me to compile and edit a book on Women and left the choice of the topic to me only. I had to think for weeks and months, before I decided to bring out a book on Indian women, covering all the concerning aspects. Hence this bulky study, spanning over one thousand odd pages and comprising three volumes. Notably each of these volumes is an independent book in itself.

Study of the prevailing status of women in our society is one of the core areas in women studies today. In order to make the work exhaustive and more comprehensive, I have divided it into three separate volumes, titled: (1) Society and Law, (2) Education and Empowerment, and (3) Work and Development.

The first volume approaches the study of women problems and prospects and the legal aspects have been examined in the socio-cultural settings.

The second volume provides information on women education and empowerment in a historical perspective.

The third volume is designed to provide information on gender and economic participation and the related problems of working women at various levels.

This voluminous book is the outcome of a painstaking research for years and compilation of materials from hundreds of sources, spread all over. In fact, I had begun this project, nearly a decade ago and finished it in over a five year period. So, for the last five years or so it has been lying for a thorough revision of the whole work, an excercise, which I carried out in the previous year only and that too at a fast pace, thanks to my overwhelming engagements in public life. One confession, I wish to make here is that I have not been able to devote my full attention to this work in its last phase and could not collect new data and other latest figure. I am afraid, if I would have opted for it, perhaps this book would not have been able to see the light of the day for another five years. So, I had to make a compromise and I regret for it. Truly speaking, this is the price, we 'politico-academics' have to pay, as public life is always taxing upon one's scholarly pursuit.

I hope this petty contribution of an humble fellows, would at least be able to stir the calm waters, create a sort of awareness among men and women and appeal to those who matter in our political and social system. If this much is done, I should feel honoured and privileged to have played a small role in the continuous process of social change and be apart of an ongoing historic struggle which is slated to be extended to the next millennium.

Dr. Anita Arya

Introduction

Women, today form an active section of the society, involved in all sorts of functions and performing all kinds of duties, shouldering man at each and every stage.

As far as rights and duties are concerned, Indian Constitution has clear provisions for the same. It states:

"The State shall not discriminate against any citizen on grounds only of religion, race, caste, sex, place of birth or any of them (Right to equality) etc."

"There should be equality of opportunity for all citizens in matters, relating to employment or appointment to any office under the State".

Thus, the Constitution has bestowed upon full rights to women, equal to men, for all purposes.

Today, women are active partners in the development of the country and work for it. In fact, women constitute a vital part of the work force in any business establishment and even in industries. Now, they are joining those professions as well, which were earlier considered to be the domain of males only. In a responsible manner they share the burden of man.

Some of the scholars of women's studies have even gone to the extent to call women, the 'Workforce of India in Future'. I too agree with the expression.

In this volume, an effort has been made to present an analysis of various aspects of women, in the context of work and development.

What I strongly feel is that the biggest factor, involved in the change of the world of work is the existence and presence of women workers in our society. The women are today , managers, secretaries, assistants, clerks, peons, mechanics, operators and even guards.

Incidentally, this editor is not the first to think about or work on this subject. A few scholars have already done it, but, perhaps no one has so far dealt it as extensively and exhaustively, as I have made efforts to. Most probably, Mahatma Gandhi was the first to recognise the importance of the women power. He worked for the Indian women's emancipation tirelessly. He saw to it that the women in large numbers play a significant role in the movement for the freedom of the country, including Satyagraha and non-cooperation etc. Actually, he believed that women's participation in political life would pave the way for their overall upliftment and guarantee a respectable status for them.

Significantly, the increase in the number of female workers all over the world and in India, as well, has been registered through the last two decades and during the present decade in particular. In India, in 1991, there were 91.39 million women workers, while the total female population stood at 402 million (This is the latest authentic figure, which is available). After that a considerable increase in this number has been witnessed in all spheres. Certainly, this a good sign.

In view of the women's working potential and their vitality as workers and partners in development, this volume has been designed to provide information on gender and economic participation and the related problems of working women at various levels through the ages.

Editor

List of Tables

One

Women and Development

Policies, Procedures and Programmes

> We talk about a welfare State and direct our energies towards its realisation. That welfare must be the common property of everyone in India and not the monopoly of the privileged groups as it is today. If I may be allowed to lay greater stress on some, they would be the welfare of children, the status of women and the welfare of the tribal and hilly people in our country. Women in India have a background of history and tradition behind them, which is inspiring. It is true, however, that they have suffered much from various kinds of suppression and all these have to go so that they can play their full part in the life of the nation.
>
> —Jawaharlal Nehru, Foreword to *Social Welfare in India*, 1954

Indian planners have generally seen development as a process comprehending the entire social system. According to the Planning Commission on the First Five-Year Plan:

> Maximum production, full employment, the attainment of economic equality and social justice constitute the accepted objective of planning ... plan for development must place balanced emphasis on all these.
>
> Development touches all aspects of Community life and has to be viewed comprehensively. Economic planning thus extends out into extra economic spheres — educational, social and cultural. Second Five-Year Plan.
>
> This broad approach to development was to give shape to the policy of transforming India into a welfare State, as directed by the Constitution.

The overall development process envisages a share in the development generated by the Plan equally for women and men. Since the Constitution stresses the need for promoting with special care the educational and economic interests of the weaker sections of the people, the welfare and development of women received particular attention from the beginning.

The Planning Commission's 'Plans and Prospects for Social Welfare in India, 1951-1961' spells out social welfare services as intending to cater for the special need of persons and groups who by reason of some handicap—social, economic, physical or mental—are unable to avail of or are traditionally denied the amenities and services provided by the community. Women are considered to be handicapped by social customs and social values and therefore social welfare services have specially endeavoured to rehabilitate them.

The Planning Commission defined three major areas under which they have paid special attention to women's development: (a) education, (b) social welfare, and (c) health. The development of education for women has been already discussed. In this Chapter we shall examine the policies, provisions and programmes for women's development, in the fields of social welfare and health including the administrative agencies created by the Government of India to implement the overall policies regarding women's development, in order to assess the achievements in this regard.

The First Plan emphasized that, in order to fulfil women's legitimate role in the family and the community, adequate services needed to be promoted for her welfare. Well organized social service departments were needed in the States to initiate comprehensive programmes of women and child welfare. It recognized that the problem of high infant and maternal mortality was mainly due to malnutrition and undertook to develop (a) school feeding schemes for children and creation of nutrition sections in the State Public Health Departments; (b) maternity and child health centres; and (c) family planning.

The Second Plan emphasized the need for special attention to problems of women workers, since they were comparatively less organized and suffered from certain social prejudices and physical disabilities. They were also paid less because of the feeling that they were less suited to heavy work and were more vulnerable in situations which produced fatigue. The Plan stated therefore that women should be protected against injurious work, should receive maternity benefit and creches for children. It also suggested speedy implementation of the principle of equal pay for equal work, provision of facilities for training to enable women to compete for higher jobs and expansion of opportunities for part-time employment. Table 1.1 gives the allocation and expenditure on social services in the Five-Year Plans.

The main thrust of the Third Plan as regards women's development was on the expansion of girls' education. In social welfare, the largest share was provided for expanding rural welfare services and condensed courses of education for adult women. The health programmes for women mainly concentrated on provision of services for maternal and child welfare, health education, nutrition and family planning.

The approach in the Fourth Plan was a continued emphasis on women's education. As regards social welfare, the approach was to let the voluntary sector operate the bulk of departmental programmes. Governmental efforts were confined to the provision of institutional services for destitute women and women rescued from prostitution. The basic policy was to promote women's welfare with the family as the base of operation.

The outlay on family planning was stepped up to reduce the birth rate from 40 to 25 per 1000 through mass education and motivation, and with cooperation of voluntary agencies and local leadership. High priority was assigned to immunization of pre-school children and supplementary diet for children and expectant and nursing mothers.

The Draft Fifth Five-Year Plan indicates that priority will be given to training women in need of care and protection, women from low income families, needy women and dependent children and working women. A programme for functional literacy to endow women with necessary knowledge and skills to perform the functions of the housewife (including child care, nutrition, health care, home economics, etc.) will be launched for the age group 15-45. Special steps will be taken for the placement of follow-up of successful candidates under the exciting scheme of condensed courses of education and the socio-economic programmes.

In addition to production-cum-training units, managerial and sales training will be introduced to promote the marketability

TABLE - 1.1

ALLOCATION AND EXPENDITURE ON SOCIAL SERVICES IN VARIOUS PLANS

(Rs. in crores)

Head of Development	First Plan		Second Plan		Third Plan		Fourth Plan		Fifth Plan	
	Allo-cation	*Expdtr.*	*Allo-cation*	*Expdtr.*	*Allo-cation*	*Expdtr.*	*Allo-cation*	*Expdtr.*	*Allo-cation*	*Expdtr.*
1	2	3	4	5	6	7	8	9	10	11
1. Education and Scientific Research	149 (7.6)	-	273 (5.8)	-	660 (7.7)	-	98.22 (8.50)	-	1826 (3.46)	-
2. Health	98 (5.0)	-	216 (4.6)	-	226 (2.6)	-	226 (2.6)	-	816 (1.53)	-
3. Family Planning	0.65	0.15	4.97	2.16	26.98	24.85	315 (1.9)	-	516 (0.97)	-
4. Social Welfare	4.0 (1% app.)	1.60	19.70 (2.2)	13.44	32.00 (2.3 app.)	19.40	88.94	48.24* (1969-73)	229 (0.43)	-
(Social Services & Miscellaneous)	472 (24.1)	459 (23)	855 (18.3)	830 (18)	1492 (17.4)	1492 (17.4)	2771 (17.4)	-	5910 (11.17)	-
(Women's Welfare under Social Welfare Sector)	** 4.00	-	** 1900	-	** 21.70	-	** 73.06	-	** 62.91	-

Sources: (a) Planning Commission Government of India (Allocations on Women's Welfare Under Social Welfare Sector of Five-Year Plans)
(b) India—A Reference Annual 1974, pp. 159 (Allocation and % of the First three Plans)
(c) Draft-Fifth Five Year Plan-1974-79, Vol. I (Allocation and % of the Fourth & Fifth Plans) Govt. of India, pp. 83-85.
(d) *Indian Economy* - Datta, R. and Sunderam, K.P.M., p. 228 (Exp. & % on Social Services of First three Plans)
(e) Year Book—Family Welfare Planning in India—1972-73 (Allocation & Expdtr. of First three Plans) Govt. of India, pp. 6, 7, & 8.

* 1972-73 (Expenditure on Fourth Plan) is anticipated.

** Includes provision for other categories, e.g., children, physically handicapped, etc.

Note: Figures in parentheses indicate percentage of total allocation and expenditure.

of goods produced in different units. Under the Health programmes, the primary objective is to provide minimum public health facilities integrated with family planning and nutrition for vulnerable groups, children and pregnant and lactating mothers. The plan emphasizes the need to correct regional imbalances and provide services to meet the minimum needs of the community.

An examination of the Five-Year Plans reveals that in spite of the policy emphasis on welfare or investment in human resources, the share of investment in the social services in terms of the actual allocation has been steadily declining in successive plans. The objectives emphasized in the various plans, as well as the share of allocations indicate that among programmes specifically designed for women's development, the order of priorities up to the Fourth Plan has been education, then health, and lastly other aspects of welfare because it was generally assumed that all other programmes will benefit women indirectly, if not directly.

Programmes for Women's Welfare and Development: A Classification

Programmes for women's welfare and development may be classified as follows :

Programmes under Statutory Obligations

The suppression of Immoral Traffic in Women and Girls Act, 1956 provides for institutional custody and after-care programmes. The Maternity Benefits Act, 1961 has a provision for leave and cash benefits. Under the protective laws, women in organized industries are entitled to provision of creches and family welfare facilities.

Programmes for Development

Under this category can be included the largest number of programmes which provide essential services and opportunities to women for development, such as education, health, maternity and child welfare, family planning, nutrition, socio-economic training and certain community organizations.

Programmes for Special Group

These vary from State to State. Some special assistance programmes have been initiated to serve groups like widows, the aged and the destitute, in the way of pensions or homes. A programme to provide hostels for working women in urban areas was initiated in the Second Plan, and has been continued over all successive Plans. For girls from backward communities, Scheduled Castes and Scheduled Tribes, there is provision for scholarships, and free residential schooling in Ashram schools.

While there have been additions and shifts in emphasis regarding the concept of women's welfare and development under the various Plans, and in some cases programmes have been expanded or integrated with others under a new nomenclature, the nature and content of the programmes have not changed.

Agencies for Women's Welfare and Development

In pre-independence India, while provisions of health and educational services had been increasingly demanded from the State, social welfare programmes were administered mainly, by voluntary agencies. There was no comprehensive nation-wide programme to provide welfare services. After the attainment of independence, it was felt that social and economic uplift of the masses required Government assistance to strengthen the services rendered by voluntary agencies. The administrative structure inherited from the colonial Government was clearly not equipped for this task. The Central Government therefore created a new agency—the Central Social Welfare Board in 1953 to promote welfare and development services for women, children and other underprivileged group by providing assistance to voluntary agencies, improving and developing welfare programmes and sponsoring them in areas where they did not exist. Following the creation of the Central Social Welfare Board, the State Government set up, at the request of the Central Social Welfare Board, State Social Welfare (Advisory) Boards for the same purpose. This was necessary, as welfare is a State subject.

Even after creation of these Boards, there is no clear pattern in social administration. The responsibility for planning and administering women's welfare and development is scattered in various departments and other agencies of the government. The federal framework, and the need to involve voluntary or community organization in this task generally results in a three-tier structure of administration, with agencies at the centre, the State and the local level.

Agencies at the Centre

At the Centre, the major responsibility for planning and implementing women's welfare and development programmes rests mainly with the following: (i) Planning Commission; (ii) Ministry of Education and Social Welfare with its two specialized agencies — the Central Social Welfare Board and the National Council for Women's Education; (iv) Ministry of Health and Family Planning; (v) Ministry of Home Affairs; (vi) Ministry of Labour and Employment.

Agencies at the State Level

At the State level, there is no uniform pattern. Programmes for women's and children's welfare and development are administered by a large number of departments. All States have separate departments for Health, Family Planning and Education. With the exception of a few States, the Department of Agriculture and Community Development also is responsible for some women's programmes. In some States, the department of Local-Self-Government is involved in these programmes. Social Welfare departments or directorates as well as Social Welfare (Advisory) boards have been set up in most States. In some cases, they exist independently while in others they have been combined with education, tribal welfare, etc. A few States have set up separate directorate for Women's Education, or Women's Welfare.

The Committee endeavoured to collect information from all Central and State Departments concerning their special programmes for women's welfare and development. 12 Ministries of the Central Government indicated that they have some programmes for women's welfare. 19 States and one Union Territory indicated the existence of similar programmes. The replies were not comprehensive and often did not provide full answers to our questions. Two things, however, clearly emerge from these replies:

(a) These programmes, even when they have common objectives, are supervised and implemented by many Government departments without any effective machinery to coordinate their functions.

(b) Government departments, by and large, are not at all clear in their understanding of what constitutes welfare or development for women. Some adopt a comprehensive view, some a very limited one. A few regard improvement of earning power as essential for any development. Most are, however, content to adopt a somewhat charitable approach to welfare and equate it with assistance to women in distressed condition.

Since the major responsibility for social welfare and development lies with the Ministries of (a) Health and Family Planning and (b) Education and Social Welfare, we have examined them in some detail. The rest are only briefly enumerated.

Evaluation

It was impossible to use quantitative indices to measure progress in the implementation of these programmes. Owing to data. Particularly in the field of development, programmes specifically meant for women are very few and do not give a total view of governmental effort to improve the condition of women. The general programmes, designed for all sections of the population, do not maintain separate records of allocations or expenditure for women, nor has any attempt been made so far to evaluate their impact.

We were, however, surprised to note that with the exception of the Second Plan, all the others have confined their concern for women's development to only education, health and welfare. Conspicuous by its absence is any reference to the need for generating and improving employment of women. Even the Fifth Plan, which gives highest priority to employment generation, appears to accept the present low representation of women in the labour force as a natural order of things, which will continue unchanged in the years to come. This expectation appears to be in direct contradiction to the Planning Commission's own view, that utilization of idle manpower would be a tremendous force to speed up the process of development. It is also a denial of the Government of India's stated objective of the total involvement of women at all levels of national development.

It is interesting to note that all the agencies engaged in programmes exclusively for women, inevitably attach the highest priority to increasing women's earning power. But since these programmes are classified as welfare and therefore non-productive, they invariably enjoy lower priority.

This ambiguity and confusion springs from traditional middle class attitude regarding women's roles in society. It will continue to affect both planning and administration of women's welfare and development unless the objectives of such policies are clarified and given concrete shape.

Health Programmes

According to the World Health Organization, health is "a state of complete physical, mental and social well-being and not merely the absence of disease and infirmity." Health is both an important factor in the achievement of status as well as an indicator of social status, particularly for women, whose health is conditioned to a great extent by social attitudes. The health status of women includes their mental and social condition as affected by prevailing norms and attitudes of society in addition to their biological and physiological problems. Societies delineate women's roles partly according to their biological function and partly from prevailing attitudes regarding their physical and mental capacity. These social attitudes also influence the provision and use of preventive and curative health care, including maternal care. The health care facilities offered by a community in the form of medical, particularly maternity services for women, is a significant index of the emphasis that community places on the health of its women. Some studies in both the developed and developing countries have shown a definite link between low status of women and deficiencies in the knowledge and utilization of preventive health services.

In 1957 a study was made of the percentage distribution of ailing males and females both adults and children according to expenditure for treating the illness in six rural communities covering six districts in Maharashtra State with a total population of 37,000. The survey revealed that in the year under study there were 730 ailing females and 513 ailing males in the age group below 15 years. The percentage of males getting medical treatment was higher than females. The study also showed that more adult women had to be content with free or traditional treatment or no treatment as compared to the medical facilities used for the males.

Cultural Norms and Attitudes

The cultural norms that particularly affect women's health are the attitudes to marriage, age of marriage, the value attached to fertility and sex of the child, the pattern of family organization and the ideal role demanded of the women by social conventions. They determine her place within the family, the degree of her access to medical care, education, nutrition, and other accessories of health. In India, marriage is almost a universal function because of cultural and religious influences. The age at marriage and fertility rate have important demographic implications. The largest number of children are born to women who marry at the age of 19 years. Cultural insistence on the marriage of women in the early phase of their child bearing period leads to high fertility rate and each additional child is a burden on the mother, affecting her physical and mental health. Barrenness is regarded as a curse and the woman is always blamed for this. Though the desire for many children may not be, the desire for sons is widespread. The joint family system also has in many ways contributed to high fertility in India. It encourages early marriage and large sized families which appears as a source of collective economic security as well as emotional security.

The lower status of woman is the result of her dependence and lower educational and social position. Tradition idealizes her role as the mother, housewife and the distributor of food. It is customary in all Indian households for the women to serve the family first and then to eat whatever is left. According to our survey, 48.53 per cent of persons stated that in their families males eat first. In families affected by poverty, this generally results in still greater malnutrition for the women. The young girls as they grow up are taught subservience and self-effacement.

The process, therefore, starts at an early age and has very adverse consequences on women's health particularly at the time of pregnancy and child birth. From their childhood, girls are taught to be uncomplaining and to maintain strict secrecy about their physical troubles. With menstruation, taboos are enforced and restrictions placed on their movement. They are unable to either discuss their health problems, if any, or even visit the doctor. Later as a mother, with children depending on her for care and attention, the woman has a tendency to carry on until ailment overtakes her. Reluctance to visit a doctor, particularly a male doctor, arises out of these restrictions imposed on women from the beginning. Such social attitudes, therefore, lead to a general neglect of women's health and in view of their child bearing role, they are the greatest sufferers as compared to men.

A study of data from particularly the developing countries indicates that other health problems of women—the higher maternal and infant mortality, maternal morbidity, lower expectation of life at birth, malnutrition, mental disorders, suicide rate and certain sex-selective diseases are linked to their status and role in the society. Child bearing and rearing is still the dominant rolc assigned to most women in developing nations. In the context of low socio-economic status of the bulk of the population, this factor becomes adverse to good health in the case of women. All the developing nations are faced with rapidly growing population. Inadequate housing sanitation and poor medical facilities adversely affect the vulnerable segment of the community. Maternity, therefore, constitutes a special problem. The bulk of the stress and strain falls in the women who suffer from extremely poor health.

Health Indicators

The indicators of women's health status in India are drawn from two sources:

(a) Demographic trends, and
(b) Access to health services

They should be examined separately.

Demographic Trends

We have already drawn attention to the adverse and declining sex-ratio, higher mortality rate and lower life expectancy of women. The high birth and fertility rates, beyond doubt, contribute to the low health conditions of women. Starting with 1871, almost every census report has emphasized:

(i) The crucial role of female mortality;
(ii) The significant contribution of mortality in the age group 15-44 to aggregate female mortality;
(iii) The crucial role of neglect of female health in determining female mortality; and
(iv) The insignificant role of under numeration to explain the adverse sex-ratio.

Neglect of women was proved by customs like female infanticide then prevalent in certain parts of the country. Child marriage, premature consummation resulting in early child-bearing, overwork and malnutrition were cited as other causes of women's poor health. The census of 1931 drew attention to higher female mortality in the age group 5-10, and "at the reproductive age". Tables 1.2 and 1.3 indicate the high increase in female deaths in the age group of 1-4, in spite of some fluctuations, the mortality figures are higher than the 1960 figures throughout. Table 1.4 indicates that in total deaths under one year, female deaths increase with age group from one week to 6 to 12 months. This is true for all areas and over the time period.

The apparently low sex-ratio of deaths (female deaths per thousand male deaths) is actually due to large under-reporting of female deaths as compared to male deaths. The doubtful accuracy of SRS data on age-wise and sex-wise mortality rates has been demonstrated in a recent study. The difference between estimated and reported deaths of females is sometimes said to be as high as 75.69 per cent for rural areas and 59.07 per cent for urban areas in the lowest age group; 46.57 per cent and 35.47 per cent in the age-group 1-19; 58.56 per cent and 37.94 per cent in the 20-49 age group; and 50.2 per cent and 28.54 per cent in the 50+ age-group. This difference in the case of males is consistently lower.

All the available evidence leads us to conclude that female

mortality infact is higher for all the three age groups, namely, during infancy, childhood and during the productive age particularly in rural areas. The inference from this is that female mortality is due to the consistent neglect of female health.

TABLE - 1.2
SEX RATIO OF DEATH BY AGE, ALL INDIA

Age Groups	*1960*	*1961*	*1962*	*1963*	*1964*	*1965*	*1966*	*1967*	*1968*
> 1 year	850	871	864	857	834	856	825	836	840
1-4 years	986	993	996	987	989	997	1016	1012	988
5-14 years	898	952	901	912	874	892	905	901	868
15-29 years	1136	1190	1121	1141	1119	1109	1107	1102	1076
30-49 years	861	970	892	891	855	843	839	828	873
50-59 years	769	773	750	755	739	694	680	669	653
60 + years	884	927	895	895	860	870	848	851	835
Age not stated								850	796
Total	904	943	910	911	886	1139	881	878	859

Source: Vital Statistics of India

TABLE - 1.3
SEX RATIO OF DEATHS BY AGE, RURAL INDIA

Age Groups	*1960*	*1961*	*1962*	*1963*	*1964*	*1965*	*1966*	*1967*	*1968*
> 1 year	840	869	862	353	825	850	939	859	842
1-4 years	972	979	988	976	982	989	1015	1009	984
5-14 years	899	958	902	916	876	892	910	913	875
15-29 years	1127	1205	1110	1136	1116	1100	1109	1099	1074
30-49 years	887	952	925	927	888	877	876	877	924
50-59 years	806	817	801	807	795	748	731	730	714
60 + years	893	943	906	909	870	887	868	870	852
Age not stated								861	797
Total :	908	948	920	922	896	1240	898	897	880

Source: Vital Statistics of India

It is observed that the maternal mortality rate is high enough to raise the overall death rate for females and accounts for the low sex ratio. It was reported to be 252 per 1,00,000 live births in 1964 for the country as a whole, but for rural areas, it is as high as 573 in 1968. It is unfortunate that no later figures are available for this.

The SRS data for 1968 and 1969 also reflects the same pattern as reported in the various censuses, namely that female mortality continues to be higher in the age groups 0-4 and 15-34.

TABLE - 1.4

SEX RATIO OF INFANT DEATHS BY AGE FOR TOTAL, RURAL AND URBAN AREAS 1960-68 AGE GROUP

Year	One Week			One Week-One Month			1 Month-6 Months			6 Months-1 Year			Total Death under Year 1		
	Total	Rural	Urban	Total	Rural	Urban	Total	Rural	Urban	Total	Rural	Urban	Total	Rural	Urban
1	2	3	4	5	6	7	8	9	10	11	12	13	14	15	16
1960	771	760	1768	798	830	804	853	929	869	921	1000	943	842	888	852
1961	774	788	741	809	802	839	899	887	941	940	923	1005	860	855	878
1962	796	810	761	825	825	825	880	872	913	939	925	994	864	862	870
1963	766	782	760	807	802	827	896	391	910	933	917	998	856	853	867
1964	789	803	755	810	806	824	1050	899	1802	913	896	982	892	855	1027
1965	774	779	761	813	808	831	893	881	932	928	908	1015	855	849	877
1966	778	782	768	801	796	819	898	897	902	935	919	1001	858	856	865
1967	779	588	1485	808	809	806	899	896	907	946	671	990	856	789	1089
1968	937	778	1426	782	780	789	887	885	894	918	911	946	840	842	833

Note: Since the comparable data for Rural and Urban areas is unavailable, figures for certain areas (noted below) have been excluded from the totals:

1966 : Orissa, Chandigarh, Jammu & Kashmir, Rajasthan, Himachal Pradesh, Laccadive, Minicoy, and Amindivi Islands and Dadra & Nagar Haveli.

1965 : Orissa, Jammu & Kashmir, Rajasthan, A. & N. Islands, Laccadive, Minicoy & Amindivi Islands, & Dadra & Nagar Haveli.

1964 : Jammu & Kashmir, Rajasthan, Laccadive, Minicoy and Amindivi Islands.

1962 : Jammu & Kashmir, Rajasthan, Pondicherry, Goa, Daman & Diu, Laccadive, Minicoy and Amindivi Islands.

1960 : All the Union Territories except Himachal Pradesh.

TABLE - 1.5
AGE SPECIFIC SEX-WISE DEATH RATES : RURAL INDIA-1965-67

Age Group	*Period*	*Male*	*Female*
Under 1	65-66	178.2	192.4
	66-67	162.7	173.1
1-4	65-66	29.4	42.7
	66-67	35.3	46.0
5-14	65-66	3.1	3.5
	66-67	3.3	3.8
15-44	65-66	3.7	5.1
	66-67	3.8	5.7

Source: Mehta, D.C. and Ghosh, M.H., Sample Registration in Vaidyanathan- KE (edited) *Studies on Mortality in India: Madurai* 1972, p. 64.

TABLE - 1.6
AGE AND SEX SPECIFIC DEATH RATE (PER 1000 POPULATION)

Items	*Sex*	*Period*	
		1968	*1969*
0-14	M	24.3	24.1
	F	27.9	29.6
15-34	M	2.8	3.3
	F	5.3	5.4
35-49	M	8.5	9.0
	F	7.6	7.5
49+	M	40.3	44.9
	F	37.1	41.1

Factors Contributing to Women's Ill-Health

Recent medical research has tried to identify particular contributory factors to the problem of women's ill-health and higher mortality. Since maternal mortality in India continues to be so high, it is understandable that the bulk of this research has concentrated on this aspect of women's health. The specific factor that have been identified by various studies are firstly pregnancy wastage, caused by abortions and still births. The incidence of this phenomenon has remained constant over the period 1957-68, a period which witnessed intensification of family planning activity. In fact there was even an increase in actual numbers. Such foetal wastage prevails more in low income groups. One study reported that pregnancy wastage of malnourished mothers was 30 per cent as late as in 1972. Still births are reported as constituting 11 per 1,000 live births. Much of this pregnancy loss and prenatal mortality and still births result from premature births, itself a consequence of maternal malnutrition, particularly iron deficiency during pregnancy. Haemoglobin estimations carried out on about 5,000 pregnant women in different parts of the country show that 30 per cent of them are anaemic, i.e., they have haemoglobin levels below 10 per cent. There is evidence that this is largely due to iron deficiency. Premature births have consistently been a very high proportion among the cause of infant deaths.

A second group of causes for both infant and maternal mortality relate to higher birth orders. Frequency of pregnancies causes protein malnutrition of the mothers. As it is, the majority of Indian women are victims of malnutrition. 10-20 per cent of maternal deaths are known to be due to nutritional anemias. This has been borne out by a series of studies of the National Institute of Nutrition. Table 1.7 indicates the gap between the actual and recommended intake of nutrition in the case of pregnant and nursing women.

It has been estimated that if causes of maternal mortality are eliminated female mortality will decline substantially, since pregnancy complications still constitute 16.44 per cent or the second highest contributor to female morbidity. The Bhore Committee had observed that even psychiatric morbidity among Indian women was the result of malnutrition, frequent pregnancies and anaemia. While data on this aspect of women's health is scanty, a WHO Report indicates that psychiatric morbidity is more prevalent among women than men.

TABLE - 1.7
NUTRIENTS INTAKE GAP

Nutrient	*Actual*	*Recommended*	*Actual*	*Recommended*
Calories	1440	2500	1425	2900
gms	37	55	39	65
Iron (marriage.)	18	40	18	30
Calcium (gm.)	0.2	1.0	0.2	1.0

Source: For data on Pregnant women : Leela Iyengar 1969 *Nutrition*, 3 (3), p. 2, for data on Nursing Women: Annual Report of Nutrition Res. Lab. 1965-66; for Recommended Allowances, see report of the Nutrition Expen. Group ICMR (1968)

All the demographic indicators thus point to a low health status of women. In particular they suggest that child bearing in

India, for the majority of women, is more a health hazard than a natural function.

Access to Health Services

The broad objectives of the health programmes so far have been to control and eradicate communicable diseases, to provide curative and preventive health services in rural areas through the establishment of primary health centres in each block, and to augment programmes for the training of medical and para-medical personnel. In the Fifth Plan the main thrust was to improve the deficiencies in building, staff, equipment, drugs and medicines in the primary health centres and to integrate family planning and maternity and child health services. Health is a basic component of the proposed minimum needs programme. Any assessment of the impact of these programmes on the health of women has to take both quantitative and qualitative factors into account. Any

Table 1.8 presents a comparative picture of available basic medical facilities in selected countries of the world. It is clear that India's position is more backward than even some of the developing countries.

TABLE - 1.8
POPULATION HEALTH PERSONNEL RATIOS IN SELECTED COUNTRIES OF THE WORLD

Sl. No.	*Name of the Country*	*Year*	*Bed Population Ratio*	*Doctor Population Ratio*	*Dentist Population Ratio*	*Pharmacist Population Ratio*	*Nurse Population Ratio*
1.	India	1970-71	2027	4730	74864	10275	7695
2.	Pakistan	1968	2900	6180	442310	290360	18130
3.	Burma	1966	1190	9580	1009840	*	11610
4.	U.A.R.	1968	490	2080	18500	6530	3900
5.	Japan	1968	70	910	2820	1650	400
6.	Indonesia	1967	1470	27560	146380	131830	8310
7.	Thailand	1968	1030	8530	100580	31080	3750
8.	U.K.	1967	100	860	3870	3060	330
9.	Australia	1966	90	850	3350	1390	150
10.	U.S.A.	1967	120	650	2020	1630	200
11.	Canada	1968	100	740	3050	1960	170
12.	U.S.S.R.	1968	100	50	2850	*	250

* Information unavailable.

Source: World Health Statistics, 1968, 9.69 Pocket Book of Health Statistics, Ministry of Health & Family Planning.

TABLE - 1.9

ACHIEVEMENTS DURING THE 1ST, 2ND, 3RD AND 4TH PLAN PERIODS

Sl. No.	Category	1st Plan 1951-56	2nd Plan 1956-61	3rd Plan 1961-66	4th Plan Achievement 1970-71	4th Plan Target 1973-74	Population per Unit of End of the 4th Plan	Desired Norms as per the Mudaliar's Committee
1	2	3	4	5	6	7	8	9
1.	Institutions	10000	12000	14600	@	@	-	-
2.	Hospitals & Dispensaries	125000	185000	240000	269370	281600	0.49 per 1000 Population	1:1000 Population
3.	Medical Colleges	42	57	87	96	103	5.75 million	107
4.	Annual Admissions	3500	5800	10520	11850	13000	-	-
5.	Dental Colleges	7	10	13	15	15	-	-
6.	Annual Admissions	231	281	536	680	800	-	-
7.	Doctors	65000	70000	86000	115725	137930	1:4300	1:3500
8.	Nurses	18500	27000	45000	71000	88000	1:6400	1:5000
9.	Auxiliary - Nurse-Midwives	12780	19900	22000	42000	54000	1:11700	1:5000
10.	Sanitary Inspectors	4000	6000	14000	25000	32600	1:18300	1:10000
11.	Health Assistants Pharmacists	-	42000	48000	57000	66000	1:9060	1:10000

* Unavailable, @ Number unfixed

Source: Pocket Book of Health Statistics, Ministry of Health & Family Planning, 1973, p. 20.

In spite of the achievements during the last Four Plans (Table 1.9) indicates that medical care remains inaccessible to a large section of the population.

Any increase in personnel or medical facilities is nullified by increase in the population. The quality of the existing health services is reduced by inadequacy of staff, medical supplies and equipment, and by overcrowding. In rural areas not even the minimum medical facilities by trained personnel is available in all districts. Distance and inaccessibility remains a major problem, particularly in hilly and difficult areas.

The lowest unit of the Health Service structure or its rural arm is the Primary Health Centre which is supposed to provide integrated and comprehensive curative and preventive health services in rural areas. The Bhore Committee which proposed the setting up of primary health centres had recommended that, to start with, each centre should cater to a population of 40,000 with a 30 bedded hospital to serve four Primary Health Centres. It visualized district level hospitals with a strength of 500 beds. Among other staff, primary health centres were to include four public health nurses, two medical officers, four midwives and four trained *dais*. Describing these requirements as the 'irreducible minimum', the Committee had recommended the key importance of developing preventive health services, with 'the country-side as the focal point.'

The Mudaliar Committee reiterated these recommendations, adding further the provision of three specialists in medicine, surgery, obstetrics and gynaecology, and 75 maternity and 50 paediatric beds to each district hospital.

In fact, when the primary health centres were established, the 'irreducible minimum' requirements were not provided. They had to serve a far larger population of 60 to 70,000 with only one lady health visitor and four auxiliary nurse-mid-wives, six beds and three sub-centres. Each sub-centre was put in charge of one ANM. Their functions were wide, including medical relief, maternity and child-health, control of communicable diseases (including the major national programme of Malaria control), school health, environmental sanitation and health education. By 1961, 2,800 primary health centres had been established.

Though the recommendations of the Mudaliar Committee were not implemented due to shortage of trained personnel and funds, from 1963 family planning services were initiated with additional staff (one woman medical officer, one extension doctor, one ANM, and two family planning workers to supervise four sub-centres). The sub-centres were to cater to a population of approximately ten thousand and were more than doubled in number, but with family planning as their major activity. The emphasis on family planning was strengthened further in 1966 by treating it as a crash programme, providing additional staff, and delinking it from Malaria control activities. In most States, the existing four health assistants were transferred to the family planning side.

Though the number of primary health centres increased from 67 in the First Five Year Plan to 5195 in 1972 and the sub-centres from 17,522 in 1967 to 32,218 in 1972, their impact on the health of the rural population has not been substantial. An expert Committee observed in 1973 that apart from West Bengal and Kerala, where utilization was 50 per cent, in other States like Bihar, Rajasthan, UP, Orissa, Madhya Pradesh and Jammu & Kashmir, the net utilization in primary health centres was hardly between 5-15 per cent. The reasons for this underutilization were: (a) apathy of the staff, (b) the status barrier that separates the doctor and his team from the village population, particularly the lower socio-economic groups, and (c) absence of lady doctors in many centres. Emphasizing the need to improve maternity and child health services, the committee recommended the provision of domiciliary maternity services as essential.

Critics of the present pattern of health services feel that they have deviated from the basic recommendation of the Bhore Committee, to emphasize preventive services in rural areas as the keystone of public health. Under the present system, the expenditure on curative services is thrice that on preventive services, but most of it is concentrated in urban areas. The 10 per cent of hospital beds meant for the four-fifths of the population living in rural areas are ill-staffed, ill-equipped, and ill-financed. In the sphere of women's health in particular, while all the expert Committees emphasized greater attention to maternity services, the actual position shows wide regional variations in the provision of this crucial service.

According to the estimate of the Study Group on Hospitals, there were only 45,000 maternity beds in 493 maternity hospitals and wards of general hospitals in 1968. The total number of beds at that time was 2.75 lakh, i.e., maternity beds constituted less than 17 per cent of total hospital facilities. It should also be noted that most hospitals in India provide no other beds for women. The distribution of general and maternity beds in the States of West Bengal and Uttar Pradesh (Tables 1.10 and 1.11-A&B) illustrate the general tendency.

TABLE - 1.10
MEDICAL FACILITIES BY SEX, WEST BENGAL IN THE YEARS 1951, 1961 AND 1971

Year	*No. of Beds*				*Outdoor Patients Attending Hospitals, Dispensaries*			*No. of Maternity & Child Welfare Centres*		
	Men	*Women*	*Total*	*Maternity beds*	*Men*	*Women*	*Total*	*Urban*	*Rural*	*Total*
1951	NA	NA	17107	2041	3391064	2045481	5436545	NA	NA	37
1961	NA	NA	29067	4339	5741381	4331218	10072599	NA	NA	472
1971	NA	NA	40450	6854	8402742 (Provisional)	6338910	1474162	72	284	351

Source: Government of West Bengal, Department of Health and Family Planning.

TABLE - 1.11A
BEDS ACCORDING TO SEX IN UP

Year	*Total Beds*	*Beds for Males*	%	*Beds for Females*	%
1962	72705	17998	64.96	9707	35.04
1963	29414	18773	63.82	10641	36.18
1964	30517	19228	62.99	11294	37.01
1965	30873	19688	63.77	11185	36.23
1966	33601	21284	64.95	11777	36.05
1967	33965	21988	64.74	11977	35.26
1968	34215	22068	64.50	12147	35.50

Source: Statistical Bulletin of U.P., Lucknow, 1969, p. 51.

TABLE - 1.11B
PATIENT TREATMENT BY SEX IN UP

Year	*In-patients*		*Out-patients*	
	M	*F*	*M*	*F*
1962	524589	370580	14890103	8842015
1963	477097	396785	16120016	8993631
1964	517789	392881	14984539	9499673
1965	517919	396220	15186055	9670673

Source: *Health Atlas of India.*

Still more revealing is the gap in sanctioned and actual strength of women doctors in Uttar Pradesh (Table 1.12). Table 1.13 provides comparative Statewise data on maternity services which when seen along with Table 1.14, throws some interesting light on the relative efforts of different State administrations to protect the health of women.

Giving the All-India Statewise life expectancy at birth, during the years 1951-85, Table 1.14 projects that Kerala, which stands out for provision of maternity services also, has the highest expectancy of life for women, which is 60.7 for 1971-75, and the lowest infant mortality rate. Uttar Pradesh, with the lowest provision for such services has a female life expectancy of 53.7, which is nearly the lowest in India, and the highest infant mortality rate.

There is no doubt that improvement of maternity services has a definite impact on life expectancy of women. States like Tamil Nadu, Andhra Pradesh, Punjab, Assam, Karnataka and West Bengal which have given some attention to these services, have helped to improve their women's expectation of life. The impact, however, cannot be uniform, because of the operation of other factors, like education, employment, general cultural norms, etc., which exert considerable influence on women's utilization of these services.

TABLE - 1.12
WOMEN DOCTORS AND WOMEN HOSPITALS - UP

Year	*Women doctors*		*Women Hospitals*
	Sanctioned Strength	*Employed Strength*	
1962	402	235	163
1963	418	247	170
1964	428	249	182
1965	444	257	190
1966	512	268	204
1967	567	270	208
1968	588	288	211

Source: Statistical Bulletin of U.P., Lucknow, 1969, p. 61.

An important cultural norm which has a direct impact on women's health is the age of marriage. No district in Kerala has below 15 as the average age at marriage and only 3 districts (33 per cent) have an average below 20. In the case of Bihar, Rajasthan and UP, the picture is just the opposite, where 71 per cent, 65 per cent and 48 per cent of the districts respectively have an average below 15 per cent, 35 per cent and 31 per cent of the districts in Andhra Pradesh and West Bengal also come into this category.

TABLE - 1.13
SOME HEALTH STATISTICS FOR THE STATES

State	*Per Capita Government Expenditure on Medical & Public Health Measures in 1963-64 Rs*	*Number of Beds in Hospitals & Dispensaries per 1000 Population in 1964*	*Percentage of Total Births in Rural Households Attended by Trained Dai-Mid Wife Physician or Qualified Nurse in 1964-65*
Andhra Pradesh	2.88	0.53	12.24
Assam	3.28	0.45	12.88
Bihar	1.72	0.24	2.78
Gujarat	2.24	0.53	9.69
Haryana	-	-	15.32
Jammu & Kashmir	4.13	1.01	6.10
Karnataka	2.58	0.75	15.89
Kerala	3.70	0.94	25.72
Madhya Pradesh	2.27	0.41	5.14
Maharashtra	2.95	0.81	7.52
Orissa	3.21	0.43	6.79
Punjab	2.57	0.67	14.27
Rajasthan	3.80	0.52	4.07
Tamil Nadu	3.03	0.48	21.92
Uttar Pradesh	1.49	0.38	2.51
West Bengal	3.32	0.85	2.68
India	2.58	0.57	8.81

Notes: Columns (2) and (3) are taken from 'Health Statistics in India', Ministry of Health, Government of India, Column (4) is calculated from estimates given in NSS Report No. 177 for the 19th Round (1964-65). For Columns (2) Punjab includes Haryana.

Source: Bardhan, P.M.-'On Life and Death Question, - *Economic & Political Weekly*, Special number, August, 1974, p. 1297.

Kerala also has the highest female literacy rate which is 53 per cent in rural areas, and 60.6 per cent in urban areas. Tamil Nadu, though well behind Kerala, is still the second highest State in female literacy, which is 19 per cent in rural areas and 45.4 per cent in urban areas. Uttar Pradesh, Bihar, Rajasthan stand out for their low female literacy rate.

We may infer from this that the availability and utilization of medical care for women reflects the general social attitude to women in a region. There is also no doubt that the female literacy rate is an important determinant for utilization as well as supply of medical and health care for this section of the population. This is particularly true of maternity and child care.

TABLE - 1.14
PROJECTED VALUES OF EXPECTATION OF LIFE AT BIRTH ALL INDIA AND STATES, 1951-85

State		*1951-60*	*1961-65*	*1966-70*	*1971-75*	*1976-80*	*1981-85*
All India	M	41.9	48.7	53.2	57.3	61.1	63.1
	F	40.6	47.4	51.9	56.0	59.0	61.8
Kerala	M	49.5	55.5	59.5	63.1	66.4	66.9
	F	47.1	53.1	57.1	60.7	64.0	64.5
Punjab	M	49.9	55.9	59.9	63.5	66.8	67.3
	F	44.0	51.0	55.0	58.6	61.9	62.4
Rajasthan	M	49.2	55.2	59.2	62.8	66.1	66.6
	F	44.3	50.3	54.3	57.9	61.2	61.7
Maharashtra	M	40.1	52.1	56.1	59.7	63.0	63.5
	F	44.3	50.3	54.3	57.9	61.2	61.7
West Bengal	M	44.1	50.1	54.1	57.7	61.0	61.5
	F	44.5	50.5	54.5	58.1	61.4	61.9
Orissa	M	40.7	47.5	52.0	56.1	59.9	60.9
	F	41.1	47.9	52.4	56.5	60.3	61.3
Madhya Pradesh	M	41.2	48.0	52.5	56.6	60.4	61.4
	F	40.0	46.8	51.3	55.4	59.2	60.2
Karnataka	M	41.2	48.0	52.5	56.6	60.4	61.4
	F	39.2	46.0	50.5	54.6	58.4	59.4
Gujarat	M	40.8	47.6	52.1	56.2	60.0	61.0
	F	39.2	46.0	50.5	54.6	58.4	59.4
Uttar Pradesh	M	39.4	46.2	50.7	54.8	58.6	59.6
	F	38.3	45.1	49.6	53.7	57.5	58.5
Bihar	M	37.4	44.9	49.9	54.5	58.8	60.8
	F	37.8	45.3	50.3	54.9	59.2	61.2
Andhra Pradesh	M	37.8	45.3	50.3	54.9	59.2	61.2
	F	36.0	43.5	48.5	53.1	57.4	59.4
Assam	M	36.6	44.1	48.1	53.7	58.0	60.0
	F	37.0	44.5	49.5	54.1	58.4	60.4

Source: Family Planning Programme, Gujarat, Fact Book, p.9 Published by State Family Planning Bureau, Demographic and Evaluation Cell, Gujarat, 1972.

Apart from regional variations, the accessibility of health services is also affected by rural-urban and social-economic differentials, including a broad pattern of sex differential. For example, uncontaminated water is available to 40 per cent of towns, but only 9 per cent of villages. Since about two-thirds of the total number of doctors and nurses, and most hospitals are concentrated in urban areas, the four-fifths of the population living in rural areas get a much smaller share of these services. The National Sample Survey (19th Round, 1964-65) found that 46 per cent of all births in urban India are attended by trained medical personnel, as compared to 9 per cent in rural areas. The household consumption data of the same Round also shows that average per capital private monthly expenditure on medicines and medical services is Rs 1.01 in urban areas, and about half that in rural areas. Majority of doctors in urban areas are private practitioners, charging high fees. Their services can be used only by the upper and middle income groups. Private nursing homes and paying hospitals, with private doctors, are almost totally out of reach of the poorer sections of society.

A recent study on rural health services brings out the peculiar tension created by scarce supply of medical personnel in the villages. On the one hand is the unmet felt need for the services of the Auxilliary Nurse Midwife at the time of child birth. Villagers are keen to have the ANM's services because they consider her to be more skillful than the traditional *dai*. Whether the ANM's have provided the services, the *dais'* role has become less significant. During our tours we were repeatedly informed of the inadequacy in the number and services rendered by ANMs. Apart from their small number, the area covered by these personnel is too large, with consequent transport and accommodation difficulties. Night-halts and the problem of security create difficulties for most of these workers in rural areas, and effect their functioning.

Such problems very often obstruct an ANM from really attending to her duties in all places under her charge. Secondly, for an outsider to live and work in rural areas, a degree of social acceptance and security is essential. Protection extended by influential members of the village community ensures this, and prevents her being handicapped by their hostility. The result very often is that her services are monopolized by the dominant, or relatively well-to-do section of village society. It should also be remembered that the social and educational background of the

ANMs is likely to be closer to the dominant, or well-to-do groups in the village, rather than the poorest.

This sort of cornering widens the gap between the ANM and the masses of women who need her services. 'The overall image of the ANM in villages, particularly in North India, is that of a person who is distant from them, meant only for special people or for those who can pay for her services. She is not for the poor. She can be called only when there are complications and then also she has to be paid.

As for sex differentials, they are deeprooted in social attitudes regarding the needs of women for care and assistance during ailments. In many areas we were told that rural society does not always care to report women's ailments, or seek medical aid. Women themselves often prefer to be silent in such matters. The studies in nutritional deficiencies of women indicate that their requirements are often sacrificed to provide a little more nutrition to others in the family. The incidence of diseases caused by malnutrition is higher not only among adult women, but even among female infants. At the same time hospital records reveal that more male children are treated for such diseases.

The two sets of indicators—demographic trends, and access to medical care, both reveal the same situation regarding the health status of women.

This increase in comparative neglect of female lives as an expendable asset, observed to persist and increase over several decades, is a matter of serious concern.

Family Planning

If the masses of Indian women are to be freed from their status as 'expendable assets' some of the obvious and immediate answers lies in releasing them from the bondage of repeated and frequent childbirth, providing them with some choice in the size of their families and in ensuring adequate medical facilities to protect them during and against maternity.

Propagators of the family planning movement in India have been keen to emphasize the improvement in the status of women as one of the direct consequences of acceptance of family planning.

The birth control movement in India, from its inception, was associated with the feminist movement, and women's organizations were among the first to start a voluntary campaign for spread of birth control techniques among women. Even now they are active partners of the government's programme to persuade more and more women to accept family planning methods.

Recent researches in this field however make it extremely difficult to establish such an a prior relationship. All recent studies seem to agree more on the obverse of the relationship, viz, that improved status of women, with rise in the age of marriage, education, employment, better living conditions and greater general awareness, have a direct impact on the adoption of family planning methods.

There is no doubt that knowledge of family planning methods enables a woman to regulate her biological function and thus gives her a greater control over life and future. This certainly helps to build up her confidence in herself and can enable her to pursue various other ways to develop her personality, e.g., training, career interests and fulfil responsibilities to herself, her family and the wider society. Above all, such control has a direct impact on her health. Ability to prevent frequent and excessive drain on her-physical resources undoubtedly helps to preserve her health, and since health is a basic necessity for any kind of development for a person, ability to plan her family ultimately contributes to such improvement of a woman's personality. A third consequence which is sometimes emphasized is the possible change in husband-wife relationship, leading to improved position of the woman in decision making within the family.

All these results could certainly lead to a general improvement of a woman's status. But each of them are integrally connected with other socio-economic factors and developments, and the relationship between family planning and status improvement depends, in the ultimate analysis, on the presence and behaviour of such variables as social attitudes and opportunities for women's education, employment, pursuit of independent interests and career, size and sex of the family, accessibility of health services, and general economic development.

If the sexual role were the main determinant of male

dominance and authority in a society, there would have been no communities in the world where the women are dominant, or equal members. The status of women in any society depends on a complex set of social, economic, demographic and political variables, among which the woman's ability to control the size of her family could be a contributory factor. But in our view, emphasizing it as a direct cause of improvement of women's status is somewhat exaggerated, and ignores the evolution of women's status in different societies. The matriarch of many ancient civilizations and primitive communities certainly enjoyed a much higher status than the women with complete control on the size of their families in the developed, modern societies of the West today. Knowledge of family planning techniques may have liberated Western women from excessive pregnancies, but it has not basically changed their status in these societies either economically or politically. Even in the sphere of social attitudes, with all the progress in education, and different types of social freedom and changing roles, their image as sex-symbols has been intensified, not eliminated.

In India, there has been an enormous volume of research on degree of acceptance of family planning, to assist the continuous evaluation of the Family Planning Programme. In one such research by the Ministry of Health and Family Planning, it was concluded that:

> The focus of evaluation of the Family Planning Programme at present is on the purposive assessment of impact of the programme, identification of areas of success and failures and reasons thereof, and feeding back this information for motivation and improvement or programme implementation. Family Planning Programme can be evaluated in terms of its objectives, viz., (a) the immediate objectives, including efforts and performance, objectives set for developing resources and activities for achieving the decision made; (b) the intermediate objective of spreading knowledge, developing favourable attitudes towards encouraging practice of family planning methods; (c) the ultimate objective, which is reduction of fertility so as to bring down the birth rate to 25 per thousand by 1978-79.

Apart from continuous assessment of information received from the States regarding the success of the programme in quantitative terms, i.e., actual number of couples protected by various methods, provision of services in the way of personnel and equipment, etc., the evaluation includes field surveys on knowledge, attitudes and practices (KAP Studies). The Central Family Planning Institutes, the National Sample Survey, the various demographic and communication action research centres in the country, as well as a large number of individuals and institutions in the university system have been engaged in periodical assessment of the impact of this programme at both local and national levels since its inception. As a result, family planning is now the most heavily documented and evaluated among all major programmes of the Government of India.

One common trend in the results of these studies has been to expose the differentials in knowledge, acceptance and practice of family planning methods between different sections of the population. The results from the national survey conducted by the Operations Research Group, Ministry of Health and Family Planning during 1970-71 indicate that the percentage of couples using any family planning method increases with:

(i) Age of wife (from 7 per cent among those below 25 years of age to 17 per cent among those aged 30 years or more);

(ii) Number of living children (from 2 per cent among those without any living child to 25 per cent those with 5 or more living children);

(iii) Education of wife (from 10 per cent among wives without any education to 56 per cent among those who have gone to college);

(iv) Family income (from 10 per cent among those with monthly income of Rs. 100 or less to 30 per cent among those with monthly income of Rs. 1,000 or more);

(v) Size of city or village (from 10 per cent among those living in villages of 5,000 or less to 32 per cent among those living in cities of 1 million or more);

(vi) that the percentage of current users among the Hindus is higher than among the Muslims.

The survey revealed notable differences in the characteristics of current users, past users and non-users of contraception as indicated in Table 1.15.

TABLE - 1.15
CONTRACEPTION: CHARACTERISTICS OF CURRENT, PAST AND NEVER USERS, 1970-71

Characteristics	*Current Users*	*Past Users*	*Never Users*
Average age of wife (years)	32.0	31.0	29.7
Live birth per wife	4.4	3.9	3.3
Living children	3.8	3.0	2.5
Living sons	2.1	1.7	1.4
Per cent desiring more children	21	48	64
Per cent with literate wife	42	42	13
Per cent earning over Rs. 200 per month	41	43	21
Per cent non-manual workers	45	44	25
Per cent Urban couples	36	34	14

Source: KAP Survey, operations Research Group Baroda, 1970-71.

In our discussions with Muslim women in different parts of the country, we did not get the impression that there was any organized resistance to family planning on religious grounds. Some of the very poor women told us that they had heard about the religious propaganda but they could not see their children starve. In every state we asked the lady doctors about the response to family planning from different sections of society. The answers were interesting. Those doctors who had some kind of social commitment and sympathetic attitude invariably said that women from all classes and all regions came to them for advice while the others complained that Muslim women and women from the poorer sections of society were not interested.

Our general impression has been that men, particularly, Muslims, are not very much concerned about family planning, though in Kerala an enthusiastic collector informed us that in the Family Planning Camps a number of Catholic and Muslim men came to him for vasectomy but they did not want anyone to know about it and requested that the operations may be performed at night. He agreed to make the necessary arrangements and the response was good. According to him there was no significant difference in the percentage of acceptors from different communities. In a village in West Bengal while a B.D.C. was complaining that Muslims were not coming forward for family planning, an old, poor Muslim woman came up and asked where she could take her daughter-in-law for advice, so that she would stop having any more children. She already had 5 children. In Kashmir, the educated and working women are very much interested in family planning and we did not come across any group of women expressing disapproval on religious grounds.

An analysis of variance in five factors, viz., educational level of spouses, family income, number of children, urbanization and exposure to mass media simultaneously has shown that the effect of each of these factors on the use of family planning methods is significant at 1 per cent level. Some studies have suggested that the differential in adoption and use of family planning methods between States may be due to the differences in socio-economic characteristic of couples in actual implementation of strategies or combination of both.

While some of the studies occasionally contradict findings of previous research, one factor which is generally emphasized by most is education, particularly the education of women. The Regional Fertility Survey conducted by the Demographic Research Centre, Lucknow 1966-67, indicated that mean number of live births varied inversely with the mother's education. The educational level of both husband and wife was found to have a very large influence on their attitudes towards family planning.

The Delhi Fertility Survey conducted by the Demographic Research Centre, Institute of Economic Growth, Delhi in 1969-70, based on a total sample of 9,000 households, indicated the inverse relationship between a couple's educational level and average number of live births in a pronounced way only when both husband and wife were educated beyond matriculation level, the variation being 2.73 for this group and 4.47 for literate couples. The Mysore Population Study reported that among the social and economic factors studied, the one which appeared to be the most significant in relation to fertility in Bangalore City was educational status, but education below the high school or university stage was not found to be related significantly to the average number of children born.

Education may affect fertility in two ways:

(i) by increasing knowledge and advantages of family planning; and

(ii) by generating deliberate efforts for a planned family.

The first is effective at lower educational levels, while the latter operates probably when a sufficiently high level of education is achieved by the couple. The National Sample Survey indicated that the percentage of husbands desiring additional children after 2, declined from 60 when they were illiterate to 41.59 when they were intermediate and above. However, the decline was neither consistent nor pronounced when the educational level was below intermediate and above (Table 1.16A). A comparitive study on attitude towards family planning and educational level, done by the ORG is given in Table 1.16B.

TABLE - 1.16 A
PERCENTAGE OF HUSBANDS (WITH WIFE UNDER 45 YEARS OF AGE) DESIRING ADDITIONAL CHILDREN AFTER TWO SURVIVING CHILDREN BY EDUCATIONAL STANDARD

Sl. No.	*Educational Standards of Husbands*	*Per cent Husbands Desiring Additional Children after Two in each Category*
1.	Illiterate	60.00
2.	Literate but below primary	52.44
3.	Primary	60.91
4.	Middle	53.65
5.	Matriculate	54.21
6.	Intermediate and above	41.59
7.	Total (All-India Urban)	55.89

Source: National Sample Survey

TABLE - 1.16 B
ATTITUDES TOWARDS FAMILY PLANNING AND EDUCATIONAL LEVEL OF WIFE

Attitude Towards Family Planning	*Percent of Couples Educational Level of wife*			
	Illiterate	*Gone to Primary School*	*Gone to Secondary School*	*Gone to College*
Per cent desiring three or less children	34.8	54.3	66.7	76.0
One must have a son	89.2	87.1	85.4	72.4
Disapprove adoption of birth control methods	46.5	23.0	1.43	6.4

Source: Operation Research Group, Baroda, Family Planning Practice in India. The First All India Report, p. 5.

The Dharwar Surveys on the attitudes towards family planning undertaken by the Dharwar Demographic Research Centre in 1962 and 1969 indicated that educational level was the most important factor associated with awareness about family planning.

Role of Education

While all the major surveys found a positive relationship between education and knowledge, acceptance and practice of family planning, most of them have revealed the existence of other associational factors which may have influenced this relationship. Education is generally associated with one or more of the following: (a) rise is the age of marriage; (b) diversification of consumption pattern of people, involving both material and non-material aspects which can lead to a decline in the psychic utility generated by the birth of children; (c) urbanization; (d) possible increase in work force participation of women; (e) higher socio-economic status of the couple; (f) higher mobility; (g) higher exposure to mass media and (h) more diversified knowledge of family planning methods. It has been found that couples with primary level education or below have very limited knowledge of family planning and are most often aware only of sterilization and IUCD (Intra Uterine Contraceptive Device).

Methods of Contraceptions

Most of the methods for contraception affect women directly, and acceptance by them would indicate the success or failure of a method.

IUCD

This was introduced in 1965 and initially was very popular. Later the level of acceptance showed a reverse trend. Various studies indicate that the failure of I.U.C.D. was largely because enough information on certain side effects of the insertions was not adequately published. Table 1.18 gives the break up in Rural/ Urban India, regarding the IUCD insertions.

During our tours, the doctors and field workers told us that this method was unpopular and it was a failure. Their observations were as follows:

(1) The careless handling of IUCD insertions by the paramedical staff led to complications and there was a whispering campaign everywhere that it was harmful for the health of the women.

(2) Proper arrangements were not made for a follow-up treatment in case of bleeding or other side effects.

We found, however, that wherever it was handled by properly trained personnel, e.g., in Haryana and Punjab, it was found to be the most successful method, specially because it was reversible and inexpensive.

TABLE - 1.17
RURAL-URBAN BREAK UP OF IUCD INSERTIONS IN INDIA

Year	*Rural*	*Urban*	*Total*	*Percentage of rural of total*
1966-67	542228	367498	909726	59.6
1967-68	394027	274952	668979	58.9
1968-69	286181	192550	478731	59.8
1969-70	267982	190744	458726	58.2
1970-71	279622	196226	475848	58.2
1971-72	311099	177269	488368	63.7

Source: Year Book - Family Planning Welfare in India, 1972-73 Government of India Ministry of Health and Family Planning, Department of Family Planning, New Delhi, p. 46.

Sterilization

This has been performed as part of the family planning programme since 1956. Tubectomies accounted for two-thirds of all sterilizations in 1956, and up to 1960, they exceeded the number of vasectomies, but since then the number of vasectomies has increased more rapidly, and in 1965, they accounted for more than 80 per cent of all sterilizations. We would like to point out, however, that the validity of these figures has been often questioned.

Since sterilization is a terminal method which is often believed to have consequences on the health of the woman, the possible constraints that may develop in taking recourse to this method are obvious. During our tours we received evidence of this apprehension from a large number of women. They were reluctant to end their chance of child bearing because of an underlying fear regarding the survival of their existing children. They were also apprehensive of the possible consequence of their health. This fear has occasionally been aggravated by the experience of the mass tubectomy camps which very often did not provide adequate medical care or follow-up measures.

Two specific arguments regarding sterilization were brought to our notice by women doctors. A group of these doctors in West Bengal mentioned a number of cases of 'post ligation syndrome' where the women developed psychological disturbances after tubectomy, particularly if any untoward incidence like illness or death of a child happened in the family. In their view, this was due to the tremendous hold of traditional values on the minds of these women, who developed a sense of guilt and regarded these tragedies as being the consequences of their 'unnatural' act. Yet another argument by doctors in the rural areas of Rajasthan was the impossibility of undertaking sterilization for a large number of women, particularly tribal ones, because of their extremely anaemic condition. Table 1.18 gives the sex-wise break up of sterilization operations done in India during 1951 to 1973.

TABLE - 1.18
SEX-WISE BREAK UP OF STERILISATION OPERATIONS DONE IN INDIA SINCE 1956

Year	*No. of Sterilizations*			
	Vasectomy	*Tubectomy*	*Total*	*% of Tubectomies to total*
1956	2395	4758	7153	66.5
1957	4152	9584	13736	69.8
1958	9189	15959	25148	63.5
1959	17633	24669	42302	58.3
1960	37596	56742	64338	41.6
1961	63880	40705	104585	38.9
1962	112357	45590	157947	28.9
1963	114621	55625	170246	32.7
1964	201171	68394	269565	25.4
1965	401741	75141	476889	15.8
January to March 1966	174861	19073	193934	9.8
1966-67	785378	101990	887368	11.5
1967-68	1648152	191659	1839811	10.4
1968-69	1383053	281764	1664817	16.9
1969-70	1055860	366258	1422118	25.8
1970-71	878800	451114	1329914	33.9
1971-72	1620076	567260	2187336	25.9
1972-73*	2611631	504731	3116362	16.2

* Provisional Figures

Source: Year Book, Family Welfare Planning in India 1972-73, p. 42.

Other Methods

About 2.3 million couples are estimated to be using various other types of conventional contraceptives during 1972-73. This is 2.3 per cent of the estimated couples protected in the reproductive age group. For women the most significant is the use of oral contraceptive pills. A number of trials have been conducted to study the medical and social acceptability of oral contraception among Indian women. The pill as a method of oral contraception is useful for the educated urban rather than rural women. It is also comparatively more expensive and constant medical supervision is necessary to check the side effects.

Abortions

The objectives of the Medical Termination of Pregnancy Act 1971 is to reduce the incidence of criminal abortions which pose grave risks to pregnant women by liberalizing the provision of the Indian Penal Code which restricted medical practitioners from terminating pregnancies legally. The Shanti Lal Shah Committee has estimated that for every 73 live births, 25 abortions take place of which 15 are induced. "In a population of 500 million, the number of abortions per year would be 6.5 million, 2.6 million spontaneous and 3.9 million induced." From hospitals records it has been observed that 15 to 20 per cent of the direct obstetric causes of maternal deaths are from abortions. Of these, 98 per cent were from septic abortions usually resulting from abortions undertaken by unqualified persons. According to the Registrar General Census (vital statistics for 1966-67); abortions form a high percentage of causes of all deaths due to child birth. According to two studies of the National Institute of Nutrition, Hyderabad, pregnancy wastage from miscarriage and abortions ranges from 16 to 19 per cent to 32 per cent among poor income groups.

The Act allows termination of pregnancy on:

(a) Therapeutic grounds, where the continuance of pregnancy would involve a risk.
   (i) to the life of the pregnant mother or,
   (ii) of grave injury to her physical and mental health.

(b) Genuine grounds where there is substantial risk that the child, if born, is likely to suffer from such physical or mental abnormalities as to be seriously handicapped.

(c) Humanitarian grounds, where the pregnancy has been caused by rape; or

(d) Social grounds:

  (i) where the pregnancy in a married woman is the result of contraceptive failure, or

  (ii) that the environment of the pregnant woman during the continuance of pregnancy at the time of childbirth and thereafter, so far as is foreseeable, would involve risk of injury to her health.

Termination can be done only by registered practitioners certified for the purpose in approved places, mainly government hospitals.

While the Act emphasizes its importance as a health measure, the permission granted under section 3(2) to permit such termination for married women in cases of contraceptive failure, has emphasized its importance as an instrument of population control. This has given rise to a strong difference of opinion among medical personnel who are averse to using abortion for such a purpose. Many of them insist on tubectomy as a condition for abortion. In their view, based on experience, abortions often lead to frequent pregnancies, apart from its health hazards.

There is considerable evidence that the measure is being used more for birth control than for other reasons. According to a study undertaken by the Government and Children Hospital, Egmore, Madras, out of 7,957 abortions only 11 were for therapeutic reasons. 617 were cases of induced abortions admitted to the hospital only after complications had set in.

A study undertaken by the International Research Fertility Programme revealed that 88 per cent of abortion cases were among married women, of whom 55 per cent were between the age of 25 to 33, 81 per cent were urban, 19.1 per cent rural; 37 per cent had three or four children. In another study it was found that 72 per cent were married, of whom 60 per cent were in the 20 to 29 age group. The average total pregnancy of these groups was 4.3, where the average number of living children 2.5 and 0.8 had previous abortions. 50 per cent of all the patients had a previous abortion in their record 17.8 per cent had 2 to 5.

All the studies indicate "that most pregnant women who go

in for induced abortions are fully motivated for small family norms if not planned parenthood. These people are very amenable and can be fully motivated for adoption of family planning methods, more often sterilization, if they have two or more living children or other temporary methods of spacing children."

We have given serious consideration to this matter and discussed it with several representatives of the medical profession. While we appreciate the ethical considerations which make some of them reluctant to perform this operation, we feel that it is a woman's right to have control over the size of her family. At the same time it is important that doctors should have the authority to discourage such operations when it posses a definite risk to the health of a particular patient.

We, however, feel that the condition being imposed in many hospitals, that abortion will only be performed if the patient agreed to sterilization, should not be compulsive, particularly where a woman has only one child. It would be far better to adopt methods of persuasion through expert counselling rather than compulsion. Compulsive conditions of this kind will only drive women to unqualified persons, thus defeating the main purpose of this Act.

We have been informed that there are serious psychological hazards posed by both pregnancies as well as sterilization. It is, therefore, imperative to organize systematic research on this field, to ascertain the impact of these situations and operations on the physical and mental health of women.

The difficulties placed before us by medical personnel regarding the recording procedure and paper work involved in these operations, lead us to suggest that these procedures need to be simplified. It is also necessary to extend facilities for authorized termination of pregnancies, particularly in the rural areas. We have also been informed that though the law does not require it, many hospitals insist on the husband's consent before performing these operations. A special effort needs to be made to convince the medical profession of the social value of this law, from the point of view of both individuals and society.

We have also been informed that most doctors are reluctant to perform these operations in the case of unmarried girls. It is necessary to clarify the point that rape is not the only ground to justify termination in cases of unmarried girls nor is there any legal obligation on the doctor to inform the police of an abortion done in a rape case. We note that the All India Medical Council has introduced this Act in the syllabus for medical jurisprudence, with the object of setting up new norms for the medical profession. This will go a long way in breaking down the resistance of doctors.

Recommended changes in Law

We would also like to recommend the following changes in the Law:

(a) According to Section 4(a) of the Act — consent of a minor girl is not required for operation, while in other surgical operations on children above 12, such consent is necessary. In our view this distinction is uncalled for and may lead to guardians' compelling young girls to undergo this operation even when they do not want it. The consent of the patient should be essential. In the case of a minor girl nearing majority, if the doctor and the patient are in agreement, the consent of the guardian may be dispensed with. In all such cases, greater discretion should be permitted to the doctor.

(b) Section 8 of the Act provides an overriding protection to the doctor for any damage caused by the operation. Since no such protection is given for other operations, this seems an unnecessary clause and may lead to negligence. It may, therefore, be dropped.

Change in Policy

During the First and Second Five-Year Plans, Government's approach to the problem of population growth, and the need for family planning, was a long-term objective, depending as much, if not more, on 'improvement in living standards and more widespread education especially among women', as on positive measures for 'inculcation of the need' and techniques of family planning. Admitting that rates of population growth could only be altered over a period, it was agreed that programmes to restrain population growth had to complement a massive development effort. Table 1.20 gives the Allocation of funds for Health and Family Planning during the First to the Fifth Five-Year Plans.

From the Third Plan, however, restraint of population growth received a much greater emphasis and priority, with time-bound targets for reducing the birth rate and heavy investment in the administrative network to mount the programmes on the lines of a military operation, and the adoption of practices like mass sterilization camps, financial incentives and appointment of promoters, to make sterilization acceptable to the people. The legalization of abortions in cases of contraceptive failure was also a step to promote reduction in the birth rate. Some State Governments even adopted measures to deny maternity benefits to Women Government Servants after the third child. We feel strongly about this measure, for the denial of maternity benefits to a working woman is likely to affect both the health of the mother as well as that of the child. In Madhya Pradesh, we met a group of women teachers who complained bitterly that this measure has resulted in a number of them having to work till the day before the child was born. We have already pointed out the results of the absence of this benefit to construction workers.

The result of this change in emphasis was to put excessive reliance on the clinical rather than the welfare approach to family planning. Heavy investment in services, personnel and propaganda, exclusively devoted to family planning, led to a relative neglect of the other health and welfare services. In the case of women, the maternity and child health services, family welfare, adult education, and economic progress, all suffered relative lack of attention and resources, and Family Planning came to be described as the most important governmental programme for women. Table 1.19 indicates the inroads made by this programme on the investment of health services as a whole, resulting in the "unfinished public health revolution" in India.

TABLE - 1.19

ALLOCATION FOR HEALTH & FAMILY PLANNING IN VARIOUS PLANS

(Rupees in Crores)

	I Plan	*II Plan*	*III Plan*	*IV Plan*	*V Plan*
(a) Allocation for other Health Programmes	98	216	226	226	816
(b) Allocation for Family Planning	6.50	49.70	269.70	315	516
Ratio of allocation for Family Planning to other Health Programmes	6.63	23	114.91	139.38	63.23

The Draft Fifth Plan has changed the emphasis again, mainly in view of a growing realization that the programme is becoming increasingly unpopular among many sections, and is failing to achieve the unrealistic targets. It is also admitted that a purely clinical approach cannot overcome the socio-psychological resistance caused by poverty, ignorance, low survival rate of children among the poor sections, and the economic and social dependence on children.

Though integration of family planning with maternal and child health care was suggested in the Fourth Plan, the policy of integration could not be achieved, since the family planning services had been already placed under a different administrative machinery from the other health services. A new strategy evolved for the Fifth Plan visualizes the integration of family planning into the general health services, particularly its maternal and child care component including nutrition. The principle of integration will be extended to other fields, in particular to efforts at mass motivation through the existing channels for functional training programmes to train multipurpose health workers to deliver the integrated health care services under the Minimum Needs Programme. The impact of this decision to see family planning in its proper perspective is clearly visible in the allocation of resources proposed for the Fifth Plan. According to the Draft Fifth Five-Year Plan:

> The primary objective during the Fifth Plan is to provide minimum public health facilities integrated with family planning and nutrition for vulnerable groups — children, pregnant women and lactating mothers. It will be necessary to consolidate past gains in the various fields of health, such as communicable diseases, medical education and provision of infrastructure in the rural areas.

During our tours we found that wherever the medical personnel and the village level workers were mature and sympathetic in their approach and worked with a sense of social commitment, their persuasive power evoked a great degree of response. On the other hand there was considerable criticism of the 'motivators', most of whom are very young and inexperienced as well as purely untrained persons. It was a frequent observation that they were responsible for criminal mistakes like persuading extremely young persons both male and female to undergo sterilization, or bringing elderly women who were long past the child bearing age for the same, entirely because of the financial incentives. According to Banerjee (1948):

> Perhaps the greatest mistakes in the formulation of family planning programmes has been a gross overestimation of the effectiveness of the `motivators and equally gross underestimation of the resistance to be encountered motivating a community as a whole ....Motivation techniques were viewed as some sort of a magic which would be applied by a person to induce another to accept family planning.

We understand that it has been decided to introduce community incentives and group awards for the programme personnel with a view to increasing the involvement of the community and strengthening the commitment of the staff and institutions in order to improve the quality of the services. Most of the doctors and the women with whom we discussed problems of family planning were of the opinion that while payment to acceptors should continue particularly for daily wage workers, the payment to motivators is not only a waste but has been responsible for much of the unpopularity of this programme. There were also severe criticisms of the lack of adequate follow-up measures. We also came across large gaps both in areas and communities where the family planning services have not reached. One group of women whom we met in Bangalore had never heard of family planning.

During the course of its tours in the States, the Committee met a number of health and family planning officials, social workers, as well as a cross-section of rural and urban women. An analysis of the tour reports reveals that the message of family planning has reached almost everywhere, but access to health and family planning services was most inadequate. Even in slum areas of big cities, there were no family planning clinics in the vicinity, and the women did not know where to go, though they were anxious to avail themselves of the information. In the rural areas, there was an acute shortage of maternity facilities, and trained medical personnel.

In Bastar district, and in some tribal areas of Himachal Pradesh, we were informed that the birth rate is 29 per 1000, which is well below the national target for the Vth Plan, and yet we found money being spent on family planning projects in these areas. There were huge hoardings and posters advocating the small family norm, when this money could very well have been utilized for other welfare activities in these extremely backward areas.

In our view, the inadequacy of qualified medical personnel and mature counselling presents the greatest internal drawback to the success of this programme. We are entirely in agreement with the Draft Fifth Five-Year Plan, that integration of family planning with more positive health services like maternal and child health and nutrition, and improvement in the life expectancy of children and mothers, will provide a far greater incentive to the adoption of family planning measures than the hitherto adopted negative approach.

Welfare Programmes

Programmes for women's welfare and development can be classified under the following broad base :

A. Programmes in the rural areas

Welfare Extension Projects, Family and Child Welfare Projects, Organization of Mahila Mandals, Training Schemes for Workers.

B. Programmes in urban areas

Welfare Extension Projects, and Working Women's Hostels.

C. Other Programmes

Grants-in-aid to voluntary organizations, Condensed Courses of Education for Adult Women, Adult Literacy and social education for women. Craft training centres, Socio-economic programmes, Nutrition Programmes, Social Defence Programmes, Border Area Programmes, Homes for Women.

Rural Areas

The concept of rural development as conceived in India covers a wide field and history. Both Mahatma Gandhi and Rabindranath Tagore had seen rural development as an important method of social mobilization which could build the social infrastructure for independence. According to Tagore, it was an effort to make the village a self-reliant and self-respectful unit, with knowledge of its culture and history, and to enable the people to make use of modern resources for their full upliftment — physical, social, economic and intellectual. Gandhi viewed rural development as aiming to make every village a 'Republic', in which no person would be unemployed, and everyone would enjoy sufficient nutritious food, houses with adequate hygiene and sanitation, and enough *khadi* for their clothing. Thus, rural development was not seen only in its micro-dimension, but as a new philosophy for society, which was to bring social consciousness or a revolution among the rural people. Tagore's Shriniketan and Gandhi's Village Construction Programmes were the forerunners of rural development that was to be taken up by the government after independence. The Community Development Programme undertaken by the Government of India drew heavily from the Gandhian concept.

The application of Gandhian ideas to the field of women's development had been done by the Kasturba Memorial Trust after the death of Kasturba Gandhi, which had been given a concrete form in the objectives and activities of the Kasturba Memorial Trust. This Trust was born with the objective of serving rural women by providing:

(i) education for women and children;
(ii) medical and health services; and
(iii) socio-economic programmes in the form of *khadi* and village industries to relieve economic distress.

The Trust trained a number of *gramsevikas* and mid-wives and the training centres were specially conceived to train and mobilize village women, specially widows and deserted wives. The health programmes aimed at prevention of diseases as well as promotion of positive health through maternal and child welfare programmes.

When the Central Social Welfare Board decided to launch the Welfare Extension Projects in 1954, this threefold approach was adopted as the basic framework for provision of services. The activities included Balwadis, maternity services and general medical aid, social education and craft training for women. The original Welfare Extension Projects (WEP) were to serve a unit of 25-40 contiguous villages, with a population of 25-30 thousand through five centres. At the end of the Second Plan, there were 420 such projects with 2004 centres. Eight of these projects, with 40 centres, continue to be operated by the Central Social Welfare Board, while others have either been closed or handed over to Mahila Mandals and voluntary organizations which receive 75 per cent financial assistance.

Since the general objectives and methodology of this programme were similar to those of the larger programmes of community development initiated by the government during the First Plan in 1952, and to eliminate duplication of work, it was decided that Welfare Extension Projects should be started in Community Development Blocks on a coordinated basis. All original Welfare Extension Projects were converted into this pattern as soon as the area was covered by a C.D. Block. These projects covered a block of 100 villages with a population of about 60,000 through 10 centres. The work and the functionaries were supervised by a Project Implementing Committee which consisted of representatives of block officials and local voluntary workers. For the first year the budget was shared by the Central Social Welfare Board, the State Government and Community Development Block in the ratio of 12:6:5 and at the end of 5 years the total expenditure was shared in the ratio of 24:12:5. At the end of March 1971, there were 264 projects with 2,800 centres.

Since greater importance was increasingly attached to the role of voluntary organizations in the continuance of welfare programmes, 1,629 centres of the Welfare Extension Projects (original and coordinated pattern) were handed over to Mahila Mandals by 31st March, 1966. 442 Mahila Mandals, who have taken over one or more activities of this project were given a grant of Rs. 25.69 lakh during 1972-73.

On the recommendations of the Central Social Welfare Board and an Evaluation Committee of Social Welfare on the Welfare Extension Projects in 1964, it was decided to revise services existing in rural areas in different patterns aiming to develop a country-wide programme of integrated welfare services for children. Thus the Family and Child Welfare (F&CW) scheme was initiated in November, 1967, whereas extension projects provided services for women and children, the Family and Child Welfare Projects aimed at integrated development of the pre-school child, training to young mothers and all services that were necessary for the proper growth and development of the child and rural family.

The family and child welfare projects were funded by the Central and the State Governments in a 75:25 ratio and aided by UNICEF with equipment, stipends and training facilities. They have progressively taken over the functions of the earlier projects of the Central Social Welfare Board and the Ministry of Community Development. The services provided are:

(a) Integrated services to rural children; specially pre-school;

(b) Basic training to women and young girls in home management, health education, nutrition education, child care. General health and maternity services for women were also to be provided with the aid of the Primary Health Centres. Similar collaboration was also envisaged for nutrition.

(c) Assistance to women through Mahila Mandals, specially established centres and existing welfare agencies, for getting supplementary work to augment their income.

(d) Cultural, educational and recreational activities for women and children.

There were 221 projects in existence at the end of 1970-71 and during 1971-72, 20 coordinated welfare extension projects were added to this scheme, bringing the total to 240. On 31st March, 1973, 281 projects were functioning.

Maternity and Child Welfare Services

With the integration of the First Plan, Maternity and Child Welfare Services were taken up by the Ministry of Health as part of the overall development programme in health. These services were augmented by WHO and UNICEF. A number of Maternity and Child Welfare Bureaus were established in States, staffed by qualified women medical officers. At the same time, the then Community Projects administration also undertook these services in the

Community Development and National Extension Service Blocks. Other Ministries like Railways, Defence and Labour also promoted Maternity and Child Welfare Programmes through the Ministry of Health. The number of Maternity and Child Welfare Centres increased and these services were given an important place in rural development programmes. The Union Government assisted the States in establishment of primary health centres and sub-centres covering a C.D. Block. At present 5,195 centres are functioning in the country. Maternity and Child Welfare Services are also undertaken by the Ministries of Railways, Labour (under Labour Welfare and the various Acts in this section) and public sector undertakings.

Mahila Mandals

Practically from the beginning it was realized that the objectives of these rural development programmes could not be achieved without the active participation and leadership of the local community. Government functionaries, however, efficient and dedicated, can only provide some stimulus and act as catalytic agents to train and release efforts for self-help of the people. This was particularly true of women who had been paralysed by generations of social oppression, and denial of basic rights. Both the Central Social Welfare Board and the department of Community development concluded that the proper agency for the success of this programme would be a committee of local women. The organization of Mahila Mandals thus became one of the objectives of these rural development programmes.

The declared objective of community development is to enable rural women to organize themselves at the village level to assemble on a regular basis to learn from each other and from workers appointed by the Government. The basic idea is to create opportunities for rural women to improve their status as housewives and to take part in public affairs. The department therefore organizes Mahila Mandals, imparts training facilities to their members and provides incentive awards for performance.

Mahila Mandals were organized in villages and blocks for promoting women's programmes. Nutrition, education, health, mother and child care, home improvement, adult literacy, recreation and cultural activities and training and house and family planning were part of their programmes. By the end of 1972-73, there were about 53,000 Mahila Mandals with a total membership of 14,00,000 averaging 11 Mahila Mandals per block. Under the Applied Nutrition Programme, additional facilities are being provided for the promotion of economic activities of Mahila Mandals towards development and management of kitchen and school gardens, organization of fishery units, etc. During the Fourth Plan 7,500 awards in various categories were given to Mahila Mandals.

The Central Social Welfare Board and the State Social Welfare Advisory Boards also realized the importance of Mahila Mandals and after 1961 they are being given grants up to 75 per cent for running some programmes of the Board. In 1972-73, 442 Mahila Mandals received a grant of about Rs 25.69 lakh. They are also running some Welfare Extension Projects of the Board.

Voluntary agencies like the Bhartiya Grameen Mahila Sangh have also established a large number of Mahila Mandals. The representatives of the Village Mahila Mandals form the District Mahila Samities and the representatives of the District Mahila Samities constitute the State panel or State branches. According to the Bhartiya Grameen Mahila Sangh, its branches in the 17 States now cover 7,000 villages.

Training Scheme for Workers

The various functionaries required for these rural development schemes are trained at centres located in different parts of the country. The training is organized by some government agencies like the Directorate of Extension of the Ministry of Agriculture and various schools of social work, non-governmental organizations like the Kasturba Memorial Trust, Visva Bharati, Jamia Millia with assistance from the Central Social Welfare Board.

The Department of Community Development in the Ministry of Agriculture has a programme for training associate women workers to enable members of Mahila Mandals to come forward to become organized. The members of Mahila Mandals get to know about the organization of Balwadis, health and nutrition, education, nursery, kitchen gardening, etc. About 20,000 women received training in the Third and Fourth Plans and a sum of Rs 11.17 lakh was spent during the Fourth Plan.

The Directorate of Extension of the Ministry of Agriculture also provides training for village level workers of Community Development Block at 25 centres. The emphasis is on the protection of Agricultural production and nutrition education. In service, training facilities are provided after 2-3 years service and two-week refresher courses are given to Mukhya Sevikas. Refresher courses are also given to Instructresses for Gram Sevika and Mukhya Sevika training centres for six weeks. Associate workers such as Gram Lakshmis or Gram Kakis are also given one month's training. Under the nutrition education scheme of 1969-70, training was given to associate women workers.

Farm Women's Training Courses for one week are organized at about 100 training centres for farm women. This farmers' training was started in 1968-69 in a few districts and is now being implemented in almost all districts. The emphasis is on agricultural production, reproduction patterns of high yielding variety cereals, stock managements, nutrition, etc. Radio broadcasting is also used for educating the farm women and organizing discussion groups.

The Bhartiya Grameen Mahila Sangh also holds various training camps for rural women. Among these are leadership training camps sanctioned by the Department of Social Welfare in border areas. Similar programmes have also been sponsored by the CSWB. The increased agricultural production programme is a seven-day camp sanctioned by the Ministry of Food and Agriculture for training in improved agricultural methods and covered 650 villages till March 1973. The Ministry of Health has sanctioned the family planning orientation programme to train village women in methods of family planning.

Urban Areas

The structure of welfare programmes in urban areas varies from region to region. The municipalities and local administration are responsible for providing basic formal education and health facilities like schools, hospitals, dispensaries, etc. Welfare programmes as such have already been left to voluntary organizations, which in some cases receive grants through the Central Social Welfare Board or the State Governments.

In 1958 the Central Social Welfare Board started Welfare

Extension Projects in the urban areas to meet the needs of people living in the slums, particularly in new industrial areas. These projects provided balwadis, creches, arts and craft classes and family planning and maternity advice for women; they also do placement of destitutes. 65 such projects were in existence at the end of the Third Plan. They were reduced to 33 by 1971-72 and 1972-73. In 1972-73, 34 Welfare Extension Projects received Rs 2.78 lakh benefiting approximately 70,000 families.

Working Women's Hostels

An increasing number of women are leaving their homes and entering employment. The problem of accommodation in metropolitan areas, particularly impelled the Central Social Welfare Board to provide grants for hostels for working women as one of its services. The Board viewed this service as a preventive measure against the possibility of young girls in urban areas being exposed to undesirable and anti-social influences.

The scheme was started during the Second Plan and the Board sanctioned grants to voluntary welfare institutions willing to provide healthy accommodation at reasonable rates for working women of lower income groups. At the end of the Third Plan, 101 grants amounting to Rs 9.76 lakh had been sanctioned. During 1972-73, 29 hostels received a grant of Rs 66,000 from the Board. During 1971-72, the Department of Social Welfare initiated a scheme for financial assistance to voluntary institutions for the construction of hostel buildings in capital cities and cities with a population of over ten lakh. The pattern of assistance is under review at present and in the Fifth Plan a sum of Rs 5 crore has been set aside for hostels for working women.

Other Programmes

Condensed Courses of Education for Adult Women

The very high percentage of illiteracy amongst women as well as various difficulties in imparting education to them gave rise to the condensed courses of education for adult women which are being implemented by various governmental and non-governmental agencies. The programme was initiated by the Central Social Welfare Board in 1958 with the dual objective of opening new vistas of employment for needy women and to create a band of trained workers for various projects in the rural areas.

Under the scheme, adult women between the ages of 18 and 30, who have some schooling, are prepared for middle schools, matriculation or equivalent examination within a period of two years. Grants up to Rs 35,000 per course for two years are given for maintenance, stipends, salaries to teachers and educational equipment. Women who complete these courses can go in for vocational training as nurse, mid-wife, *gramsevikas*, etc. In the Second Plan Rs 58.82 lakh were sanctioned for 271 courses, though only Rs 28.88 lakh was released. In the Third Plan, a provision of Rs 150 lakh was made for 500 courses. Up to the end of February 1973, 1,386 courses were started and Rs 3 crore were spent. Of 33,000 women enrolled about 25,000 completed their studies. The programme has been extended to wives of Jawans killed or disabled in action. The Community Development Department also has established adult literacy centres in blocks which cover women.

Socio-Economic Programmes

It was realized at an early stage of the welfare programmes that they would not have the desired impact unless the women were imparted some craft or technical training. This was a part of the three pronged approach of the earliest programmes. While health received some attention and resources from the Ministry of Health, and Family Planning, as well as welfare agencies, the economic schemes did not receive corresponding attention from the concerned governmental agencies. On a very minor scale, some socio-economic schemes were initiated by the Central Social Welfare Board and its grants-in-aid schemes and also organized on a small scale by the Department of Community Development and some voluntary organization. Initially started by the Ministry of Rehabilitation for refugee women, it was taken up by the Central Social Welfare Board in 1954, to provide leisure time employment to women in lower income groups and help them supplement their income. This was undertaken in cooperation with the Ministry of Commerce and Industry which provides them necessary assistance in technical training, finance and marketing. The scheme was working in co-operation with State Governments and State Social Welfare Advisory Boards. 95 demonstration-cum-training centres set up on 26 pilot projects for industries in the Community Development Project areas have benefited women.

At present the socio-economic programme of the CSWB provides financial assistance to voluntary welfare institutions and Co-operative Societies for setting up small production units where needy women or handicapped persons are given initial training and subsequently provided with employment. In the implementation of this programme, the Board as well as voluntary institutions and Cooperative Societies obtain technical assistance from the National-Small Industries Organization and regional offices of the All-India Handicrafts Board and All-India Handloom Board. The categories of the scheme that are being implemented under this programme are:

1. Production units of small-scale industries, such as manufacture of toys and articles, printing books, binding, fruit preservation and canning, bakery, confectionary, ready-made garments, etc.
2. Handicrafts training-cum-procurement and production units; for example, cane and bamboo articles, mat — weaving, traditional embroidery, etc.
3. Handloom training-cum-production units;
4. Units ancillary to large industries; and
5. Industrial co-operative societies set up under the voluntary welfare programmes started by the Board in 1953-54.

Up to the end of March 1972, the Board had approved grants to 130 institutions for setting up production units with an employment potential of about 4,000 under various categories of schemes. By the end of March 1973, an amount of Rs 54.60 lakh had been sanctioned for 140 approved units with an employment potential of 4,235.

The Annual Report of 1972-73 of the Central Social Welfare Board mentions that the attention of the State Governments have been drawn to the need for extending some sort of protection or patronage to socio-economic units run by voluntary institutions buying their products. The problem of marketing remains unsolved and unless this is overcome, the objective of a number of socio-economic programmes will remain unfilled. A number of Ministries such as Railways, Ministry of Labour, apart from the Ministry of Agriculture and Community Development have small schemes for providing craft training to women. The Mahila Samities of the Ministry of Railways have handicraft centres to help women in learning some trade to enable them to supplement the family income. Some public sector undertakings have Mahila Mandals which also provide such training. While the emphasis on these programmes to improve women's earning power indicates awareness of the dimension of women's problems, it is doubtful whether these programmes are having the desired impact, since most of these women are unable to obtain the raw-material or market the finished goods. It is also remarkable that the governmental agencies responsible for promoting industrial development have completely ignored and the reality of the problem that they are trying to solve.

Nutrition Programmes

The Plan emphasized nutrition as a major problem particularly in rural areas, and among the lower income groups. The Department of Social Welfare and the Central Social Welfare Board, the Ministry of Health and Family Planning, the Department of Community Development of the Ministry of Agriculture and the Ministry of Education are all operating various nutrition schemes for women and children.

The Special Nutrition Programme of the Government of India was introduced in 1970-71 to provide supplementary nutrition to children in tribal areas and urban slums, by the Department of Social Welfare. This scheme covers a number of pre-school children in 0-6 age groups and nursing the expectant mothers. Over 19,600 feeding centres have been set up in the tribal areas and about 7,500 in urban areas. The Department of Social Welfare also implements a nutrition programme for children in the age group 3-5, through the Balwadis and day-care centres run by the CSWB, the Indian Council of Child Welfare, the Harijan Sevak Sangh, and the Adimjati Sevak Sangh, covering 2,00,640 children and 5,577 instructions. The Balwadis of the Family and Child Welfare Projects were generally excluded from this Programme because provision for nutrition was already provided in the scheme. The Board, however, feels that it has not been possible to build up adequate machinery for implementation and supervision of this programme at the State and Central levels and it requires greater provision by the Government.

The Directorate of Extension of the Ministry of Agriculture has been running a Composite Nutrition Programme since 1969-70, to provide nutrition education in areas not covered under the Applied Nutrition Programme. It includes nutrition education, through Mahila Mandals, strengthening the supervisory machinery for women's programmes, encouragement of economic activities of Mahila Mandals, training of associate women workers and demonstration feeding. The Applied Nutrition Programme of the Department of Community Development was introduced in collaboration with UNICEF, FAO and WHO. It was intended to educate the rural people in improved nutrition by promoting the production and consumption of protective foods like fruits, vegetables, fish and poultry. From 1966-67, steps were taken to co-ordinate the operation of the Applied Nutrition Programmes with other schemes like the Mid-Day Meal Programme of the Ministry of Education, and Family and Child Welfare Projects of the Department of Social Welfare. During the Third Plan period, the ANP covered 221 blocks and by the end of 1972-73 it covered, 1,101 projects and spent Rs 1.46 crore for this purpose. Under this programme, demonstration, in cooking and feeding is held, particularly designed to give direction on nutrition through the Mahila Mandals and to train women workers.

The Ministry of Health has increasingly emphasized nutrition particularly for pregnant women, lactating mothers and pre-school children of the weaker sections, through an integrated programme of supplementary feeding, health care, immunization as well as nutrition education. During the Fifth Plan, concentrated attention will be given to these vulnerable sections in rural areas, urban slums, tribal development blocks and school going children of the weaker sections. Within the resources allocated, it should be possible to cover about 11 million additional beneficiaries in the

Fifth Plan. This programme is under the budgetary control of the Department of Social Welfare.

The Fourth Plan Special Nutrition Programme for pre-school children and expectant and nursing mothers has been redesignated and included in the Integrated Child Development Programme in the Fifth Plan. The services include supplementary nutrition feeding, immunization, health check-up and referral services, health and nutrition education. The entire expenditure for the ICDP during the Fifth Plan will be made by the Centre and implemented through the State Governments and Union Territories. It is proposed to cover about 7,000 nursing and expectant mothers in each project. Women between 15-44 years numbering approximately 23,000 will be provided nutrition and health education. In the tribal areas 2,450 nursing and expectant mothers and 7,000 women in the 15-44 age groups are the target population for each project. The ICDP depends on interdepartmental coordination between the Ministry of Health, State Health Departments, Community Development Department and the Department of Social Welfare. The existing 33,000 feeding centres of the Special Nutrition Programme and Balwadi nutrition programmes in operation in organized slums, tribal areas and other rural areas will initially be included into ICDP centres in the project areas.

Social Defence Programmes

Among the services available in the country for the correction and reformation of persons who come into conflict with the law are the following which apply directly to women:

(a) Suppression of Immoral Traffic;
(b) After care services; and
(c) Welfare Services in Prisons.

These services are provided by the Department of Social Welfare and Rehabilitation Directorate at Central level.

The Suppression of Immoral Traffic in Women and Girls Act of 1956 provides for protective homes and reception centres. There are at present 33 protective homes and 68 reception centres and district shelters in the country. A scheme for short stay homes for rehabilitation of women and girls facing moral danger was approved in 1969-70 and two pilot projects — one in West Bengal and the other in Madhya Pradesh were provided grants of Rs 1.10 lakh in 1972-73. During the Second Plan, programmes were drawn up under Social and Moral Hygiene and After Care Programmes not only for those under the SIT Act, but also those discharged from Correctional and non-Correctional Institutions. The State Governments were assisted to set up special homes such as protective homes.

We visited some of these protective homes. In the Protective Home in Lucknow and in the Nari Niketan in Delhi, efforts are made to rehabilitate the inmates by providing training in sewing and embroidery. There is no formal procedure for marketing of these products, nor are the inmates given any training either to organize production or marketing. We were informed that sewing machines are presented to the inmates when they are discharged to help them to become self-employed. This practice was reported to be prevalent in many States. According to reports by social workers in different parts of the country, most of these young women find it difficult to earn an adequate livelihood from this occupation. Quite a number are compelled to dispose of the machines, and revert to their original profession. We were rather distressed to find that these homes house women rescued from immoral traffic as well as young girls sent under the Children's Act. Even insane women are housed in these homes. We consider this to be a very unhealthy and undesirable situation. We also feel that the training provided for rehabilitation in these homes is not adequate and requires much greater attention and planning as well as resources. We were informed that in some of the homes, efforts are made to return these young women to their families wherever possible, or to arrange marriages for them.

There has been considerable discussion on these programmes for rehabilitation of victims of immoral traffic. During a recent Judicial Seminar on Correctional Services, the speakers, who included representatives of the Association for Social Health, the Director of Social Welfare, Delhi Administration and members of the staff of the Delhi School of Social Work, pointed out the inadequacy of the arrangements for the employment of these young women. Without economic rehabilitation, much of the efforts made for their rescue is wasted. Some social workers have suggested to us that the best way for rehabilitation would be to set up production-cum-marketing centres along with these homes. It is also necessary to diversify the types of training provided to the inmates, since over-dependence on tailoring and embroidery has led to considerable waste. Economic independence is the only way to protect these women from the clutches of persons who have a vested interest in this traffic.

Homes are also provided for the aged and destitute women in various States though the total number of such homes is inadequate in terms of the population to be covered. A scheme for the welfare of destitute women between the ages of 18-44 and 45-65 providing for basic amenities of food, shelter, clothing, besides education and training in craft to enable the younger group to become self-reliant, as also services for dependent children up to 7 years was finalized in 1970-71. For the first group, residential institutions to accommodate 200 persons were to be provided. The scheme was to be implemented by giving grants-in-aid to voluntary organizations up to 75 per cent of the expenditure. The total Fourth Plan provision was Rs 100 lakh. We regret to note that the scheme remains unimplemented.

Grants-in-aid

Grants-in-aid are extended to registered voluntary institutions working for welfare of women, children and handicapped persons. Under the grants-in-aid for women's welfare during the First and the Second Plans, assistance was provided for expansion, development and improvement of activities of voluntary organizations. On the basis of the recommendations of the grants-in-aid Committee, the Board decided to limit the assistance during the Third Plan to consolidate and improve the activities initiated during the First and the Second Plans. Generally all grants except those given for developing special schemes were given on a matching basis.

The amounts allocated to these schemes during the four Plans indicate that while the First and Second Plans brought in a number of voluntary institutions within the network for administration of welfare services, Government's dependence on these bodies has registered a decline during the Third and Fourth Plans.

Grants sanctioned to Voluntary Organizations by the Central Social Welfare Board under Grants-in-aid Programme

1st Plan	Rs. 75,54,000
2nd Plan	Rs. 294,00,000
3rd Plan	Rs. 246,00,000
4th Plan	Rs. 159,61,000

Voluntary Organizations

Voluntary welfare services in India have always been an integral part of the cultural and social tradition. The bulk of the social services were provided by the voluntary sector prior to independence. Social welfare services have always been present in some form or the other for the well-being of the weaker sections of society who, because of various handicaps, social, economic, physical, etc., could not make use of, or were traditionally denied, normal facilities. The weaker sections included women, children, the aged, infirm and handicapped, Scheduled Castes and Scheduled Tribes.

Voluntary organizations may opt for several alternative roles according to their objectives and composition. They may be innovational and experimental activities in fields where government has not entered. They may co-exist with the public sector and the private sector for social development because they may have some advantages over the former or they can provide the government with a supportive base, i.e., they can work like agents of the government at local levels and operate programmes of the government as their own.

Soon after independence, on the basis of a survey made by the Planning Commission, it was estimated that there were about 10,000 voluntary organizations in the field of social welfare. In order to strengthen and encourage these agencies the Central Social Welfare Board was established in 1953, with a nationwide programme for grants-in-aid. It was realized that the voluntary organizations, with the qualities of flexibility, of experimentation, human touch, nearness to the clientele, sensitiveness to the new problems and capacity to discover new ideas could be of great assistance, since it was impossible for any government to take care of all the welfare needs of the people. The voluntary agencies could also mobilize resources from within the community for social welfare.

The relative importance of the role of the State and the role of the voluntary agencies has been engaging the attention of policy makers, planners, social thinkers, administrators and voluntary workers. In 1959, a Study team on Social Welfare and Backward Classes, appointed by the Planning Commission, recommended that whereas all programmes of social welfare arising out of the statutory responsibility of the State should be sponsored by State departments of Social Welfare, other social welfare services to meet local needs should be implemented through voluntary organizations. A seminar on Social Administration in Developing Countries held in New Delhi in March, 1964, felt that the co-operation of the State and voluntary agencies in meeting social needs would always bring out better results in promoting welfare services on a larger scale.

We met representatives of some national voluntary organizations working for women's welfare and the welfare of socially deprived groups. We also met representatives of voluntary welfare organizations in every State during our tours. Most of the women's voluntary organizations have been confined to the urban areas, with its membership drawn mainly from educated urban middle-class women. Their main activities are conducting literacy classes, adult education centres, Balwadis, promoting women's cooperatives, small savings, handicrafts, etc. Some of these organizations have also taken up family planning programmes. In times of emergency, such organizations have organized canteens, blood banks and other services. These organizations seek to raise the status of women in the social, economic, political and educational fields. They have passed numerous resolutions for the uplift of Indian women, but their constructive activities have suffered from limitations of resources, personnel, and failure to reach rural areas.

Only a few organizations have endeavoured to work amongst rural women, to improve their living conditions, promote leadership and assist them to take part in developmental activities. The government has given grants for some voluntary welfare activities. In some cases, the grant has been for administration and maintenance while in other cases it has been allotted for programmes only.

Apart from the Central Social Welfare Board's grants-in-aid programme, there is no machinery to coordinate and distribute the services provided by these bodies, to ensure greater efficiency and even distribution. Nor are the resources of the majority of these organizations adequate to maintain trained workers for their complex types of work. Initially, the important organizations were able to act as pressure groups in directing the attention of the government to social problems, and to mobilize support for social legislation. Our investigation has shown that these laws still remain unknown to the large mass of Indian women, who have not been able to take advantage of them. Most of these organizations operate independent of each other and as such have not been able to fully benefit the community.

Governmental Administration of Welfare Programmes

Expenditure for welfare programmes, including programmes meant for women is low in comparison to other sectors, since it has been viewed as a non-productive item in comparison to the economic sectors. In times of stringencies, financial cuts are made first in this sector, since returns from investments are not immediate. A break-up of allocations indicates that a major part of the expenditure is on maintenance and establishment charges, leaving only a small percentage for actual services. The administrative tradition in India has tended to emphasize maintenance of law and order, and economic development, and departments dealing with welfare programmes generally occupy a relatively less important position in the governmental structure. The training imparted to the administrators also emphasizes the same aspects. It has now been realized that administration must also be welfare oriented and recently a working group has been set up to frame a syllabus for social administration for the training of service probationers at the National Academy of Administration and other State level training institutes.

The administration and handling of welfare programmes has become increasingly technical. Administrators have to acquire technical orientation for successful implementation of social welfare programmes. The lack of emphasis on the required technical competence and the limitation of resources have had an adverse impact on the quality and success of welfare programmes.

Certain factors impede realization of a high degree of rationality in organization and flexibility in operation. The federal nature of our policy vests responsibility for implementing social policy and programmes with State and local authorities, but resources and agencies for planning are at the Centre. The weakness of local authorities further complicates the problems. There is dire need for greater coordination between voluntary agencies and organizations built up by Government, between activities of States and the Central Government and of the district or local level organizations and the States.

State Level

At present the majority of the States have a Minister-in-charge of Social Welfare, though this portfolio might include other subjects. State governments give still lower priority to social welfare programmes, and are reluctant to allocate sufficient resources. It has also been found that in the operation of the democratic process, the interests of the weaker sections are sometimes neglected, as they are relatively less vocal and less powerful than the dominant section of the population. Due to existing social prejudice and attitudes towards women, any policy regarding their welfare and development is limited either to education or welfare of special groups like handicapped or destitute women. Therefore, though social welfare is a State subject, the major share of the State's allocations go towards the maintenance of the existing social welfare activities initiated generally by the Centre.

As an illustration, it may be mentioned that during Shri Charan Singh's tenure as Chief Minister in UP, all women's welfare programmes of the Government were summarily discontinued. The State Social Welfare (Advisory) Board was however allowed to continue because of strong representation from the State Finance Department that its abolition would result in stoppage of Central assistance. The closure provoked a protest from the women functionaries whose services were held up as a model to other States, because of their success. The result of the closure has left only skeletal services for women in the States.

Most State governments do not have any machinery for collection of data or planning of welfare services. The State Social Welfare (Advisory) Boards, which might have fulfilled this role, serve mainly as a link organization to supervise, implement and report on the working of aided voluntary organizations in the State as an agency of the Central Social Welfare Board. The relationship between Central and State Governments, the Central Social Welfare Board and the State governments are also not clearly defined and the status of the State Boards differ from State to State.

Local administrations have shown even less interest in women's welfare programmes in general and local bodies authorized to allocate resources have given very low priority to them. Everywhere we were told that the Mahila Mandals were being starved of funds and not being provided even with accommodation. The process of co-opting women into the Panchayats has also not been very successful as their small numbers has prevented them from being more effective in emphasizing the needs of women. As a rule, they have not had an effective voice in policy making or the allocation of resources. The male members of the rural elite are by and large not favourably disposed towards improving and changing the position of women and consequently women's programmes are prone to be neglected.

Increase in Role of Centre

The neglect and indifference to welfare activities by the local and State Governments has led to an increase in the role of central agencies in this field. Within the federal framework the Central government's role should normally be planning, monitoring progress of activities, stimulating particular activities to ensure a national minimum standard, and guiding States through policy directions, giving advice and providing technical and financial help. The reasons for this increase in the role of the Centre can, therefore, be summed up as follows:

(a) Limitation of resources of State Governments;
(b) Indifference and low priorities for welfare programmes on the part of most State Governments;
(c) Absence of proper welfare agencies in most of the States.

The experience of the Central Social Welfare Board suggests that the Coordination Committees as envisaged at the local level of some of the projects of the Board were not very useful since local administrations were not willing to take up women's welfare programmes. The State Boards were not in a position to function autonomously and the State Governments were disinterested in women's welfare programmes.

Under the system of financial relations between the Central and the State Governments, the Centre provides assistance for development programmes during a Plan period either on sharing or on full basis. At the end of the Plan period full responsibility for continuing the programmes devolves on the States. In the case of the women's programmes initiated by Central agencies, State Governments have not always been willing to accept the responsibility for continuation. In such cases, these programmes have had to be discontinued or redesignated as a new programme so that Central assistance could be continued.

Standardization of Programmes

The concept of a local need-based approach to social welfare has gradually been overshadowed as a direct consequence of this centralizing trend. Programmes and policies are initiated at the Centre, and there is increasing distance between the level of policy making and the levels of implementation. National programmes are framed without adequate reference to local variations and needs and this defeats the very purpose of social welfare. It particularly affects the initiative of the local community and the voluntary sector, and leads to increasing bureaucratization. It has also prevented the State Governments from admitting their responsibility in the field of welfare.

Because of this bureaucratization and centralization, the authority and initiative of the field staff is considerably impaired. As an example, the field staff at the State level are not taken into confidence nor are their suggestions considered at the level of policy and planning. For a number of schemes of the Central Social Welfare Board, the State Boards have little authority for initiating and reviewing the programmes.

The delays inherent in routine procedure and functioning of the Government hampers the progress of the programmes. Government organizations and procedures, with rigid rules governing sanctions and expenditure by their very nature, are not suited to the essentially informal and personal approach required for welfare work. Generally the approach of the voluntary workers and organizations is more flexible and personal. Once funds have been allotted for a particular project, they cannot be diverted for any other purpose and these agencies have to function within the rigid framework of the government sanction.

Lack of Coordination

An examination of welfare and development activities undertaken in the country so far indicates that there is a multiplicity of programmes, agencies and functionaries. A large number of these programmes have very similar objectives and functions.

These programmes are run by different departments, have separate allocations, and the field staff belong to different agencies. Areas of implementation in many cases are not rationally demarcated. Since most of these are Central programmes, planning and policy making is carried out by separate Ministries and Departments at the Centre. There is very little or no coordination between these Ministries and Departments, except where a coordinated programme has been envisaged (as in the case of the Fifth Plan Integrated Child Development Programme). This leads to a waste of funds in the duplication of administrative machinery, leaving a relatively small amount for the actual implementation of the programmes.

There is very little coordination at the State level also. Even though the State Social Welfare Advisory Boards have some government officials as members, this has failed to ensure any substantial coordination of governmental effort in the welfare of women. At the project level, the functional committees and implementation committees are constituted with representatives of the State Governments and State Boards. They have to work in collaboration with the Panchayats or other local organization. The experience of these committees has not been always happy. Besides, their scope of activities is limited only to the programmes of the Board.

There is little justification for the vast number of agencies for implementing welfare programmes with almost similar objectives. A division in administrative agencies can be justified on one of the three following grounds:

(a) territorial distinction, i.e., each agency functioning in clearly demarcated territory;
(b) methodological distinction, i.e., if the method of work has to be different;
(c) functional distinction, i.e., if the objectives of the agency are such as to warrant a separate organization.

The present allocation of work amongst various agencies has followed no such principle of clear distinctions.

The Central Social Welfare Board

As one of the most important agencies for the implementation of social welfare activities, the status of the Social Welfare Boards is currently under consideration. Though in practice the Board has enjoyed some autonomy, legally it has no independent existence. It was given the status of a charitable company in 1969 to meet audit objections in the way of giving grants. This has not solved its problems and its relationship with the Department of Social Welfare in regard to policy, planning and approval of programmes and financial allocations clearly indicates its status as a subordinate agency of the Department.

The justification for creating an agency outside the ministerial framework of the Government lay in the peculiar nature of welfare work, which required a flexible, personalized and committed approach, not easily possible within a government department because of procedural rules and regulations. The intention of the government was thus undoubtedly to create a specialized agency with its membership drawn from the ranks of social workers, with direct experience of voluntary welfare activities. Some other specialized agencies created by the government have been given statutory autonomous status. The unfortunate vagueness of the status of the Central Social Welfare Board, created administrative difficulties and led to its registration as a company in 1969. This arrangement has been admittedly unsatisfactory, and there is an increasing demand for a more autonomous status.

It may also be noted that at the time of the creation of the Central Social Welfare Board, the Government of India had no central department responsible for social welfare. With the establishment of the Department in 1966, and its increasing rôle in planning and execution of various welfare programmes, the Central Social Welfare Board's position has become still more anomalous. Uncertainty regarding its ultimate status and consequently of the State Boards has had a very adverse effect on their functioning.

At a Conference of State Ministers of Social Welfare held in July, 1992, recommendations were made for the reorganizations of the Central Board. This reorganization was dependent upon the adoption of a general enabling enactment. The State Governments, who had been advised to implement recommendations of this Conference with regard to the State Welfare Boards, were asked to defer action until the reorganization of the Central Social Welfare Board.

At a second Conference of the Social Welfare Ministers and Secretaries held in January 1974, discussion covered four major points. In regard to functions of the Central Social Welfare Board, it was decided that in addition to its executive functions, the Central Social Welfare Board should be responsible for the following:

(a) To advise the government on the problems and provision of measures for the welfare of women, children and handicapped.

(b) To promote investigation into the study of problems in specific areas, particularly those affecting women and children.

(c) To arrange training for social workers at all levels for promoting the involvement of women in national activities.

(d) To provide technical guidance to voluntary organizations for effectively rendering welfare services.

In regard to the composition of the Central Social Welfare Board, the Conference urged that all the Governments of States and Union Territories by rotation, should be represented on the executive committee and the General Council of the Central Social Welfare Board. In conformity with their demand for greater control over the State Boards, the States and Union Territories wanted a greater voice in the nomination of State Board members. With regard to relationship between the Central and State Social Welfare Boards, some States wanted them to be set up by State Governments, while others wished to register them as independent societies.

Procedures and Difficulties Faced by Field Agencies

Because of the present variations in status and functions of these multiple agencies for welfare and development activity, the field staff experience many difficulties. The procedure for the release of grants to a voluntary agency often takes about six months and a great deal of hardship is faced by the voluntary agencies whose meagre resources often do not permit continuation of the programme. The uncertainty felt by the staff seriously hampers their work. Many voluntary agencies informed us that they do not have trained workers to manage the accounts in the manner required by the government.

The ad hoc nature of the programmes, their frequent conversion under the various Plans, and the reluctance of State Governments to take over maintenance have also caused a great deal of uncertainty among the field staff. For example, in the case of the Family and Child Welfare Projects, at the end of the Fourth Plan period, 13 States and 3 Union Territories have agreed to accept the responsibility. Six States have not agreed and the continuation of 74 projects are now uncertain. It is proposed to absorb them in the Integrated Child Development Programme. The feeling of the Board in this matter is clear. "With more time, more projects could have been started in consultation with State Governments. The proposed change in the nomenclature and contents of the programme and transfer of all the programmes from the Board to the State Governments, without ensuring continuity by allowing sufficient time for the existing schemes to achieve their objectives, only tend to confuse the rural population."

The staff of the Central Social Welfare Board and the State Boards are not considered on par with government employees and do not enjoy the same facilities and benefits. Their status at the field level is also temporary and dependent on the allocation for the year or the life of the projects. They have a feeling of uncertainty because of the temporary nature of their appointment which is dependent on the continuance of the scheme. They face a number of difficulties, particularly accommodation problems.

We met a large number of these field workers in various States. In our experience, the workers from voluntary organizations and the Board's staff have, on the whole, established better relationship with the village community, since they are better motivated and dedicated to welfare work, as compared to government functionaries who are more concerned with their service conditions, promotion, etc. The Board's cadre are more knowledgeable about the programmes in their areas and can give a better idea about the difficulties with regard to their implementation.

In recognition of this problem, the Department of Social Welfare has, recently examined the service conditions of the staff of the Board, and some of recommendations of the Third Pay Commission have been made applicable to employees of the CSWB. An officer on special duty was appointed by the CSWB in 1973 for drafting service regulations for its employees. The draft is now under examination by the Department of Social Welfare and is expected to be finalized in the near future.

Deficiencies of the Programme

While most programmes for women have emphasized acquisition of knowledge and skills to improve their efficiency as housewives and mothers, and to improve their earning power, they have neglected the dissemination of information, particularly regarding their rights and duties, which could increase their awareness and improve their participation as citizens. The objective of improving their earning power has also not been adequately fulfilled.

The Role of Voluntary Agencies

Though it would be difficult to demarcate territories, the relationship of the voluntary and the Government sector should be all along complementary and mutually supportive. The present relationship between these two have not been very satisfactory and a number of complaints have been voiced on both the sides. Ideally the Voluntary Sector should provide services for implementation of welfare programmes, while the financial contribution should come from the Government. Further, the voluntary agencies have a surveillance role to play to see to what extent social legislation and the Government have contributed and can contribute to social welfare.

Voluntary organizations complain of lack of involvement with Government programmes since they are not consulted at the planning stage. Being totally outside the decision-making process, they have been reduced to the level of grant receiving agencies. Due to paucity of funds many voluntary agencies have come to rely heavily on the Government and in this process, the initiative and humanitarian impulse of voluntary welfare work has been considerably reduced. The basic concept of social work is that it should arise out of the local community needs. Voluntary agencies have repeatedly stressed that they should be equal partners with the Governments in the fields of welfare and accountable only for rendering proper accounts for grants. At the policy planning level, voluntary agencies desire that their experience and advice should be taken into account.

The voluntary agencies also express difficulties faced by them because of lack of training of their workers. Training facilities should be provided by the Government, if possible. Without technical and organizational competence, they are unable to utilize resources in the most productive manner. One of the representatives of a voluntary organization needed to review their organizational structure with a view to improving the managerial and professional competence of their workers.

The rising cost of living has reduced funds from private sources. It has also affected the ability of women to devote the same time and resources to voluntary work. Consequently, the area of constructive work of most of these voluntary agencies is limited to their neighbourhood.

The Conference of State Ministers and Secretaries of Social Welfare held in January 1974, earmarked the following programmes as of interest to voluntary organizations :

1. Socio-economic programmes organized broadly on a cooperative basis;
2. Condensed courses of education for adult women;
3. Functional literacy for women; and
4. Integrated Child Development Service Programme.

It was also agreed that the procedures and rules for making grants should be liberalized, and new ways found for raising and training voluntary workers, to ensure greater coordination amongst them and to improve the dialogue between governmental and non-governmental sectors at all levels, particularly at the district level. This can succeed only with a change in the approach to the voluntary sector.

Recommendations

Health and Family Planning

While welcoming the proposed integration of family planning and maternity and child health services in the Fifth Plan, we wish to offer certain suggestions with regard to its organization at different levels, so that the objective of integration is not defeated by organizational separatism.

1. The rank of the Chief Executive for the integrated maternity and child health services, including family planning, should be upgraded to at least that of an Additional Commissioner, so that this service does not again become subordinate to Family Planning. This procedure should be adopted at all levels of the administration at the Centre and the States.
2. A separate budget head for maternity and child health services should be created, drawing on the provisions now made for family planning and the general health services. It is important to increase the provision for these services to avoid their being neglected, as has been the trend so far. Since programmes for immunisation and nutrition of infants yield better results when they form a part of general maternity and child health services, we see no difficulty in increasing the allocation for these services.
3. At the level of the primary health centres, the maternity and child health services should be separated for purposes of administrative supervision, provision of medical personnel and budget. While they may share the same buildings and equipment, a separation of the administrative structure required for maternity and child health services will ensure greater priority of treatment. It has often been found that the services of the lady doctor, lady health visitor and the auxilliary nurse-mid-wife, are unavailable to the poorer sections of the rural community. The primary health centres have to cater to the whole population, and women and

children do not always get the priority of treatment in the way of medical attention or medicines and other facilities. Separating the MCH Unit will limit the clientele to the women and children, and make the services more accessible to these weaker groups. The allotment of facilities in the way of maternity beds, equipments for immunization of children and family planning for women could be allocated to the MCH Unit. The PHC could be responsible for sterilization operations for men along with other general health services. The proposed Integrated Child Development Programme calls for a coordinating agency at the implementation level, to coordinate all the nutrition and immunization measures which form a basic component of the programme. If the MCH Unit is separated as suggested above, these functions could be allotted to it.

Yet another function that could be undertaken by these Units with suitable provision of staff, is that of maintenance of fertility and morbidity statistics for women and children, the absence of which has made it impossible to undertake any substantial research and evaluation in these fields.

4. We recommend that each MCH centre should collect this data which should be studied and evaluated at the district level by persons of required competence. This will call for a health statistics Section at the district level.

   The separation of the MCH Services with family planning as a component at all levels will be a step towards a system of health services which would be reasonably accessible to women and children for preventive, diagnostic and supportive treatment, no matter at which point or stage the patient enters the system.

5. We recommend the abolition of the present practice of providing financial incentives to promoters of family planning.

6. We also recommend that incentives to women who accept family planning should be in the shape of a token or certificate to ensure them higher priority in health care facilities for both the mothers and their children. Such a step will promote greater acceptance of family planning and correct the social

attitude towards these practices. Compensation for loss of wages during sterilization operations should however be paid to daily wage earners. Others should be given paid leave for this purpose.

7. The qualifications prescribed for recruitment of personnel for these services in rural areas need to be gradually raised. Until women of requisite higher qualification are available, the present requirements may continue, but they should be reviewed and progressively increased after every 3 years. Attempts should also be made to obtain the services of older and mature women for these services in the rural areas.
8. We further recommend the promotion of research in the field of female disorders, e.g., puerperal psychosis and the ill-effects of family planning methods on their health.
9. We disapprove the denial of maternity benefits to women in government service after three children, as adopted by some State Governments, and recommend rescinding of such orders.
10. We also recommend that mass campaigns for family planning should also aim to correct prevailing social attitudes regarding fertility and metabolic hereditary disorders, and the sex of the child for which the woman is generally blamed. Correct information in these matters would go a long way to improve the status of women.

Welfare and Development

1. Any programme for women's welfare and development must have an integrated approach. In order to prevent any ambiguity in the understanding of what constitutes women's welfare and to prevent the development of policies that sometimes go against the basic objective, we recommend that the Government of India should evolve a National Policy on women's development in the light of the Constitutional Directives and pledges made to the women of this country and to the international community from time to time.

   We also feel that in the absence of a general policy for social development, the weaker sections of society tend to receive inadequate attention. Economic development has sometimes contributed to elimination of social inequalities, but has also aggravated them. Adoption of a policy for social development would clarify matters, and provide a frame of reference for assessment of governmental and voluntary effort in these fields.

2. In view of the need to maintain links between governmental and voluntary and community effort for promotion of women's welfare, and to assist the process of government planning with actual knowledge and experience of the problems and needs of women at different levels, the following steps are recommended:
   (a) Reorganization of the Central Social Welfare Board as a statutory and autonomous specialized agency for planning, co-ordination and management of welfare and development programmes for women and children.
   (b) Reorganization of the State Social Welfare (Advisory) Boards as statutory autonomous agencies at the State level with similar functions. In addition, the State Boards may also serve as links among the Central agency, the State Government and the local bodies.

Supportive Services for Women

Issues involving women are closely related to supportive services. These refer to the gamut of services and amenities that make the women more functional and productive, while at the same time reduce the overburdening drudgery of the daily chores which she is expected to perform for the survival of her family. The major supportive services that require attention are fuel, fodder, water, creche and housing services. One of the major hurdles to women's development activities is the difficulty of providing economically viable means of releasing them from day to day drudgery and survival activities which are neither awarded an economic value nor are shared by men. Data indicate that women are unable to avail of tubectomy services in the absence of a substitute who can care for the children while the woman is away. Similarly, the education of girls is impeded because they are invariably required to help the mother to look after younger children. It is well known that besides adult women, children are also expected to fetch fodder, fuel and water. Cooking also accounts for a large chunk of the woman's time. The use of inefficient smoky *chulhas* affect their lungs, eyes and health in general. This also interferes with social interaction.

The factors affecting women's advancement are thus critically linked to the socio-cultural environment. In keeping, with her sex-stereotyped role as a housewife and home maker, an Indian woman irrespective of clan, creed, region, religion, spends, most of her time on household chores. Table 1.20 indicates the rural women's work time distribution. While the actual time distribution would vary from place to place, undoubtedly many women are subjected to the drudgery of a day to day subsistence working up to 16-18 hours per day. Unfortunately, such 'shadow work' brings her no monetary returns nor does it enhance her prestige in the family or society which is necessary for her to participate in decision making.

TABLE - 120
WORK-TIME DISTRIBUTION OF RURAL WOMEN IN HRS/DAY (SRIVASTAVA, 1982)

Sl. No.	*Work*	*Landless Agricultural Labour*	*Small & Marginal Farmer*	*Average Farmer*	*Land Holder*
1.	Sweeping and cleaning	1.0	1.5	1.5	2.0
2.	Drawing and fetching water	1.5	1.5	1.5	1.0
3.	Washing clothes	1.5	1.5	1.5	1.0
4.	Cooking and serving	2.0	2.0	3.0	4.0
5.	Collecting fuel and making dung cakes	2.5	2.0	1.0	-
6.	Work for cattle	-	1.0	2.0	-
7.	Repair and maintenance of house (Average of year)	0.5	1.0	2.0	1.0
8.	Caring for children and looking after household chores	0.5	2.0	2.0	3.0
9.	Marketing food	-	3.0	2.0**	3.0**
10.	Work in the field/farm	8.0	2.0	*	*

* Stands for seasonal jobs of sowing, transplanting, harvesting and threshing.

** Covers cleaning, drying and storing food grains, making milk products, curd and butter and selling.

In addition, women are often left to fend for the household's basic needs and sanitation, especially in the rural context. The Seventh Plan notes that women play an important role in agriculture, animal husbandry and other related activities such as storage, marketing of produce, food processing, etc. About 54 per cent of rural women and 26 per cent urban women are engaged in marginal occupations in order to supplement family income by collection of fodder, firewood, cowdung, maintenance of kitchen gardens, tailoring, weaving, teaching, etc. It is not easy for a woman to take up employment, unless there are alternative ways to saving time at home and sufficient remuneration to justify her employment outside. Thus all programmes for women, be it education, health, family planning, nutrition, social welfare or legislation are necessarily interrelated support structures for reducing the household drudgery.

Since drinking water, fuel and fodder are the basic requirements especially in the rural areas, a major portion of women's time is spent on collecting these. Strategies which help overcome such problems by providing the necessary support services need to be carefully devised and effectively integrated in development strategies/plans for women.

In the previous plan periods, the emphasis was mainly on issues concerning education, employment and social aspects, without giving commensurate attention to supportive services. For example, the section dealing with the 'Infrastructure for Women's Participation in a Modernizing Economy', the Report on the Status of Women, touched only upon childcare services. The National Plan of Action (1976) was also silent on the structuring of various supportive services. However, the Sixth Five-Year Plan recommended separate Science and Technology (S&T) inputs for women (Item 19.35) as a part of Science & Technology for Human Resource Development. The Plan suggested the setting up of special cells for promotion of Science and Technology for women under the aegis of different organizations such as the University Grants Commission (UGC), Council of Scientific and Industrial Research (CSIR), Indian Council for Medical Research (ICMR), Department of Adult Education (DAE), etc. Although it was proposed to apply Science and Technology for the improvement of the living conditions and status of women, support services were not specifically discussed. The Seventh Plan is more emphatic on women's development and has a separate section on 'Socio-Economic Programmes for Women'. It notes that in giving Science and Technology inputs for women, special efforts have to be made to reduce their drudgery.

The interlinkages between various sectoral and support services have to be fully understood so that an integrated purposeful view is taken of women development. The programmes have to be planned on the basis of a detailed analysis both at micro and macro levels. The analysis should identify critical factors including resource availability, appropriate technologies, skill constraints, public awareness and organizational, institutional and policy supports.

Fuel and Fodder

Fuel and fodder are best taken up together since they are biomass based and often the same plant provides both. This system also integrates with food which, in turn, is linked to fuel through cooking. Hence the discussion here also touches upon forestry and wasteland utilization for growing a variety of biomass in the broader perspective.

Women participate in fodder production as a part of their activities in agriculture and in cutting and fetching fodder for feeding the animals. Generally green fodder is raised as one of the crops or in grasslands and is gathered from the fields as and when required. Alternatively a variety of straws and other agricultural residues are collected and stored as fodder or converted into silage or hay. Often women also have to visit the nearby forests to cut fodder from trees and bushes. This is generally done along with fuel collection. The harder biomass like twigs and firewood are used as fuel and the palatable leaves, as fodder. As for fuels, as indicated by a number of studies, cowdung (*gobar*) and agricultural residues and firewood form the major fuel for cooking and are gathered and stored mainly by women. The act of making and storing cowdung cakes has developed into an art, with 'bitodas' (cowdung storage structures) prominently standing out in the rural landscape. Cowdung cakes are preferred for slow cooking on low fires or heating milk, while firewoods and agricultural residues serve to produce more intensive heat. Depending on resource availability, the utilization pattern varies with cowdung being more prominent in the northern regions. The major portion of total energy consumed is through such 'non-conventional' sources which, in rural areas, accounts for 90 per cent of the domestic energy expenditure.

The three plans (Fifth, Sixth and Seventh) have generally discussed the fodder under 'Animal Husbandry', fuel under 'Energy', and biomass under 'Forestry'. The Fifth Plan observed that the 'forestry' development has assumed a significant dimension as a source of timber and fuel and for the maintenance of the natural ecological system. Special plantations have been given high priority. Under the section 'Energy' it has been proposed to adopt a multipronged approach to develop biogas technology and tap new sources such as solar energy, tidal and wing power. The Sixth Plan noted that feed and fodder constitute 60 to 70 per cent of the cost of production of various livestock products and that the area under fodder crops has remained more or less static during the last two decades. It also stated that emphasis will continue to be placed on the promotion of fodder production as an integral part of crop husbandry through a mixed farming system, particularly, on the small landholdings. Effective farmer-oriented extension programmes will be taken up by the Government for evolving and popularizing high yielding varieties of fodder crops, and introduction of leguminous fodders in existing crop rotations. Production and distribution of high quality fodder seeds will also receive priority attention. Accordingly, a Central Fodder Seed Production Farm and Centres for Forage Production and Demonstration were set up during this plan. The development of extensive grasslands and creation of grass reserves were taken up by the State Forest Departments. Under the social forestry programmes marginal and degraded forests were allocated for cultivation on fodder trees.

As for fuel, the Sixth Plan (item 9.248 under social forestry) proposed: (i) Mixed plantation of wasteland; (ii) Reforestation of degraded forests and raising of shelter belts. In the districts where shortage of fuel wood was particularly acute, new centrally sponsored schemes of social forestry including Rural Fuel Wood Plantation and Farm Forestry were introduced in selected areas. New thrusts in the form of Tree for Every Child Programme, Economic Development Force, Eco-development Camps and Agro

Forestry programmes were devised during the Sixth Plan. The concept of organic recycling (Item 9.36) and the propagation of biogas technology (Item 9.40, 9.41) were also envisaged. Further, this plan dealt with the new and renewable energy sources and suggested that energy forestry, biogas and biomass conversion technologies have to be taken up along with solar and wind energy and a variety of other technologies. For example, item 15.95 on 'Energy Forestry' notes that firewood is the most important traditional fuel accounting for two-thirds of the total energy contribution from non-commercial sources and is becoming scarce. In view of the pressure on land, all available unutilized pockets of land could be used for energy plantations. Considering that rural communities will continue to depend heavily on such resources, it was proposed to decentralize energy production and distribution as a part of an Integrated Rural Energy System (Item 15.105) which considers all energy resources in a given area.

In the Seventh Plan also, emphasis has been given to social forestry, agro forestry and various renewable energy technologies and the necessity of creating awareness among people through mass media. The Plan notes that a proper implementation of some components of forestry programmes may be entrusted to local and voluntary bodies (NGOs). Concepts like 'social fencing' may be tested. Infact the revised 20-Point Programme (1986) has advocated a "New Strategy for Forestry" (Point No. 16).

In recognition of the importance of renewable resources, a Department of Non-conventional Energy Sources has been set up. Also a National Wasteland Development Board was created with the objective of bringing 5 million hectares of land every year under fuelwood and fodder plantation.

In many of the above programmes, the role of women in the production, collection and utilization of fuel and fodder and the related problems are not adequately emphasized. However, it is heartening to note that the Department of Science and Technology set up a cell on "Science & Technology for Women" in 1982. This cell divided the various technologies required for women into the following four areas: Technologies for Drudgery Reduction; Employment Generation Technologies; Health and Sanitation Technologies; and Technologies for Minimizing Occupational Hazards.

Under the first category, the problems of fuel, fodder and drinking water were perceived from the point of view of women. Besides a number of projects funded through individual institutions, an 'All India Coordinated Project' was also undertaken on 'Fuel and Cooking Aspects' through Science and Technology Department. More than 20 institutions from all over the country participated, analysing the date based on micro level surveys. The local specific and general problems of women in dealing with fuels were identified and the viability of a variety of technologies were field tested. Similarly, some of the selected technologies like the improved *chulha*, biogas solar cooking biogas based technologies, etc., are being taken to the people through the Department of Non-Conventional Energy Sources. Apart from various governmental institutions like Department of Science and Technology (DST), Indian Council of Agricultural Research (ICAR) Council, for Scientific and Industrial Research (CSIR) and Department of Non-Conventional Energy Sources, a number of relevant State departments are also taking up the implementation of such projects. Some reports analysing the reasons for the success as well as failures of experiments undertaken are available.

It is encouraging to know that recently a number of NGOs have taken up programmes with funding support from the various Government bodies noted above. A Bio-energy Society of India has also been established with a view to promote research and development as well as public awareness. Bio-energy education dealing with the production, conversion and utilization of biomass with special emphasis on fuel aspects is being given prominence. People's participation is being promoted through social forestry and other programmes. However, the linking of women with these activities is still weak. A few movements like 'Chipko' stand out, emphasizing that much can be achieved by organizing women at the local levels.

The agricultural universities, dairy development institutions and forest institutes undertake research in fodder and fuel production and have a network of extension centres such as Krishi Vigyan Kendras for taking these technologies from the lab to land. While agriculture provides fodder crops, special attention is also paid to trees and plant species like 'subabool' which can cater to both fuel and fodder needs. Researchers on social forestry and agro-forestry all over the country now recognize the need for integrating the food, fodder, fuel, fertilizer, fibre and other biomass based production and utilization aspects.

The various technologies developed are being compiled into suitable directories for dissemination, e.g., the Science and Technology Women's Cell has listed a number of technologies for women. Council for Advancement of People's Action and Rural Technology (CAPART) has undertaken the publication of several volumes of National Directory of Rural Technologies, the first volume titles 'Post-Harvest Technologies' has already been printed.

However, the scope exists for designing and developing more technologies appropriate to women taking into consideration the agronomy, ease of handling, economics, etc. A special mention must be made of Agricultural Tool Research Centre at Bardoli, which has tried to make efficient agricultural tools especially suited for women.

Drinking Water

Although India is one of the wettest countries in the world with an average annual rainfall of 1170 mm, it still faces and is expected to face in future the threat of acute water shortage. Among the various usages of water in rural areas, drinking water followed by irrigation, sanitation and agriculture are of importance for the overall developmental process.

Water resources are generally dealt with as a part of irrigation in agriculture. In addition to this, the Sixth Plan laid special stress on rural water supply as a part of the 'Minimum Needs Programme'. As in the Sixth Plan, the Seventh Plan also highlights the importance of drinking water. The supply of drinking water to all problem villages features at Point 7 of the Twenty-Point Programme (1986). A 'Technology Mission on Drinking water in Villages and Related Water Management' was established in 1986-87 under the Department of Rural Development, Ministry of Agriculture, Government of India. The collaborating agencies identified were Council of Scientific and Industrial Research, Ministry of Science and Technology, Department of Environment and Forests, Department of Defence Research and Development, Ministry of Health and Family Welfare, Ministry of Water Resources and State Governments. The 'problem' villages were identified as those with: (i) No source of water; (ii) Water sources more than 1.6 km. distance, 15 km depth and 100 metres elevation difference; (iii) Biological contamination (guinea worm, cholera, typhoid); and (iv) Chemical contamination (fluoride, brackishness, iron). The number of such problem villages amounts to 39 per cent of the total villages (2.27 lakh out of 5.57 lakh). In respect of these problem villages, some basic targets envisaged are:

Eradication of guineaworm	9,920 villages by 1989
Control of fluorosis	8,700 villages by 1988
Control of brackishness	17,500 villages by 1990
Removal of excess iron	2,900 villages by 1988

Apart from these, the strategy has focused on 50 project areas (Mini missions) to evolve new, cost effective science and technology techniques, to apply and replicate these techniques in the rest of the problem villages and to implement an integrated approach to water conservation.

A booklet outlining the project objectives, background, strategy, management structure, targets, methodology, milestones, accomplishment, resources and policy needs, has been brought out by the Ministry of Agriculture. Already this mission has started working with the State Departments concerned. In addition, universities, research institutions and voluntary organizations are also being involved. A first Regional Seminar to focus on these issues for Southern States and Union Territories was held at Gandhigram in Tamil Nadu in July 1987.

Most of the above efforts, however, are not directly addressed to women. Although in the Sixth Plan, special mention has been made about assuring the weaker sections of their due share of water, only a few organizations like the Science and Technology Women's Cell have looked at this problem from the women's development angle. In addition to sanctioning some institutional level projects on various aspects of potable water, an "All India Coordinated Project on Drinking Water" has also been proposed by this department.

Ideally, as in the case of urban services, the Government should be in a position to supply potable water to all households through pipelines and taps right at the doorsteps. However, considering the current constraints of finance and non-availability of suitable water sources, problem terrains, etc., this may not be feasible in the near future. Hence constructing and maintaining smaller water sources like wells, water tanks, hand pumps, etc., are to be given due consideration.

As with the implementation of any project, there is always the problem of ensuring people's participation in both maintenance and the distribution systems. Merely installing different kinds of units and equipment does not lead to sustained water supply. Thus, organizing women to adopt different technologies is a key issue. In this context, a successful experiment by a voluntary agency in Rajasthan could be considered as a model for replication. In this case, the people were involved in identifying the locations for tube-wells. A few persons were then trained in their actual construction and maintenance. The system of giving due remuneration for subsequent management to these trained personnel was also evolved. This ensured sustained working of the pumps/tube-wells and equitable distribution of water. Other case-studies worthy of note are the "Water Harvesting Systems" employed at Banwasi Sewa Ashram and the "Water Sharing System" evolved at Sukhamajari.

Although a number of technologies are available, only a few have reached the villages. More research and development is needed on issues like devices for carrying water in hilly terrain, water purification techniques suitable for different problem areas, storage at home levels, and rapid methods of water testing.

A list of available technologies have been compiled in a volume brought out by the Cell on Science and Technology for Women. The CAPART has also brought out publications on drinking water and the third volume of its National Directory of Rural Technologies will be on Drinking Water. The Technology Mission on Drinking Water has brought out two publications entitled *Sub-Mission on Desalination of Water* and *Sub-Mission on Eradication of Guineaworm.*

Creche/Daycare

With the advent of industrialization and modernization, and with the gradual disappearance of the traditional joint family and with its inbuilt security system, the problem of working mothers has become increasingly serious. Although it is mainly an urban phenomenon, rural India is beginning to experience it too. With increasing economic pressures more and more women have to take 'out of home' jobs. The situation is serious because the majority of women who need daycare for their children are from economically backward strata of society.

Working mothers of low-income groups need day care most as they cannot afford to hire or pay for labour-saving devices. Thus, in addition to the general need for child care for all working mother's, there is also a more specific and strong need for child care for those belonging to the poorest sections of the society.

Rural mothers struggle hard not only in the fields but also to collect fuel, fodder and water. Thus their time "out of home' is much more and the majority of them are forced to either take their infants along or to leave them under the 'supervision' of elder children who stay at home, or even alone. This situation not only keeps older children away from the educational system, but endangers the health of infants and small children. The need for childcare services had already been accepted, but the legal provision exists only for women in the organized sector, which comprise approximately 10 per cent of the working women.

After the submission of the CSWI report (1974), and the International Women's Year, childcare has been recognized as an important and essential support service in women's development. The CSWI report has stated that despite the laws and ILO Convention, maternity and childcare benefits are available only to 3-5 per cent of Indian women workers in the organized sector. The other 3-5 per cent of the organized sector (mainly in services) do not get creche facilities because they are not covered by labour laws. To the 90 per cent of women workers who are in the informal sector, these facilities have so far never been provided as highlighted in the report of the National Commission on Self-Employed Women and Women in the Informal Sector.

In 1950, creches were run by four national level voluntary organizations — The Indian Council for Child Welfare, Bhartiya Grameen Mahila Sangh, Bhartiya Adimjati Sevak Sangh and Harijan Sevak Sangh. The then Ministry of Social Welfare launched a scheme of creches/day care centres for children of working and ailing mothers in February 1975. The aim of the scheme was to promote healthy all round development of such children. The scheme caters to the basic needs of young children of poor working and ailing women in the unorganized sector. The services under the scheme include health care, supplementary nutrition, sleeping facilities, immunization, entertainment and nursery school facilities for children. Starting in 1974-75 with 247 creches to cover 6175 beneficiaries, the scheme has been considerably expanded since then. In the year 1987-88 there were 3,137 agencies running 10,210 creches in the country which included both permanent and mobile units. The Department of Women and Child Development which now deals with the scheme had on its plan that by the end of 1988-89, 12,000 creches would cover 2,82,800 children. The training of creche workers under this programme commenced from September, 1986. Grants-in-aid to certain all-India level institutions were released for conducting training courses. In the statutory sector, around 55,000 children are taken care of in creches/day care centres.

The Balwadi Nutrition Programme is another programme being implemented since 1970-71 which looks after the social and emotional development of children in the age group of 3-5 years, apart from providing supplementary nutrition to them. About 5.045 balwadi centres are functioning in the country covering about 2.29 lakh children.

The Integrated Child Development Services (ICDS) scheme launched by the government in 1975 is designed both as a preventive and developmental effort. It extends beyond the existing health and education systems to reach children below six years and their mothers in villages and slums and delivers to them an integrated package of services — non-formal pre-school education, immunization, health checkups, supplementary nutrition, medical referral services and nutrition and health education for women. As on 31 March, 1988 information received from 1,455 ICDS projects indicate that 1,46,693 Anganwadis were providing supplementary nutrition to 96.10 lakh children. In these Anganwadis, 18.40 lakh nursing mothers were receiving supplementary nutrition. Though focused on the all round development of the pre-school child, it is also the largest scheme providing part time creche facilities to children in rural and tribal areas and in slums. As an employment generation scheme for women, it employs nearly 2,00,000 women at the Anganwadi level.

The National Policy on Education' 1986 (NPE), for the first time took note of the growing awareness that the performance of household chores, specially care of younger siblings, is a major reason for the stagnation in enrolment of girls in schools. At two, places in the policy document, (vide para 5.2 in Early Childhood Care and Education (ECCE) and para 4.3 in Education for Women's Equality, reference is made to the need for child care, attached to or near primary schools, as a support service to encourage and allow girls to attend school.

Housing

The rapid rate of urbanization in India, coupled with large scale migration of people into the metropolitan cities, has created a tremendous pressure on the housing situation in the country. On the one hand, is the ever increasing shortage of housing which is estimated to be to the tune of 5.1 million dwelling units in urban areas alone (NBO 1981), and on the other, is the steep cost of housing and new construction which is unable to keep pace with the increasing demand and is beyond the reach of the urban dwellers.

In the successive Five-Year Plans, the Government of India has launched several social housing schemes for different income groups under which, loan/subsidy is given to the low income and economically weaker section families. The implementation of these schemes on a countrywide basis has created great awareness of the desirability of improving the housing and environmental conditions among all sections of the populations including women.

Several other measures which have been taken include providing house building advance, housing finance at low rates of interest through financial institutions, fiscal incentives, bulk acquisition and development of land and ceiling on land, land use regulations, promotion of housing through cooperatives, setting up of Housing Boards and City Development Authorities and Slum Clearance Boards to augment the housing stock.

A Central Scheme of assistance for construction of hostel buildings for working women was initiated in 1972. The scope of the scheme was widened in 1980 by including a provision for day-care centres for children. Financial assistance is given to voluntary organizations for construction/expansion of hostel buildings for working women. Local bodies are also eligible for taking up these programmes. The total number of hostels sanctioned so far is 429 with a total capacity of 27,292 working women with day-care centre facilities for 2,920 children, since the inception of the scheme in 1972. It has been decided to reserve 5 per cent seats in the hostels for widows and other women in distress who are otherwise, eligible for hostel accommodation.

Under the Minimum Needs Programme to ameliorate housing and environment conditions, the Government of India has been implementing various schemes, viz., Slum Clearance Improvement Scheme, Scheme for Environmental Improvement in Slum Areas and the Schemes for Provision of House Sites to landless workers in rural areas and other social housing schemes for improving the living conditions of the urban and rural poor. The benefits of the schemes accrue to women also.

In the Twenty-Point Programme (1986) high priority was accorded to provision of drinking water supply (Point No. 7), improvement of housing conditions for 14.6 million rural landless families (Point No. 14) and those living in slums and squatter settlements (Point No. 15).

Large-scale housing programmes was taken up in different states under the National Rural Employment Programme (NREP) and Rural Landless Employment Guarantee Programme (RLEGP). Housing schemes with employment as the main feature have also been taken up in many States. For implementing the Indira Gandhi Grih Nirman Awas Yojna, an allocation of Rs. 125 crore annually has been provided in the Seventh Five-Year Plan to build one million houses for Scheduled Castes and tribal families.

Improvement in the quality of life of people depends to a great extent on the quality of housing and related facilities which determine the physical environment. It is in recognition of this fact that the world conference of the International Women's Year adopted a World Plan of Action in 1975 which included aspects related to housing amongst its recommendations. The Plan suggested that settlement planning and policies should be formulated keeping in view the trend to recognize women's role in the development process and should prioritize investments in infrastructure therein according to the needs of women. Subsequently, following the declaration of 1987 by the United Nations as the International Year of Shelter for the Homeless, the Ministry of Urban Development of the Government of India formulated a Draft National Housing Policy (March, 1987) with a view to ensuring every family a shelter by the end of this century. Nowhere in its text, however, had the draft acknowledged that housing and women's needs required to be closely linked. Passing references to women was made only at page 12 para 13.4 of the draft wherein it stated that special efforts would be made to improve women's skills and working conditions in the housing sector.

For women, housing has a wider meaning. It implies their working and living environment to which they are confined for a greater portion of their lives, performing their multiple roles that of production which is often home based and therefore implies the use of the shelter and its environs as the working space; that of reproduction which is traditionally viewed as their primary role and includes child rearing activities linked to domestic chores; and that of management of resources and assets within the family unit which includes activities such as storage, managing domestic provisions, processing, etc.

Women's housing needs, arising from their multiple roles, have been listed as follows; as child bearers, they need access to sanitary facilities and a healthy living environment; as child rearers, they need space for childcare and recreation within or outside the house; as managers of households, they need water, fuel, waste and garbage disposal, proper light and ventilation and space to perform domestic chores; and as producers, they need a working space as well as space for storage of raw materials and finished products, besides space for processing of materials. In addition, women also need privacy and security as well as facilities for education, recreation, production and training within the housing space. Housing thus, implies space beyond the confines of the immediate shelter.

An effective public distribution system for essential commodities like rations and cloth is a necessary support for women, especially women workers in the unorganized sector. Poor women are denied ration cards which forces them to purchase basic necessities from the open market at exorbitant prices. Even women with ration cards are often denied rations due to understocking or diversion of stocks.

Each of the above roles indicates that women's efficiency and effectiveness in performing the productive and reproductive tasks are linked to the quality of housing. Since they are in effect the primary users of housing, women must have a role to play in decisions regarding housing as well as ensure that they have access to ownership of the same.

In planning for women's development, priority needs to be given to creating access to assets for single women and female headed households. An estimated 30-35 per cent of households in rural India are headed by women according to available micro studies. Women have hitherto had no rights to ownership or inheritance of property within the framework of customary law. Recent legislative provisions have tried to remedy this situation but ancestral property still remains inaccessible to women. By and large, the patriarchal patterns of land ownership and transfer have implied that land is transferred to males. This pattern has been adopted by the planners in formulation of housing programmes so that men are recognized as heads of households and land is distributed in their names. Although distribution of land deeds or pattas has been legally sanctioned for men and women jointly, in effect, women are not given land titles. Where women are able to gain access to land or assets, they are often required to have a man stand surety for the same, as also for loans and credit.

Within the patriarchal norm, women may not customarily claim ownership of the matrimonial home. This has often denied women access to shelter in times of crisis. In cases where women have been deserted and are destitute, they have not had any legal right to claim access to shelter, housing or any such assets. Only recently have policy makers and legislators realized that, it is imperative to accord priority to the provision of housing for single and women headed households.

Various strategies have been evolved to augment the housing stock in the country by urban planners and specialists especially for economically weaker sections. The target groups have however seldom been involved in planning for such housing. The norms applied to make such houses affordable for the identified target groups have ignored women's needs for space in the dwelling unit. It is necessary to scrutinize established standards and develop norms in housing especially for economically weaker sections, and to determine their adequacy for women. There must also be visible participation of women in the planning and execution of housing programmes in order to ensure that women's needs are adequately considered in the housing designs.

Women have had no traditional access to capital assets or to institutional finance and credit for housing. They have had to resort to borrowing from traditional credit sources at exorbitant rates of interest. Institutional sources of credit such as banks have not recognized women as credit worthy individuals in their own right so that they may borrow through existing schemes at differential rates of interest. Various agencies have tried to play an intermediary role in creating access for women to institutional credit but their out reach has been limited. It is essential, therefore, that institutions such as HDFC and HUDCO recognize women in their individual capacities as beneficiaries for housing credit and finance.

The housing market also offers a vast potential for employment, especially in the rural areas. Expanding construction activity in housing would ensure that greater opportunities for employment are created, while also creating shelter for the rural populace.

Recommendations

Fuel, Fodder, Water

Problems specific to women have to be highlighted in considering issues like fodder, fuel and drinking water. Since these directly concern women, their involvement in all programmes related to such issues must be given prominence. The interlinkages among fuel, fodder and drinking water with other aspects of the development of women such as education, employment, food and nutrition, health and sanitation must be recognized and integrated programmes worked out on a holistic basis for optimal utilization of personnel and financial inputs.

As has been stressed by the Seventh Plan, the government must ensure public participation and draw upon the resources of voluntary agencies, educational (especially Science and Technology) institutions, industries and financial organizations in implementing various programmes for the development of women. Various funding agencies may consider sponsoring All India or regional projects on a coordinated basis wherein, Science and Technology experts could collaborate with the NGOs and the people in designing and implementing programmes based on micro-level surveys.

Women must be specifically organized by involving the NGOs wherever necessary to participate in the implementation of social forestry programmes, water sharing projects and in the maintenance of various gadgets and devices. The necessary formal and non-formal education has to be appropriately matched with their time schedules, seasonal occupations and socio-cultural constraints.

In training programmes, in addition to NGOs, educational institutions could play an important role. Agricultural extension centres, home science colleges, and youth forums like NSS should be purposefully involved. Science and Technology institutions can take up the task of training and provide the technical back up in technology transfer as well as monitoring and evaluation.

A data bank may be set up with such resource centres where information may be made available not only on technologies but also on manufacturing availability of training facilities, etc. These centres must have working models readily available for demonstrations, and requisite resource persons. Interaction among the centres will enable them to serve as a national network.

Research must be undertaken both in improving and developing hardware and software systems. All the necessary technologies on collection, processing, storage and utilization of fodder, fuel and drinking water may be carefully analysed and gaps identified. Many issues are regional and location specific and tackled best at the micro level. For example, carrying water is more problematic in hills than in plains; fuel problem is more acute in arid zones. The choice of fuel and fodder generating plants would depend on the agroclimate and terrains. The type of improved *chulha* required depends on the food and cooking practices. Perhaps an area based approach can be taken combining locations with similar type of problems into groups or clusters.

The necessary industrial support in the manufacturing of various small equipments should be created, e.g., manufacture of small water storage systems forage harvesting system, etc. Women and small entrepreneurs should be involved in such ventures with suitable subsidies.

The decision makers both at the bureaucratic and political levels should be sensitized to the importance of programmes specifically targeted for women in the context of national development.

The socio-cultural and traditional practices must be suitably modified for conservation of various resources and more efficient utilization of time, energy and capital. For example, cooking recipies which require more fuel and time in cooking have to be pointed out and corrected. Where possible, community kitchens should be encouraged. Especially in the periphery of towns, the food prepared in neighbouring areas can be brought in packages. This would reduce the load on fuel, provide employment to women in the surrounding areas while benefiting many working women.

Many of the local hardware and software problems especially with respect to fuel and drinking water are not easily solved at the household level. The right level of scaling has to be planned, keeping in view both the economic viability and the consumer's convenience. For instance, in a biogas system, a $80m^3$ community biogas plant is more economical than a $2m^3$ household plant but the former calls for a more elaborate management system. Perhaps a subcommunity biogas plant of $15\text{-}20m^3$ for 15-20 families could be a solution. Thus for each problem, a suitable community or sub-community system has to be worked out.

Some of the above recommendations have been noted both in the 'Country Report of 1985' presented at Nairobi and "Forward Looking Strategies for the Year 2000". However, at the level of implementation, the programmes of various governmental departments tend to get superimposed. Hence it is important to identify one of the Ministers as the 'Nodal Ministry' for coordination and keeping abreast of all programmes related to women. The Ministry of Human Resource Development could perhaps take this up so that a Master Table could be prepared of all action/projects having a bearing on women, noting the time schedules for implementation, and the agencies involved in planning and action at the central, state, regional local levels. This "Nodal Ministry" for women may constitute sub-committee with members drawn not only from government but also from other participating agencies to discuss the various issues and evolve strategies.

Creche/Daycare

Creche services must be universally provided to all women, especially in the poverty sector. This would enable some of them to augment their family income and, at the same time, ensure proper care of their children. The children's health, sanitation, nutrition and early stimulation would get attention. Increasing the number of creches would also generate more employment opportunities for women. In view of the above, it is recommended that in rural areas, wherever ICDS infrastructure already exists, creches should be opened and attached to the Anganwadis. These creches should make provision for babies below 3 years age. The timing of Anganwadis which provide pre-school services for children of 3-6 years, should be adjusted according to the working hours of rural women. These creches will help in containing morbility and mortality rates and malnutrition of infants and small children. They will also relieve the children in the school going age group from child care responsibilities, and give an opportunity to them to utilize the ICDS pre-school services.

The existing law that stipulates provision of a creche for employment of thirty or more women should be changed to thirty persons (men and women). This would ensure that employers do not use loopholes in the law to their advantage and would extend creche facilities to children of men workers whose wives, if they are not in the organized sector do not otherwise have access to such facilities.

The Government of India, being an employer of a large number of women, must provide creche facilities in or near all workplaces.

Creche service must follow an integrated approach to childcare.

Creche workers should preferably be local women to whom appropriate skill-oriented, on the job training should be imparted.

Technical institutions and home-science colleges should be utilized to train creche workers as also provide inputs for systematic monitoring and supervision of the creche programmes.

Organizations running creches should be given flexibility to adopt timings suitable to the needs of the working mothers.

Local women's groups and mothers of the children attending creches must be given training in preparation of toys, play materials out of low cost/no cost indigenous material. Employment for women can be generated by employing local women to prepare the midday meals, etc.

Action research projects, such as, a study of the impact of day care services on the education of girls should be initiated.

Housing

Traditionally, women have had a significant role in resource management including housing management. It is important to recognize this role and provide for women's participation in development programmes, and for incorporating their needs in schemes for improvement of housing and environmental conditions in the following manner:

Identify the needs of women in relation to housing and community facilities and build them in an integrated manner into housing development programmes.

Integrate environmental factors into development planning for women including their requirements in settlement planning.

Involve women at all levels of decision making and bring about their participation in programme implementation so as to ensure that the benefits of housing, essential services, and community facilities are directed to women in general and to the poor and vulnerable among them in particular.

The special needs of women should be identified and

adequately catered to while formulating minimum housing standards.

Necessary facilities in homes should be provided to lessen the burden and drudgery of women in performing productive and reproductive roles.

Priority investment in infrastructure such as water supply, sanitation, energy, transportation, working women's hostels, public distribution of basic needs, etc., should take into consideration the needs of women.

Provision of housing for working and/or single women is recommended on priority basis. In addition, women in difficult circumstances such as widows, refugees, destitutes, victims of social oppression, seasonal migrant workers, victims of natural disasters, etc., must be provided shelter as part of an integrated rehabilitation programme.

The National Housing Policy which has been formulated, must pay adequate attention to the special needs and roles of women in the implementation of housing programme.

The social and economic constraints which come in the way of women's participation should be removed and their active involvement in housing should be promoted by:

- — Allotting house-sites in the joint name of wife and husband;
- — Mobilizing savings of women for housing;
- — Organizing self-help in undertaking house construction work;
- — Imparting training so that women could become skilled labour (including masons and other skilled labour); and
- — Ensuring access for women to institutional credit at low rates interest without collateral.

In India, rural women constitute nearly 80 per cent of the female population. They contribute largely to the country's economy which is mainly agriculture based. Although distributive justice has been categorically underlined in all the development plans, the needs of women have not been adequately addressed. While laying emphasis on enhanced agriculture production in which the involvement of women is high, the plans have fostered a target group and area oriented approach to reduce regional and ecological imbalances disregarding women's equality as embodied in the Constitution. Rural development programmes for women have only in recent decades recognized the crucial role of organization and mobilization as strategies for women's empowerment and development. Rural women's organizations are also mechanisms for restructuring and redistributing power and have been utilized pressure groups that influence and/or bargain on behalf of rural women.

Situational Analysis

The launching of the Community Development Programme in 1952 was a landmark in the history of India and ushered in an era of development with the participation of the people. The Community Development Programme adopted a systematic integrated approach to rural development with a hierarchy of village level workers and block level workers drawn from various fields to enrich rural life. Agriculture, animal husbandry, public health, women's development, rural industries, etc., found a special niche in the framework cast for this purpose. Five thousand National Extension Service Blocks were created under the Community Development Programmes by the end of the Second Five-Year Plan. During the Third Five-Year Plan the momentum was maintained through a series of developmental schemes though allocations under the NES programme tapered. This was succeeded by the Small Farmers Development Agencies followed by Marginal Farmers Development Agencies, Crash Schemes for Rural Employment, Food for Work Programme, Drought Prone Areas Programme and Desert Development Programme in the early seventies. The contents of all these programmes were to strengthen the rural base of the economy, specifically the primary sector comprising agriculture, animal husbandry, etc., and employment through labour intensive works that would create the infrastructure of roads and other community assets for the benefit of the rural people.

It was recognized that the skewed pattern of landholdings stood in the way of creating an egalitarian society and obstructed modernization and intensification of agriculture. Land reform measures for abolition of intermediary tenures, tenancy reforms, imposition of land ceiling on agricultural holdings, distribution of surplus land to the landless agricultural workers and consolidation of landholdings were introduced through a series of State Legislations under Central guidelines.

Certain areas of the country are characterized by soil-erosion, water stress and environmental degradation. The Drought Prone Areas Programme was started in 1973 aiming at an integrated area development for optimum utilization of land, water, livestock and human resources through a watershed management approach to mitigate the effects of drought. A few years later the Desert Development Programme, a wholly centrally funded scheme, specifically to cover extremely arid areas for controlling desertification and restoration of ecological balance, was also started.

The emphasis shifted to fulfilling minimum needs of the people during the Fifth Five-Year Plan.

A systematic analysis and examination of the status and role of women within the agriculture and rural development strategies in India started with the National Plan of Action (NPA) for women which followed the report of the Committee on the Status of Women in India (CSWI), Subsequently, efforts of women activists, social science institutions and researchers produced enough documentary support to persuade the Sixth Plan document to include a chapter on 'Women and Development' for the first time in the country's history of planned development.

A strategy of direct attack on poverty was adopted in the Sixth Plan as the theory of trickle down benefits of general development programmes had not proved as a successful strategy for the removal of poverty. Forty-eight per cent of the population were found to be living below the poverty line at the beginning of the Sixth Five-Year Plan.

One positive outcome of these developments has been the recognition that rural women are not a homogeneous group to justify a uniform development strategy. The development plans in the case of women must be based on the assessment of their actual role and participation in socio-economic activities.

Women's employment has been recognized as the 'critical entry point' for women's integration in mainstream development.

The low and deteriorating status of rural women is attributed to their declining economic participation and other factors like the modernization of the agricultural sector. The need for giving a better deal to the rural women is beginning to be widely recognized. It is now accepted that the participation of women themselves in the development activities is the most effective tool for the promotion of the access of women to the benefits of development. A working group set up by the Deptt. of Rural Development, Ministry of Agriculture and Rural Development in 1978 recommended that the major objectives of the development plan for rural women should be: (i) The improvement of their economic status; and (ii) The promotion of women's organization to have the collective strength to articulate their needs and promote their participation in the development process.

The Integrated Rural Development Programme initiated in 1978-79 and extended to all the development blocks in the country in 1980-81 was conceived as one of the instruments for a direct attack on poverty. It dealt with individual rural families below the poverty line. Credit from banking institutions and subsidy from the Government were given to the families for self-employment and income generation. Under IRDP, a special place was accorded for training rural unemployed youth for employment with the introduction of TRYSEM. An exclusive scheme for the social and economic uplift of women belonging to families below the poverty line, DWCRA (Development of Women and Children in Rural Areas) was launched in 1982 as a subcomponent of IRDP.

The Sixth Plan accepted poor rural women to be targets of rural development strategies. The specific problems identified concerning rural poor women were:

- (i) Marginality of attention and services to them in rural and agricultural development;
- (ii) Special constraints that obstruct their access to available assistance and services such as, lack of training to develop their awareness and skills; lack of information and lack of bargaining power;
- (iii) Low productivity and narrow occupational choices;
- (iv) Low level of participation in decision making;
- (v) Inadequate finance and expert guidance for promoting

socio-economic activity of rural women and their participation;

(vi) Inadequate monitoring of women's participation in different sectors;

(vii) Wage discrimination;

(viii) Inadequate application of science and technology to remove drudgery; and

(ix) Low health and nutrition status.

The Sixth Plan document stated that one of the most important means of achieving improvements in the status of women would be to secure for them a fair share of employment opportunities, to earmark a percentage of allocation for women, and to fix for them a quota in all the poverty alleviation programmes. The Seventh Plan reiterated the strategies suggested in the Sixth Plan with a sharper focus on the increased coverage of women in various rural development programmes.

Simultaneously, the National Rural Employment Programme (NREP), assuring wage employment to the unemployed rural population was introduced in 1980. Subsequently, concentration on the rural landless was attempted by the introduction of the Rural Landless Employment Guarantee Programme (RLEGP) in 1983. The Indira Awas Yojana was added as an important component of the programme in the Seventh Plan for constructing houses for SC/STs and free bonded labourers. Social Forestry was added as another component of the RLEGP with national emphasis on greening fuel and fodder.

The establishment of the Technology Mission on Drinking Water and Related Water Management gave a new thrust to the Rural Water Supply Programme. Safe and adequate drinking water is to be provided to the entire rural population by the end of the Seventh Five-Year Plan.

The impact of the poverty alleviation programmes coupled with the development in various sectors reduced the rural population below the poverty line to 37 per cent by the beginning of the Seventh Plan. The target is to bring this down to 28 per cent by the end of the Seventh Plan Period.

Agriculture and allied fields provide the largest sector for women's employment. It largely determines the rural women's socio-economic status. This is the sector where women's role as unpaid labour in productive activities is most prominent and is responsible for conferring women a non-working status. In case of both agriculture and animal husbandry, development strategies have provided very little attention to women in comparison to their active involvement in both the sectors. Some training is imparted to women in agriculture and animal husbandry under the programmes for Farmer's Training and Krishi Vigyan Kendras. But the Farmers Training Programme has lost much of its importance after the introduction of the new extension system of Training and Visit (T&V). Though women constitute a major work force in agriculture which with regional variation is estimated to be around 60 per cent, they are invisible in the T&V system. Currently there is one major extension programme for women in Karnataka and 2-3 such programmes on the anvil in other states. There is an inbuilt resistance observed in them in viewing women within their home making role. Even the visual presentations (slides, filmstrips and films) which are used for the orientation of the functionaries, often depict the women in the field and the extension agent talking to the contact farmer on the same field, fail to project the full dimension of women's role.

While rural women have become marginally visible in the anti-poverty programmes, they have not been adequately recognized in agricultural development, land reform, or rural industrialization. Non-recognition of women in agriculture has many implications. Intensive agriculture and the green revolution have reduced women's participation in on-farm activities but the work load related to the home based farm activities has increased considerably. That has only reduced them from the 'working' to a 'non-working' status. Limited employment opportunities created by technology resulting in the means of production being concentrated in the hands of a few, and increased landlessness for the poor led to men replacing women in many of their traditional areas of employment. But women have had to work and survive. They are thus found to be gradually moving to the non-traditional sectors seeking employment for survival.

Following the Sixth and Seventh Plans, the Department of Rural Development issued directives to the State Governments to give priority to women headed households, enhance the share of women under the anti-poverty programme (IRDP), and the programme of Training for Self-Employment (TRYSEM). Guidelines for NREP and RLEGP envisage increasing participation of women in wage employment and creation of assets specific to the needs of women's groups. At present the share of employment generated under NREP for women is approximately 20 per cent. A special programme for women entitled DWCRA was also introduced in 1982, as a sub-component of IRDP to accelerate the process of integration of women in the rural development programmes. Up to 1987, 11,553 groups are reported to have been organized in 106 districts under this scheme.

The Integrated Rural Development Programme meant for the poorest in the rural areas has been formulated for creating assets with a view to increasing the productivity and income generation abilities of the beneficiaries. Efforts have been made under this programme to select female headed households. The scheme of DWCRA could be strengthened and modified in order to ensure that the benefits reach more target groups. The National Rural Employment Programme (NREP) and Rural Landless Employment Guarantee Programme (RLEGP) would generate additional employment to women in the lean season. Under Training of Rural Youth in Self-Employment (TRYSEM), one-third of the beneficiaries were expected to be women and special attention was to be given to improve existing skills of women and imparting to them new skills under the programmes of farmers training, fodder production, post harvest technology, application of pesticide, budding and grafting, training in horticulture, fisheries, poultry, dairy and social forestry, etc. The training of women under TRYSEM exceeded the target to 44 per cent in January 1988. Out of a total of 37.23 lakh families which received benefits under the IRDP during 1986-87, the number of women-headed families was 5.67 lakh which amounts to only 15.23 per cent as against the target of 30 per cent. On assessment of the programmes, it is observed that considerable efforts are required to elicit the participation of women in these activities. The training provided under TRYSEM and DWCRA is not always viable and there is a tendency to limit to a few traditional crafts, though the Department of Rural Development is laying greater stress on taking up innovative activities too. Therefore, a fresh look is needed to be given to identification of trades and activities which may gainfully be taken up by women. Many income generating programmes have not succeeded due to full thought not being given to the input availability, training and marketing of products.

Special development projects linked to certain ongoing activities need to be taken up on a project basis to improve the effectiveness of the programmes related to women. Specific projects such as sericulture for tribals in certain states like Bihar and Orissa, development of dairy units linked to Operation Flood areas, fruits and vegetables cultivation linked to marketing through Mother dairy, prawn farming and fishing in the coastal region were commended. Agro-based industry schemes, etc., are essential.

The scheme of Training of Rural Youth for Self-Employment (TRYSEM) should be revamped with a view to organizing training in trades with assured employment potential to women in rural areas, as well as for wage employment in peripheral metropolitan and urban areas. State Emporia, marketing channels of KVXIC, etc., should be tapped to ensure elimination of middlemen and better prices.

The Accelerated Rural Water Supply Programme (ARWSP) and the Minimum Needs Programme (MNP) are of special significance to rural women who are the victims of drudgery, such as fetching water from distant locations. The Technology Mission on Drinking Water and Related Water Management lays emphasis on purification of water to make it potable, training in the use of water and maintenance of water sources. Women are the target of the awareness creation programmes as well as agents for creating awareness in conservation of water and maintenance of water sources. The low cost sanitation programme is also of great importance to women, who are otherwise subjected to a lot of privation due to lack of appropriate sanitation facilities. Rural Technologies and innovation promoted by CAPART aim at relieving the drudgery to women in several areas of their households and economic activities. They include the improved varieties of stone grinder, wheel barrow, ball-bearing pulley, groundnut shelter and smokeless *chulhas*.

The limited performance of the programmes introduced to achieve the integration of women in the development process suggests that only policy directives do not achieve the desired objectives. Programmes do not get implemented due to the lack of comprehension of the relevance of women's contribution to national development. Although the concern for development of women is well articulated at the central policy making level, an ambivalence is observed at the implementation level. The policy directives issued by the Government of India for the increased share for women in the development programmes and the promotion of a participatory approach, do not provide for corresponding development in the infrastructure, extension, training information support and a strong monitoring system which is particularly lacking at the State level. The programmes for rural women still continue as a separate exercise within the sectoral programmes with marginal attention, resources and inadequate monitoring.

The major shortcomings noticed in the implementation of the programmes for women with development objectives are:

(i) Perpetuation of the concept that women need only welfare services;

(ii) That the developmental benefits will automatically accrue to the women as a result of economic development of the family;

(iii) Inadequate knowledge and skills for designing socio-economic activities for women and in group organizations; and

(iv) Lack of supportive services such as credit, childcare, marketing, training and technology for reducing the drudgery.

Methodological Issues

The approaches used for integrating women in the mainstream of development have raised some methodological issues. These relate particularly to the organization of groups, involvement of the voluntary sector, and the household approach in development programmes for rural women.

The organization of women's groups is considered to be one of the most effective tools for integrating women in the development process. Yet it has raised several issues which are not fully resolved. Some of the questions which are being asked repeatedly are:

(i) Who will organize the groups (the role of intermediaries)?

(ii) What will be the size, structure and status of groups — formal or informal?

(iii) Should the groups be organized first and the choice of activities to be undertaken by the groups come next?

(iv) Should women be assisted individually under the IRDP, etc. or be formed into groups.

Apart from these unresolved issues, there are problems in selecting and working out economically viable group projects. Women activists argue against giving individual projects to be carried out within the household as it would only perpetuate their subordination in the household hierarchy. They claim that assistance to the voluntary agencies, which was expected to provide grass-roots structural support in this regard, is either not forthcoming or has not been sought.

It is logical that the size of the group to be mobilized should be such as to enable close interaction amongst the members which is only possible when they come from the same background and from one cluster of villages. It is also evident that poor women acquire confidence when they get organized. The delivery system will respond positively even if they are informally grouped. But in the interest of economic viability, and to strengthen their earning capacity, it is desirable for the group to be formalized. It is however, impossible or advisable to suggest one organizational model for all situations. The experience by and large is that the organization based on personal interface and on localized issues is more effective, more flexible and functional than the highly structured and impersonal form of organization.

Some of the processes under IRDP, such as identification of beneficiaries/productive activities, preparation of loan applications, sanction of the same and procurement of assets have not been given much attention in terms of proper planning, particularly of the linkage required after the asset is given, to make the same optimally productive. Such linkages include most critically the supply of raw materials and facilities for marketing. These processes and linkages are more effective when implemented through the group approach.

The crucial question in the field of land reforms is how rural poor women should get land and have access to land. Power structures in the villages are dominated by the relatively better off classes. Considering that implementation of land reforms measures leaves much to be desired, there is an urgent need for people's participation more specifically of the women, by promoting their groups organizations and through Panchayati Raj institutions. Each village should have a village plan which should include cultivable lands, gochar lands and forest lands with clearly demarcated boundaries.

The involvement of intermediaries in development programmes for rural women has been considered vital, particularly in demonstrating and promoting the participatory model and to provide support to the grass-root structure. Here too, there are basic issues which need to be carefully resolved. Among others, it is queried whether the role of the intermediary organizations has been understood by the Government, or whether it is feasible for the voluntary organizations to function in partnership with the government, given the differences in approach.

There is no uniform understanding and acceptance of the role of the voluntary agencies in the States. In some cases, there is a complete lack of rapport between the Government and voluntary agencies. In others, there is the tendency of associating the women's programmes entirely with voluntary action, showing a lack of initiative on the part of the Government. There is little doubt that the voluntary agencies are committed to the cause of women and have expressed a real concern for the enhancement of women's status. They have also demonstrated skills for mobilizing women, and in trying innovative projects. In view of this, the association of the voluntary agencies with the programmes is bound to enrich the programmes as well as the delivery mechanisms. Yet, they cannot be a substitute for Governmental action. To end women's isolation from rural development, the Government must work in partnership with voluntary agencies.

Currently debated issues in the context of women in rural

development and in the anti-poverty programmes, is the household versus group approach; some argue in favour of ensuring a share of developmental resources and benefits to women in all sectoral programmes, while others argue in favour of having separate investments for women.

In India, the family is hierarchical, traditional and the status in the family is determined by sex and age. In the patriarchal society, it is the man who holds the position of the head of the family and the bread-winner. Therefore, it is the man who gets attention in the investment of developmental resources, training, extension and other supports. Women's contribution to the family's earnings goes unrecognized. This bias, in fact, is responsible for the earlier programmes not taking note of women headed households whose number is currently estimated at 30-35 per cent of all rural households. With mounting pressure on the government to give priority to this group, it has been convincingly argued that an improvement in the income of the household does not necessarily mean development for women. The household approach instead of creating equitable conditions, perpetuates the subordination of women and limits their opportunities for self-growth and self-expansion.

Having a special component within sectoral plans can stimulate action for women provided the components are monitored separately. The introduction of the scheme of DWCRA within the programme of IRDP was aimed at stimulating the response of the State Governments to integrating women into anti-poverty programmes. Therefore, in case of women, it can be contended that a combined approach is desirable. This would allow women to be adopted as a target in all sectoral programmes, with earmarked resources along with special component plans aimed exclusively at women. Such dual approaches can be continued until women acquire sufficient power to articulate their needs and demands, and until such time as women's concerns get to be internalized in the planning and administrative structures.

Women Access to Land: Inheritance and Ownership Patterns

In the economic sphere and in particular in the rural sector, the empowerment of women relates mainly to their access to means of production and control over the fruits of their labour. The access to the means of production implies ownership of land, other productive assets, access to capital and access to technology and acquisition of various skills required to make labour power more productive.

The aspect of ownership of land relates to rights of inheritance which are governed by personal laws of different communities. These personal laws at present are discriminatory against women and have a bias in favour of the male heirs. The State Governments of Kerala and Andhra Pradesh have sought to remove some of these discriminations with a view to give daughters in the family, coparcenary ownership in the family property on the same level as the sons. But even these changes do not go far enough and still discriminate against a married daughter and a widow and do not apply equally to the separate properties of the father in the Hindu Customary Law. There is discrimination against women of different types in the personal laws of other communities also. In the customary law of certain tribes, only male agnates in the male line are recognized as valid heirs and an unmarried daughter is only entitled to usufructuary maintenance. It would be necessary to introduce correctives to overcome the discrimination, in order that the gap between the State's proclamation to achieve equality of the sexes and its laws which deny it, is bridged. Women's undiluted access to land, the most productive resource, would undoubtedly bestow on her necessary economic independence and power and would improve her social position in the family as well.

Regarding access of women to land, the land records do not incorporate the rights of women in the landed property shown in the name of the husband or the father. Only where a woman is a widow and happens to be the *'karta'* of the family, her name may figure in the record of rights as the owner of property.

Co-ownership of property by women, should not merely be confined to land but also to other productive assets like house, family wealth, shops, factory or any other income generating establishment or asset. This would provide sufficient conditions for women to participate in and influence the decision concerning the use and disposal of such properties.

As regards access to capital, there is a general reluctance on the part of the public financial institutions to extend credit to women independently of the male head or guardian of the family.

The existing land ownership pattern in India is largely male oriented except in some areas of the North-east and a few other places where matrilineal system is in operation and inheritance of property passes through the institution of the mother. The land records, to the extent they reflect the ownership and other interests in land, only record the names of men. Similarly, where share-holders of such lands are recorded, it is usually the male shareholder who finds mention in the land records. The processes of preparation of land records, i.e., the survey and recording of rights also deal with such male holders of interests in land. The only exception would be in such cases where a widow with no other male person, manages the land. Her name is recorded as the owner and manager of land. Land reform measures have also not taken into cognizance interests of women as co-owners or cultivators of land, and to this extent land reform measures seem to have bypassed the women. The most prominent example where this inherent discrimination in land reforms has been noticed is the case of ceiling laws where most State laws have provided for a separate unit of ceiling for major sons in the family but not major daughters married or unmarried. Although from the point of view of implementation of such ceiling laws, addition of yet another unit in the name of major daughters would have further defeated its objectives, nonetheless, the discrimination cannot be denied. Further, in the matter of distribution and allotment of various lands, it is usually the male head of the family who gets the 'patta' in his name. Recently, of course instructions have been issued to give joint 'patta' on the name of both husband and wife while allotting land and house-sites. Similarly, in the matter of collection of minor forest produce and enjoyment of rights over common property resources, the rights of women are not focused, even though it is the women who have to collect fuel-wood and fodder and minor forest produce from such lands.

Tribal social structures are more egalitarian and open and less stratified than social structures of larger and more advanced communities in India. The status and position enjoyed by tribal women in society is, therefore, in certain tribes, much better than their counterparts in other communities. This is on account of many reasons. Tribal society has a tradition of both men and women working on an equal footing whether in agriculture or in other vocations. Thus tribal women have access to income and are therefore, economically independent. There are also no restrictions on women going out for work independent of men, and not necessarily along with them. Usually tribal women go out for work in large groups. In social matters and family life also tribal women are far more emancipated. They have a much greater say in the decision making in family and community matters and are not subjected to the same degree of social control by male members of the family as women in other communities are.

Despite this, in matters of inheritance of father's/husband's property and in access to land, there is a certain built-in discrimination against women in some tribal communities. The customary law of some tribal communities excludes women from inheritance rights, such inheritance rights being restricted to "male heirs in the male line". These customs are even enshrined in tenancy laws wherever enacted and applicable to these communities. This discrimination against women has a harmful effect on their lives, rendering them economically and socially powerless and driving large numbers of them into destitution. Infact, in certain tribal communities, for example, the Ho Tribe in Singhbhum district of Bihar, a large number of women remain unmarried so as to ensure to themselves usufructuary rights available to them as unmarried daughters. Many of them are harassed by their husband's and father's male agnates who wish to deprive them even of this usufructuary right. A number of women are forced to migrate in order to earn their livelihood, since their hold over the family land is so insecure and dependent on the attitude of their male relatives even though these women do the bulk of agricultural work. Sometimes, the women are declared witches, the concealed motive being to drive them out of the village or even to kill them in order to usurp the family property.

The married women also enjoy limited usufructuary rights in the deceased husband's property. Even these usufructuary rights cannot be freely exercised by them since the husband's male agnates often harass them and try to get rid of them in the hope of asserting their inheritance claims to the land. If the married woman has a son, he inherits the land from his father, and she has no legal claim to it. If the husband has one or two or more wives, the sons of other wives have inheritance rights to the land, and she is dependent on them for maintenance. In case, the marriage breaks up, or a man remarries or deserts his first wife, the woman is absolutely without land rights, since she has, by marriage, lost the usufructuary rights in her father's house, and she is also deprived of rights in her matrimonial home. Since tribal communities have their customary laws, the Hindu Succession Act, the Indian Succession Act, or any other succession Act do not apply to them.

The discrimination against women in the customary law of tribal communities, historically speaking, may have evolved with a view to preserve the integrity of the tribe and to prevent land passing from the tribal to persons outside the tribe which would have the effect of disintegrating the tribal society. While, it is necessary to preserve the integrity of the tribe and to protect the interest of the tribals in land against any encroachment by non-tribals, it is also necessary to protect the interest of tribal women in land by giving them rights to inheritance in father's and husband's property. But safeguards will have to be provided in the event of marriages outside the tribe.

Therefore, provision in law and customary practices which discriminate against women in matters of inheritance of property and restrict such inheritance to male agnates in male line should be changed, while at the same time preserving alienation of tribal land to non-tribals.

Women, especially tribals, migrate in search of work. They are employed in large numbers in the unorganized sector like brick-kiln, road construction, irrigation works, agricultural operations, forestry operations, stonecutting, domestic labour, etc. They are subjected to brutal exploitation at places of work by contractors and the middlemen who recruit them. The exploitation is not merely confined to payment of low wages, long hours of arduous work and other dismal working conditions. They are also subjected to sexual exploitation. It is necessary, that for each category of employment in the unorganized sector, specific institutional mechanism be built-in to protect women's interests.

Perspective for 2000 A.D.

Poverty alleviation in the rural sector remain central. It is targeted to bring down the percentage of rural poor below 10 per cent by 2000 A.D. The Department of Rural Development has already suggested that in case of women, poverty alleviation goals for 2000 A.D. should be to:

(i) Bring all women-headed households (estimated to be 30-35 per cent) above the poverty line; and

(ii) Attain the target of having women constitute 30 per cent of all beneficiaries to be assisted under IRDP.

In addition, the endeavour should be to bring in the women's development dimension into the sectors particularly, agriculture and allied sectors which have hitherto not responded adequately to women's needs. Women's access to productive resources must also be ensured.

Political power and access to positions of decision making and authority are critical prerequisites for women's equality in the processes of nation building. Hence it is crucial that the representation of women in local bodies up to the district level be ensured.

Health and Family Welfare

Women's health status is basic to their advance in all fields of endeavour. Any serious attempt to improve the health of women must deal firstly with biased social customs and cultural traditions that have an impact on their health status. Though the health problems of women have been identified for priority attention and efforts made for maternal and child services since the beginning of planned development in India, much remains to be done to improve health care for women both in qualitative and quantitative terms. However, in subsequent plan periods it has been observed that resource allocations for health have been decreasing. There is need for a more comprehensive integrated approach to health issues if there is to be a significant impact on the present conditions of Indian women.

The cultural norms that specially affect women's health are the attitudes to marriage, age of marriage, the value attached to fertility and sex of the child, the pattern of family organizations and the ideal role demanded of women by social conventions. They determine her place within the family, the degree of her access to medical care, education, nutrition and other accessories of health. Improvements in female health status are, therefore, critically dependent on a number of non-health development components such as education, opportunities for skill-building, income generation and decision making and the availability of basic support services to carry out women's multiple roles. Thus it is essential to address the causes of women's ill-health. Measures to improve the social and health situation would have to form an integral part of a multi-sectoral package operationalized simultaneously, in complementary thrusts. Earlier analysis have emphasized this aspect. But gaps have existed in preceding plans and even more in the implementation of strategies.

Situational Analysis

The demographic trends are important indicators of women's health status. The sex ratio which illumines the survival scene for women versus men was 933 females per 1000 males in 1981. Not only is this ratio unfavourable, but its steady decline from 972 in 1902 to 930 in 1971 is a cause for great concern (Table 1.21). Marginal improvement has taken place in the last decade, but even today fourteen States and Union Territorics have less females per 1000 males then the national average (Table 1.22), and in eleven States and Union Territories, the ratio has further declined (Table 1.23).

TABLE - 1.21
SEX RATIO IN INDIA

(Female per 1000 male)

Year	*Sex ratio*
1901	972**
1911	964
1921	955
1931	950**
1941	945**
1951	946
1961	941
1971	930
1981	933

** Excludes Pondicherry

Source: Registrar General of India, Reported in "Health Statistics of India" (1985), Central Bureau of Health Intelligence, Directorate General of Health Services, Ministry of Health and Family Welfare Government of India, New Delhi.

TABLE - 1.22
SEX RATIO IN STATES AND UNION TERRITORIES OF INDIA

Sl. No.	*India/State Union Territory*	*Total*	*Rural*	*Urban*
	India*@	933	951	878
1.	Andhra Pradesh	975	984	948
2.	Assam	901	917	768
3.	Bihar	946	963	832
4.	Gujarat	942	959	905
5.	Haryana	870	876	849
6.	Himachal Pradesh	973	989	795
7.	Jammu & Kashmir @	892	897	875
8.	Karnataka	963	978	926
9.	Kerala	1032	1034	1021
10.	Madhya Pradesh	941	956	884
11.	Maharashtra	937	987	850
12.	Manipur	971	971	969
13.	Meghalaya	954	965	904
14.	Nagaland	863	899	688
15.	Orissa	981	999	859
16.	Punjab	879	884	865
17.	Rajasthan	919	950	877
18.	Sikkim	835	864	697
19.	Tamil Nadu	977	987	956
20.	Tripura	946	945	957
21.	Uttar Pradesh	885	893	846
22.	West Bengal	911	947	819
Union Territory				
23.	Andaman & Nicobar Islands	760	774	720
24.	Arunchal Pradesh	862	881	629
25.	Chandigarh	769	688	775
26.	Dadra & Nagar Haveli	974	981	884
27.	Delhi	808	810	808
28.	Goa, Daman & Diu	981	1013	919
29.	Lakshadweep	975	986	963
30.	Mizoram	919	928	893
31.	Pondicherry	985	977	992

* Includes projected figures of Assam where census could not be held due to disturbed conditions prevailing there at the time of 1981 census.

@ The population figures exclude population of area under unlawful occupation of Pakistan and China where census could not be taken.

Source: Registrar General of India, Reported in "Health Statistics of India" (1985), Central Bureau of Health Intelligence, Directorate General of Health Services, Ministry of Health and Family Welfare Government of India, New Delhi.

TABLE - 1.23
SEX RATIO IN SELECT STATES AND UNION TERRITORIES IN INDIA — 1971 AND 1981

(Females per 1000 Males)

Sl. No.	*State and Union Territory*	*1971***	*1981**
1.	Andhra Pradesh	977	975
2.	Bihar	954	946
3.	Manipur	980	971
4.	Nagaland	871	863
5.	Orissa	988	981
6.	Tamil Nadu	978	977
7.	Dadra & Nagar Haveli	1007	974
8.	Goa, Daman & Diu	989	981
9.	Lakshadweep	978	975
10.	Mizoram	946	919
11.	Pondicherry	989	985
	India	930	933

Sources: * Registrar General of India, Reported in "Health Statistics of India" (1981), Central Bureau of Health Intelligence, Directorate General of Health Services, Ministry of Health and Family Welfare Government of India, New Delhi.

** Registrar General of India, Reported in "Pocket Book of Health Statistics of India" (1971), Central Bureau of Health Intelligence, Directorate General of Health Services, Ministry of Health and Family Welfare Government of India, New Delhi.

Life expectancy has increased over the decade from 44.7 years in 1971 to 54.7 in 1980 for women. It was estimated to be slightly higher in 1980 for women than men: 54.7 and 54.1 years at birth respectively (Table 1.24). A general reduction in female mortality, as well as the greater differentials in death rate was observed over 1970-82 in both rural and urban areas (Table 1.25). However age specific death rates indicate higher mortality for female children and women for every five-year period till 35 years of age (Table 1.26). This higher mortality experience of female children and younger adult women during the prime reproductive years is largely preventable through appropriate health and other interventions, and points to the continuing neglect of female health.

Women face high risk of malnutrition, retardation in growth and development, disease, disability and even death at three critical stages in their lives, viz., infancy, early childhood and adolescence and the reproductive phase. In old age, they face threats of cancer, breast cancer and uterus cancer and menopause related problems.

TABLE - 1.24
EXPECTATION OF LIFE (YEARS) - INDIA — CENSUS - 1901-1980

Census	*At birth*		*Age 10*		*Age 20*		*Age 30*		*Age 40*		*Age 50*	
Year	*M*	*F*	*M*	*F*	*M*	*F*	*M*	*F*	*M*	*F*	*M*	*F*
1901	23.63	23.96	34.73	33.86	28.59	28.64	22.90	23.82	17.91	19.12	13.59	14.50
1911 (a)	22.59	23.31	33.36	33.74	27.46	27.96	22.45	22.99	18.01	18.49	13.97	14.28
1921	19.42	20.91	29.64	29.21	25.46	25.41	21.64	21.78	17.93	18.31	14.30	14.95
1931 (a)	26.91	26.56	36.38	33.61	29.57	27.08	23.60	22.30	18.60	18.23	14.31	14.65
1941	32.09	31.37	41.20	38.56	35.02	33.11	29.03	27.89	23.27	22.91	17.77	18.17
1951	32.45	31.66	38.97	39.45	33.03	32.90	26.58	62.18	20.53	21.06	14.89	16.15
1961	41.89	40.55	45.21	43.78	36.99	35.63	29.03	27.86	22.07	22.37	16.45	17.46
1971 (b)	46.40	44.70	48.80	47.70	41.10	39.90	33.50	32.00	25.90	25.40	19.20	19.70
1981 (c)	54.1	54.7	56.1	58.0	47.0	49.2	38.0	41.0	29.3	32.5	21.4	24.3

Note: Excludes Sikkim

(a) Expectation of life during the Census years 1911 and 1931 relates to birth and age 0, 10-19, 20-29, 30-39, 40-49, 50-59, 60-69

(b) Based on 10% rural and 20% urban sample

M- Male; F- Female

(c) Population projections for India 1981-2001, Paper 1 of 1984

Source: Registrar General of India, Ministry of Home Affairs Reported in Health Statistics of India (1985). Central Bureau of Health Intelligence, Directorate General of Health Services, Ministry of Health and Family Welfare, Govt. of India, New Delhi.

TABLE - 1.25
AGE-SPECIFIC DEATH RATES FOR FEMALES : 1976 AND 1982

Age Group	*Rural*		*Urban*		*Combined*	
	1976	*1982*	*1976*	*1982*	*1976*	*1982*
0- 4	55.9	45.7	30.1	20.5	51.9	40.2
5- 9	5.4	4.3	3.3	1.8	5.1	3.2
10-14	2.6	1.9	1.5	1.0	2.5	1.7
15-19	3.1	2.7	2.0	1.6	2.9	2.4
20-24	4.4	3.8	3.3	2.4	4.1	3.5
25-29	5.0	3.5	3.0	2.2	4.6	3.2
30-34	5.1	3.9	3.3	2.2	4.8	3.5
35-39	5.3	4.5	3.8	2.5	5.0	4.0
40-44	4.9	5.5	6.3	4.0	4.7	5.2
45-49	8.1	7.6	7.2	4.6	8.0	7.0
50-54	12.7	12.1	11.8	8.4	12.6	11.3
55-59	18.7	16.5	16.7	11.5	18.5	15.5
60-64	35.0	27.6	23.7	21.7	33.2	26.4
65-69	47.3	39.6	40.3	36.3	46.4	38.9
70+	85.7	90.2	83.4	71.2	85.5	86.1
All ages	16.6	13.2	9.6	7.1	15.3	11.9

Source: Sample Registration Scheme, Registrar General of India.

TABLE - 1.26
AGE-SEX SPECIFIC DEATH RATES IN INDIA - 1982

Age Group	*Rural*			*Urban*			*Combined*		
	M	*F*	*P*	*M*	*F*	*P*	*M*	*F*	*P*
0- 4	42.2	45.7	43.9	21.2	20.5	20.9	31.9	40.5	39.1
5- 9	3.4	4.3	3.8	1.4	1.8	1.5	3.0	3.7	3.3
10-14	1.9	1.9	1.9	0.8	1.0	0.9	1.6	1.7	1.7
15-19	2.1	2.7	2.4	1.1	1.6	1.3	1.8	2.4	2.1
20-24	2.5	3.8	3.1	1.6	2.4	2.0	2.3	3.5	2.9
25-29	3.0	3.5	3.2	2.2	2.2	2.2	2.8	3.2	3.0
30-34	3.7	3.9	3.8	2.4	2.2	2.3	3.4	3.5	3.4
35-39	4.8	4.5	4.6	2.8	2.5	2.6	4.5	4.0	4.2
40-44	6.7	5.5	6.1	5.0	4.0	4.5	6.5	5.2	5.7
45-49	9.7	7.6	8.7	8.0	4.6	6.5	9.3	7.0	8.2
50-54	14.7	12.1	13.5	12.9	8.4	10.9	14.4	11.3	12.9
55-59	21.7	16.5	19.2	16.8	11.5	14.4	20.7	15.5	18.3
60-64	34.6	27.6	31.2	28.2	21.7	25.1	33.4	26.4	30.0
65-69	49.4	39.6	44.6	42.7	36.3	39.5	48.5	38.9	43.6
70+	98.1	90.2	94.2	83.4	71.2	77.2	95.5	86.1	90.8
All ages	13.1	13.2	13.1	7.7	7.1	7.4	11.9	11.9	11.9

Note: M Male; F - Female; P - Person

Source: Sample Registration System 1982. Registrar General of India, Reported in "Health Information of India" (1986), Central Bureau of Health Intelligence, Directorate General of Health Services, Nirman Bhavan, New Delhi.

Infancy and Early Childhood

Discrimination starts even before birth in the form of sex determination tests misusing the high technology of aminocentisis, resulting in a new kind of femicide, i.e., abortion of female foetuses. A survey carried out in Bombay during 1984 revealed that out of 8,000 abortions 7,999 were of female foetuses. Considering that this test facility has spread to even small towns and people from rural as well as urban areas are utilizing it, the magnitude of the problem can be imagined.

Micro studies have shed light on the fact that sex is the main determinant of infant nutrition, irrespective of economic development. It is worse in a situation of poverty. Studies indicate that while both boys and girls get less than recommended daily dietary allowances, girls are more deficient and suffer more from related disorders and illnesses (Table 1.27). However, more girls go without treatment when ill, than boys (Table 1.28).

TABLE - 1.27
PERCENTAGE DISTRIBUTION OF AILING MALE & FEMALE NON-ADULTS

	Area 1		*Area 2*		*Area 3*		*Area 4*	
	M	*F*	*M*	*F*	*M*	*F*	*M*	*F*
No treatment	30.8	58.1	18.7	62.1	13.0	27.8	7.6	16.0
Treated free	3.8	2.3	3.7	3.1	19.5	27.2	4.2	2.3
Household treatment	15.4	16.3	54.2	19.2	8.9	9.4	29.2	28.0

Source: Mankekar, Purnima (1985), "The Girl Child in India—Data Sheet on Health", National Media Centre and UNICEF.

TABLE - 1.28
MALNUTRITION IN CHILDREN IN PUNJAB

		Male %	*Female %*
Severe Malnutrition	Infants	2.35	18.35
	Toddlers	7.98	14.71
	Pre-Schoolers	4.26	6.71
Moderate Malnutrition	Infants	15.33	30.38
	Toddlers	21.00	35.29
	Pre-Schoolers	21.57	38.16
Mild Malnutrition	Infants	25.64	30.47
	Toddlers	34.42	35.67
	Pre-Schoolers	39.48	37.20
Normal	Infants	56.67	20.81
	Toddlers	36.62	14.33
	Pre-Schoolers	34.68	27.93

Source: Shanti Ghosh, "Discrimination Begins at Birth", Presented in the Conference on the girl child, UNICEF, 1985.

Boys are breast-fed longer, given more of weaning foods, and get a bigger share of whatever food is available (Table 1.29 to 1.32). Consequently, although the female children are biologically stronger when born, their morbidity and mortality rates are worse than that of male children. Age specific death rates are higher for female children, as noted earlier. Whereas, no male/female breakup is available for immunization rates, the total figures themselves are low. By 1982, only 25 per cent of all children below 3 years were given DPT, 5 per cent of infants were immunized against Polio, and 65 per cent were given BCG (Table 1.33).

TABLE - 1.29

COMPARISON BETWEEN THE NUTRITIONAL STATUS OF MALE AND FEMALE CHILDREN

	Normal Nutrition		*70-80% of the Expected Weight for Age*		*Less than 70% of the Expected Weight for Age*	
	M	*F*	*M*	*F*	*M*	*F*
Privileged	86%	10%	10%	11%	4%	13%
Underprivileged	43%	26%	43%	24%	14%	50%

Source: 7th Annual Report Community Health Department, CMC, Ludhiana, 1978.

TABLE - 1.30

SEXWISE COMPARISON OF FOOD INTAKE OF CHILDREN IN THE AGE GROUPS 3-4 AND 7-9 YEARS

Food Items	*Age in Years*					
	3-4 years			*7-9 years*		
	Male	*Female* (*Wt. in grams*)	*RDA*	*Male*	*Female* (*Wt. in grams*)	*RDA*
Cereals	118	90	175	252	240	250
Pulses	22	18	55	49	25	70
Green Leafy Vegetables	3	0	62	0	3	75
Roots and Tubers	15	13	40	42		50
Fruits	30	17	50	17	6	50
Milk	188	173	225	122	10	250
Sugar and Jaggery	13	16	22.5	30	12	30
Fats and Oils	5	2	30	23.3	8	50

Source: Rajmal Devedas and Godavari Kamalanathan
NA Women's First decade, Presented in the Conference on Women's KESI, UNICEF, New Delhi, April 1985.

TABLE - 1.31
AVERAGE PER CAPITA INTAKE OF CALORIE FROM MEALS PREPARED IN HOUSEHOLD KITCHEN BY AGE AND SEX AND PER CAPITA MONTHLY EXPENDITURE CLASS

Age	*Sex*	*Per capita expenditure (Rs.)*					
	(1)	*20 or Less*	*20-40*	*40-60*	*60-100*	*Above 100*	*All*
Less than six months	m	173	248	222	281	441	254
	f	223	246	245	279	323	255
Six months to less	m	313	343	387	613	617	428
than 1 year	f	375	401	451	506	740	455
1 year to less	m	451	529	601	710	871	597
than 2 years	f	407	479	580	620	771	565
2 years to less	m	613	715	855	852	993	790
than 3 years	f	638	723	772	855	937	776
3 years to less	m	813	883	936	1150	1193	968
than 5 years	f	764	834	986	1091	1280	952
12-16 years	m	1046	1258	1498	1585	1950	1446
	f	1017	1166	1350	1498	1748	1346
17- 21 years	m	1250	1406	1623	1669	2025	1615
	f	1078	1273	1455	1643	1831	1498
22-56 years	m	1317	1453	1684	1761	2018	1696
	f	1121	1351	1476	1657	1794	1549
57 years and above	m	1043	1261	1529	1745	2020	1611
	f	1018	1195	1344	1464	1633	1355

m - male; f - female

Source: Maitra, Tarses, Devadas, Rajamal and Kamalanathan, Godawari (1985). "A women's First Decade" presented at UNICEF during the "Women's MEC Consultation."

The shadow of the girl child's deprivation looms throughout her later life, but most particularly increases her vulnerability to the risks of child bearing, which in turn create risks for the child to be born. Thus is set into motion the vicious cycle of deprivation, debilitation, disease and disability. Leading to greater deprivation and debilitation and often death. That is the depressing lot of a significant numbers of mothers and children today.

Adolescence

As girls attain puberty, they go through a second spurt of growth when their bodies grow much more rapidly to prepare them for child-bearing. But unfortunately, in addition to the poor economic conditions, their gender denies them proper nutrition. Even in situations where food is available, girls are taught to eat less so that they remain slim to rate better in the marriage market. Nutritional deprivation at all growth stages gets compounded during the inset of puberty resulting in severe growth retardation in girl children.

TABLE - 1.32
GOALS FOR HEALTH AND FAMILY WELFARE PROGRAMMES

Sl. No.	*Indicator*	*Estimates in 1982*	*Goals*	
			1990	*2000*
1.	Infant mortality rate	Rural 136 (1978) Urban 70 (1978) Total 125 (1978)	87	below 60
	Prenatal mortality	67 (1976)		30-35
2.	Crude death rate	Around 14	10.4	9.0
3.	Pre-school child (1-5 years) mortality	24 (1976-77)	15-20	10
4.	Maternal mortality rate	4-5 (1976)	2-3	below 2
5.	Life expectancy at birth (years)	Male 52.6 (1976-81) Female 51.6 (1976-81)	57.6 57.1	64 64
6.	Babies with birth weight below 2500 gms. (percentage)	30	18	10
7.	Crude birth rate	Around 35	27.0	21.0
8.	Effective couple protection (percentage)	23.6 (March 82)	42.0	60.0
9.	Net Reproduction Rate (NRR)	1.49(1981)	1.17	1.00
10.	Growth rate (annual)	2.24(1971-81)	1.66	1.20
11.	Family size	4.4(1975)		2.3
12.	Pregnant mothers receiving inite Natal care (%)	40-50	60-75	100
13.	Deliveries by Trained Birth attendant (%)	30-35	80	100
14.	Immunisations status (% coverage)	20	100	100
	TT (for Pregnant women)			
	TT (for school children)			
	10 years		100	100
	16 years	20	100	100
	DPT (Children below 3 years)	25	85	85
	Polio (infants)	5	70	85
	BCG (infants)	65	80	85
	DT (new school entrants 5-6 years)	20	85	85
	Typhoid (new school entrants 5-6 years)	2	85	85
15.	Leprosy-percentage of disease arrested cases out of those detected	20	60	80
16.	TB-percentage of disease arrested cases out of those detected	50	75	90
17.	Blindness-Incidence of (%)	1.4	0.7	0.3

Source: Statement on National Health Policy, Government of India, Ministry of Health and Family Welfare, New Delhi (1982).

TABLE - 1.33
INTAKE OF NUTRIENTS IN DIFFERENT DEMOGRAPHIC GROUPS

	No Land	*Less than 5 Acres*	*5-10 Acres*	*More than 10 Acres*	*Labourers*	*Cultivators*	*Others*
Calories *(per consumer unit per day)*							
Kerala	1824	1904	2232	1589	1718	2040	2015
Tamil Nadu	2108	2320	2671	2718	2012	2548	2321
Karnataka	2312	2576	2860	3099	2338	2901	2526
Andhra Pradesh	2274	2480	2824	2974	2358	2805	2338
Maharashtra	2006	2178	2251	2517	1948	2413	2150
Gujarat	1999	2042	2234	2444	1941	2219	2097
Madhya Pradesh	1977	1939	2108	2403	1905	2221	2059
West Bengal	1866	2346	3055	3052	1806	2543	2414
Uttar Pradesh	1991	2116	2227	2377	2000	2192	2043
Protein *(gm per consumer unit per day)*							
Kerala	44.2	44.3	57.5	34.6	37.7	49.3	49.0
Tamil Nadu	52.3	56.6	66.7	67.2	49.6	62.4	57.7
Karnataka	63.3	65.3	76.3	86.5	63.2	77.0	67.0
Andhra Pradesh	53.8	59.7	72.3	74.3	55.7	70.4	55.9
Maharashtra	58.8	62.5	65.7	73.8	57.5	70.3	62.3
Gujarat	57.2	60.1	64.5	70.6	56.9	65.0	58.0
Madhya Pradesh	58.0	59.9	67.1	74.5	57.3	69.5	61.5
West Bengal	48.7	59.2	76.3	75.2	46.7	63.3	61.3
Uttar Pradesh	64.2	66.2	73.9	77.7	64.4	69.9	65.1

Source: Annual Report (1979) of National Nutrition Monitoring Bureau, National Institute of Nutrition, Hyderabad, Reported by Rajaram Dasgupta, *Economic and Political Weekly*, Vol. XVIII, No. 28, July 9, 1983.

The half grown, uneducated, adolescent girl is married early and becomes pregnant soon. Teenage pregnancy interrupts the physiological growth spurt which brings a girl to her genetically determined maximum stature. As of 1981, 7 per cent of girls in the age group 10-14 and 43 per cent in the age group 15-19 were already married. They enter into sexual life and child bearing with no knowledge about sex and the reproduction process. As estimated, 10-15 per cent of all the annual births (around 25 million) are attributed to these teenage mothers. With their malnourished status, small pelvis, undernutrition, and overwork during pregnancy, these adolescent mothers run a high risk of life. Their babies are of low birth weight and suffer risk of mortality many times higher than those of fully grown, well nourished, educated mothers.

Girls who marry before the age 18 are twice as likely to end up with a large family than those who marry after completing 20 years, and therefore not only face much higher risks in pregnancy when they first conceive, but also compounded risks and related ill-health over their lifetimes.

Maternal Health

The Indian woman on an average has 8-9 pregnancies, resulting in a little over six live births, of which 4-5 survive. She is estimated to spend 80 per cent of her reproductive years in pregnancy and lactation.

Dietary surveys have shown that the intake of women in low income groups is deficient by 500 to 600 calories. The corresponding findings for pregnant and lactating women reveal daily deficiency of 1100 calories and 1000 calories respectively. Deficits in nutrient intakes have been observed in various occupational groups, particularly in those without land and are labourers (Table 1.34). Women belonging to the lower socio-economic groups gain around 3-5 kgs. during pregnancy as against 10 kgs. in the developed countries. Over 50 per cent of pregnant women have a haemoglobin level of less than 10 grams. Anaemia in pregnancy accounts directly for 15-20 per cent of all maternal deaths in India, and indirectly for a much larger proportion.

TABLE - 1.34
PERCENTAGE OF DEATHS BY CAUSES RELATED TO CHILD BIRTH AND PREGNANCY (MATERNAL) 1976 TO 1983

Specific Causes	*1976*	*1977*	*1978*	*1979*	*1980*	*1981*	*1982*	*1983*
Abortion	11.6	8.2	11.0	11.7	12.5	13.7	10.1	10.7
Toxaemia	10.4	11.2	21.2	16.1	12.4	8.0	12.5	12.1
Anaemia	22.1	15.9	14.6	15.0	15.8	17.7	24.4	18.9
Bleeding of pregnancy and puerperium	17.2	20.6	18.2	20.0	15.8	23.4	26.2	23.8
Malposition of child leading to death of mother	8.6	9.4	9.5	10.5	13.4	9.2	7.2	8.3
Puerperal sepsis	13.5	18.8	12.4	11.7	12.4	13.1	8.3	11.6
Not classifiable	16.6	15.9	13.1	15.0	17.7	14.9	11.3	14.6
Total	100.0	100.0	100.0	100.0	100.0	100.0	100.0	100.0
Sample No. of Deaths	163	170	137	180	209	175	168	206
Percent to total Deaths	1.1	1.0	1.0	1.1	1.2	1.0	1.0	1.2

Source: Survey of Causes of Deaths (Rural) 1980, 1983 — A Report, R.G. India.

With the fairly high fertility levels during the reproductive span prevailing in India, maternal mortality accounts for the largest to near largest proportion of deaths among women in their prime years. Official estimates place maternal mortality at 400-500 per 100,000 live births but figures as high as 1000-1200 have been reported from certain rural areas. A woman in the subcontinent runs a lifetime risk of 1 in 18 of dying from a pregnancy related cause. Anaemia, haemorrhage, toxemia, sepsis and abortion are the major causes of maternal deaths in India (Table 1.35). It has been estimated that 70 per cent of these deaths can be prevented. Multiparity increases maternal illnesses and deaths which rise significantly with the fourth pregnancy and reach very high levels after the fifth. In India, 38.4 live births in rural areas and 33.0 live births in urban areas are of the fourth order and above (Table 1.36).

TABLE - 1.35
DISTRIBUTION OF LIVE BIRTHS BY ORDER OF BIRTHS — ALL INDIA

Order of Birth	*% Rural 1978*	*% Urban 1978*
1.	23.45	25.75
2.	20.63	23.33
3.	17.49	17.88
4.	13.38	12.22
5.	9.69	7.93
6. or more	15.36	12.89
All	100.0	100.0

Source: Registrar General, India, New Delhi, Survey on Levels, Trends and Differentials in Fertility, 1979, Government of India, Ministry of Health and Family Welfare, New Delhi.

TABLE - 1.36
PERCENTAGE OF BIRTHS BY TYPE OF ATTENTION AT BIRTH BY RURAL/URBAN, INDIA, 1983

Sector	*Institutional*	*Attended by Trained Professionals*	*Attended by Untrained Professionals*
Rural	12.6	16.3	71.1
Urban	45.4	25.4	29.2
Total	19.2	18.1	62.7

Source: Sample Registration Bulletin

Accurate assessments of maternal morbidity are unavailable but evidence from available studies points to an appallingly high incidence of pregnant women not in contact with health services. Around 71.1 per cent of deliveries in rural areas and 29.2 per cent of deliveries in urban areas are conducted by untrained personnel outside the health system (Table 1.37). In Rajasthan, one-third of pregnant women reported illnesses lasting on an average for over two weeks. The maternal mortality rate was 592 per 100,000 live births; for every maternal death some 60 episodes were related directly to pregnancy and childbirth and together represented both the leading cause and over a quarter of overall morbidity.

Abortion has been legalized in India as a health measure since 1972 by the Medical Termination of Pregnancy Act, 1971. Even so, because of non-availability of MTP services within easy reach for most of the rural population and ignorance of the law, 'illegal' abortions continue to be performed by incompetent persons under unhygienic conditions. As a result, abortion-related mortality and mobidity remain major problems. Only 507,719 terminations were performed through the health services in 1986-87 which is around 9 per cent of the induced abortions that were likely to have been performed during the same period. Since the inception of the programme, 5.1 million abortions have been performed under the MTP programme, which is less than the total number of induced abortions likely to be performed in one year. Induced abortions indicate an unmet need of women for family planning, highlight a gap between the availability of services and their accessibility to those in need, and demonstrate women's inability to make use of the services they need acutely.

Respite from pregnancy, and rest and care during pregnancy emerge as major needs. Studies have clearly shown that women engaged in hard physical labour during pregnancy did not gain much weight, and delivered low-birth-weight babies, as compared with women doing less work but having the same food intake. One study on energy consumption and expenditure per household per day, found the energy expenditure to be 5.68 units for men, 9.69 for women and about 3 for children. The major part of domestic energy consumption was for survival-cooking, fetching water, firewood, etc. Technology for reduction of drudgery in women, and providing water and fuel within the easy reach of all, could go a long way in energy conservation for women.

Hardly any information is available for the health hazards of women engaged in different occupations, in agriculture and industries, birth during pregnant and non-pregnant states. In agriculture, they are exposed to heat and rain and have to work in standing and bending postures for long hours, which are hazardous to health. They also work in large numbers in industries such as beedi, carpet, jute, coir weaving, slate, electronics, etc. Micro studies have indicated that workers of these industries suffer from several health hazards.

The health services for children and women, particularly during pregnancy, childbirth and after are inadequate. About 40 per cent of pregnant women receive tetanus toxoid. Although data are unavailable separately on the proportion of pregnant mothers receiving iron and folic acid, it is roughly estimated that around 25 per cent of pregnant and nursing mothers receive iron and folic acid. About 46 per cent of pregnant women are estimated to register for antenatal care. Facilities and basic equipment for mid-wives have been found to be grossly inadequate.

The situation regarding women's health may be summarized as:

(i) Major disparities in health care in population groups in rural and urban areas; remote, backward, hilly and desert areas; and in socio-economically deprived groups.

(ii) Social attitudes and prejudices inherent in our milieu which are unfavourable towards girls and women, effect their health and nutrition negatively.

(iii) Poor health of women due to the synergistic effects of high levels of infection, malnutrition and uncontrolled fertility extending over a prolonged span.

(iv) Inadequate basic health care facilities (including facilities for MCH, family planning, MTP and nutrition) for women and children, in terms of outreach, range of services, quality, availability, etc.

(v) Inefficient use of resources available for health care of women, resulting in a slower pace of health development for them.

(vi) Ignorance and lack of knowledge related to health

nutrition and family planning, affecting self-help efforts in health; and resulting in underutilization of existing resources.

(vii) Absence or inadequacy of essential non-health facilities which affect health, such as potable water, sanitation; female education; food supply, etc.

Policy Guidelines for Health Care for Women

Health care has been accepted as an important intervention for women's development since the First Five-Year Plan. It was recognized that the high infant and maternal mortality would have to be reduced through the provision of maternal and child health services and family planning. The basic strategy for providing health care to the general population as well as women, in the 1950's during the first and second plan periods included:

(i) Expansion of physical infrastructure for health (including opening MCH centres);

(ii) Initiating the family planning programme;

(iii) Communicable disease control (for malaria, filaria, tuberculosis, leprosy and venereal diseases); and

(iv) Establishing facilities for training (attention was given to training female health personnel including nurses, auxilliary nurse midwives, health visitors and *dais*) and having more manpower.

The need to link hospitals at different levels into an effective "coordinated hospital system", and correlate their functions with those of "clinics, domiciliary care services and public health activities", was recognized. The maternity centres which were established during the first two plan periods, were to be linked up with district and referral hospitals. MCH services in urban areas were generally provided through maternity and child health centres, in isolation from the rest of the services. 4500 maternity centres had been established, one-third of which were in urban areas; and about 2800 health units were also established in rural areas. In rural areas, the "health units" in the block were expected to provide MCH services in addition to other health services. During the decade 1950-60, female health personnel were increasingly trained and employed, which resulted in availability of 27,000 nurses (from 5,000 in 1950); 19,900 auxiliary nurse midwives (from 8,000 in 1950); 1,500 lady health visitors (from 52 in 1950) and 11,500 nurse-*dais* and *dais* (from 1,800 in 1950). From the First Plan itself, family limitation and spacing of children were noticed to be "essential steps for securing better care in bringing up children, and therefore, as an important part of public health." Though initially, family planning services were provided primarily through specialized family planning clinics, the need to integrate it with the general health services was realized; and when the fourth plan was put forth, maternity and child health services were stated to be integrated with family planning.

The basic strategies for health care in terms of expansion of physical infrastructure, training more female health personnel, communicable disease control and family planning were continued during the Third and Fourth Plan periods. Specific prophylaxis programmes were initiated to prevent anaemia in pregnant women, and vitamin deficiency in children 1-5 years of age during this period. Also, programmes were started to control smallpox were also formulated, which included a component for instruction of school teachers.

The primary objective of the Fifth Five-Year Plan was to provide minimum public health facilities integrated with family planning and nutrition for vulnerable groups — children, pregnant women and lactating mothers. The accent during this period was similar to previous plan periods — increasing the accessibility of health services to rural areas; correcting regional imbalances; development of referral systems for health care; and communicable disease control. The need for qualitative improvement in the education and training of health personnel was also recognized. Several schemes were initiated during this period to give increased emphasis to the health of mothers. The Integrated Child Development Services Scheme was accepted for countrywide application in 1977. Though primarily for child development, this scheme provides a package of health, nutrition and family planning services for pregnant women and nursing mothers who are socio-economically deprived. Since a large proportion of deliveries are conducted by traditional birth attendants (TBAs) particularly in rural areas, a scheme was initiated during this time to train them for safer mid-wifery practices; the target was to have atleast one TBA per 1000 population. In order to involve the community in health care, and to further promotive and preventive health care at village level, the health guides scheme was initiated. The norm of one health guide per 1000 population was suggested.

The guiding principles for the first two and a half decade of planned development in health in India included measures to:

- (i) Make health services more accessible to the population;
- (ii) Developing the needed human resources;
- (iii) Provision of services for health, including maternal and child health, and family planning.

Over time, the need to interact more closely with people, has been felt, and somewhat more emphasis was given to preventive and promotive aspects of health care.

Committee on the Status of Women in India — 1974

The Committee on the status of women in India highlighted the impact of social attitudes on the health of women, which clearly revealed the poorer lot of women, from the time of birth. The demographic analysis brought into sharp focus the deterioration in the condition of the majority of women despite the advances in medical care and the general improvement in health services, pointing to the criticality of the social conditions.

On the health side, it was pointed out that more resources were being spent for curative than preventive and promotive services; and that major rural/urban and regional disparities existed in health care was noted to be an unfortunate distortion. The report further underlined that lack of security and mobility are major problems of female health personnel in rural areas.

However, their recommendations, while emphasizing the need for an integrated thrust for MCH, nutrition and family planning, were limited mainly to upgrading the posts of MCH officers at Central and State levels; the provision of a separate budget for MCH and separate units for MCH at primary health centres. Some modifications in the MTP Act were also recommended. However, while the legislative aspects were gone into detail, the main problems with medical termination of pregnancy, that is the wide availability of services and ignorance of the law, did not get sufficient attention. Altogether, while the analysis of problems was a powerful indictment of the existing situation, this was not matched by comprehensive suggestion to bring about the desired changes in women's health.

The Plan of Action for Women — 1976

The National Plan of Action recognized that the health profile of women (and girls) in India was poor. While giving attention to the salient issues in the social and health areas, it did not however, develop the needed coordinated thrust for actions in each sector converging to achieve common goals. In fact, while emphasizing that the plans of action would have to cover a wide spectrum of programmes and needed to integrate with other strategies, it did not even attempt to provide any directions and made the action plans for health under six separate categories, namely:

(1) Provision of Services
(2) Development of the needed human resources
(3) Mass Education Programmes
(4) Legislative Measures
(5) Role of Voluntary Organizations
(6) Areas of Research

Broadly, it stated that services for women, including mothers and female children, should be part of the general health system. It was recommended that the physical infrastructure be expanded and manpower for health care be augmented. However, their emphasis on the qualitative aspects of maternal care as well as training was inadequate. The necessary infrastructure strengthening at village, primary and secondary levels, linked by an affective referral system, did not receive much attention. Instead, they recommended the establishment of various types of clinics. The need to modify medical undergraduate curriculum, in order to cater to the needs of mothers and children in rural areas, was rightly stressed, so also, the need to orient doctors in services. The TBA was identified as one of the most important person, in the provision of maternity services, and steps to involve her were outlined. The Committee underlined the need to have mass education programmes for mother and child care. Several legislative measures were suggested.

They referred to the MTP Act, age of marriage, and provision of MCH services in municipalities and local bodies. However, the main issue remains operationalizing the law, ensuring that the necessary developments take place. This includes better services for MTP, specially in rural areas; more resources for MCH services through local bodies; and providing education as well as income-generating opportunities to women to raise the age of marriage. Some legislative measure have been taken to ensure that advertisement of baby foods is curbed — this was also a recommendation. The committee suggested some areas in which the voluntary organizations could be involved, such as school health services, MCH care in urban slums, training health workers and information dissemination. Though some efforts have been made to involve them, much more remains to be done on this aspect. Areas for research were suggested, on which only limited action has, followed.

Health Care for Women 1977-87

During the Sixth and Seventh Plans, the major strategies for health care, including that for women, continued to be:

(i) Expansion of physical infrastructure;
(ii) Increasing the availability of trained health manpower;
(iii) Strengthening services for communicable disease control, as well as other diseases; and
(iv) Provision of family planning as well as MCH services.

During the Sixth Five-Year Plan period, in 1983, the National Health Policy was formulated and accepted for implementation. The policy for the first time, defined goals for women's health; reduction in maternal mortality, crude rate and crude birth rate; coverage with antenatal care and immunization of pregnant mothers, and the control of leprosy, tuberculosis and blindness (from which women also suffer), were specified. The levels to be achieved over time were also specified. The policy stated that:

> "the highest priority" would have to be given to "efforts of launching special programmes" for the improvement of maternal and child health, with a special focus on the less privileged sections of the society. Such programmes would required to be decentralized to the maximum possible extent,

their delivery being at the primary level, nearest to the doorsteps of the beneficiaries. While efforts should continue for providing refresher training and orientation to the traditional birth attendants, schemes and programmes should be launched to ensure that progressively all deliveries are conducted by competently trained persons, and that complicated cases receive timely and expert attention, within a comprehensive programme providing antenatal, intra-natal and postnatal care. Also, "organized school health services, integrally linked with a general, preventive and curative services, would require to be established within time-limited programmes.

The Seventh Five-Year Plan clearly states that primary health care will be the main sphere of action in health. It was stated that "women would be organized around available economic activities to enable them to actively participate in the entire process of socio-economic development, including health." Care of pregnant and nursing mothers, young children and school-age children (both in and out of school) was stated to be a priority.

Issues Needing Attention

Some of the critical factors and issues related to women's health have evidently not received the necessary attention in the existing health programmes. Girls need adequate care so that they can enter motherhood without physical and social inadequacies. Optimal reproductive and child-bearing patterns (age of the mother at first childbirth — 20 years; interval between pregnancies at least 3 years; a small family; and no pregnancy after 35 years of age, which influence the health of mothers and their children) need to be advocated, and backed by policies that make them feasible for women. Measures to reduce the workload of women have to be promoted to conserve their energy. Adequate and appropriate information for decision-making, particularly during pregnancy and lactation, needs to be made available.

Recognizing that the renewal of the human race is the unique contribution that women make at considerable personal cost to the nation's existence and productivity, it must be taken as a national obligation to ensure that the fulfilment of this role occurs with minimum personal risk to women's lives and health. Control, over reproduction is a basic right for all women, as this right forms an important basis for the enjoyment of other rights. The enormous wastage of female life and well-being occurring at present has, however, been demonstrated to be containable within human capacity and existing resources.

Women are victims of possessive syndrome and many other kinds of neurosis. The majority of women face mental depressions due to family related problems which are the outcomes of the present social attitudes. Particularly, in the rural areas, such depressions are believed as "possessed by spirits". This encourages many cruel practices and treatment which often lead to physical harm to the women. The primary health centres are ill-equipped to deal with even simple mental disorders.

With rapid urbanization and commercialization, the nutritious foods produced in the villages like fruits, vegetables, milk and so forth are being exported to urban areas thereby denying them to the rural poor. Growing poverty in the countryside is also encouraging such exports. This results in a further drop of nutritional levels of the rural poor.

The Bhore Committee way back in 1946 recommended establishing a Primary Health Centre for each 30,000 population which has not yet been achieved.

Health for All goals and indicators have already accepted and accorded primacy to maternal and child health care, inter alia including a halving of maternal mortality, hundred per cent coverage for ante-natal care and delivery by trained birth attendants by year 2000 A.D. The health services programmes are already committed to work towards the achievement of these goals. The Technological and Societal missions for eradication of illiteracy, immunization and safe water supply include certain critical indicators that will have impact on maternal and child care. However, as in the past, the present efforts lack in scale and systematic organization of the various components that together could radically alter the situation for women and children. Therefore, a comprehensive programme of health care of women needs to be developed with a special technological and societal mission to halve maternal mortality and morbidity and ensure optimum child bearing patterns by the year 2000. This mission, the details of which would have to be worked out by an expert working group, would need to, simultaneously gear the health services to reduce maternal, infant and child mortality and address the conditions that can assist women not to bear a child when this event will increase the risk to the health of the women and/or the child to be born/already born. Inter alia, the observance of the small family norm through proper education of its impact on the health of women and children, will be an integral part of this mission.

Family Welfare

It is unfortunate that the family planning policy is oriented towards fertility control and not concerned with providing a means for women and men to have control on their own bodies. A reflection of this policy is the encouragement of injectable contraceptives like Net-en which have been banned in most developed countries.

Though the family welfare and planning programmes have been a part of development planning since the First Five-Year Plan, actual achievements are below expectations. By March, 1987, the effective couple protection rate was only 34 per cent. From the beginning, emphasis has been placed on sterilizations rather than on temporary methods. Whereas in the early phases more vasectomies were performed, during the last decade, female sterilizations have been promoted at a very high rate. With the introduction of laproscopy, female sterilizations have reached high numbers amounting to almost 90 per cent of all sterilizations.

Research studies have shed light on the fact that the knowledge regarding family planning/methods is low despite the huge amounts of money spent on propaganda. The only method known to all is sterilization. The higher rates of abortions show the desire and need of the women for family planning and the failure of the family planning information and services to reach them in time. Laproscopic operations are being performed in several family planning camps without proper care and follow-up. Consequent problems tend to create apprehension among people. More intensive propagation of spacing methods together with innovative strategies for delivery of supplies has to be taken up and spread of information about temporary methods accorded high priority.

The shift towards female sterilizations has to be reversed. Ironically, while that programme mainly provides female centred methods most of the women using these are not really happy due to the side effects. Hormonal reactions to oral pills, pain and heavy bleeding due to IUD, etc., are common complaints. In many areas women suffer from post-operative problems following tubectomy. The health personnel also concentrate most on sterilization (female) as it helps them to realize their target and earn cash rewards.

Recommendations

Infancy & Early Childhood

1. Using amniocentesis for sex determination tests should be banned as in Maharashtra. Practitioners indulging in and abetting such acts should be punished severely and their medical licenses should be revoked.
2. Incentives should be considered to encourage parents to have female children. A couple who opts to limit their family to one female child may be given a regular monthly cash subsidy to attend to the girl child's needs. The amount must be given to the family over a period of time and not in a lump sum, as this might result in misuse of the female child as an instrument for getting easy money and later to neglect the child.
3. Infants' and small children's growth and development should be monitors by recording their weights and heights at regular intervals. Proper corrective interventions should be made wherever necessary.
4. Universal immunization should be enforced to encompass all children.
5. Oral Rehydration Therapy (ORT) should be widely disseminated. ORT salts in packed form should be made available at a large scale in order to reduce the mortality from diarrheal diseases.

6. The ICDS should be strengthened and priority access should be provided to the girl child. Higher participation of women would also result from expansion of the programme.
7. Efforts should be made to bring a qualitative change in the attitudes against girl children. Media should be used for this purpose aiming to get the girl child to be accepted in the family and the society as an equal to the male child.
8. Focus is needed on the adolescent girl (12-18 years), so that she attains her maximum physical and mental capacities. It is necessary to provide alternative options to an early marriage. This can be ensured by a mix of education and employment opportunities and enforcement of the law on minimum age of marriage (18 years). The younger girl child needs to utilize health and education programmes more fully. It has been proposed that the ICDS will also address this issue in specific areas.
9. Adequate nutrition should be ensured for adolescent girls during the pre-puberty and pubertal growth phase to ensure 'catch up' on physical development by providing supplements to deprived groups.
10. Health and nutrition education should be promoted to ensure that preventive and promotive measures are adopted. The necessity of safe water, sanitation and personal hygiene also should be advocated.
11. Immunization against tetanus and rubella should be introduced for this age group.
12. Linkages with basic health care must be developed at the village level in the view of the special problems of mobility faced by young girls.
13. A massive communication campaign to create widespread awareness of the law prohibiting the marriage of the girl before 18 years and boys before 21 years and generate consciousness on the severe health implications in children and women of such early marriages must be launched.
14. The aim should be to implement the present legal minimum age of marriage effectively by creating a social consciousness for the desirability of marriage for girls only after 20 and for boys at 25. Preferential employment for unmarried males

and females and priority in other developmental schemes for such youth, need to be seriously examined.

15. The comprehensive school health scheme which is being formulated, should be speedily implemented. Special efforts must be made for the health services to reach girls of the school-going age who are out of school. Each child should be examined and screened at least three times — at primary school entry, before leaving primary school and at completion of high school. Similarly, a girl child out of school should be examined and screened three times — at around 6, 10 and 15 years of age. Screening kits and medicines should be made available. School teachers and non-formal education functionaries should be trained in the required areas of health care. The health programme for school and non-formal education systems should be integrally linked with the general health services.
16. It is necessary to impart information about reproductive processes, ways to prevent conception, need for spacing between children, optimum age of child bearing, necessary care for pregnant women and lactating mothers and small family norm, etc. This may be introduced as a part of the regular curriculum in school, colleges and universities. For girls/boys who are not in school, Anganwadi workers/female CHWs may impart this knowledge.
17. To improve women's health status, there is no doubt that the general health services have to be made to respond to women's specific problems. A strategy for improving the health of women in the reproductive age group would be to reduce the risk of death and illness associated with pregnancy as well as to reduce the exposure to pregnancy itself. Comprehensive minimal care during pregnancy, childbirth and thereafter, steps to ameliorate malnutrition as well as decrease the workload of women, and improved access to health services, particularly family planning services, should be the salient instruments for improving the health of women.
18. Since women are severely restricted in their mobility, basic health care services must be made available to them as close as possible to their homes. Therefore, resources should be

allocated as a priority to health services at the village, as well as at the first level of referral. The services would be provided by the female health workers, supported by the functionaries and the community from the village, as well as supervisory echelons within the health sector. Measures should be taken to reduce the incidence of low birth weight babies.

19. A minimum package of services should be available for pregnant women at village level. This should include at least
    — Facilities for early detection of pregnancy, with low-cost pregnancy detection kits;
    — Antenatal registration;
    — Minimum of three antenatal check-ups in the second and third trimester;
    — Screening of high-risk cases;
    — Anaemia prophylaxis with iron and folic and tablets;
    — Tetanus toxoid coverage;
    — Prophylaxis against malaria in high endemic areas;
    — Advocacy of adequate rest;
    — Health and nutrition education;
    — Priority attention to locally endemic diseases affecting women; and
    — Adequate safe drugs for her illness.
20. ANMs should be trained to assess pelvic proportions of pregnant women to identify the high risk cases and refer them to competent institutions. This will help in saving women from maternal deaths and also to reduce the incidence of still births.
21. The emphasis will have to be on providing better care to the pregnant woman in her home, as well as to ensure that adequate facilities are available at the first level of referral to deal with obstetric emergencies such as toximias, sepsis, obstructed labour and haemorrhage. In order to improve village level care during childbirth, the following are suggested:
    — Continuous training, supervision and support for better mid-wifery practices to the TBA and female health workers;
    — Provision for sterile delivery kits to the TBA, health workers and even to mothers;

- — Stocking adequate drugs and supplies with the health workers, and providing a restricted number to the TBA; and
- — Pre-arranged transport (or reimbursement of transport costs) for any emergency, when a woman has been registered for antenatal care.

Post-natal services should be available as close to the homes of mothers as possible. In rural areas in several parts of India, women do not leave their homes for 40 days after delivery. Post-natal care should include:

- — A minimum of three contacts with the mother by the TBA and/or female health worker within the first 10 days after child birth;
- — One massive dose of vitamin A within one month after delivery to all mothers;
- — Iron and folic acid for 50 per cent of mothers;
- — Adequate drugs to deal with puerpural sepsis;
- — Education for the mother's nutrition and contraception as well as for infant feeding and health care, particularly immunization.

Women's Health Care

23. The health of women who are not pregnant or nursing, is an area which has received inadequate attention so far. Interventions thus made can cause a significant difference to women's health status not only between pregnancies, but also improve the outcome of future pregnancies. Moreover, the woman's right to health care as an individual must be promoted.
24. Women with chronic or serious illnesses, such as tuberculosis, leprosy, viral hepatitis, anaemia, sexually transmitted cases, etc., should be promptly treated and advised to postpone their pregnancy for a suitable safe period.
25. High priority should be given to women for treatment/ control of all endemic diseases, specially those which have a harmful effect on the next generation (for example, goitre, sexually transmitted diseases, etc.)
26. Doctors of the Primary Health Centres be given in-service training to handle the cases of possessive syndrome and

neurosis. Mass education programme be taken up to change the negative attitudes prevalent against mental illness.

27. Nutritious foods produced in the villages should be primarily utilized to cater to the nutrition needs of the rural poor. Only the surplus should be allowed for export to urban areas. A widespread public distribution system would be essential to make basic foods available at affordable costs.
28. Emphasis should be placed on Science and Technology research pertaining to sex linked diseases, occupational hazards, and indigenous methods of family planning as affecting women. Undergraduate level programmes should introduce courses relevant to women, i.e.:
    (i) Work physiology (ergdonomics) as related to health, and occupational hazards.
    (ii) Basic tenets of genetics, related to family studies, genetic disorders and environmental effects.
    (iii) At the postgraduate level and above, research needs to be conducted in ergonomic abnormalities in women such as spinal strain after carrying loads. Also, work is needed on sex-linked, genetic disorders like muscular dystrophy and haemophilia, where women are the carriers.
29. More Primary Health Centres should be set up in the rural areas to achieve the target of having one Primary Health Centre for each 30,000 population as recommended by the Bhore Committee in 1946.
30. The timings of the dispensaries and hospitals should be fixed in a way which would be convenient to working women.
31. There should be a 24 hours creche facility for women patients with children in every hospital and PHC.
32. There is a need for a humane Drug Policy and check on the pharmaceuticals industry that at present operates on the profit principle like any other industry.
33. It is necessary to provide safety equipment including powerful exhausts to remove harmful dust from the work environment and personal protective equipment like masks, feet protectors, eye glasses, ear muffs and gloves and strong contraceptions for the safety of women workers.

34. There should be Refreshers/Orientation courses for the doctors on the subjects of women's work and health.

Family Welfare

35. Family planning policy should be such that it will help women have greater control over their bodies and enable them to make conscious choices on having or not having children and declining the number of children they want.
36. Injectible contraceptives as well as other contraceptives banned in developed countries should not be permitted in the country.
37. More research needs to be carried out to develop contraceptives that can be used by men and they should be propagated more widely.
38. Family Planning counselling needs to involve married and older women, selected from local surroundings for effective transmission of the concept and its urgency.
39. Laproscopic operations should be followed up.
40. Disseminating information about temporary methods of spacing should be accorded high priority.
41. Male sterilizations (vasectomies) need to be encouraged.
42. Recommended measures in the non-health sectors that critically influence health are as follows:
    - Drinking water supply is a prime essential;
    - Fuel should be made available within easy reach to all;
    - Progressively more latrines should be made available and their use encouraged by special education efforts aimed at women;
    - Energy-saving devices for household work should be actively promoted for conserving women's energy.

Social Welfare

As recognized in the Fifth Five-Year Plan, even with expanded employment opportunities, the poor will not be able, with their level of earnings, to buy for themselves all the essential goods and services which should figure in any reasonable concept of a minimum standard of living. The measures for providing larger employment and incomes to the poorer sections will, therefore, have to be supplemented up to at least certain minimum standard, by social consumption and investment in the form of education, health, nutrition, drinking water, housing, communications and electricity, and social welfare services. Social welfare services are intended to cater for the special needs of persons and groups, who by reason of some handicap—social, economic, physical or mental—are unable to avail of or are traditionally denied the amenities and services provided by the community. Women are handicapped by social customs and social values and therefore social welfare services have and should specially endeavour to rehabilitate them by inducing a change in the attitudes of society towards women, their role and contribution.

Identification of Problem Areas

A statement of a plan of social welfare programmes relating to women even if it is within the purview of the overall social welfare programmes, will help in providing the correct emphasis on the problems and development needs of the weaker sections of women and provide voluntary organizations and voluntary effort "a certain" direction. The problems and consequently the developmental action required are, it appears, unlimited and the resources are limited. As such, priorities have necessarily to be assigned.

Among women, the following categories and some of the problems faced by them, call for special attention on a priority basis. The categories are:

- (A) Working women. To include
  - (i) The low-income women living in tribal and backward rural areas and urban slums.
  - (ii) The migrant women.
  - (iii) The divorced/separated.
- (B) Physically and mentally handicapped women.
- (C) Widows with or without children.
- (D) Destitute women.
- (E) Women who come into conflict with law.
- (F) Exploited women and unmarried mothers.

The problems faced by each of the above categories are numerous and some of them are common to other categories. To decide on action plan priorities, the handicaps and/or the factors which impose constraints need to be understood.

Working Women

5. According to 1971 Census, women workers constitute nearly 12 per cent of the total women population and well over 90 per cent of the women workers are found employed in rural areas. It should be recognized here that the problems faced by women workers in rural areas are altogether different from those in the urban areas.

Rural areas including tribal and backward areas: Women workers in rural areas are largely landless agricultural labourers; members of households with uneconomic holdings; those engaged in traditional household industries like hand-spinning, hand-weaving, oil pressing, rice pounding, leather, tobacco processing, etc. These household industries-which are predominantly female labour intensive and which have been a major source of employment in villages appear to have declined in importance during the post-Independence period. This is also evidenced by the distinctly declining trend in employment of women workers in the rural areas between the decennial Censuses 1961 and 1971. It has not been possible to reverse this trend because:

(i) Almost all the women workers in the rural areas are handicapped by illiteracy and lack of mobility.

(ii) In addition to this, incessant child bearing coupled with hard domestic work does not provide them any time to go through formal education/training to acquire new skills. Facilities for acquiring new skills are still sparse.

Urban Areas: Women workers in the urban areas fall into three distinct categories:

(i) The first category consists largely of migrants from villages and members of families whose economic position has deteriorated to near starvation. The women of this class work mainly as domestic servants and as unskilled labour in various unorganized industries.
This category of women workers, who are largely slum dwellers, are below subsistence level. Their problems are to find a job which is secure or provides them regular income at least to subsist, a place for comfortable living, as most of them are away from their homes located in villages; and rehabilitation facilities for their

families, particularly children and preparing them for better livelihood, through better education and training; in that order.

(ii) The second category consists of women, who need employment either to keep their families away from starvation or to ensure better standard of living. Most of such women are found employed in industries, services and professions. Some are even self-employed. In the case of this second category of women workers in urban areas, their existence ranges from subsistence to security. Some of these women, particularly those residing away from their families, are likely to be exposed to the dangers of exploitation from undesirable and anti-social elements. Personal security is therefore a major problem for them.

(iii) The third category consists of women who are highly educated and work in higher ranks of services and professions for personal satisfaction and independence. Belonging as they do at least to the upper middle-class families, they do not as group face any serious problems requiring immediate attention here.

Divorced/separated women are part of each of these categories.

Physically and Mentally Handicapped Women

There are several types of physical handicaps like blindness, deafness, orthopaedic handicap, leprosy, mental retardation, etc., which hinder two persons from even entertaining the hopes of equal participation in the overall social activity. These problems are common to both men and women.

Estimates of physically handicapped women are not separately available. To provide a basis for the formulation of Fifth Five-Year Plan, the working group on the Handicapped - constituted for the purpose, estimated that "India may have well over 12 million blind, deaf and orthopaedically handicapped persons. In addition, an estimated 2 million suffer from moderate to severe retardation. The number of persons suffering from leprosy is believed to be around 2.5 million".

The basic problem concerning these physically handicapped persons is lack of adequate facilities for differential medical care, education, training and rehabilitation programmes and a lack of knowledge about these facilities by handicapped persons. Further, it is widely known that though the existing facilities are largely used by men, a majority of physically handicapped women are not coming forward to utilize the available facilities.

Widows With or Without Children

The 1971 Census distribution of women according to marital status indicates that roughly about 9 per cent of the women are widows. Further, they are almost evenly distributed between the rural and urban areas.

Widowhood is a curse for most of the women in India for various reasons:

(i) It is almost invariably accompanied by economic disaster. This is because a large number of the families in India survive at below subsistence level and hence death of a male earning member pushes down the families concerned to near starvation. Also many of the females are voluntarily out of work force, and illiteracy remains the greatest barrier for the improvement of the economic position of widowed women, particularly in the rural areas.

(ii) Age-old traditions, social prejudices and cultural practices almost exclude widowed women from any socially productive work. Social acceptance of women is reduced with widowhood. In some communities/ regions. There is almost a sort of social boycott of widowed women.

Problems faces by Widows of Different Age Groups: The problems faced by widowed women are not all the same as between different age-groups; and as between rural and urban areas:

(a) For widows in the younger age group — particularly those belonging to 15-44 years of age the problems are more related to economic independence and rehabilitation in the society — preferably through remarriage.

(b) For widows in the age group 45 and above, the problem is more of social acceptance and security. Most of such women, if not previously employed, will be unfit for employment. Even in respect of employed women — widowed after 44 years of age — it is difficult to impart of the needed training/skills for more remunerative jobs within the existing framework of education/ training facilities.

Problems of widowed women in the rural areas are even move severe than those in the urban areas. In addition to economic dependence and the social stigma attached to widowhood, there are no opportunities for their emancipation. Many of them are possibly not even aware of the efforts being made by the government agencies through voluntary organizations to redress their miseries.

Destitute Women

These destitute women can be classified into three age-groups as their problems are different:

Below 15 years: Persons in this group can be categorized as children. They are mostly orphans and are, therefore, deprived of the tender parental care. They are also subjected to malnutrition and the consequent diseases. This age group, viz., below 15 years of age constitutes the formative years in a person's life, as the process of development and learning are most rapid during these young years. During these formative years, the effects of environment greatly influence the personality development, mental attitudes, moral character, etc. Often, destitute persons in this age group fall a prey to the environmental disadvantages.

15-44 years: This second group of women are both in the productive and reproductive age group. Their main problems are those pertaining to economic independence, social acceptance and security.

45 years and above: In the case of third group of destitute women, their major problem is social security. They are mostly unfit to be employed. They cannot even be trained to earn their livelihood.

Women Who Come into Conflict with Law

Women who fall under this category are: (i) juvenile delinquents, (ii) women in moral and social danger—particularly those who indulge in immoral traffic and (iii) women prisoners.

Juvenile delinquents: are again a creation of the society and the environment in which they are brought up; the deprivation of proper nutrition and training/education which would enable them to earn a better livelihood, etc.

Prostitutes: Women subjected to severe economic distress and hardships often come into the clutches of persons who have vested interests in immoral traffic. Once they succumb they do not receive proper health care — curative and preventive treatment for the diseases associated with immoral traffic; many of them are not aware of the existing health care facilities and added to it is the innate fear of being exposed to the general public and the resulting social reactions. The existing health facilities are also not adequate and are not perceived as being sympathetic towards their health problems.

Female Prisoners: Many of the problems faced by female prisoners are in common with male prisoners. However, some of the problems are peculiar to females alone. For example, women prisoners with children — particularly in case children are below five years — have problems in arranging for the care of their children. Also, problems in getting rehabilitated, after they are free, are more severe in the case of women prisoners than men prisoners.

Exploited Women and Unmarried Mothers

(i) Out-of-wedlock pregnancies are on the increase, judging from the number of abortions and live births among single women recorded at various institutions. Estimates of medical termination of pregnancies (MTP) in the case of single women alone range from 10 to 30 per cent of total MTP cases. In respect of live illegitimate births estimates based on hospital records range from 2 to 3 per cent of the total confinements. In reality many more clandestine live illegitimate births may be taking place which are not brought to public notice.

(ii) Premarital pregnancies, are as generally believed, no longer confined to the illiterate and depressed classes. According to some case-studies in this field, nearly 50 per cent of the pre-marital pregnancies were observed in the case of women who are at least matriculates. A few were graduates. Some of them were observed to be belonging to the privileged classes of the society. A more distressing feature, however, is that pre-marital pregnancies are being observed even in the case of school girls.

Among the reasons attributed to premarital pregnancies are: interactions between various social, psychological and economic forces like break down of joint families; overwhelming poverty, rapid urbanization bringing in its wake the social transformation which leads to increasing permissiveness, lack of communication between children and parents; emotional immaturity and craze for excitement among the youth; antipathy towards the introduction of basic sex education among school children, etc., are the most important reasons cited.

Permissiveness and promiscuity increase with rapid urbanization and measures to avoid such premarital pregnancies is a long drawn social education problem and cannot be expected to decline rapidly. However, the problems concomitant to pre-marital pregnancies can and should at least be tackled effectively.

The action plans should be directed primarily to solving the problems of these six target groups of women.

Broad Groups of Action

There is considerable overlap both in terms of the causes and programmes and agencies concerned with eliminating the problems and building rehabilitation/development plans for these target groups. As such, the action plans are classified under broad groups of actions rather than in terms of categories of women discussed above:

I. Provision of Services/Infrastructure.
II. Education/Training Programmes for the Target Groups.
III. Promoting Voluntary Effort : The Role of Women.
IV. Development of Human Resources.

V. Administrative Set-up and Coordination.
VI. Legislative Measures.
VII. Areas of Research.

The Fifth Five-Year Plan has rightly emphasized the need for a shift in the approach towards social welfare, from a mere provision of curative and rehabilitative services — the kind of approach adopted during the past two decades of planning — to promoting the needed preventive and developmental aspects of social welfare. The action plans should necessarily have such a preventive and development orientation.

Action Plans

Provision of Services/Infrastructure

21. (i) Services for the care of girls below 15;
(ii) Facilities for women in the productive age group, i.e., 15-45 years;
(iii) Programmes for the care of aged and infirm women; and
(iv) General welfare programmes.

Services for the Care of Girls below 15

There are three categories of children who need particular attention, viz., children of working women, destitute children — particularly female children and juvenile delinquents. The following action plans are suggested:

(1) The child population below 6 years of working mothers in urban and rural areas is estimated to be around 20 lakh and 166 lakh, respectively. With a view to helping the working mother discharge her duties — both as a mother and worker better family aid services like Anganwadis, Balwadis, creches and day care centres might be launched in a big way.
Both in the rural and in the urban areas efforts should be made to cover more than 40 per cent of the children of working mothers.

(2) There are about 11 lakh destitute children in the country. The girls among them need particular attention, because they are likely to be exposed to social and moral dangers when they grow up. Efforts should be made to provide institutional

facilities whether through the foster care programmes or otherwise for taking care of a majority of the destitute female children.

(3) It is impossible to discriminate between male and female juvenile delinquents, as the problems are common to both. However, the approach towards juvenile delinquency as such should be to provide the needed atmosphere for a child to develop personality, character and social conscience through setting up of clubs, play centres, juvenile guidance units, workshops, etc.

(4) Holiday homes schemes initiated earlier to provide organized and guided recreational facilities to children and be one of the measures to prevent juvenile delinquency. Such facilities should at least be extended to cover all the children residing in the slums of major cities.

Facilities for Women in the Productive Age Group

In some selected urban areas, hostel facilities are available for working women of the lower income groups earning Rs. 50 to Rs. 800 per month. However, the coverage of the programme in terms of the proportion of working women needs to be stepped up considerably. Similarly, district-wise investigation would be undertaken about the need for working women's hostels and appropriate facilities set up. The matching contribution for grants for construction/addition/alterations should be stepped up.

Socio-economic programmes were initiated in 1958 with the objective of providing full or part-time work to the needy/destitute women and the physically handicapped either through full wage or a wage sufficient to supplement the meagre income of their families. These programmes should be expanded considerably in both rural and urban areas, as they have the potential to provide the needed economic independence to women belonging to the weaker sections and thus act as a preventive measure to many of the social evils.

For effectively implementing these socio-economic programmes, active collaboration should be sought from agencies like Handicrafts Board, Handloom Board, Khadi and Village Industries Board, Small Industries Service Institutes, Small

Industries Development Corporations at the State level and the nationalized banks.

To increase the employment potential for the following types of schemes additional steps should be undertaken within the purview of socio-economic programmes:

(i) Small-Scale industries.
(ii) Units as ancillary to large production of handicrafts.
(iii) Units for the procurement and production of handicrafts.
(iv) Handloom training-cum-production units.
(v) Agro-based industries like dairy, poultry farms, etc.
(vi) Traditional female labour intensive industries like rice pounding, oil-pressing, etc.

Attempts must be made to revitalize and activate the existing sick units falling under the purview of socio-economic programmes.

Ways to improve the working, efficiency and effectiveness of Mahila Mandals must be studied and necessary action taken. They should be reoriented to aim at increasing the earning power of women in the rural areas.

It is suggested that by the end of the Fifth Plan, about 10,000 Mahila Mandals should be developed throughout the country to provide an effective media for organizing women welfare activities in the rural areas.

Scholarship programmes of the Central and State Governments for the handicapped should be expanded considerably and efforts should be made to encourage women to make use of the scholarships available.

Sheltered workshops should be organized.

Schemes for the welfare of destitute women between the ages 18-44 and 45-65 providing for basic amenities of food, shelter, clothing, basic education and training in crafts should be implemented through voluntary organizations who may be given grants to cover 75 per cent of the expenditure. It is suggested that this scheme should be revived and implemented in all the States.

Homes for the rehabilitation of rescued and released women prisoners should be started in all towns with a minimum of 5 lakh of population. Apart from providing shelter, food and clothing, the inmates should also be provided training in crafts like sewing, embroidery, knitting, etc. Efforts should, however, be made in the direction of making inmates self-sufficient and earn independent livelihood.

In some such protective homes, insane women are housed along with other women which is an unhealthy and undesirable practice and should be discontinued.

Programmes for the Care of Aged and Infirm Women

Women in the age group 65 years and over constitute roughly 85 lakh according to the 1971 Census. Many of the women lack absolutely any security. They are mostly dependent on their children who often desert them. Thus, even women belonging to upper middle classes are sometimes reduced to the status of destitute. Efforts should therefore be made at least in a modest way to initiate social security measures through old age pension with the objective of providing economic independence to at least 25 per cent of women in the age group particularly in the rural areas.

For the women retired from active service and for those who are in need of some residential facilities, hostels should be started in all the major cities. If necessary, subsidies may also be extended under the grants-in-aid programmes.

General Welfare Programmes

Slum clearance programmes should be initiated in all the major cities and towns with a minimum of 5 lakh of population. People displaced should be provided alternative sites, with proper environmental sanitation, for building their homes.

Zila Parishads and youth in the districts should be entrusted with drinking water supply projects.

A vigorous campaign of education and action should be launched in favour of community sanitation and hygiene. Public utility services should be expanded. The practice of carrying night-soil as headloads must be eradicated.

Education/Training Programmes for the Target Groups

Analysis of the problems faced by the target group of women indicated that illiteracy, inadequate education/training, lack of facilities for training in alternative skills and lack of knowledge about the existing facilities are some of the major problems that have hindered the progress of women in India. There is, therefore, the need for accelerating the efforts in this regard with renewed vigour. With this in view, the following action plans are recommended:

(1a) The Fourth Plan introduced a programme of functional literacy built round farmer's training in selected districts where high yielding varieties of crops were being cultivated. It is estimated that about 90,000 women received this training during the Fourth Plan and about 5 to 7 lakh of women are likely to be trained under this programmes during the Fifth Plan. This programme must be extended to all the rural areas.

(1b) Apart from imparting knowledge about farming, the curriculum for women should include courses of training in occupational skills like kitchen gardening, food cultivation, poultry keeping, animal husbandry; household arts like cooking, nutritional values of foods locally available, sewing, knitting, etc.; and family planning.

(1c) Preference should be given to women belonging to Scheduled Castes, tribal wcmen, widowed women and destitutes under this functional literacy programme.

(2a) For the non-student young girls without any education and school drop-outs — particularly for girls in the age group 11-14 years, the pre-vocational training programmes should be reviewed and strengthened by enlarging the scope of training and by increasing the number of trades.

(2b) In respect of girls in the age group 11-14 years, the objective of pre-vocational training should also be to train them to be self-sufficient in home management by organizing courses of training in sewing, cooking, nutrition, minor repairs of the house, motherhood, child care, etc.

(2c) Pre-vocational programmes should be extended to cover girls in this age group in the rural areas. In urban areas, preference should be given to girls in the slum areas and destitute girls.

(3) Condensed courses of education were started in 1958 with the twin objective of (a) opening new vistas of employment to a large number of deserving and needy women, and

(b) creating a band of competent trained workers required to man the various projects in the rural areas in the shortest possible time. Under the scheme, women in the age group 18-30 who have studied up to classes IV and VI are trained for middle school/matriculation examinations within a period of two years. The scheme was found very useful but the statistics reveal that the beneficiaries have been mostly women belonging to the middle-class families. Preference should be given to women belonging to backward classes, widowed women and destitute women.

(4) Special efforts should be made to cover women belonging to Scheduled Castes and Scheduled Tribes through condensed courses. An incentive of Rs. 1,000 (as recommended by the Review Committee), be given to the institution for every successful Scheduled Caste/Scheduled Tribe candidate trained.

(5a) The condensed courses should be organized in a big way and for smaller groups of say 5 to 7 with the help of high schools and colleges for girls. Efforts should be made to cover about 215 lakh women under the condensed course programmes, during the Fifth Plan period.

(5b) Apart from imparting general education, condensed courses should also aim at imparting job-oriented training with the active cooperation of existing vocational training institutions.

(5c) Under this programme of condensed courses, short-term courses should be organized to retain women who have been temporarily out of job-market to fulfil child bearing responsibilities.

(5d) For the failed candidates, short-term course of six months to one year should be organized.

(5e) Special efforts should be initiated to follow-up successful candidates with a view to helping them in securing jobs.

(6) Pre-examination training facilities should be offered to duly qualified poor women with the objective of equipping them to successfully compete in examinations for public jobs. It is suggested that about 80 lakh girls in the age group 14-17 may be covered under this programme during the Fifth Plan period.

(7) The school curricula in various States in India should encourage the doing away of traditional prejudices of inequality of the sexes.
(8) Sex education should be introduced at the appropriate stage with the objective of also educating the young girls about the social and moral dangers they are likely to encounter.
(9) The value of physical training in the school curricula should be emphasized.

Promoting Voluntary Effort: The Role of Women

Voluntary welfare service organizations have been an integral part of the cultural and social traditions in India. Soon after independence, it was estimated that there were 10,000 voluntary organizations engaged in social welfare. In fact, all the schemes of Central Social Welfare Board are implemented only through voluntary organizations. The reorientation given to social welfare in the Fifth Plan calls for more effort on the part of both voluntary organizations and the State agencies involved. The following action plans are, therefore, warranted in this regard:

(a) Efforts should be made to promote a large number of voluntary organizations throughout the country. They have a critical role in mobilizing public opinion in favour of equality among men and women, and eradicating superstitions, social evils and waste. The motivational strategy for encouraging voluntary organizations needs to be well thought through and support facilities provided. Women should be promoted to take the initiative and responsibility for organizing voluntary effort, for not only can they bring to the tasks the necessary dedication commitment and empathy; but their very presence will provide their socially handicapped sisters a source of inspiration and set in a cycle of social rejuvenation. All voluntary organizations particularly those concerned with social welfare vis-a-vis women must be encouraged to have women members. Women Panchayats, Mahila Mandals, working women, etc., should be encouraged to spearhead such voluntary activities. Mahila Mandals should be promoted in every village so that they can function as field level agencies for social and economic transformation.

(b) Most of the voluntary organizations have been operating independently of each other. They have, therefore, not been able to fully benefit the community. The role of existing organizations should be determined and measures should be initiated to coordinate/supplement the efforts of various organizations at each district level.

(c) Many of the women's voluntary organizations are located in urban areas, while only a few organizations have endeavoured to work amongst rural women. Efforts should be made to promote a large number of voluntary women's organizations in the rural backward and tribal areas and urban slums to mobilize public support for different programmes and to implement them. This calls for liberation of the rules regarding the matching grant through voluntary contributions, simplification of the rules and procedures of obtaining the grant as well as administering the organizations, provision of trained staff, organization of leadership training programmes, etc.

Development of Human Resources

Administration of various social welfare programmes have become increasingly technical. During the past two decades of developmental planning lack of technically competent workers has had an adverse impact on the quality and success of welfare programmes. With a view to provide the necessary support to various agencies, the following action plans are suggested:

(1) Training facilities for the workers attached to all the voluntary agencies, like Mahila Mandals should be initiated immediately. The training needs of workers, however, differ from organization to organization depending on the nature of tasks required to be performed.

(2) Through a proper investigation training requirements of workers in each district should be assessed and suitable training programmes designed.

(3) These training programme should, as far as possible be organized at each district level.

(4) Trainees should preferably be local candidates.

(5) Effective implementation of the various socio-economic

programmes require two cadres of workers: the grass-root workers and supervisory staff. The grass-root workers should be provided training in the latest techniques and methods of production with the active collaboration of well established industrial units and Industrial Training Institute. The supervisory staff, on the other hand, should be trained in advanced techniques of production, business management, personnel management, etc.

(6) In the case of handicrafts units under the socio-economic programme, practising craftsmen should be trained as instructors and appointed.

(7) Short-term orientation should also be given to the members of the managing committees of the units — socio-economic programmes — about the general working of such units.

(8) Senior level officers in charge of the socio-economic programmes should also be exposed to short-term orientation courses in business management and allied fields through Small Industries Service Institutes, University departments of business management, etc.

Administrative Set-Up and Coordination

Administrative traditions in India have tended to attach least importance to departments dealing with social welfare. This is reflected even in the training imparted to administrators. Only recently it has been realized that administration must also be welfare oriented. The federal nature of our policy vests a large responsibility for implementing social policy and programmes with State and local authorities. There is, therefore, the need for reorganizing the administrative set-up with a view to effectively implementing the various welfare programmes. The following action plans may be taken up for consideration:

(1) Orientation/training programmes should be organized for social welfare personnel, particularly at decision making levels, to sensitize them to social welfare needs and adopt the extension approach of reaching out to the clients. The new developmental and preventive concept of welfare also needs to be imparted.

(2) Every State Department of Social Welfare should have a

Women's Welfare Division with responsibility for planning, programming and monitoring the implementation of schemes of women welfare.

(3) The Central Social Welfare Board is one of the most important agencies for the implementation of social welfare activities. It should be reorganized and strengthened, and vested with larger funds and responsibilities for promoting and developing voluntary effort particularly in rural, backward and tribal areas and among the weaker sections of the community.

(4) The Central Social Welfare Board should launch a massive campaign for onlisting and developing a cadre of voluntary social workers who should be provided some normal assistance to enable them to carry out this work.

(5) State Social Welfare (Advisory) Boards should also be reorganized and strengthened.

(6) The State Board should also be made to function as liaison among the State Government and the local agencies.

(7) Suitable infrastructure should be developed at each district level and block level for implementing and expanding the programmes of Central Social Welfare Board.

(8) Trained social welfare workers should be associated with all the committees to be set-up by the Central Social Welfare Board.

Legislative Measures

(1) International experience indicates that evolving a sound social security system takes a long period of time. However, suitable enactment can be initiated to provide public assistance to select groups like destitute women and people above 65 years but without any means of livelihood. Assistance here need not be in the form of cash. It should be in the form of medical, housing, feeding and recreational facilities, etc.

(2) It should be open to the States and Union Territories to go in for taxation or special levy to finance such public assistance schemes without prejudice to any assistance made available to States and Union Territories from the Central Government under plan schemes.

(3) No child should be tried in adult courts nor should any child be sent to a jail.
(4) State Governments should enact legislation for apprehension, institutional treatment and rehabilitation of beggars, particularly women.
(5) Machinery should be set up for speedy and effective adjudication in all cases concerning the family, including the setting up of family welfare courts since the ordinary judicial procedure is not suited to handle such cases. Women, particularly in rural areas, should be protected against harassment.
(6) A vigorous campaign should be launched to educate women about their rights and the machinery through which they can seek their realization.
(7) Active public support should be mobilized by government agencies, voluntary organizations and public leaders against child marriage and dowry to support the legislative measures for the eradication of these undesirable practices. Ostentatious weddings and other wasteful social ceremonies should be banned.

Areas of Research

Primary data available with sources such as the Census and National Sample Survey, are insufficient and are very scanty for social welfare planning, particularly on the needs and requirements of handicapped women, destitute women, women under the purview of the suppression of Immoral Traffic Act, etc. In view of this, the following areas of research are suggested:

(i) Studies on 'Social profiles' with district as unit, wherein information on the prevailing conditions of social needs and requirements, etc., are investigated.
(ii) Studies on the requirements of physically handicapped children and women.
(iii) Studies on the requirements of destitute children and women.
(iv) Studies on the training requirements of workers in voluntary welfare organizations.
(v) Studies on the socio-economic and psychological factors behind the problem of premarital pregnancies.

(vi) Studies on the magnitude of problems facing prostitutes and their children such as problems of children of prostitutes, particularly female children.

Voluntary Action

Voluntary action in India has always been an integral part of the cultural and social traditions. A variety of social services were provided by voluntary agencies prior to independence and in the first few decades of planned development in India. Traditionally, voluntary agencies undertook a wide variety of activities in the areas of social reform in the pre-independence period. Independence resulted in government policy and commitment to support and strengthen voluntary agencies. Voluntary agencies have currently opted for several alternative roles depending on their objectives, location (rural/urban) and resources available.

The role of voluntary agencies in national development has been considered vital due to their direct and first-hand experience and knowledge of local needs, problems and resources at the grass-roots. Further the commitment and zeal of the voluntary action movement is considered effective as it is not bound by rigid bureaucratic systems and is more responsive to people. The voluntary sector is observed to operate with great flexibility and bases its activities on felt needs. There is a process of continually learning from past experiences in programme planning and implementation, etc.

The essential strength of voluntary agencies derives from the fact that they are closer to the community and people. They represent in many cases the needs and aspirations of the people. Voluntary agencies often function more effectively than the government managed agencies in areas such as motivation, problem identification and analysis, project formulation, innovative methods of service delivery and involvement of the community, due to their spirit.

There are a number of lessons to be learned in such areas such as the demystification of technology; demphasizing formal educational qualification in favour of experience, capabilities, aptitude and ability to work with people; expansion of activities without adding on cumbersome bureaucracy; and reliance on community based and non-institutional approaches. The unique strength of the voluntary sector is its ability to pressurize the government without succumbing to it and losing its identity and lobbying on issues and ideas to make them acceptable to government and the people. The decentralized administration in the voluntary sector not only facilitates effective grass roots, delivery mechanisms but also ensures the participation of the beneficiaries in the programmes.

Voluntary agencies in India have evolved as a result of a historical process that has brought them to their present status and role in the country's development. In the 1950s, most of the organizations provided either relief work or were involved in institutionalized programmes such as schools, destitute homes, hospitals as well as welfare activities. In the 1960s, many of these organizations realized that families with a weak economic base would be unable to procure the benefits of institutional welfare and relief services. It led them to the conclusion that services should enable beneficiaries to be productive and self-reliant through income generating programmes. In the 1970s, many of the voluntary organizations began to feel that economic inputs alone could not overcome poverty and a critical roadblock to development was the unequal social structure. A new type of education geared to raising the consciousness of weaker sections on their situation and rights so that they become active agents of their own development, and change was considered essential. Activist groups built around these considerations, subsequently came into existence in the voluntary sector.

The organization of women by voluntary organizations has acquired importance as the need has emerged for organizational structures to ensure women's participation in the development process. Many old established voluntary agencies have undertaken the task of setting up welfare development services for women in the country.

New Trends

From the mid 1970s onwards there was an emergence of many newly established organizations and activist groups. A large part of the activities of these groups has centered around combating atrocities and violence committed on women, dowry murder, brutal forms of maltreatment and exploitation. In many cases, women in distress have approached such groups for assistance in registering and follow up of cases, providing shelter, etc. These activist groups have identified themselves with oppressed, victimized, and harassed women and awakened new hopes, aspirations and consciousness among women on these issues. Recently many formal and informal groups have emerged throughout the country which have successfully mobilized women's awareness and have preferred to work directly with the women, relying less on material inputs from the outside and more on increasing the internal capabilities and resources—economic, social, cultural and political. These activist groups have also elicited the intervention of the State, especially of the judiciary and of the fourth estate, to project the rights of women and ameliorate their situations. At the same time, they have organized the women themselves for struggle.

Besides voluntary agencies and activist groups, there are many other functional groups such as Mahila Mandals, Youth Clubs, Nehru Yuvak Kendras, National Service Schemes, cooperatives and other people's institutions that have effectively taken up the issues of women in development with varying degrees of success.

Government's Stance on Voluntary Action

The Planning Commission has recognized the role of voluntary action in accelerating the process of social and economic development in most of its plans, particularly so in the Sixth and Seventh Five-Year Plans. Voluntary agencies at their best have played an important role in providing a basis for testing and devising innovative projects and new models and approaches in programme implementation and in ensuring feedback, as well as in securing the participation of women living below the poverty line. They have developed competence in many non-traditional areas and played a vital role in supplementing governmental efforts so as to offer the rural poor choices and alternatives. They have often served as the eyes and ears of the people at the village level. By adopting simple, innovative, flexible and inexpensive means to suit their limited resources, they have tried to reach a larger number of beneficiaries with minimal overheads and with greater community participation. In the process they have successfully demonstrated how village and indigenous resources, rural skills and local knowledge are grossly underutilized at present, in a cost-effective manner. Voluntary agencies have also managed to mobilize and organize the poor to some extent and to generate in them the awareness to demand quality services and improve accountability of the local level functionaries. They have helped to train a cadre of grass root workers that believe in professionalizing voluntarism.

The increasing interest of the government in enhancing the role of voluntary agencies in the development of women is quite evident. Considering the magnitude of problems faced by women the government has rightly felt that it cannot assume the entire responsibility of service provision and development. It has sought to associate voluntary agencies in the various programmes aimed at women. The thrust of the current programmes is more towards development of women's potential and their productive participation in development rather than merely providing welfare services to them. A meaningful partnership with the voluntary sector has thus been an avowed goal and an essential variable in government's attempts to integrate women in development.

Women and the Voluntary Sector

Voluntary agencies have contributed immensely to the new directions and impetus provided to women's programmes during the decade for women. A number of innovative features in several government formulated schemes/programmes are based on the experience of the projects run successfully by voluntary agencies.

The rationale for involvement of voluntary agencies in women's development is quite clear. Women in India suffer from multifarious constraints such as a low level of literacy, lack of access to resources and obstacles caused by the cultural and social customs and traditions that are discriminatory of women. In a situation such as this, the role of voluntary agencies in creating awareness among women of their rights and mobilizing women as well as developing in them appropriate motivation and leadership to realize those rights cannot be minimized.

The process of creating an environment conducive to the progress of women is dependent on a multitude of socio-economic factors, starting with a political will to enforce the development of women as a priority. The long-term objectives of the Seventh Plan spell out that raising the economic and social status of women is a critical goal of national development. The basic approach suggested is to inculcate confidence among women and bring about an awareness of their own potential for development. Within this framework, gainful employment to women is accorded the highest priority as an effective strategy. Various ministries and departments have formulated programmes for the development of women with an emphasis on the involvement of voluntary agencies as delivery mechanisms. The role of voluntary agencies in the mobilization of women in particular is seen as a critical factor for the development strategies of the future.

A higher involvement of voluntary agencies is thus envisaged in the implementation of such government programmes as the Integrated Rural Development Program (IRDP), Training of Rural Youth in Self-Employment (TRYSEM), Development of Women and Children in Rural Areas (DWCRA), Integrated Child Development Services Scheme (ICDS), and Adult Literacy programmes. Besides their involvement in these schemes, voluntary agencies can also assist in effective enforcement of minimum wages, supply of safe drinking water, afforestation, social forestry, consumer protection, promotion of science and technology, rural housing, legal education, etc. With the new focus on women, some funds should be earmarked for implementation of these programmes in the concerned ministries/departments for voluntary agencies. Further through the Central Social Welfare Board (CSWB), Council for Advancement of People's Action and Rural Technology (CAPART) and the National Rural Development Fund, the activities of and cooperation with voluntary agencies should be expanded and strengthened. To the extent that voluntary agencies are dependent on public funds, accountability has to be ensured but without cumbersome and rigid methods.

Voluntary Action in the Organization of Women

Empowerment of women cannot be ensured until they are enabled to organize themselves. Collective organizations spell strength. This is a prerequisite for initiating action, lobbying, pressurizing and bargaining. Grass roots organizations can greatly enhance the opportunities for poor women to participate in development programmes by providing an organizational base to operate from. By organizing, working together, sharing experiences and resources, building pressure groups and so forth, women can find independent access to opportunities for their betterment.

A large number of women are engaged in the unorganized sector working and living under precarious conditions and with no legal protection. The unorganized sector denies women all benefits of collective action. Dispersed and unorganized, they have no political power and no bargaining strength. As a result, it becomes much more difficult to implement protective labour laws relating to wages, conditions of work, insurance, provident fund, maternity leave, and creches, etc., and also to channelize economic inputs such as credit, technical training and marketing. In such a situation, the need for collective action becomes critical, and is dependent upon the organization of women in the unorganized sector. Many spontaneous and organized struggles have been launched by some voluntary organizations for the articulation of the needs of poor women, particularly the need to organize them for their interaction into the mainstream. For instance, the whole issue of women in the unorganized sector has been debated and seriously addressed through the awareness generated by certain organizations in different parts of the country.

Uncovered Territory

The issue of gender disparity at work is yet to be voiced effectively in the organized voluntary action movement. Of the vast masses in the category of the working poor, the unskilled ranks contain a larger proportion of females. These women are much less organized for any kind of market leverage or wage bargaining and even when organized, less inclined to redress gender inequalities at work sites. There is the need to replicate the success stories of voluntary action in organizing women in different parts of the country and to take up the issue to parity at work in a larger way.

The participation of women in development requires an all round transformation in the consciousness of both men and women as also in the socio-cultural norms, the mass media and pattern of education all of which at present tend to perpetuate a passive unequal role of women in social, economic and political affairs. There is a need for a strong voluntary action involvement in order to evolve a specific strategy based on the local situation, in this area, of women. Any voluntary agency that is serious about promoting women's participation would have to seriously consider the challenge of recruiting and training women catalysts, extension agents and functionaries for reaching and eliciting women's participation.

Voluntary Action for Legal Aid

The majority of women have no knowledge about their rights and very few have resources to obtain legal redressal. It is now being strongly felt that laws by themselves cannot bring about the desirable change in the status of women unless women become aware of their rights. At the same time, it is also felt that since most of the women cannot afford legal representation in courts due to high financial costs and lack of access to knowledge pertaining to the legal process, the countrywide network of voluntary agencies can play an effective role in providing legal aid and legal education to women. One of the priority areas for the legal aid movement in the country should be the mobilization of women through voluntary agencies. Voluntary organizations also have an important role in providing counselling, para-legal support and rehabilitation of women in distress. In fact, in the absence of such help, neither police nor courts can effectively help women. In many such cases, women are compelled to withdraw cases under the dowry prohibition act and compromise with unjust situations due to lack of alternatives. This situation could be remedied if women could be assisted through counselling support, employment training, and rehabilitation and development support by voluntary agencies.

The upsurge of interest in women's issues which characterized the decade, has left its mark on the legal scene. Voluntary organizations and activist groups are beginning to initiate action on various legal issues. It is felt that the Government should provide financial assistance to women's organizations for setting up legal aid cells. Evidently, there is a need for many more voluntary agencies to take up the issues of women and provide necessary legal aid to women.

Environment and Women

It is well recognized that the management of the environment requires the participation of people as they are closest to it and have a stake in its preservation. Active involvement of women and their organizations in environment protection is of paramount significance since women are most affected by the issue. There is a serious threat to the environment due to its degradation and pollution arising from various factors such as policies of government as well as the private sector, unplanned discharge of residual and waste, handling of toxic chemicals, indiscriminate construction of dams, large-scale deforestation, expansion of settlements and unplanned mining and quarrying work. Such conditions have pushed great number of women into marginal environment where floods, droughts, shortage of fuel, and excessive utilization of grazing land have deprived women of their livelihood.

Many voluntary agencies have taken up the issue of environment protection. Among these agencies are the Dasholi Gram Swarajya Mandal that has started the Chipko Movement in which women play a very important role. This movement has received international acclaim and was initiated by hill women. Women embraced (Chipko) trees to prevent them being felled and some women were killed while thus protecting these with their own bodies. Trees to these women and others are the source of life. The impact of environmental degradation and of soil erosion is first felt by women. Many grass root level women's organizations have begun to take up environmental issues in addition to their continuing concern for rural poverty due to the intrinsic link among environment, poverty and gender.

The responsibility for creating awareness, mobilizing public opinion and building a strong people's movement lies mainly with the voluntary agencies. The awareness generated by individual women pioneers/leaders and all types of women's organizations on environmental issues has focused on the fact that women and men have the capacity to manage their environment, and their access to productive resources should be sustained and enhanced. It is also recognized that the requisite knowledge and information can be disseminated by voluntary organizations to reinforce the self-help potential of women in conserving and improving the environment.

Demystification of Technology

A number of voluntary agencies are involved in commendable work in the demystification of appropriate technology for the advancement of rural women. The programmes implemented by voluntary agencies in this area include, providing opportunities for gainful employment and self-employment for women, reducing the drudgery in their lives, ensuring adequate medical and nutritional facilities, improving sanitation and environmental conditions and protecting women from occupational hazards. However, there is a need for further voluntary action in this direction that can develop and disseminate appropriate technology for women. Since the technological marginalization of female work is endemic in both the agricultural and the non-agricultural informal sector, voluntary agencies should be involved in overcoming gender differentials in the application and generation of technology. There is a need to actively deploy technology to reduce the drudgery of the poorest working women in back breaking tasks such as gathering of fuel, fodder and water.

Training constitutes another important input, particularly for upgradation of skill and augmentation of earning capacities of women. There is a strong need for a diversification of training undertaking by voluntary organizations. Their role should be particularly geared to the sensitization of administrators functionaries and catalysts on the issues and needs of women in development and in the delivery of comprehensive training programmes that have a component of knowledge, attitudes and skills for women's development.

Recommendations

The increase in the number, expansion and diversification of activities of the voluntary agencies has not necessarily equalized the disparities between them. There are not only regional imbalances in the growth of the voluntary sector but within a particular state, the growth of this sector has not been even. It is also well known that a majority of voluntary agencies are urban based and that relatively few have taken up the issues of women. It is recommended that the focus of voluntary agencies move from urban to rural areas, as the situation of rural women warrants immediate support. There is also need for the government to encourage voluntary action for the development of women by provision of adequate financial and structural support.

There is an urgent need to improve the effectiveness of voluntary action. Improvement will have to be brought about both in the organizational structures as also in the quality of services offered. Voluntary workers need to be professionals, equipped with appropriate skills for managing women's projects and sensitivity towards women's issues. National and State level institutions and training organizations should provide adequate facilities for research and training relating to women's issues. They should take up activities guided by the felt needs of women and those that can make a qualitative difference to women's lives, rather than be confined to traditional areas of support and action. Their work should be related to contemporary issues and thinking on women. As a caution, they should resist the temptation of initiating more work than they can effectively manage.

Voluntary action should be directed particularly towards preventive rather than purely curative measures. Efforts of voluntary agencies should also be geared towards generating self-reliance rather than to create dependencies. To improve their capabilities in planning and implementation of programmes, voluntary agencies are in need of expertise and technical guidance as much as financial assistance. Unfortunately, in the existing system of grants-in-aid, financial assistance to them assumes over-riding importance vis-a-vis other forms of assistance such as technical guidance in the area of programme planning, project formulation, financial planning, administration, monitoring and evaluation. The proposed Resource Centre at the national level could also facilitate in the training needs of functionaries and in providing necessary managerial and technical assistance to voluntary agencies.

The process of grant-seeking and receiving is considered by a number of voluntary agencies as a frustrating experience. There is an urgent need to review the working of the grants-in-aid system. Wherever needed, modifications should be introduced to ensure that rules are simplified, grants released on time and the amount provided is commensurate and proportionate to the needs of a particular programme. While a system of accountability for government funds is unavoidable, it need not be painful. Further, it should be ensured that financial assistance from the government does not seriously affect the basic character of voluntarism, its flexibility and innovativeness.

A number of programmes implemented by conventional voluntary agencies have emphasized imparting skills to improve the efficiency of women as housewives and mothers, and or to improve their earning capacities. Voluntary agencies have, tended to neglect the participative potential of women in the development process as well as conscientizing women on their rights and roles. There is the need for such efforts that could increase the awareness of women and improve their participation as equal citizens in national development. Further, voluntary agencies should play a surveillance role and observe, explore and analyse the extent to which social legislations implemented for women have actually benefited them. They should also act as pressure groups to better enforcement of laws for women.

At present, there is no proper mechanism of coordination among different voluntary agencies working for the development of women. An effective mechanism for coordination between the government and the voluntary agencies is also to be ensured. CAPART and CSWB are appropriately situated to make efforts for more effective coordination and implementation of various programmes for women through voluntary organizations. For them to perform this role effectively, there should be a proper representation of grass roots women's organizations in CAPART and CSWB, that can serve as pressure groups. There is also the need for a continuous flow of information from government to voluntary agencies and vice versa through such mechanisms as a clearing house for information.

A focal point is desirable in the rural areas to encourage women's voluntary activities. Mahila Mandals and women's groups at the village or community level should be organized or revived and encouraged to register and function as women's institutions for undertaking socio-economic programmes. These institutions should be effectively linked with the various development and service agencies, offering training facilities for income generations as well as enhanced awareness among women. This linkage will enable women to absorb institutional finance for the development of viable economic activities. Particular attention will need to be given to the training of the Mahila Mandal functionaries and women's group organizers and provide them an orientation to development perspective rather than purely welfare approaches.

The CSWB which has been the coordinating agency for voluntary action for women and children, must respond to the new thrust of government policy meant for women and recast its own programmes.

Greater coordination and cooperation among NGOs is called for to avoid duplication of services. Greater funding for net-working among NGOs must be provided. This will ensure more efficient utilization of funds and greater coverage of programmes, Government support to voluntary agencies for providing assistance to women in distress, including the running of crisis centres and short stay homes must be expanded. Para legal training must be an integral part of such efforts.

Voluntary agencies must be increasingly involved in the provision of employment and supportive services for women.

The National Literacy Mission must involve women's organizations in a big way.

The voluntary sector should increasingly be involved to act as a catalyst/intermediary in organizing women for collective action.

There is the need to document success stories of major NGOs in India and learn from their success and failures. Further, it is necessary to analyse the cost-benefit of NGO Projects versus governmental projects, i.e., both economic and social costs. It would also be critical to total the overall number of women reached by NGOs in India. The areas of activities and fields of success would also highlight their strengths and limitations.

In order to ensure that the security and integrity of the nation are preserved, there is a need to adopt suitable policies to ensure that voluntary agencies abide by the rules governing the receipt and utilization of foreign grants and submit audited accounts, returns and reports periodically.

Identity cards should be issued to workers of voluntary agencies who are dealing with cases of atrocities against women, as is already being done in some districts.

In order to have sufficient infrastructure and facilities, there is need to mobilize more resources for voluntary agencies who are engaged in welfare and development of women.

There is a need to decentralize the planning process to stimulate local people's participation in planning, implementation, monitoring and evaluation of development projects. A suitable mechanism should be evolved to involve voluntary agencies and other people's institutions at various stages of developmental programmes/projects. Voluntary agencies should further ensure the participation of poor women in the development process.

General Recommendations

In the preceding chapters recommendations have been made sectorally with a view to strengthening women's roles therein. Certain important issues, however, impinge on all spheres of women's lives and work. With a view to enhancing women's status and capacities to participate in the process of nation building, the following general recommendations are made:

The overall approach of this National Perspective Plan is to perceive women in a holistic manner. While the programmes for women will continue to be implemented by different ministries as part of their department plans, it is essential to have a strong inter-ministerial coordination and monitoring body along with its own supportive facilities service by the Department of Women and Child Development (Proposed infrastructure at Annexure I).

All ministries must reflect the concern for the all round development of women. The concerned ministries must have women's cell which currently only exists in the Ministries of Labour, Small-Scale Industry, Science and Technology and Rural Development. It is essential that the new policy thrust for women's development should be reflected in the Planning Commission as well as the State Planning Boards. The National Commission on Self-Employed Women and Women in the Informal Sector, has also independently concluded that the Planning Commission and State Planning Boards need to focus their attention sharply on the realistic situation of (labouring) women.

An essential prerequisite for the implementation of these new policy directives would be a women's unit in the Planning Commission, to redefine categories of data collection for women, modify existing terminology and identify gaps in data collection relating to women and to give direction to plans and programmes for women's development. It is also essential to analyse the impact of the different macro policies on women while planning new endeavours.

Financial and fiscal resources should be apportioned and preferential allocations for women's employment in mainstream programmes and projects should be made. This would imply the rationalization on resource allocation within mainstream programmes so as to benefit women, rather than only seeking separate allocations for women. Critical emphasis must be placed on rate of investment in women preferred industries and occupations.

At the State level, the Departments/Directorates of Women's Development should be initiated. Currently, there is no separate department of women in many States. Social welfare, handicapped, Scheduled Castes and Scheduled Tribes are subjects that are bracketed together with the development of women at the State level. This new department could also be the State level implementation body for the programmes/policies of the Department of Women and Child Development of the Government of India.

In terms of programme implementation, the two major implementing bodies envisaged, are the Social Welfare Boards and the Women's Development Corporations. There can be a rationalization of service provision between these two bodies. The State Social Welfare Advisory Boards could eventually concentrate on implementing welfare/supportive programmes for women (homes for women in distress, working women's hostels, counselling centres for legal aid and paralegal training, condensed courses, etc.). Women Development Corporations would be responsible for the implementation of economic programmes through non-governmental and governmental agencies/ departments wherever necessary, concentrating on technical inputs like credit, marketing, design development, etc., and reaching out to women at the district and village levels.

Women should be entitled to a package of services at the block level created by the convergence of schemes such as

Development of Women and Children in Rural Areas (DWCRA), Integrated Child Development Schemes (ICDS), Adult Education, Health Care, etc., at the grass roots administrative level. Every district should have a coordinator to assist in the integration of these programmes aimed at the development of women. The coordinator will also be responsible for motivating local planning of programmes and assist in their implementation and provide feedback for effective planning and evaluation. Since decentralization of planning monitoring and implementation of development programmes for women is suggested as also devolution of finance at district level, appointment of District coordinators for women's programmes would facilitate this process, and control over finance would empower them. The National Commission on Self-Employed Women and Women in the Informal Sector has also recommended the appointment of District Coordination Officers to be responsible for planning, monitoring, coordination and evaluation of the programmes affecting women. Rationalization of functionaries at the block and village levels to ensure coordination of programmes affecting women at the grass roots level also needs to be undertaken.

There are today sufficient number of programmes in the Government of India as well as innovative programmes in many States and sectors. What is needed is not merely larger resource allocation but technical inputs for greater effectiveness of these programmes, to guarantee better resource utilization. Emphasis has to be placed on more effective planning, monitoring and evaluation of existing programmes through a result oriented mechanism operating at different levels.

Recognizing that a critical input for women's development would be a new thrust to training and wider dissemination of information backed by research data and documentation. It is proposed to set up a National Resource Centre for Women. This resource centre would translate national developmental needs of women into a systematic grid of programmes and schemes for training at different levels in skills/knowledge/attitudes. The centre would identify and if necessary, strengthen existing governmental and non-governmental agencies including women's universities/women's centres and colleges through which the training, research/dissemination could be carried out. The National

Commission on Self-Employed Women and Women in Informal Sector has also recommended the need for a National Institute to cater to women's training as well as formulate guidelines and help the other constituent units at the State level, Divisional levels and district level to carry out training programmes.

Reorientation and sensitization of the administrative machinery at all levels in the Government of India, the States, as well as specialized technical agencies (both Government and Voluntary) to the issues of women in development is essential. Three levels of orientation are necessary, i.e., at the policy and planning levels, at the district or intermediary level, and at the block and village levels. The training of functionaries and their orientation to women's issues must also be in the right perspective, i.e., women should be perceived as producers and participants, not clients for welfare. The dynamic role of women's contribution to the national economy as partners and equal citizens must be reiterated and translated into programmes and projects. The National Resource Centre would be responsible for revamping the existing content/ methodology and monitoring of training at all levels.

A special division should be created in the Department of Women and Child Development for the enforcement of law for women. The officer in charge may be designated Commissioner for Women's Rights and must liaise with the various Special Cells for women created by the police, the CBI as well as with the Departments of Public Grievances at Centre and State levels as also the Women's Cell in the Home Ministry. This division will be concerned with the enforcement of law to ensure women's rights, to facilitate action oriented research in needs such as discrimination against women, protection at work, etc.

This Plan recommends that the Census in future must take into account women's unpaid work in the household and outside as well as the value added in performing her many survival tasks for the family. A greater conceptual clarity has to emerge on 'work' and 'non-work' as well as a distinction between work that produces economic value and other activities that are consumption oriented. Data relating to women, especially in the unorganized sector should be reflected in the data of the National Sample Survey and the Central Statistical Organization.

ANNEXURE I

- National Committee on Women
- Inter-ministerial Coordination & Monitoring (Department of Women & Child Development)
- Cells in Mainline Ministries
- State Departments for Women
- District Employment Committees for Women
- District Coordinator for Women's programmes

DEPARTMENT OF WOMEN & CHILD DEVELOPMENT
(Policy, Planning Programmes, Training, Information Monitoring at the National Level)

↓ Programme Implementation
↓
- ↓ CSWB (Welfare and Supportive Programmes)
- ↓ Women's Development Corporations (Economic Programmes)

↓ Training & Information
↓
National Resource Centre for Women
Functions:
- Documentation/Policy research
- Advocacy and coordination
- Information dissemination
- Training and sensitization

↓ Enforcement of Women's Rights
↓
Commissioner of enforcement to liaise with special Cells for Women (Police) and with the Department of Public Grievances etc.

↓ Planning Policy
↓
Monitoring

Two

Gender and Economic Participation

The status of any given section of population in a society is intimately connected with its economic position, which itself depends on rights, roles and opportunities for participation in economic activities. The economic status of women is now accepted as an indicator of a society's stage of development. This does not, however, mean that all development results in improving women's economic status.

Patterns of women's activity are greatly affected by social attitudes and institutions, which stem from the social ideology concerning basic components of status in any given period. These may differ according to the stage of economic development. For example, at certain stages of development, capacity for work may provide the highest claim to status. At other stages, when society becomes inegalitarian, leisure may substitute work as a basic indicator of status.

Need for Equality of Rights

The debate regarding women's economic role and the need for equality of rights and opportunities for economic participation has centred round three basic arguments:

Human Rights and Social Justice

Women's economic subjugation, or dependent position is the result of a rigid distinction in men's and women's roles in society and leads to exploitation. According to Karl Marx aand Freidrich Engels:

> The emancipation of women and their equality with men are impossible and must remain so as long as women are excluded from socially productive work and restricted to house work, which is private.

M.K. Gandhi had stated in Young India, 26.2.1918, that:

> Today the sole occupation of a woman amongst us is

> supposed to be to bear children, to look after her husband and otherwise to drudge for the household .... not only is the woman condemned to domestic slavery, but when she goes out as a labourer to earn wages, though she works harder than man she is paid less.

Utilization of Human Resources

It is in the interest of the society to make full use and most effective use of its human resources. The full benefit of development can only be realized with people's participation and the economic role of woman cannot be isolated from the total framework of development. In a UN declaration on "Elimination of Discrimination against Women" in 1967, it was stated that:

> Discrimination against women is incompatible with human dignity and the welfare of the family and of society, prevents their participation on equal terms with men in the political, social, economic and cultural life of their countries and is an obstacle to the full development of the potentialities of women in the service of their countries and humanity.

According to Supra:

> To maintain the proper quantitative balance between various economic activities was one of the principal functions of the economic system, which, it was felt, should operate to give equal freedom of choice to men and women. The orientation of a society as a whole regarding the desirability that women should play an equal part in the country's development was taken as very important precondition for the development not only of the women but of the country as well.

Implication of Social Change

Socio-economic and political change creates a need to extend the spheres of knowledge and activity of all members of a society. Modern trends in demographic and social changes call for a redefinition of women's roles in family and society. Changes in the age of marriage, size of families, urbanization, migration, rising costs and standards of living and the call for greater participation in the decision-making process within the family and the wider society, all lead to subtle but major changes in roles and responsibilities. These have to be recognized and provided for in order to avoid social crises. Absence of adequate opportunities and the inability of women to meet these challenges because of social handicaps present obstacles to a balanced and smooth adjustment to the process of social change.

Why Opporunities to Women are Opposed?

The opposition to increasing opportunities for women's participation in economic activities springs firstly from a conservative view regarding women's 'proper role' in society, where 'proper' imposes clearly, and often rigidly defined limits to the activities that women may or may not perform. For example, the elite classes in most societies limited the activities of women to the home only. In the same societies, women of the labouring sections did participate extensively in economic activities outside the home, but their spheres were often clearly defined by a customarily accepted division of labour between the sexes. The patterns of this division have however varied, not only from society to society but among different sections of people within the same society. (Margret Meads, 1950 and Ester, 1970).

Secondly, this opposition comes from situations of chronic unemployment, or apprehensions of unemployment, where the prospects of a large-scale entry of women in the labour market is regarded as a potential cause of economic disorganization. A typical manifestation of this attitude is the theory of women's marginal role in the economy. According to an Internationl Labour Conference (1963) announcement: in Women Workers in a Changing World:

> This concept of women as a sort of balancing force in the family or national economy has a whole series of practical implications which have the net effect of making it difficult for women to become integrated as a permanent part of the work force and of rendering them particularly susceptible to unscrupulous or discriminatory treatment in the employment market.

The Report of the National Commission on Labour, Government of India, 1969 states that:

> In countries which are marked by labour surpluses, the need

for providing employment for women when many men are available for work raises questions which cannot admit of categorical answers. It is in these developing countries that incomes by and large are low and the family requires the assistance of an additional earner. Where social conventions do not weigh oppressively against bringing women into paid employment, the family income can best be supplemented by a draft on the female population in the working age group.

In agrarian societies the family is the unit of production. The place of work being close to the home, men, women and children all participate in the production process. As a society moves from the traditional agricultural and household industry to organized industry and services, from rural to urban areas, the traditional division of labour ceases to operate, and the complementary relationship of the family is substituted by the competitive one between individual units of labour. The scarcer the jobs, the sharper is the competition. Technological changes in the process of production call for acquisition of new skills and specializations which are very different from the traditional division of labour. Women, handicapped by lack of opportunities for acquisition of these new skills, find their traditional productive skills unwanted by the new economy.

Women in the Indian Economy

Economic Role

A review of the economic roles played by women in India reveals certain clearly distinct trends. The traditional village community in India consisted of the cultivators, the artisans and those performing menial services. In each of these, the women played a distinctive and accepted role in the process of earning a livelihood for the family, putting in sometimes more, sometimes less and often an equal amount of labour in both production and marketing of products of agriculture and handicrafts. Markets were mostly local or within accessible distance. By and large this pattern is still found prevalent in the traditional forms of the economy. The marketing of vegetables, processed and semiprocessed foodstuffs of the traditional type (dried and pickled fish and vegetables, preparations of rice and pulses, etc.) and handicrafts mainly produced by women (baskets, hand woven fabrics, etc.) are still marketed by women in most parts of India.

Amongst most tribal and Scheduled Caste communities, the production of handicrafts as well as their marketing is mainly carried on by women. In Nagaland, Manipur and among the Galong in Arunachal Pradesh weaving is exclusively practized by women. It may be noted that handwoven fabrics constitute an important export of these States and are the most important export item of Manipur. Though weaving is a traditional industry in other parts of India also, the general pattern is for women not to weave, but to take part in other operations.

Among the agricultural classes in most parts of the country and particularly among marginal and landless agriculturists, earning a livelihood is till a family endeavour with or without division of labour among men, women and children.

The patterns of women's participation vary according to regional and cultural norms. Throughout the Himalayan region, the major role in agricultural production is played by women. In areas where the 'jhum' (shifting) system of cultivation still prevails, the men's contribution to the production process ends with the chopping down of the trees and burning the soil. The entire process of dribbling (planting) and gathering of crops is done mainly by women. With terraced cultivation the men's activities increase as they usually undertake ploughing, but women engage in all other agricultural activities. Among the Khasis of Meghalaya, women dominate the economic process and even educated women holding high positions in offices do not hesitate to do manual work in agriculture.

There is a general taboo on women engaging in ploughing but the degree of taboo differs from region to region. In Himachal Pradesh women informed us that sometimes they have to undertake ploughing in the absence of male members in the family or inability to hire male labourers. But this could result in some loss of social prestige. In most parts of the country the jobs traditionally done by women are generally transplanting, sowing, weeding, harvesting, winnowing and threshing.

The cultural norms that influence women's engaging in manual labour outside the home vary according to their position in the social hierarchy. Historians and sociologists agree that withdrawal of women from active participation in manual labour outside the home is a consequence of social stratification. (Altekar, A.S., 1963) Gradually this process of excluding women from labour outside home has itself become a symbol of higher social status. (Gadgil, D.R., 1965)

The general decline of handicrafts from the eighteenth century led to increasing pressure of population on agriculture and increase of poverty in the rural sector resulting in migrations. The Royal Commission on Labour in India attributed the migrations from village to city to three causes: economic pressure, the decay of village crafts and the social disabilities of the outcastes. The first cause, that of economic pressure was the most important. According to the Royal Commission on Agriculture, "the numbers who have no other employment than agriculture are greatly in excess of what is really required for thorough cultivation of the land." The Report of the Royal Commissionn on Labour (1931) states that:

> The driving force in migration comes almost entirely from one end of the channel, i.e., the village end. The industrial recruit is not permitted by the lure of city life or by any great ambition. The city as such has no attractions for him, and when he leaves the village he has no ambition beyond that of securing the necessities of life. Few industrial workers would remain in industry if they could secure sufficient food and clothing in the village; they are pushed, not pulled to the city.

Effect of Industrial Development

When there was prospect of employment of the women also as in plantations, mines, jute and the textile industry, the migration was of families. Similarly the women migrated with their husbands who went as indentured labourers to other colonies in the British empire. When only men migrated the women left behind continued to depend on agricultural work as cultivators or wage labourers.

In the initial phase of industrial development, most industries continued the traditional pattern of family participation and employed a considerable number of women and children. While they confined them to certain unskilled and semi-skilled types of work at lower rates of wages, in terms of proportions of total labour employed, women constituted an important segment of the labour force in these industries.

Technological changes have affected the employment of women in these industries adversely. In the absence of training opportunities, the women, already handicapped by illiteracy and lack of mobility cannot acquire the new skills demanded by modern industry. This creates a gap in the earning power of men and women and is responsible for the widespread belief that female labour associated with backward economies is less productive. (Supra)

Development has, however, opened some new avenues to women. Modernization, social change and education, have enabled some women to enter new profession, or occupations which were totally closed to them earlier. For example, the presence of women in the public services, and other jobs in the tertiary sector is now an accepted fact. For certain limited jobs, women are even preferred.

Social attitudes to women's work reflect to a great extent the current needs being faced by society. In some sections, economic pressure has precipitated withdrawal of the traditional prejudice against women working outside the home. Since this is also the class which has generally been more exposed to education and other instruments of modernization, they have benefitted more from change and development unlike the women whose world has remained confined to the limits set by tradition.

These factors pose difficulties in using any uniform indicators to assess the economic status of women. Apart from the limitations of quantitative data, a macro-analysis of women's economic participation purely on quantitative terms would not be valid for all sections of women. The heterogeneous character of the Indian economy and the uneven rates of development have had varying degrees of impact on different segments of the labour force. It would "not justify aggregation into a single dimensional magnitude". (Report of the Committee on Unemployment, 1973) The different segments need to be estimated separately, taking into account such important characteristics as region need to be estimated separately, taking into account such important characteristics as region (State), sex, age, rural-urban residence, status or class of workers and educational attainments. The relative importance of these components differ considerably between rural and urban areas.

In the Committee's opinion any appraisal of women's economic roles to be meaningful must take into account the socio-economic status of different categories of workers. The largest of these categories consists of the women below subsistence level. We have attempted to identify some components of this vast group who are generally found in unskilled work, in both the organized and unorganized sectors. In rural areas, they are the landless agricultural labourers, members of households with uneconomic holdings, those engaged in traditional menial services performed by particular castes. A large majority of workers in traditional village and cottage industries also come within this category.

In urban areas they consist largely of migrants from villages, and members of families whose position has deteriorated due to the break down of joint families. Some of these families in previous generations, used to work in urban areas but left their families in the village to share in agricultural incomes of joint families.

A rapid rise in the population of rural areas, coupled with a steeply rising cost of living has made this difficult now, and urban workers are being compelled to bring their families to the cities along with them. The women of this class work mainly as part-time domestic servants, or in various unorganized industries. Majority of them are handicapped by lack of education or any other skills that could fit them for work in urban areas.

The second category is a most heterogeneous class. It consists of both white collared and manual workers whose existence ranges from subsistence to security. Most of them are to be found in industries, services and professions. Some are self-employed. They are mostly found in urban areas. In the rural areas, they consist of land owning cultivators and the handful of women engaged in health, education and welfare services. The level of aspiration and employment opportunities of women in this group differ with their social background and educational attainment. All of them need employment either to keep their families from starvation or to ensure a somewhat better standard of living. Some are able to achieve security by improving their earning power, others remain handicapped by lack of education and other skills.

The third category is not burdened by insecurity. It consists of the minority of women who seek employment mainly to improve their standard of living. Some do so to achieve personal independence and satisfaction. They are generally highly educated, enjoy high status both in their families and work life, and are mostly found in the higher rungs of services and professions. In recent years, a few have entered the field of commerce and business management.

Limitations of Data

The three major sources of data on employment and unemployment are the Census, various rounds of the National Sample Survey and the Employment Market Information Programme of the Directorate General of Employment and Training. The comparability of census data is limited because of conceptual differences in the definition of workers, and lack of uniformity in cross-classification of workers by sex, 5-year age-groups, educational level, marital status and industry. The National Sample Surveys apart from the smaller size of the sample and shorter reference periods, do not take into consideration the sharp seasonal variations in the labour force participation rates, which are even more pronounced in the case of women, specially in the agricultural sector. Starting from the 11th Round (1956) the N.S.S. started collecting data on persons 'not seeking but available for work', which is of particular significance for rural women because of the predominance of self-employment, unpaid-family work and limited opportunities for paid employment in rural areas.

Data on women workers from these two sources also suffer from reporting bias, particularly for the large unorganized sector of the economy where the majority of women are employed and does not permit an evaluation of the total women labour potential and its relevant characteristics. A sizeable proportion of the labour input in household enterprises is provided by family workers who have only partial attachment to the labour market. While their inclusion in the labour force would be misleading, their total exclusion would also fail to reflect the reality of the economic situation. As an example, we may mention the case of women from hawkers' families, who help the family enterprises by actually producing the material for sale. As this work is done within the home it is not recorded as economic activity. Expert committees on unemployment have been repeatedly emphasizing the need to use identical concepts for collecting information on different sections of women workers to understand the complex problems of employment, unemployment and under-employment.

The Employment Market Information Programme of Directorate General of Employment and Training covers all public sector establishments and private sector establishments which employ 10 or more workers, excluding all self-employed persons and unpaid family workers engaged in small non-agricultural establishments, agriculture, small plantations and private construction activities. These estimates are useful only for assessing the employment situation in the urban organized sector. The National Employment Service has not yet penetrated the rural areas. Even in the urban areas its coverage of women is minimal. The National Sample Survey and the National Employment Service data are not comparable because they adopt different norms for classifying educational level of workers.

Trends in Economic Participation

The long-term trend in economic participation of women indicates an overall decline both in percentage of workers to total female population and in their percentage to the total labour force after 1921 (Table 2.1). When we look at their distribution in different sectors of the economy, however, there are significant variations. Explanations of these trends have to be found in the totality of interconnected factors both (a) during the pre-1947 and post-1947 period separately, and (b) the nature of development of our economy from the first to the second period. We can only briefly describe the major factors.

Agriculture continued to receive the burden of the surplus labour force all through the period of 71 years. Variations in participation rates in agriculture during different decades mainly show a decline before 1947 and a steady rise after 1947. This is generally explained by the pattern of industrialization of our country.

The participation of women in industry, however, shows a general stagnation, and a distinct decline after 1961. One reason for this lies in the transformation of the role of household and small scale industry in the national economy. It is well known that ruination of domestic industry has been a constant factor of our history during the British period, which naturally affected both men and women. But domestic industries like hand-spinning, weaving, paper, jute articles, etc., which were relatively more female labour intensive were more effected by the process than industries like smithy, carpentry, pottery, etc., which hardly used any female labour.

TABLE - 2.1

TREND IN DISTRIBUTION OF WOMEN WORKERS 1911-1971

(in thousand)

Year	*Agriculture*	*Industry*	*Service*	*Total*	*Female Workers Percentage to Total Female Population*	*Percentage to Total Labour*
1911	30,898	6,137	4,767	41,802	33.73	34.44
	(73.9)	(14.7)	(11.4)	(100)		
1921	30,279	5,409	4,407	40,095	33.73	34.02
	(75.5)	(13.5)	(11.0)	(100)		
1931	27,177	5,147	5,276	37,600	27.63	31.17
	(72.3)	(13.7)	(14.0)	(100)		
1951*	31,062	4,554	4,923	40,539	23.30	28.98
	(76.8)	(11.2)	(12.1)	(100)		
1961	47,274	6,884	5,244	59,402	27.96	31.53
	(79.6)	(11.6)	(8.8)	(100)		
1971	25,060	3,307	2,931	31,298	11.86	17.35
	(80.1)	(10.5)	(9.4)	(100)		

1941 Figures are omitted as they are based on 2% of the population on sample basis.

Note: Figures within brackets denote percentages of women workers.

* Figures do not include Jammu and Kashmir.

Sources: (1) Census of India 1961 - Paper No. 1 of 1962-Final population.

(2) Pocket Book of Population Statistics-Census Centenary 1972 totals.

In the period before 1947 both displacement of labour from small scale and cottage industry including domestic industry and corresponding increase in labour force employed in organized industries moved at a slower pace. During the 30-year period between 1917 and 1947 the total number of industrial enterprises increased from 4,827 to 11,961 and the number of small enterprises rose from 538 to 2990. Of the total participation in industry on the eve of 1947, the overwhelming majority was constituted by domestic industry.

In the post-independence period with rapid increase in the modern and organized sector of industry, the share of household industries declined rapidly. Since they constituted the biggest traditional source of women's employment outside agriculture, women were the greatest victims of this process of economic transformation. Many of these household industries like hand weaving, oil pressing, rice pounding, leather, tobacco processing, etc., had to face stiff competition from factory production.

The other reason for the exclusion of women from industry was technological change and rationalization of the processes of production which reduced the demand for unskilled labour. Since the majority of women in the modern industrial sector were employed as unskilled workers they were the main victims of this change.

Column three of Table 2.1 however requires some explanation. According to census occupational categories, there has been a marginal increase in the proportion of women in white-collared occupations, e.g., doctors, nurses and other health personnel, teachers, office workers, etc. The effect of this has, however, been neutralized by the virtual disappearance of women from trade and commerce. With the development of modern organized markets and increase in the number of intermediaries and wholesale trade, the marketing of the products of traditional and household industry, which was one of the important avenues of earning for women in the earlier period has been gradually disappearing. As a result, the participation rate of women in the service sector has recorded a steady decline.

During the decade 1961-71 while the male and female population increased by 25 per cent and 24 per cent respectively (20 per cent and 21 per cent in the working age-group), the number of men workers increased by 15.2 per cent while that of women declined by 41.4 per cent. It has been argued that this decline is the result of changes in the definition of workers adopted by the Census of 1971. The Census basically measures the level of employment of men and tends to ignore the interchangeable roles of women as housewives and gainful workers. Since many of them participate in family enterprises an unpaid helpers, changes in the definition of workers which exclude secondary activity has an adverse effect on the recording of female employment. For example, the Census of 1971 included 2.3 million women among non-workers, whose main activity was house work but who were engaged in some secondary activity in rural and urban areas as indicated in Table 2.2.

TABLE - 2.2

NUMBER OF WOMEN ENGAGED IN SECONDARY WORK IN RURAL AND URBAN AREAS CLASSIFIED BY THEIR MAIN ACTIVITY, 1971 CENSUS

Main Activity	*Total Rural Urban*	*Secondary Work*				
		Cultivators	*Agricultural Labourers*	*House hold Industry*	*Non-House hold Industry Trade Business or Service*	*Total*
1	2	3	4	5	6	7
Cultivators	Total	—	100	34	36	169
	Rural	—	99	33	35	167
	Urban	—	1	—	1	2
Agricultural Labourers	Total	18	—	32	46	96
	Rural	18	—	30	44	92
	Urban	—	—	2	2	4
Household Industry	Total	11	26	1	3	41
	Rural	11	25	1	3	40
	Urban	—	1	—	—	1
Non-Household Industry Trade Business or Service	Total	11	26	3	7	46
	Rural	11	24	2	5	41
	Urban	—	2	1	2	6
Non-Workers	Total	444	1190	347	330	2311
	Rural	439	1163	282	253	2137
	Urban	5	27	65	77	174

Source: Estimated from 1 per cent sample data. Census of India, 1971, series, 1-India, Paper 3 of 1971. Economic Characteristics of Population (Selected Table) page 83.

Note: Total may not tally due to rounding off. Figures in hundreds.

While the 1961 definition of workers was regarded as very liberal, according to census analysis it did not make much difference in the collection of data except in the States of Andhra Pradesh,

Mysore and Tamil Nadu. It may be noted that the reported female activity rate of 27.5 per cent usually accepted as an over estimate, agrees with the rate of 27.72 per cent in the comparable round of the National Sample Survey of the same year. As for the rather restrictive definition of 'workers' in the Census of 1971 even when the figures are corrected by the inclusion of secondary workers, the fall in activity of females remains almost the same. We may, therefore, conclude that the declining trend has been a continuous one to which the 1961 figures are the only exception. The ratio of female to male workers has registered an overall decline in all categories in the rural and in most categories in the urban areas (Table 2.3).

The Age specific workforce participation rates (1961 and 1971) are given in Table 2.4. Table 2.5 presents state-wise percentage of female workers to their total population in 1961 and 1971 separately for rural and urban areas. It is obvious that the participation rates have recorded an overall decline in all States for both rural and urban areas though in most states the decline is sharper in urban areas.

TABLE - 2.3

RATIO OF FEMALE TO MALE WORKERS ACCORDING TO ACTIVITY IN 1961 AND 1971

Category of Activity	*Female Workers per 100 Male Workers*			
	Rural		*Urban*	
	1961	*1971*	*1961*	*1971*
1. Cultivators	50.10	13.34	38.88	9.25
2. Agricultural Labourers	81.84	49.92	85.62	41.60
3. Livestock	31.22	23.43	20.06	14.41
4. Mining & Quarrying	—	17.93	—	11.96
5. Industry				
(a) Household	63.77	27.96	61.33	26.87
(b) Other than household	19.33	14.42	7.70	6.14
6. Construction	14.96	9.89	11.59	8.89
7. Trade & Commerce	19.52	8.04	6.78	4.89
8. Transport, etc.	1.93	2.16	2.35	2.46
9. Other services	35.25	15.41	20.53	18.70

The sharp difference in the participation rates of men and women is reflected in all the age groups except the youngest (0-14) both in 1961 and 1971. The data also indicates wider difference in the women's participation rates between rural and urban areas in all age-groups, than in the case of males. When we compare women's participation in 1961 with that in 1971, the decline is clear in all the age groups.

TABLE - 2.4
AGE SPECIFIC WORKING FORCE - PARTICIPATION RATES 1961 & 1971

(A) 1961

Age Group	*Males*			*Females*		
	Total	*Rural*	*Urban*	*Total*	*Rural*	*Urban*
Total	57.1	58.2	52.4	28.0	31.4	11.1
0-14	9.4	10.6	3.5	6.6	7.6	1.6
15-34	81.1	91.1	76.9	43.6	49.8	15.8
35-59	96.7	97.5	93.3	47.6	49.6	22.9
60 plus	76.6	79.9	58.4	22.4	24.3	11.4

(B) 1971

Age Group	*Males*			*Females*		
	Total	*Rural*	*Urban*	*Total*	*Rural*	*Urban*
Total	52.5	53.4	48.7	11.8	13.1	6.6
0-14	6.6	7.5	2.8	2.6	3.0	0.8
15-34	82.9	86.1	72.8	18.9	21.3	10.1
35-59	95.8	96.7	92.5	21.2	22.8	13.8
60 plus	73.8	77.4	55.4	10.5	11.3	6.4

Source: Census of India 1971. Paper of 1972.

The other significant aspect of this decline is the variation in the order of states according to level of participation over this decade. Kerala, whose position in rural participation was the last in 1961 has improved its position to 11th in 1971 and in urban participation from the 21st position in 1961 it has improved to 5th in 1971. Manipur has also improved its position in rural participation from 21st to 4th and in urban from 22nd to 1st. Rajasthan, on the other hand, lost position from 9th to 13th in rural participation but has improved its place in urban participation from 20th to 7th. Similar is the case for Andhra Pradesh, Mysore, Tamil Nadu. Maharashtra has, however, improved its position in the rural sector but lost ground in the urban sector.

Table 2.6 indicates that while the trends vary in different industrial categories the decline of women's participation in most industries is not merely in percentages and ratios but also in absolute numbers. The distribution of women workers by broad categories shows their increasing dependence on agriculture and a decline in both the industrial and the service sector.

TABLE - 2.5
STATEWISE PERCENTAGE OF FEMALE WORKERS TO THEIR TOTAL POPULATION IN 1961 AND 1971 IN RURAL AND URBAN AREAS

Sl. No.	*State/Territory*	*Rural*				*Urban*			
		1961		*1971*		*1961*		*1971*	
		%	*Rank*	%	*Rank*	%	*Rank*	%	*Rank*
1.	Andhra Pradesh	64.32	1	31.69	2	52.40	10	11.60	4
2.	Assam	53.98	17	6.36	18	55.36	5	4.32	20
3.	Bihar	56.00	14	11.04	14	51.74	12	6.45	15
4.	Gujarat	55.30	15	13.58	12	48.37	19	6.32	16
5.	Himachal Pradesh	63.47	3	22.58	6	56.44	3	7.61	13
6.	Jammu & Kashmir	59.28	10	5.94	19	50.78	15	3.60	22
7.	Kerala	47.42	23	14.92	11	45.98	21	11.20	5
8.	Madhya Pradesh	61.58	5	23.73	5	52.44	9	8.09	11
9.	Maharashtra	58.07	12	28.70	3	54.83	6	9.72	9
10.	Mysore	60.40	8	17.60	9	51.57	13	10.08	8
11.	Nagaland	61.04	6	50.22	1	52.13	11	9.08	10
12.	Orissa	61.02	7	8.55	16	57.22	2	10.73	6
13.	Punjab	53.44	19	1.27	23	50.93	14	3.03	22
14.	Rajasthan	60.13	9	11.95	13	48.04	20	10.45	7
15.	Tamil Nadu	62.19	4	21.19	7	53.16	7	16.40	2
16.	Uttar Pradesh	59.20	11	9.54	15	51.74	12	4.16	21
17.	West Bengal	53.46	18	5.64	20	55.38	4	4.75	19
18.	Andaman & Nicobar	64.27	2	8.01	17	66.17	1	7.25	14
19.	Delhi	47.82	22	5.37	22	52.80	8	5.18	18
20.	Goa, Daman & Diu	71.77	20	29.78	48	48.75	26	13.04	3
21.	Manipur	47.93	21	27.33	4	40.99	22	18.00	1
22.	Pondicherry	57.13	13	15.61	10	48.74	17	7.80	12
23.	Tripura	55.24	16	52.39	21	46.84	18	5.42	17

Note: Figures for 1971 are corrected by including 'non-workers' with secondary activity.

Source: Report of the Committee on Unemployment, 1973 Appendix IX.

The variations in trends according to mode of classification of sectors confirms our opinion that the census categories are not really useful for any proper assessment of the nature and extent of women's participation in our economy. This is corroborated by the views of the expert committees on unemployment.

The number of women in the organized sector constitutes a very small fraction of the total women working force. In 1971 out of 31 million women workers 19.24 lakh only were employed in the organized sector constituting approximately 6 per cent of the total women workers. A predominant section of this group were engaged in the tertiary sector and the services alone accounted for 50 per cent.

TABLE - 2.6

DISTRIBUTION OF FEMALE WORKERS BY BROAD INDUSTRIAL CATEGORIES FROM 1911 TO 1971

(In thousands)

Year	*Total Female Pop.*	*Total No. of Female Workers*	*Cat.I Cultivators*	*Cat. II Agricultural Labourers*	*Cat. III Mining, Quarrying, Livestock, Forestry, Fishing, Hunting, Plantations*	*Cat.IV Household Industry*	*Cat.V Manufacturing Other than Household Industry*	*Cat. VI Construction*	*Cat. VII Trade and Commerce*	*Cat. VIII Transport Storage and Communication*	*Cat. IX Other Service*	*Total of Cat. I & II (ag. sec.)*	*Total of Cat. III to IX (ag. Sex) on (agr. sec.)*
1	*2*	*3*	*4*	*5*	*6*	*7*	*8*	*9*	*10*	*11*	*12*	*13*	*14*
1911	123898	41802	18090	12808	1452		4391	294	2266	79	2422	30898 (73.9)	10904 (26.1)
1921	122749	60085	20276	10003	1431		3689	289	2189	67	2151	30279 (75.5)	9816 (24.5)
1931	136075	37600	12180	14997	1575		3281	291	1914	49	3313	27177 (72.3)	10423 (27.7)
1951*	173549	40539	18368	12694	1357		2906	291	1153	123	3647	31062 (76.8)	9377 (23.2)
1961	212467	59402	33103	14171	1187	4665	789	243	815	65	4364	47274 (79.6)	12128 (20.4)
1971(P)	263900	31298	9266	15794	907	1331	865	204	556	146	2229	25060 (80.1)	6238 (19.9)

* Figures do not include Jammu & Kashmir.

Provisional. The figures are based on one per cent sampling.

Sources: (1) Census of India 1961 - Paper No. 1 of 1962 - Final Population Totals.

(2) Pocket Book of Population-Statistics-Census Centenary 1972.

In view of the difference in characteristics and problems mentioned earlier, our classification of women workers for purposes of trend analysis divides them broadly into the unorganized and organized sectors instead of the nine industrial categories adopted by the Census. We take up the unorganized sector first as it accounts for the overwhelming majority of women workers in the country.

Women in the Unorganized Sector

94 per cent of the women workers are engaged in the unorganized sector of the economy, 81.4 per cent in agriculture, and the rest in non-agricultural occupations. The major problems that affect them spring from the unorganized nature of all industry in this sector. They are outside the reach of most laws that seek to protect the security and working conditions of labour. Labour organizations are mostly absent. Where they do exist, they are still in a formative stage and have had little impact on women.

The gradual commercialization and modernization of the economy and the efforts made by Government to replace traditional by modern institutions of credit and marketing to stabilize ownership of land, and to maintain minimum wages, have by no means succeeded in 'organising' the production relations to control the degree of exploitation of the weaker section. Nor have they solved the problems of low productivity, poverty, unemployment and underemployment. Traditional modes of production relations which defy modern classifications into employers and employees, labour and capital, rent and interest, still prevail in most industries in this sector. The impact of this intermixture has been greater on women. Wages of women are uniformly lower than those of men, even within the low wage structure of all workers in this sector.

Many of them are unpaid family workers, both in family enterprises, and in wage employment where their contribution to the family earnings as helpers of the men earners is not always realised, or admitted. These unpaid family workers are predominantly women and children. Most of them fulfil dual roles by engaging in economic and household activity. More than half of the women who enter the labour force before the age of 15 are unpaid family workers, as compared to one-third of the men in the same category. Three estimates are available regarding the proportion of unpaid family workers in the labour force. According to the National Sample Survey (except in the 19th round based on Integrated Household Schedule) the unpaid family workers in rural India were reported to form between 15 to 17 per cent of the male-labour force and between 41 to 49 per cent of the female labour force. Despite the variation in the concepts and the timings of the survey, the proportion of unpaid family workers shows a remarkable steadiness in the various rounds. (Table 2.7)

TABLE - 2.7
PERCENTAGE OF UNPAID FAMILY WORKERS IN THE LABOUR FORCE IN RURAL AND URBAN INDIA BY SEX AND AGE

	Rural India @		*Urban India £*	
Age	*Males*	*Females*	*Males*	*Females*
10-14	47.5	55.5	34.5	52.5
15-19	36.0	49.7	22.0	41.5
20-24	26.0	45.5	13.5	31.7
25-29	17.0	42.5	8.4	26.1
30-34	10.7	40.3	4.3	22.1
35-39	6.3	38.6	2.5	18.8
40-44	3.7	37.0	1.6	16.4
45-49	2.5	35.6	1.1	15.4
50-54	2.2	34.5	1.2	15.0
55-59	2.4	33.6	1.5	15.1
60-64	2.7	33.0	2.1	15.3
65-69	3.3	32.6	3.5	15.5
70-74	4.2	32.4	5.5	16.0
75+	5.6	32.2	8.8	18.0

@ Based on the NSS data from the 16th and the 17th Rounds (1960-61 and 1961-62, respectively)

£ Based on the NSS data from the 14th and the 15th Rounds (1958-59 and 1959-60, respectively)

Source: Report of the Committee of Experts on Unemployment Estimates, 1970, p. 165.

The proportion of unpaid family workers aged 10 and over, estimated from 1961 census, was about 14 per cent for males and 41 per cent for females. The degree of attachment to the labour force differs in the case of unpaid family workers. The NSS data from the 14th and 15th Rounds suggested that in rural India the proportion of females in the labour force and particularly of female unpaid family workers falls steadily from a peak during July-August to a low during May-June.

However, taking into account all these variations the one uniform trend that emerges is that the proportion of female unpaid workers is much higher than that of males and they form an important segment of the labour force. The distribution of unpaid family workers by age groups given below, indicates that their proportion declines considerably in the case of males after the age of 24 but for females, who form a higher proportion in the age group 10-19, the decline is marginal.

Agriculture has received somewhat more attention from government agencies and experts engaged in socio-economic research. Consequently, relatively more information is available on the role and conditions of women workers in this field. The non-agricultural industries and services in the unorganized sector, however, have been neglected by most investigators, with the result that there is practically no reliable data on this field.

Census data poses several difficulties, since it does not classify workers by degree of organization of their occupations. Secondly, its classification of workers by their primary activity misses the overlapping nature of agricultural with non-agricultural occupations. Even the National Sample Survey, with its short reference periods, cannot discover fully the variety of occupations that women engage in during the course of the year.

The seasonal and fluctuating nature of their different occupations, in our opinion, is one of the main causes of large scale, short distance and short-term migration of rural women particularly agricultural labourers, who are compelled to seek work outside their village during the off-seasons.

Estimates of Unemployment and Underemployment

The interplay of various social and economic factors pose difficulties in estimating employment, unemployment and under-employment of women, particularly in rural areas. In spite of such difficulties, the Committee of Unemployment found women to be a greater victim of unemployment and underemployment. The number of unemployed women in rural areas was estimated to be 4.5 million as against 3.2 million males in 1971. Thus women constitute nearly 60 per cent of the rural unemployed and 56 per cent of the total unemployed in the country. Table 2.8 shows the correct picture of unemployed persons both in rural and urban areas as per 1971 census. It should be noted that this estimate of unemployed only takes into account persons recorded as 'seeking work'. In the case of women, this category does not truly portray the number of women who need employment but cannot get it. Table 2.9 indicates that the number of underemployed women in terms of the hours of work available to them during a week becomes higher than men in the category of 22 to 28 hours in both rural and urban areas. Their proportion is however less than men when the hours of employment are less.

TABLE - 2.8
ESTIMATED NUMBER OF UNEMPLOYED PERSONS 1971 CENSUS

Area	*Sex*	*Percentage of Unemployed Persons*	*Total Population in (1971) (million)*	*Number of Unemployed Persons (million)*
1	2	3	4	5
Rural	Males	1.42	225.2	3.2
	Females	2.10	213.6	4.5
	Total	-	438.8	7.7
Urban	Males	1.35	58.7	0.8
	Females	0.98	50.4	0.5
	Total	-	109.1	1.3
All India	Males	-	283.9	4.0
	Females	-	264.0	5.0
	Total	-	547.9	9.0

Low labour utilization and seasonal unemployment are a manifestation of rural poverty where individuals are forced to take on extremely low productivity jobs which do not always ensure minimum subsistence. The basic problems that affect women's roles and opportunities for employment in this sector, spring from their helpless dependence caused by lack of adequate employment opportunities, limited skills and illiteracy, restricted mobility and lack of autonomous status. The occupational status of a woman worker is linked to that of her husband or father particularly so in the rural areas.

TABLE - 2.9

ESTIMATED NUMBER OF UNDER-EMPLOYED PERSONS IN 1971 POPULATION (ON THE BASIS OF PERCENTAGE OF UNDEREMPLOYED PERSONS DERIVED FROM 19TH ROUND OF NSS)

	Males			*Females*		
Hours of Work in a Week	*Percentage of Under-employed Workers among the Employed Labour Force*	*Percentage of Under-employed Workers in Population*	*Under-employed Persons in 1971 Population (million)*	*Percentage of Under-employed Workers among Female Workers*	*Percentage of Under-employed Workers in the Population*	*Under-employed Persons in 1971 Population (million)*
Rural						
1-7	0.65	0.34	0.77	1.49	0.36	0.77
8-14	3.15	1.63	3.67	6.18	1.52	3.25
Total 1-14			4.44			4.02
15-21	3.05	1.57	3.54	5.65	1.39	2.97
22-28	3.62	1.87	4.21	9.06	2.03	4.34
Total 1-28			12.19			11.33
Urban						
1-7	0.50	0.25	0.15	1.55	0.19	0.10
8-14	2.14	1.07	0.63	6.64	0.82	0.41
Total 1-14			0.78			0.51
15-21	1.52	0.76	0.45	5.12	0.64	0.32
22-28	2.05	1.02	0.60	11.27	1.40	0.71
Total 1-28			1.83			1.54

Source: Report of the Committee on Unemployment, pp. 156-58, Based on NSS and Census data.

The abject poverty to these workers is the result of their lack of control over adequate productive resources. The effect of possession of marginal land or landlessness, a persistent gap between income and consumption, lack of continuous employment and low social position is further enhanced by near perpetual indebtedness. The cumulative effect of all these factors is that the worker is deprived of all bargaining power and occupational and geographical mobility. The totality of this problem results in increasing pauperization and abject poverty.

Estimates of Poverty

In recent years there have been various attempts to estimate the magnitude of the problem of poverty. These estimates, measured on the basis of consumption-expenditure, have attempted to calculate the number of persons below subsistence level. According to the Planning Commission, the proportion of people below the poverty line has slightly come down in the last two decades although the absolute number of people in this condition (over 220 million) is just as large as it was earlier. While the computation of this figure is very similar in other estimates, there is difference of opinion among scholars regarding the direction of change (Minhas, B.S., 1971). While some of them agree with the Planning Commission regarding the declining proportion of persons below the poverty line, at least one has argued that in rural areas the proportion has been increasing from 30 per cent in 1960-61 to 54 per cent in 1968-69. In absolute numbers, according to this estimate, the rural people below the poverty line rose from 135 million in 1960-61 to 230 million in 1968-69. The differences in these estimates are caused by their use of different standards for determining the minimum consumption expenditure.

It is sometimes argued that such an increase in the number of the poor is impossible in view of the rise in per capita income. This argument ignores the impact of the price increase of consumption goods, particularly of foodgrains. There is some evidence that the consumer prices have risen more for the poor than for the rich.

It is difficult to estimate the proportion and number of women affected by this increase in poverty as data regarding this is not available. But the higher level of unemployment and under-employment among women leads us to conclude that their proportion below the poverty line is likely to be higher than men. The physical evidence of increasing destitution among women in recent years has been reported to us from various quarters. Unfortunately, however, no reliable data is available for estimating the size of this group. The Department of Social Welfare has estimated that about one lakh of widows become destitute every year in the age group 20-44. For the age group above 65, this number is estimated at 48.3 lakh. It is, however, difficult to understand the basis of these calculations.

While the interrelated problems of poverty, unemployment and underemployment affect the economy as a whole, we have dealt with them in the section on the unorganized sector mainly because the overwhelming mass of women workers, both by primary and secondary activity, are to be found in this sphere. Structural changes in our economy which may decrease the share of the unorganized sector, are at present very distant objectives. The special disabilities that characterize the rights and opportunities for women's economic participation are more predominant in the unorganized sector and will require special attention and remedial measures.

Three

Plight of Women Workers in different Sectors of the Economy

Agriculture

Agriculture remains the major economic activity for women. According to the census of 1971, 80.1 per cent of women workers are engaged in agriculture. In rural areas they constitute 87 per cent of the female workforce. In urban areas their proportion is 17.5 per cent. Any assessment of the role and problems of women in Indian agriculture has to take note of the nature and structure of the agricultural economy with its characteristic features of land relations, labour utilization and the roles and functions of the credit system.

The system of land relations and labour utilization are closely inter-twined, the latter being intimately related with the hierarchic structure of land ownership. "Social stratification in a village is linked with land and caste, which govern status, economic power and political influence as much as the level of living which is their consequence".

While census data classifies agricultural workers into only two categories, viz., cultivators and labourers, this classification does not, in fact, reflect the realities of the agricultural community. Cultivators include absentee land owners who do not cultivate their land themselves, or cultivate it with hired labour, lease holders, and tenants of different categories, including share croppers and marginal farmers who not only cultivate their own lands but also engage in labour on others' land. Labourers, on the other hand, include casual, daily wage labourers, 'attached' workers, whose wages are fixed by contract, and 'bonded' labour who have taken loans from land-owners and have contracted to pay off the loan by working for them. The first and the second category may include very small cultivators whose main source of earnings, due to their small and sub-marginal holdings, is wage employment. The second category gets somewhat higher wages than the first and is assured of some income in the lean seasons. The National Commission on Labour describes them as 'permanent'. Their mobility, however, is restricted as they cannot leave their masters at will. Some of this group are also share croppers. The third category, in the words of the National Commission on Labour, "can best be described in terms of debtbondage, fixed for a time or a life time, or hereditarily descending from father to son in some cases."

In spite of regional variations, this pattern of stratification of agricultural workers is found in most parts of the country. It is difficult to clearly demarcate the categories, because of a process of movement from one to the other, through changes in income position, land values, rates of return and the degree of indebtedness. Some recent studies have indicated that two separate processes have contributed to resumption of land by owners after evicting tenants: (a) increase in productivity from better methods of cultivation, and consequent prospects of higher returns from land; and (b) Governmental efforts to confer ownership rights on tenants. According to Prasad, P.H. in EPW, 1974:

> While a certain degree of upward mobility may be found among a very small minority, the general pattern of change is in a downward direction, through increasing pressure of growing families on small holdings and growing indebtedness which leads to loss of land.

P.K. Bardhan in EPW of February, 1973 has said:

> Insufficient land base is at the root of all these problems of poverty, tenurial insecurity and under-employment. Land owned being the primary collateral in loans whether from private or institutional sources, these problems are usually coupled with the problem of gross inadequacy of credit for consumption as well as production needs of the rural poor. Exorbitant rates of interest and the deadweight of outstanding loans depress the returns obtained by poor peasants from cultivation and marketing, perpetuate varying degrees of essentially bonded labour and, in general, darken their horizon for future prospects.

The impact of this process on women's participation in agriculture is visible from the sharp decline in women cultivators and the increase in the ranks of agricultural labourers over the last few decades. Table 3.1 gives the distribution of women workers in agriculture from 1951 to 1971.

TABLE - 3.1
DISTRIBUTION OF WOMEN WORKERS IN AGRICULTURE 1951-71

Category	*1951 No. of Female Workers*	*%age of Total No. of Female Workers*	*1961 No. of Female Workers*	*%age of Total No. of Female Workers*	*1971 No. of Female Workers*	*%age of Total No. of Female Workers*
1. Cultivators	18367875	45.42	33103198	55.73	9266471	29.61
2. Agricultural Labourers	12693671	31.39	14170831	23.86	15794399	50.46
		76.81		89.59		80.07

Excluding the figures for 1961 as a deviation case, which may be attributed to the broader definition of cultivators adopted in that census, the decline of women cultivators from 183.6 lakhs in 1951 to 92.6 lakh in 1971, i.e., by nearly 50 per cent, can be attributed to increasing pauperization leading to loss of land or inadequate growth of productive employment opportunities on family farms, leading to withdrawal of women from active cultivation.

The increase in the number of agricultural labourers from 12.6 million in 1951 to 15.7 million in 1971, a shift from less than one-third to more than half of the total women workforce, is the greatest indicator of increasing poverty and reduction in the level of employment and not of improving rights and opportunities for economic participation. The average opportunity for employment available to women agricultural labourers is indicated in Table 3.2.

Some incentive studies of rural households in selected districts of the country conducted by the Labour Bureau, Simla in 1967-70 indicate variations in the degree of unemployment of men and women according to regions and age groups. The percentage in the case of males and females are of the total population in each age group, and not of the male and female population respectively. The level of female unemployment is considerably higher than males in the States of Andhra Pradesh, Gujarat, Madhya Pradesh and Tamil Nadu. The increasing unemployment of women in the higher age groups in West Bengal is specially noteworthy. (Table 3.3)

TABLE - 3.2
EXTENT OF EMPLOYMENT OF MALE AND FEMALE AGRICULTURAL WORKERS BELONGING TO AGRICULTURAL LABOUR HOUSEHOLDS: BY PAID MAN DAYS IN A YEAR.

	Ag.	*Emp. (Paid mandays)*	*Non-Ag.*	*Emp. (Paid mandays)*
	Men	*Women*	*Men*	*Women*
First Ag. Labour Enquiry 1950-51	189	129	20	14
Second Ag. Labour Enquiry 1956-57	194	131	28	10
Rural Labour Enquiry 1964-65	217	149	25	11

Wage Discrimination

The most important reasons for the low rates of wages, particularly for women labour in agriculture are the unorganized nature of farm labour, the ease with which hired labour can be substituted by family labour, the seasonal nature of the demand for labour and the traditional classification of some jobs, as the monopoly of women. As per the Minimum Wages ACt, 1949 (2nd Schedule) minimum wages are to be fixed by state governments for agricultural labour and the rates are to be reviewed periodically at intervals not exceeding five years. There are still some States which have not brought large areas of agricultural employment within the ambit of the Act. The machinery for the fixation and enforcement of minimum wages is not uniform.

The National Commission on Labour had criticized the inadequate implementation of the Act. The reasons for this, in their view, lay in the poverty and illiteracy of agricultural labour, the casual nature of their employment and their ignorance of the law, all of which apply particularly to the women. According to the Census of 1971, 92.1 per cent of the women workers in rural areas are illiterate. Because of these handicaps, agricultural labour as a whole and women in particular are unable to employ methods now common to industrial labour to improve their bargaining power. There are considerable disparities in wages between men and women depending upon the region, crops and the bargaining power of labour.

TABLE - 3.3

PERCENTAGE OF UNEMPLOYED MALES, FEMALES AND TOTAL PERSONS TO THE TOTAL POPULATION OF SELECTED RURAL LABOUR HOUSEHOLD BY BROAD AGE GROUP

State	*District within which Study was Undertaken*	*Sex*	*Age Group*			
			Below 15	*15-59*	*60 plus*	*All Ages*
1. Andhra Pradesh	Mehboob Nagar	Males	1.05	1.60	2.50	1.42
		Females	2.02	8.58	5.02	5.70
		Persons	3.07	10.18	7.52	7.12
2. Bihar	Gaya	Males	0.48	6.90	4.90	3.97
		Females	0.52	2.29	1.96	1.50
		Persons	1.00	9.20	6.86	1.50
3. Gujarat	Surat	Males	0.61	3.98	1.06	2.21
		Females	1.95	6.83	2.12	4.25
		Persons	2.57	10.81	3.18	6.46
4. Himachal Pradesh	Chamba	Males	0.63	1.96	1.07	1.34
		Females	0.24	0.34	-	0.28
		Persons	0.87	2.30	1.07	1.62
5. Jammu & Kashmir	Anantnag	Males	0.80	11.77	2.22	6.52
		Females	1.04	7.66	0.20	4.40
		Persons	1.84	19.43	2.42	10.92
6. Madhya Pradesh	Rewa	Males	1.02	4.94	5.02	2.40
		Females	2.06	12.18	2.51	6.49
		Persons	3.08	17.12	7.53	7.89
7. Maha-rashtra	i. Ratnagiri	Males	1.00	7.66	1.31	3.83
		Females	-	10.03	0.66	4.88
		Persons	1.00	17.69	1.97	8.71
	ii. Wardha	Males	0.98	2.37	4.14	1.98
		Females	1.19	5.38	2.68	3.50
		Persons	2.17	7.75	6.82	5.43
8. Mysore	Hasan	Males	1.32	15.58	0.86	8.03
		Females	1.64	12.27	2.58	6.70
		Persons	2.96	27.85	3.44	14.73
9. Punjab	Gurdaspur	Males	-	0.38	-	0.19
		Females	-	-	-	-
		Persons	-	0.38	-	0.19
10. Rajasthan	Tank	Males	0.63	10.39	0.80	5.50
		Females	0.74	11.65	0.36	6.16
		Persons	1.37	22.4	1.16	11.66
11. Tamil Nadu	Dharmpuri	Males	1.73	11.19	10.55	7.04
		Females	2.53	20.02	2.78	11.37
		Persons	4.26	31.21	13.33	18.41
12. Uttar Pradesh	Etawah	Males	0.99	5.68	5.48	3.55
		Females	-	0.38	-	0.19
		Persons	0.99	6.06	5.48	3.74
13. West Bengal	Bankura	Males	0.55	3.56	9.85	1.64
		Females	-	4.22	17.33	2.06
		Persons	0.55	7.78	27.18	3.70

Source: Unpublished data from the Intensive Type Studies of Rural Labour Household. Report of the Committee on Unemployment, pp. 142-43.

In earlier times, the regional variations in wage rates were probably influenced by cultural variations in attitudes to women's work. In recent years, however, this situation has changed. As observed by the National Commission on Labour, "the fixation of statutory minimum wages by the Government has tended to narrow the gap between wages of men and women." The Commission, however, noted the continuation of wage differentials between men and women, particularly in agriculture. "In the larger sectors where women are employed, viz., agriculture and small industries, evidence shows that in fixing wage rates some State Governments have not been free from discrimination against women." Table 3.4 indicates the difference in maximum and minimum wages of men and women for the same agricultural operations in selected States:

TABLE - 3.4
AGRICULTURAL WAGES IN DIFFERENT STATES

1		2 *Maximum*	3 *Minimum*
		1. BIHAR — 1970 *(for 11 months)*	
Sowers	Men	44.05	15.95
	Women	29.50	12.50
	Children	19.25	10.53
Weeders	Men	41.30	16.12
	Women	33.76	12.90
	Children	21.00	10.25
Reapers	Men	67.00	18.75
	Women	38.95 (10 months)	13.50 (10 months)
	Children	19.31 (9 months)	8.50 (9 months)
		2. HARYANA — 1971 *(for 9 months)*	
Sowers	Men	72.20	47.00
	Women	2.50 (1 month)	—
	Children	—	—
Weeders	Men	64.00	43.50
	Women	39.60	24.50
	Children	15.00 (6 months)	3.00 (1 month)
Reapers	Men	74.80 (8 months)	30.50 (6 months)
	Women	31.50 (6 months)	10.00 (3 months)
	Children	16.50 (4 months)	8.50 (3 months)

(continued on next page)

1		2 *Maximum*	3 *Minimum*
		3. MADHYA PRADESH — 1971	
Sowers	Men (11 months)	44.75	15.25
	Women	31.25	9.25 (9 months)
	Children	23.00 (10 months)	7.75 (9 months)
Weeders	Men (12 months)	36.50	12.50
	Women	30.50	10.50
	Children	23.75	7.70
Reapers	Men (10 months)	35.00	10.50 (9 months)
	Women	31.25	9.25 (9 months)
	Children	23.75	5.75 (9 months)
		4. PUNJAB — 1971 *(for 12 months)*	
Sowers	Men	95.00	63.75
	Women	—	—
	Children	—	—
Weeders	Men	95.00	64.00
	Women	37.50 (7 months)	—
	Children	—	—
Reapers	Men	78.25 (10 months)	44.00 (8 months)
	Women	—	—
	Children	—	—
		5. TAMIL NADU — 1971 *(for 12 months)*	
Sowers	Men	48.25	23.00
	Women	30.00	12.96
	Children	24.25	12.49
Weeders	Men	42.00	12.00
	Women	27.00	12.00
	Children	24.25	10.07
Reapers	Men	58.00	24.23
	Women	44.80	14.82
	Children	44.28	16.01
		6. UTTAR PRADESH — 1971 *(for 12 months)*	
Sowers	Men	66.56	11.27 (11 months)
	Women	47.70	9.75 (10 months)
	Children	17.50 (8 months)	5.50 (7 months)
Weeders	Men	60.00	11.23
	Women	42.80	10.16 (11 months)
	Children	30.20	6.00 (9 months)
Reapers	Men	52.60	8.87 (9 months)
	Women	42.85 (11 months)	8.07 (9 months)
	Children	29.20 (5 months)	7.50 (8 months)

Source: Directorate of Economics & Statistics, Ministry of Agriculture, Govt. of India.

Apart from the differentials in wages for the same jobs, discrimination against women is strengthened by having lower rates for the job traditionally done by women, viz., sewing, weeding, transplanting, winnowing, threshing and harvesting, as against ploughing — normally done by men only. The other factor that contributes to the low wages of women is the practice of identifying a workday as equivalent of 7-9 hours. Many women are unable to report for duty on time because of household responsibilities, and do not get the full rates. It was reported to us that half an hour's delay could lead to a loss of half day's wage. This would explain the wide variations in maximum wages drawn by men and women.

In spite of inadequacy of Government enforcement machinery, there is no doubt that the Minimum Wages Act has provided an opportunity to reduce discrimination in wages. We are happy to note that some State Governments, e.g., Bihar, have not maintained any differential in wages for some jobs in agriculture.

Disabilities and Exploitation

The disabilities of women workers in agriculture stem from their occupational immobility caused by a variety of economic and social factors. The absence of alternative opportunities for employment in the rural sector has been intensified by the decline of traditional handicrafts and cottage industries.

The problem of underemployment of agricultural workers and the need to strengthen and revive village and cottage industries had formed a major feature of the economic teachings of Mahatma Gandhi and has continued to form a part of the plans for economic development since independence. The contribution of these traditional village industries to the employment needs of particularly the weaker sections of the rural population has been admitted by the Committee on Unemployment which recommended the maintenance of the present levels of employment in these industries. In spite of the policy of support from the government, however, the remnants of these industries have not been able to provide, to an adequate extent, the needed diversification of occupations to the weaker sections of the rural population.

On the other hand, disappearance of many of these industries has led to a loss of skills as a result of which the majority of women workers in the agricultural sector today do not posses any skills other than the traditional agricultural ones. We have met many such women among the landless labourers in the villages. A group of Santhal women in a village in Birbhum (West Bengal) informed us that while they could not obtain employment in agriculture, their lack of other skills had reduced them to complete destitution.

The only major alternative avenue of employment that has been offered to these women in the recent past has been through the programme of rural works. While these may meet employment needs for a short time, their impact is not continuous either in maintaining a steady level of employment or in generating new skills. Women are employed in these projects only as unskilled labourers at the lowest rate of wages.

The large majority of women agricultural workers prefer to remain in their villages seeking occasional employment available within short distance. This was repeated to us in different parts of the country and is also the finding of a number of studies on rural areas. Apart from the voluntary decision on the part of women to remain in the villages which spring from their family responsibilities and socio-psychological reluctance to move out of the familiar habitat, for many of them such a decision is involuntary because of the status of their husbands or sons as attached labour. The restriction of movement of these labourers extends to the women members of the family also, either directly or indirectly. We have been informed that in many areas the attachment covers the women of the family also who have to work along with their male members, both on the land as well as in the household of the person to whom they are attached.

The vulnerability of the woman becomes still greater when her husband has been reduced to the status of bonded labour. It was admitted by the National Commission on Labour that the system of bonded labour "grew out of acute indigence and helplessness of tribal and semi-tribal communities in the grip of a precarious subsistence economy. There was a combination of reasons for the depression of this section of the rural population:

uneconomic holdings, meagre income from forest produce, high incidence of rent, insecurity of tenure and so on. To these were added the social compulsion which constitute 'ostensible' and immediate causes of the system. These are the necessity of incurring expenditure over marriage, avoidable expenditure on birth and death and general economic depression."

It has been brought to our notice that the system of bonded labour sometimes leads to various forms of exploitation of the women. Some recent studies on the hill regions of Uttar Pradesh have revealed a close relationship between incidence of bonded labour and trafficking in women from such families.

While we do not have substantial data to establish a quantified relationship between status in the social hierarchy and economic position in the agricultural system, there are many indicators to show that a large proportion of the most vulnerable section of women agricultural labourers, namely the overwhelming majority of landless and a sizeable section of the marginal peasants, come from socially depressed communities. According to the Census of 1961, 42.9 per cent of women workers from the Scheduled Castes were agricultural labourers. In the case of Scheduled Tribes this figure was 21.33 per cent. Their representation in non-agricultural occupations was negligible. The number of Scheduled Caste women employed as agricultural labourers was over 9 lakh in Andhra Pradesh, over 6 lakh in Tamil Nadu and 7 lakh in Uttar Pradesh.

The degree of poverty and the higher participation rate among women in these sections of the population gives the large land owning families an upper hand since attached agricultural labour generally comes from these sections and wage differentials discriminating not only between men and women but between the non-scheduled workers in general is widely prevalent.

The National Commission on Labour had expressed its concern at this state of affairs. "Our concern is all the greater, since those who suffer more, even among women as a group, are ignorant, unskilled and semi-skilled workers coming from communities which convention recognizes as belonging to the lower social strata and for protecting whom Article 46 of the Constitution is presumably intended. In a way women belonging to these communities are intended to be doubly protected (a) because they are the 'weaker section'; and (b) because of the comparatively unfortunate communities to which they belong; and it is here that the protection is the least."

Before concluding our review of the agriculture sector we would like to draw attention to a problem that affects women's participation in agriculture with the introduction of modern methods of cultivation.

In the tribal areas where the traditional pattern had ensured a high participation by women, the advance of development with modern methods of cultivation is resulting in a gradual displacement of women from their traditional position in the community. Even in the matrilineal community of the Garos (Meghalaya), the development of orchards and terraced cultivation has started the process of shrinking women's activities. A similar process is visible in areas where the community is changing from shifting to terraced cultivation. It is argued by workers of the Bharatiya Adimjati Sevak Sangh that this is due to the approach of government agricultural extension workers who teach new methods to the men only.

It would appear that the Government agents, influenced by their own biases or experience limited to their home areas, are perhaps unconsciously precipitating changes in the participation pattern of these communities which will affect the economic position of the women in the long run.

Our review makes it clear that the main disabilities and source of exploitation of agricultural workers are rooted in their landlessness, lack of organization, and inequality of status. The basic solution to these problems obviously lies in redistribution of land to reduce inequalities and concentration of excessive economic power in the hands of a few.

We would like to mention here our impression of an experiment in rehabilitation of some landless families. 85 families, settled on redistributed land at Narasannapet (Rayalaseema, Andhra Pradesh) presented us with a scene not only of agricultural prosperity, but of happy, hopeful families. The women's expression, dress and above all the bright faces of the children, presented a sharp contrast to those of a group of women from landless families from the same background. The latter looked ragged, worn out and totally hopeless. The contrast remains one of the most vivid experiences during our tours. It also brought home the futility of attempts to scratch at the problem of rural poverty without the one measure that can help this destitute class, i.e., land reform.

The legislation, dealing with distribution of land is not lacking. But its implementation varies from gross inadequacy to ineffectiveness. What is more, in some of the new land ceiling laws, as for example in the laws proposed in States like Madhya Pradesh and Karnataka, undue discrimination has been shown against women. While a major son is entitled to a unit of land outside the family ceiling in his own right, no such provision has been made for a major daughter, married or unmarried.

In our opinion, no substantial improvement in the condition of women agricultural workers is possible without effective steps to redistribute land. Side by side with it, organisation of labour needs to be developed to improve the bargaining power of these workers, to prevent exploitation and low wages.

Non-Agricultural Occupations

Next to agriculture the largest number of women are employed in various industries, trades and services in the unorganized sector both in rural areas. The statistics relating to women workers in these unorganized and regulated industries and services are highly inadequate and unreliable. At present there is no agency responsible for the collection of employment statistics in the unorganized sector.

The National Commission on Labour, confessing its difficulties in identifying unorganized labour by any exact definition, took resource to describing some of their characteristics and constraints, namely: (a) casual nature of employment; (b) ignorance and illiteracy; (c) small size of establishments with low capital investment per person employed; (d) scattered nature of establishments; and (e) superior strength of the employers operating singly and in combination. Admitting the inadequacy of information in the absence of any first hand study of different categories of this amorphous group, the Commission estimated the number of their workers to be about 10 million. It also stated that there was another group of approximately 11 million who could not be described as 'employees' in the cottage and household industries and handicrafts. These estimates were based on the Census of 1961.

The Committee on Unemployment estimated that traditional village and cottage industries are "currently providing employment to more than 10 million persons among the relatively vulnerable sections of the community widely dispersed over rural and semi-urban areas." These include handloom, khadi and village industries, sericulture, coir, cashew, manufacture of *bidis*, handicrafts, etc. They suffer from a number of handicaps, including inadequacy of institutional credit, poor techniques and consequent low productivity.

It has to be remembered that one of the greatest factors contributing towards the fall in women's economic participation in India has been the decline of this group of industries as a consequence of unequal competition with the factory sector. The most developed of these household industries before independence were hand-weaving, oil pressing, rice-pounding, pottery, tanning and leather manufacture, tobacco processing, etc. Almost each of these industries had to face competition from factory production. With the establishment of oil extracting enterprises in the mid fifties, the oil mills offered higher prices for the raw-materials and thus made it impossible for the household oil-pressing industry to compete with them.

In tanning, the demand for crome tanned leather went up along with the increase in factory production of modern types of shoes. The village producers were not in a position to cater to these new demands and the industry started declining fast. The same is true of rice-pounding, which could not survive in competition with the rice mills. Metal utensils replaced earthen-ware and even traditional brass and bell-metal utensils declined through the rise of the aluminium industry. Tobacco retained its position to a certain extent because of the continuing demand for *bidis*. Hand-weaving retained much of its position but even here the introduction of power looms and the monopoly of yard manufacture by the mills sector worsened the situation. This was partly offset by the mills' growing emphasis on production of fine and super-fine cotton and synthetic textiles.

Though this trend of decline has been visible for a considerable period, data regarding women's participation in household industry is available only from the Censuses of 1961 and 71, which suffers from certain difficulties in comparability. Even after taking this into account, the decline in the number of women engaged in household industry from 4.6 million to 1.3 million during this decade presents a grim picture.

Apart from household industry, small-scale industries which are not in the organized sector, also provide some employment to women are: leather tanning, *bidi,* rice and dal mills, coffee curing, cashew nut processing, coir, match, fireworks, manufacture of Aggarbattis and paper products, etc.

According to the Draft Fifth Five-Year Plan, these industries which present a broad spectrum of varying levels of technology, scales of production and forms of organization have an important role to play in the removal of poverty and the reduction in inequalities of wealth and development.

The great difficulty in identifying different categories of this amorphous group is the variety in their pattern of organization. Some of them, e.g., the *bidi* or the match industry, have some units in the organized sector, because the establishments are sufficiently large to come under the purview of the labour laws. Others evade this by various methods, e.g., by splitting up their establishments into small units, by recruiting their labour on a casual basis, by (farming out work to be done by women at home,) or by farming out to contractors. The net result of all these methods is that they escape scrutiny, for both enforcement of labour welfare and minimum wages, and collection of information on employment and workers.

While the Censuses of 1961 and 1971 give us some estimate of women in household industries, we regret to find that no clear estimate is available regarding the actual number of women engaged in the vast unorganized non-agricultural sector. Even the special studies conducted by the National Commission on Labour did not collect any specific information regardir.g the number or percentage of women workers in these industries and services. No doubt the recommendations of the Expert Committee on Unemployment Estimates, regarding more detailed collection of data on women workers, if implemented, would provide more reliable data on this category of workers. In the absence of such information, we can only attempt a rough estimate of the number of women actually engaged in this sector.

Out of 31 million women returned as workers by the Census of 1971, if we exclude the 25 million in agriculture and the 2 million employed in the organized sector, the remaining 4 million, we may conclude, are employed in non-agricultural occupation in the unorganized sector.

The main problems faced by all employees in the various industries in this group are insecurity of employment, lack of standard minimum wages, excessive hours of work and absence of welfare amenities, most of which stem from their lack of organization particularly for women who work at home, in various industries these problems become still more acute, since they are more vulnerable to various forms of exploitation.

The Minimum Wages Act, 1948 attempted statutory regulation of wages and some control of working conditions of labour in these occupations. Minimum wages are formulated for certain scheduled employments in these industries from time to time. Though the Factories and Industrial Disputes Acts apply to many of these establishments, the National Commission on Labour's Survey of such industries revealed that the enforcement of labour laws in this sector is highly inadequate and working conditions are far from satisfactory.

The plight of the workers in these industries and occupations was noted in the Third Five-Year Plan and the intention to formulate a separate code laying down minimum service and working conditions, with an official machinery to enforce the code, was announced at the meeting of Labour Ministries in 1962, which endorsed the Plan Statement. Some attempts have undoubtedly been made by the Government to regulate conditions in this sector since then, e.g., the Contract Labour (Regulations and Abolition) Act 1970, the Bidi and Cigarette (Conditions of Employment) Act, 1966 and the various State Acts to regulate conditions of employment in shops and commercial establishments.

The success of all such attempts, however, depends on the existence of strong labour organizations to compel the implementation of these statutory provisions. Unfortunately, the lack of such organizations in this sector results in labour not having the necessary bargaining power.

In the specific industries and trades which employ a large number of women, workers are characterized by their massive illiteracy, hopeless dependence on intermediaries to obtain employment for them and ignorance of agencies or laws from which they could seek protection. Organization is undoubtedly difficult when the workers are scattered, which is frequently the case with women who do the work in their homes, or in small workplaces. Another difficulty in organizing them is the short duration of most such employment, and the high rate of turnover of most workers.

The grinding level of poverty, and the debts which they frequently have to incur from these employers, just to meet the minimum consumption requirements of their families, also act as deterrents to any form of labour organization. Under these conditions, the chances of any labour organization seem very distant, unless the initiative is taken by some committed and enlightened persons.

In the absence of any systematic and comprehensive study of the conditions of women in this complex group of occupations, we can only indicate our findings as illustrative of the situation. A fuller investigation of the workers in these occupations including the special problems that affect the women, the self-employed and the wage paid, is an imperative necessity and calls for attention by Government, social research agencies and welfare organizations.

Wage Employment

One of the most significant group of wage labourers in this sector are those employed by contractors. The practice of employing contract labour is prevalent in varying degrees in both the public and private sectors. The Labour Bureau has been studying the prevalence of contract labour in 19 industries during the last few years and has found that in iron and manganese mines the percentage of such labour was 73.9 per cent and 65.8 per cent respectively while in cotton ginning, rice mills, limestone quarries, petroleum refineries, ports and iron and steel works, their percentage ranged from 25 per cent to 48 per cent. According to the National Commission on Labour, the employment of contract labour is most pronounced in the mining and construction industry. The construction undertaken by the public works departments of the Government in 1957, employed 60 per cent of their labour on contracts.

Under the Factories, Mines and Plantation Labour Acts, contract-labour employed within the premises of establishments covered by these Acts are entitled to the benefits of working conditions, hours of work and weekly rest admissible to the labour directly employed, but they are not entitled to any leave with pay. The Contract Labour (Regulation and Abolition) Act 1970 seeks to make the principle employer responsible for the provision of essential amenities and payment of wages. The contractor will have to obtain a permit and deposit a security with the authorities and will have to pay wages at the same rate as those paid by the principal employer. In case of default the principal employer is authorised to make payments and recover the cost from the contractor.

The provision of certain basic welfare amenities like drinking water, rest rooms, canteens and first-aid are obligatory under the Act. Health insurance benefits are available to contract labour under the Employees State Insurance Scheme in establishments covered by it, but very few establishments extend this benefit to contract labour. The evasion is either by not employing them directly or employing them for short periods at a time. The Central Government is responsible for the enforcement of this Act in any industry or establishment carried on by or under the authority of the Central Government, any establishment of Railways, Cantonment Boards, major ports, mines, oil fields and banking and insurance companies. The implementation of the Act has been delayed because by 1973, 250 writ petitions have been filed in High Courts and 10 in the Supreme Court.

Construction Industry

As an illustration of women contract labourers we discuss their position in the construction industry. The number of women in this industry has declined from 2.9 lakh in 1951 to 2.04 lakh in 1971. The Government is the largest employer as public constructions — dams, bridges, roads and public buildings, make up the major share of expenditure in this industry. The Committee initiated two studies on women construction workers, one in Patna (covering 3 major projects), and the other in Delhi (covering 9 construction sites). The findings of these studies illustrate the conditions of women in this industry.

Nature of Work and Methods of Recruitment and Wage-payment: Women are employed mostly as unskilled labourers for carrying earth, mortar or bricks crushing bricks and working hand-pumps. Recruitment is mostly done either directly by the contractor or the sub-contractor (Jamadar). Wage payment is on daily or weekly basis. The Bihar study reported that the sub-contractors obtain a contract for the job on piece rate basis but pay their workers on daily basis, ensuring a higher margin of profit for themselves. Workers complain of short payment and unexplained deduction.

The system of deferred wage-payment and unjustified fines and deductions are reported in both the studies. The Bihar study reported that in the case of tribal women part of their wages are kept back to be paid at the time of termination of employment. The Delhi group reported that apart from fines, the Jamadar deducted 25-50 paise per day from their wages without giving any reasons. The existence of these intermediaries invariably depresses the wage rates. Women from all the three Bihar projects reported wage differentials between men and women. In Delhi such distinction has been abolished since 1961.

Levels of Living

The household incomes of nearly 80 per cent of the respondents in Delhi is between Rs 200 and Rs 300. The per capita monthly income is below Rs 75 for 45 per cent and below Rs 50 for a little over 20 per cent. For the Bihar group, the average household income ranges from 194.4 to Rs 334.45. Per capita monthly income ranges from Rs 38.88 to Rs 66.6. For all the families covered by these two studies, the earnings of the women constitute the major share of the families income. The expenditure pattern reported by both the studies indicate that the major part of the income is spent on food and other essential items of daily need. 37 per cent of Delhi group and 37.7 per cent of the Bihar group (58.7 per cent among non-tribals and 10.3 per cent among tribals) are in debt.

The most important reason for taking loans are sickness, to meet gaps in normal consumption and marriage expenses. These debts generally remain unpaid.

Socio-Demographic Characteristics

These women are mostly drawn from the rural poor (77.6 per cent of the Bihar group and 86 per cent of the Delhi group). The Delhi group consists of migrant labour from Rajasthan and out of 150 respondents 144 belong to the Scheduled Castes. 90 per cent of the Bihar group belong to the Scheduled Castes and Scheduled Tribes from the Chhotanagpur region. Almost all the respondents reported poverty as their main reason for taking up construction work.

One interesting feature reported in the Delhi study is that in 40 per cent cases the decision was taken by the women while in 60 per cent cases they were persuaded by their husbands and relatives. 78 per cent of the Bihar and 80.76 per cent of the Delhi group were young women below 35 as the nature of construction works makes heavy demands on physical strength. 40 per cent of the Delhi respondents became employed before reaching their 15th year, and 40 per cent had already worked for more than 7 years. At least one-fifth of them had held more than 4 jobs. Of the Bihar group, 81 per cent had begun their working life as wage labourers very early in their childhood. Of the rest, 12.7 per cent became wage labourers between the ages of 15-20. The age composition of the woman shows that of the Bihar group 8.7 per cent are below 15, 47.3 per cent between 15-25, 28 per cent are between 25-35 and 22 per cent are over 35. Of the Delhi group 40 per cent are between 15-25, 40.6 per cent are between 25-35 and 19.3 per cent are over 35.

98 per cent of all these women are illiterate. Of the Delhi group more than 90 per cent were married before the age of 15 and three-fourths cases the marriage was consummated by their 15th year. As many as 43.33 per cent were married before the age of 10. Of the Bihar group 12.9 per cent were married before the age of 10; 37.6 per cent were married between 10-15 and 31.8 per cent between 15-20. The majority of this last group are tribal women since the average age of marriages of the tribal group is 18.4 while that of the non-tribal women is 11.4. 11.3 per cent of the Bihar group are widows or deserted wives.

23.37 per cent of the Delhi group had continued working till the last day during pregnancy and 40.14 per cent till the 8th or 9th month. This indicates that the provisions of the Contract Labour Act guaranteeing maternity leave have not been applied in the case of these women. Absence of the minimum health protection during pregnancy as well as continuous malnutrition has resulted in high infant mortality. 645 children had been born to those women but at the time of the survey only 389 of them were alive. For the Bihar group, out of 233 children born to these women 67 are dead, 29 of these died before reaching the age of one year. A comparison of the tribal and non-tribal groups showed that the average number of births and deaths was nearly double amongst the non-tribal women than amongst the tribals. The Bihar study also reveals that the majority of the women continue to work even when they are ill rather than go without food for themselves and their dependents. Of the Delhi group, 30 who had suffered from some illness lasting more than one week, had received treatment in government dispensaries and hospitals and 22 had been compelled to discontinue work for periods ranging from 4 days to 6 months. They did not receive any wages during such absence. The other 8 continued to work during illness.

Working Conditions and Access to Welfare

Under the rules of the Central Public Works Department contractors are bound to provide fair wages and welfare services like creches, housing of specific standard and sanitary services. Working hours, weekly day of rest, overtime rates, wage periods and rates of payment and the name of the inspecting officer are to be notified by the department. The inspecting officer is responsible for enforcement of these rules and has to investigate cases of complaint or disputes under the Industrial Dispute and Workmen's Compensation Act. The Bihar Government has also made regulations for controlling the terms and conditions of employment of the labour force employed by the contractors. The Bihar study states that:

"But it appears that most of these regulations are more honoured in the breach than in compliance. Though the survey did not attempt to find out the reasons for the non-implementation of these regulations it is not difficult to form the observation that no serious attempt was made by the Government authorities to see that these regulations were enforced". The study which covered only government projects reports that the period of actual work has found invariably exceeding the scheduled 48 hours week. On particular days the period exceeded the maximum 9 hours by 4 or 5 hours. None of the women received pay for the weekly holidays. Though overtime is common, payment for such work was "rare, primarily because of the ignorance of the workers and the absence of the law enforcing agency". No arrangement had been made for creches in any of the 3 sites though 43 of the respondents were carrying small children with them to work. "In the case of the Ganga Bridge Project it was a clear violation of Rule 11 of the Welfare Rules."

Arrangements for living accommodations had been made by the employer for 58 per cent of the respondents. For 10.6 per cent materials for 'kuchcha' hutments had been provided by the employer. At the northern site of the Ganga Bridge Project, however, temporary living accommodation with ancillary facilities (without lighting) had been provided to all the respondents.

The Delhi study reports that:

> though in most cases women earned as much as their husbands they did not enjoy equality of status within the family. Only about 8 per cent of women said that they had a say in taking decisions in respect of matters like daily expenditure, education and marriage of children and selection of jobs. The rest of the respondents stated that the decision were taken by the husband or by the parents-in-law.

Bidi Industry

A large group of women in the unorganized sector are engaged in feeding the production of larger factories from their homes. Employers in *bidi* matches, mica industries prefer to pay women less as workers feeding their unorganized and unregulated factories. The largest of these is the *bidi* industry and consists of factories, small workshops as well as home production. Wages are on piece rate basis. Working hours and bonus payments are unregulated. Women working at home are called 'Ghar Khatas'.

This is a peculiar feature of the *bidi* industry and is prevalent over many parts of the country.

According to the Census of 1961, out of 9 lakh *bidi* workers 5.5 lakh belong to the household sector. The *bidi* and cigar industries, where employment of women exceeds men, (77.3 per cent in Andhra Pradesh, 60.9 per cent in Maharashtra, 47.5 per cent in Rajasthan) is the worst of the 'sweated industries'. A recent report on *bidi* workers in Sinar (Maharashtra) observes that out of 10,000 *bidi* workers, 65 per cent are women who generally work in their homes and are paid at the rate of Rs. 4 per thousand *bidis*. The total labour time required for rolling thousand *bidis* ranges from 12 to 16 hours.

The Committee appointed by the Government of Andhra Pradesh in 1969 for revision of minimum wages in the tobacco manufacturing industry reported that the seasonal industry of tobacco leaf handling employs nearly a lakh of workers. The factories work from February to July for a period of 60 to 180 days. The majority of workers are women. The same is true of the *bidi* industry. The revised wages recommended by the Committee are given in Table 3.5.

TABLE - 3.5

RECOMMENDATIONS OF MINIMUM WAGES IN TOBACCO COMMITTEE

Industry	*Categories of Workers*	*Revised Wage Recommended*
1. Tobacco Leaf	Men (General including packers)	Rs. 4.05 per day Rs. 115.30 per month
	Women workers (General, grading, stemming and scrap cleaning)	Rs. 3.60 per day Rs. 93.60 per month
2. Cigarette Manufacture	Men	Rs. 5.05 per day Rs. 131.30 per month
	Women	Rs. 4.60 per day Rs. 119.60 per month
3. Zarda Manufacture	Men	Rs. 4.10 per day Rs. 106.60 per month
	Women	Rs. 3.00 per day Rs. 78.00 per month

The Committee felt that the amount of work done by women workers cannot be regarded as of equal value and quantity hence higher rates were recommended for the men.

A small workshop in the house of a contractor visited by us in Kurnool (Andhra Pradesh) in 1973 was, however, paying at the rate of Rs. 2.50 per thousand *bidis*. The workers complained of frequent deductions in wages on various pretexts that the products did not come up to the required standard of quality. The workers consisted of families of men and women and small girls between the age of 5 and 15. The adults were engaged in rolling and tying the *bidis* while the children were mainly engaged in folding the tops of the *bidi*. One 12 year-old girl mentioned that she had been doing this for as long as she could remember. All the workers looked undernourished. The children particularly were extremely small for their age. A few pregnant women said they had to work till the last day of their pregnancy.

Working hours were from 6 am to 6 pm. During these hours a family of four managed to produce about one thousand *bidis*. The employer reported that young boys became restive and were therefore not found useful. The girls, however, were prepared to put in the necessary labour for 12 hours a day.

As an illustration of home production we found that in Madhya Pradesh the general practice is of distributing raw materials early in the morning to the women working in their homes, the finished products are collected in the evening. The bundles of leaves are handed over without any counting or checking of quality. The finished products are, however, carefully checked and counted, and deductions are made from wages, even for bad leaves which had been supplied but could not be used. There were also complaints that the bundles of leaves often do not contain the specified quantity for rolling the required number of *bidis*. The change for such shortages has, however, to be borne by the worker. We found the same practice in Tamil Nadu and were informed that this is widely prevalent in other parts of the country also.

The Bidi and Cigarette (Conditions of Employment) Act, 1966, which was upheld by the Supreme Court in January 1974, prescribes a working day of 9 hours and 48 hours a week.

According to this Act, the workers are entitled to a paid weekly holiday and leave at the rate of 1 day for every 20 days work during the preceding year, wages for the leave period at rates equal to overall daily wages during the month immediately preceding the leave and 3 months maternity leave for women workers. This Act which was challenged by some firms has been upheld by the Supreme Court in January 1974. Describing the 3 categories of *bidi* workers, namely those employed as direct labourers, home workers "mostly women who manufacture *bidis* in their homes with the assistance of other members of their family, including children" and out-workers, to whom material is supplied by the proprietor himself without the agency of the middleman. Chief Justice A.N. Ray observed:

> Under these systems the contractor engages labourers less than the statutory number to escape the application of the Factory Act.... Sometimes, there is no definite relationship of master and servant between the actual worker and the ultimate proprietor. The proprietor will not be answerable for the wages of the out-workers because there is no privity of contract between them. A large body of actual workers are illiterate women who could with impunity be exploited by the proprietor and contractors... Women and infirm persons can earn something by rolling beedis. The dependence of these people particularly the women shows that they have little bargaining power against powerful proprietors and contractors.

The Court also held that the provisions of the Act including maternity benefits, one month's wages in lieu of notice, etc., also applied to the home workers.

Our investigation of women in this industry confirm that the degree of exploitation has been due to their lack of bargaining power. We feel that the Supreme Court's decision regarding the applicability of the provisions of this Act including maternity benefits need to be enforced urgently but in order to do this effectively it is necessary to set up a special machinery.

Match Industry

The pattern of organization in this industry is exactly similar to the Bidi industry. We visited a factory at Sivakasi (Tamil Nadu) which presented a picture similar to that described above. We found children as young as five years and women working at home, while men work in the factory. There are no trade unions, and no protection is available to these workers.

Chikan Industry

This traditional industry, which had languished in the period before independence, revived as a result of efforts made by the Government of Uttar Pradesh after independence. It is a fine art of embroidery done on a wide variety of products such as kurtas, shirts, table linens, handkerchief, saris, etc.

The annual value of output of *chikan* goods in 1972 was estimated at about 75 lakh which was five times that of 1959. According to official sources the number of craftsmen had also increased fivefold, from about 5,000 to about 25,000 in 1972. According to the UP Handicrafts Board, however, the number of workers engaged in this craft today is about 45,000 and the annual value of their output is around Rs one crore. In the years since independence the taste for *chikan* embroidery has revived and goods like saris, kurtas, table linen are exported to Delhi, Mumbai, Calcutta as well as abroad. Chikan work is now also done on new varieties of materials like silk, voile, nylon, etc. In spite of this expansion, however, the lot of the workers has not improved but has in fact become worse. Out of the estimated 45,000 workers engaged in this industry, 31,000 to 35,000 live and work within the precincts of Lucknow Municipal Corporation. 97 per cent of them are women. The 3 per cent men are largely engaged in processes incidental to the embroidery, such as cutting, printing, sewing, washing, folding, etc. As in the case of *bidi* workers, the *chikan* workers also fall into 4 categories. 95.8 per cent are contract workers. 3.6 per cent belong to a mixed category of self-employed-cum-contract workers and only 0.5 per cent direct employees. Only 0.1 per cent can be described as fully self-employed. The contract workers work on piece rate basis while the wage employees are either on time rate or on piece rate. 70 per cent are multi-process workers while the rest specialize in particular processes of *chikan* embroidery.

Since the workers are predominantly Muslim women who

observe purdah they have no direct links with the consumers. Work is obtained through intermediaries. 65.5 per cent of the women covered by the study got work through contractors, 19.5 per cent from wholesale traders, 1.17 per cent through government agencies and only 0.27 per cent obtained it directly from the consumers. 16.5 per cent receive work through more than one agency. The study found that 46 per cent of them are contract women and wage-employees, 33 per cent of them are self-employed-cum-contract workers and 60 per cent of the self-employed are suffering from underemployment.

Only 7 per cent of the workers receive full day's work, 7 per cent get work for less than 4 hours a day. 55.58 per cent of the contract workers, 62 per cent of the self-employed-cum-contract workers and 80 per cent of the self-employed workers reported that there had been no change in the availability of work. The rest complained of decrease in the availability of work.

Levels of Living

Majority of the workers live below the poverty line. 74 per cent of the contract workers, 62.16 per cent of the self-employed-cum-contract workers and all the wage employees earn less than Rs 40 per head per month. Table 3.6 indicates the range of per capita income of these families.

TABLE - 3.6

CLASSIFICATION OF WORKERS' FAMILIES BY PER CAPITA MONTHLY INCOME

Per Capita Income Group	*Categories of Workers*				
	CW	*SECW*	*WE*	*SE*	*TOTAL*
Less than Rs. 40	728 (73.84)	23 (62.16)	5 (100.0)	-	756 (73.47)
Rs. 40-60	150 (15.21)	6 (16.21)	-	1 (100.0)	157 (15.26)
Rs. 60-80	55 (5.58)	4 (10.81)	-	-	59 (5.73)
Rs. 80-100	24 (2.43)	3 (8.11)	-	-	27 (2.62)
More than Rs. 100	29 (2.94)	1 (2.71)	-	-	30 (2.92)
Total	986 (100.0)	37 (100.0)	5 (100.0)	1 (100.0)	1029 (100.0)

(Figures in brackets denote percentage).

The earnings are lowest for the wage employees and the highest for the self-employed. The average monthly earnings of the contract workers is less than Rs 27, that of the wage employees less than Rs 15 and that of self-employed Rs 200. The self-employed-cum-contract workers earned on an average around Rs 60 per month. All the categories of workers, except the self-employed, reported decline in their incomes. The average contract workers could earn Rs 34 in 1969 as against Rs 26 in 1973. Both wage employees and self-employed-cum-contract workers experienced a decline of 30 per cent in their incomes over the period. While it is generally estimated that these women only supplement the family income by this work, a large number of them whom the Committee met in Lucknow were widowed or deserted women who were supporting their families by their own earnings. A very large number of them have to wear glasses by the time they reach the age of 30 because of the strain that this work puts on their eyes. Many of them become incapable to continue with this work by the time they reach the age of 50, because of failing eyesight.

Production and Marketing

Since production and marketing are mostly in the hands of intermediaries who are traditionally money lenders, this results in a high degree of exploitation. The study found that with a view to keeping their production costs down, wholesalers tap sources of cheap labour from rural areas. The reduced emphasis on quality work depresses the wage rates. The wholesalers' margin of profit ranges between 60 per cent and 73 per cent. The differentials between the rates paid to the workers by the wholesalers and government agencies ranges from 20-30 per cent. Deductions are made from wages on various pretexts, e.g., delay in completing work, bad craftsmanship, damage to material, etc.

This was reported by 64 per cent of the contract workers, 78 per cent of the self-employed-cum-contract workers and all the wage employees. In all 38 per cent complained of deduction in wages and 38 per cent reported disputes due to low wage rates. The group of women whom the Committee met also complained of similar treatment even from co-operatives and sometimes from voluntary organizations formed for marketing these products. In some cases the workers never received payment for goods lost by these agencies.

The UP State Industries Department organized certain *chikan* centres in 1947 to provide regular employment and fair wages and widen the market for these products. Skilled workers were enlisted and were given technical supervision and guidance. In 1964, however, this programme was abandoned since the Government felt that the aim of reviving and diversifying the craft had been accomplished. The UP Handicrafts Export Corporation set up in 1971 deals directly with the intermediaries and not with the craftsmen. A study by the Giri institute states that:

> In the specific context of work organization pattern of the craft which is characterised by the hold of indigenous moneylenders, wholesalers and multiple tiers of middlemen over the workmen, it should be obvious as to who could have been at the back of such an argument.

Majority of the women fully realize their helplessness at the hands of the middle-men. They would like to become self-employed, but find it difficult because of their lack of capital, education and the inaccessibility of the market. A large majority wanted reopening of the *chicken* centres by the Government. 73 per cent wanted the Government to help in the supply of raw materials, 45 per cent wanted financial assistance and credit through the banks and 73 per cent wanted the Government to make marketing arrangements. Nearly 16 per cent wanted fixation of minimum wages. They were sceptical about cooperatives.

It should be noted that crafts like *chikan*, *kamdani* and *zardozi* were originally practised mainly by men. This pattern still continues in *zardozi* work. As wages and income from *chikan* work declined, this work has now become practically the monopoly of women. A similar process has developed in the *kamdani* industry also, where the condition of women is very similar to that of the *chikan* workers.

Tailoring and Ready-made Garments

This is a new industry, and little factual information is available regarding the details of employment. The tailoring profession in India has always been practised by men, and still remains so. In the initial stages of welfare activities among women, in the pre-independence period, it was believed that knowledge of tailoring would make women better housewives. For the same reason, home science training in schools also emphasized this training.

It was rarely practised by women for earning purposes. In recent years, welfare agencies and all women's polytechnics have been emphasizing this as the most important avenue for self-employment. Government, and other welfare agencies present sewing machines to army widows, destitute women and women rescued from prostitution as the most respectable method for rehabilitating them. Craft training centres run by Government or voluntary agencies all over the country organized tailoring classes for women.

There is no doubt that many women are now engaged in the manufacture of readymade garments. They are generally sold by welfare organizations or a few sympathetically disposed retail shops. The income is low and insecure. As an avenue of self-employment, tailoring has proved very difficult for women, because of their inability to command sure markets, and adequate capital for investment. We were informed in several places that the sewing machines gifted by the Government were often sold, because the women were unable to use them as a means of earning a livelihood.

With the growing importance of the readymade garments industry in recent years, however, some women are able to obtain wage-employment in this field. The reports that we have received point to low wages and exploitation of workers. In the metropolitan cities like Delhi and Mumbai a few women from upper middle class families are now entering this field as private entrepreneurs.

A study conducted by the Textile Labour Association, Ahmedabad, covering a thousand women who were occupied in sewing in their homes and were paid on a piece-rate basis, yields some information. About 65 per cent of the respondents were daughters or wives of industrial workers. Most of them (60 per cent) were young women, below 25, and 13 per cent were even below 15. Majority of them were school dropouts (76 per cent) mainly due to economic reasons. Employment Exchanges are of no help to such women in getting employment, 57 per cent of them had to rely on their own efforts to procure work. Mostly they get work from contractors or shop-keepers dealing with readymade garments. Untrained women usually stitch re⁻dymade garments after cutting is done by a professional man. Lack of skill and ignorance about availability of work results in exploitation of the highest degree. Wage rate are generally very low and vary widely. The majority (86 per cent) were earning below Rs 50 per month.

Sweepers and Scavengers

While Government and municipalities are the most regular employers of sweeper women, many industries employ women under contract system and they are employed in large numbers in private capacity as domestic workers. The local bodies maintain waiting lists of sweepers who work as substitute workers in temporary capacity as road sweepers, drain and latrine cleaners. The study group of the National Commission on Labour noted that there is a growing trend among municipal bodies to discourage the recruitment of women in view of the liabilities involved in their employment in the shape of maternity benefits and other conditions of work. They are governed by the Minimum Wages Act. There is no uniformity in the wages of employees in different local bodies and complaints about irregular payment of wages, deductions and irregularity in disbursement of salaries also exist on a large scale. The hours of work also vary from one local body to another.

A study of women sweepers in seven small towns in Punjab indicates that they are severely exploited by most of the local bodies (Dang, Satya pal, 1974). They are mostly given part-time jobs, without weekly rest, maternity leave or paid holidays, uniforms or house rent allowance. On an average they get a monthly wage of Rs 80. While women sweepers constitute a substantial proportion of municipal workers, their wages and working conditions vary from one municipality to another. The study suggests enactments of a suitable legislation to regulate the conditions of work to bring them on a par with men part-time sweepers. They suffer from social disabilities and their problems are further aggravated by poverty and illiteracy.

A study undertaken by the 1961 Census in two towns of northern India found that scavengers and sweepers in private households were mainly women, since men from the families of the traditional sweeper castes have begun to take up jobs as labourers or as employees in the tertiary sector, specially in the urban areas. The study noted that male members of the families who have taken to other occupations continue to allow their women to work as scavengers.

Groups of women sweepers whom we met in Madhya Pradesh and Rajasthan also complained that local bodies discriminated against women by using them mostly as substitute, temporary or contract workers. Among the whole group of thirty in Madhya Pradesh, only four had become permanent.

A special problem that effects these women is that with the gradual introduction of modern sanitation in urban areas the demand for their services is on the decline. In our opinion, the plight of these women require close investigation and alternative avenues of employment. This is particularly important because being Scheduled Caste and illiterate their chances of finding such employment on their own are severely limited.

Domestic Servants

Domestic service, for cooking, cleaning, sweeping, washing and looking after children is a major avenue for wage employment of women, particularly in the urban areas. Considering the large numbers in this occupation, it is unfortunate that no effort has so far been made to collect data on their numbers, wages and conditions of work. They are unprotected by any law or regulations and even the modicum of protection that the Minimum Wages Act provides, is not applicable to this group. Though wages for such services have increased to a certain extent in recent years, particularly in large cities, they are still very low, considering the sharp rise in cost of living. Service is insecure and the possibilities of exploitation is high. Full-time workers may sometimes be provided with accommodation and food, though the accommodation is generally inadequate. The pattern, however, is not uniform.

There are also no limits on their hours of work. Part-time

workers generally get no accommodation or food, and their employment is subject to much greater insecurity. Their basic needs are hardly met by their meagre income. In order to bridge their consumption gap, it is common for these women to work for several families. In total their working hours often exceed 12 hours a day.

We met groups of these women in Calcutta, living in the slums. Most of them were sole-supporting mothers, who would carry on their work in several houses only with the help of young daughters. The latter have to start this work from the time they are 8-9 years old. Younger children are left by themselves near the homes. In one slum we found that the children were left tied to a tree.

Babies in arms are often carried to work. Older boys are sent to school, though due to lack of supervision there is no guarantee of their attendance. Malnutrition is high in such families, and both adults and children are exposed to all the evils of slum-living, lack of proper sanitation, pollution and congestion. One teenager we met was working in several houses to support an unemployed father, a sick mother and three young children. The normal income from one household ranges from Rs 20 to Rs 40 per month, depending on the nature of the work. The fortunate few who can obtain and maintain work in four or five households, may earn an average of Rs 150 to Rs 200 by working over 12 hours a day.

One odd feature of this group in Calcutta is that many of them are wives of share croppers, whose husbands stay behind in the village. The normal pattern in other parts of the country, is for the family to remain in the village, while the man seeks work outside.

A comprehensive investigation of this group of workers is an imperative necessity, with provision of at least the basic services for the protection and welfare of their children.

Women in Petty Trades

Petty trades like food and food products, home crafts , paper bags, *agarbattis*, making packets of incense or tobacco are all low productive occupations, returns from which are generally far below the level of subsistence. Economic pressures are pushing rural women workers and women in urban slums to seek ways to earn a livelihood.

A large group of widows in Varanasi whom we met were all engaged in such trades. Their earnings averaged between Rs 15 and Rs 20 per month. In Karnataka, we found earning 50 paise for 1,000 *agarbattis*, when they work on premises of the employer. When such work was taken home, the earnings were 40 paise per thousand. Employers justified this difference by blaming the workers for pilfering the material. Since the material is weighed on both the occasions, namely before and after production, this argument can only be described as an excuse for exploitation. A UN report on "Inter-Regional Meeting of Experts on the Integration of Women in Development" states that:

> Among these women in petty trades, crafts and personal services, the worst cases of poverty and malnutrition were to be found. A large proportion of the persons occupied in low productivity occupations were women, many of whom were the sole supporters of their families and lived in urban slums. Nearly all such women were illiterate and without any vocational training. As modern industries in most developing countries recruited mainly male workers, these women were forced to support themselves and their families on work of such low productivity that malnutrition and high child mortality became a characteristic of such families.

Casual Workers/Daily Wage Earners

Daily wage earners are found in all types of unskilled jobs in both organized and unorganized sectors with varying degrees of protection, depending on the type of industry and nature of the task. In mines, plantations, construction, stone quarries and seasonal industries employment of such labour is a common feature. While the casual workers directly employed by the larger establishments, do come under the purview of some labour enactments like wages and hours of work, the daily wage earners in unorganized industries do not get the benefit of even minimum wages and enjoy exceedingly little protection.

The casual workers are employed to fill vacancies of permanent workers and during occasional pressure of work. It is significant that the majority of women employed in mines are casual workers engaged in wagon loading or earth-removing operations whose employment is neither continuous nor regular. They are pressed into service to complete loading work within a stipulated period. The control and supervision exercised by the management is nominal. In the jute industry a large number of women work as *'budlis'*, or substitute workers. Such labour is continually employed to circumvent the provision of laws which confer certain benefits on permanent workers, or to deliberately restrict the scope for regular employment by causing artificial breaks in their service. They are deprived of the maternity benefits because the Maternity Benefits Act stipulates employment for a continuous period (160 days for factories and mines and 150 days for plantations) for eligibility. They earned 150 days leave with wages and sickness benefits. The Factories Act limits such benefits only to workers who have completed 240 days of service, and the Mines Act to those who complete one calendar year of service. The National Commission on Labour noted that all such stipulations are an invitation to an employer to arbitrarily terminate the workers' service before they complete the prescribed period to deprive them of these benefits.

Very little is known about nomadic and daily wage labourers, load carriers carrying raw material to the markets and factories or those working in village industries. A significantly large number of such labourers are living below the poverty line. They are mostly concentrated in rural and backward areas and urban slums.

In the industrial city of Ahmedabad there are about 1000 women hand-cart pullers. A survey of these women in 1973 revealed that 70 per cent of them were in the age group of 20 to 40 years. Majority of them live in huts (71 per cent) or in *pákka kholis* (14 per cent), 12 per cent of them were found to be living on footpaths and only 3 per cent of them had rooms provided by the Housing Board, 93 per cent of these women were illiterate. One woman had completed high school, which is exceptional.

It is a family vocation as in 73 per cent cases men were also cart-pullers. In 16 per cent cases, the husbands were engaged in small trades. Majority of the families are rural migrants from Rajasthan, Gujarat and Maharashtra. 88 per cent of the women work from 9 am to 7 pm and 12 per cent have no fixed time. 85 per cent take their children along with them. Their average daily income is below Rs 3 for 49 per cent , between Rs 4 and Rs 8 for 40 per cent, and Rs 9 and above for 11 per cent. Meagre income and large-scale indebtedness are common. 40 per cent of the women were casual labourers relying for work entirely upon the *mukaddam*, who claims a regular daily tax between Rs 2 to Rs 3.50.

Self-Employment

In the period before the rise of modern markets and commercialization of the economy, most traditional occupations open to women generally on the basis of their castes, could be described as self-employment. Spinning, weaving, fish curing, basket making, midwifery, barbering, etc. can be mentioned as illustrations. Commercialization, the rise of immediate producers, who could organize both production and marketing on a large scale with the aid of capital, and the introduction of wage labour, gradually eliminated many of these avenues for employment of women. The recent increase in unemployment has led to a realization of the need to promote self-employment in all areas and various programmes have been undertaken by the Government to promote self-employment, through training and credit assistance. Before discussing the possibilities for promoting more self-employment among women, we examine some of the existing occupations in which they find some opportunities.

Weaving

According to the Census of 1961 the handloom/powerloom industry provided employment to about 1.4 million workers. It forms an important section of household industries and handicrafts. The National Commission on Labour found a large proportion of workers in this industry to be family workers. The cooperative form of organization which extends to areas of small enterprises is a more recent development. A third of the total number of handlooms is found in Andhra Pradesh and Tamil Nadu. This mainly rural industry does not require much capital and the technology has remained mostly at the simple stage. The introduction of power-looms in some areas, has however, precipitated a lot of changes in the status and income of producers, making a few wealthy and capable of setting themselves up as entrepreneurs, reducing others to the level of wage labour.

In the less developed regions, particularly the north-eastern hill areas, weaving still remains the monopoly of women. Traditionally this was only for home consumption, and not for commercial purposes. Such weaving is still done, even by educated and urbanized women in Nagaland, Manipur and some parts of Assam. Some attempt for commercial production has developed in recent years, and where this is definitely linked to a system of marketing, the women develop considerable economic independence.

An excellent example of this is Manipur, where women's right to market their own products has been institutionalized for a considerable period. The women's market in Imphal, where the sellers are all women, selling various items of dress, furnishing and food products, produced by themselves and others, is only a larger replica of similar markets in the interior of Manipur. Ownership of a stall in the market is a prestigious occupation and till very recently, former Ranis of the State used to join other women in selling their goods in the women's market. The stalls are passed on from generation to generation, from mother-in-law to the daughter-in-law. In the absence of the latter, or her reluctance to accept the responsibility, it is offered to a niece-in-law on the husband's side, but not to the daughter. Some of the stall-keepers acquire the place by paying rent to the actual owners, who are fairly well-to-do. The tradition is so strong that an attempt by the Municipality to evict them provoked an organized protest from the women. The Municipality was compelled to abandon the idea. While the Imphal women, because of better market prospects both in the city and outside the State, earn more, rural women are at a disadvantage.

We were informed that some women who could market their own products could earn an average income of about Rs 400 per month from weaving. When they worked for others, however, this came down to between Rs 50 and Rs 80. Women complained of the rising prices of yarn, and demanded that the State Government should take over the yarn-trade, to prevent black-marketing. The Government's efforts to market these handloom products outside the State has stimulated this industry, but the emergence of unscrupulous intermediaries between the producers who are all women, and markets outside the State may affect the women's share of profits in the long run.

The opposite of the Manipur situation exists in the silk-weaving industry in Varanasi, another traditional occupation. There the women only reel the silk and silver yarn, but cannot touch the looms, which are operated by men only. Training in the craft for men and women begins from childhood. Though self-employed, these families are fully dependent on the intermediaries (Mahajans) who buy their products, sometimes provide the initial capital to buy the yarn and often provide loans to meet the gap in minimum consumption. The women have neither control nor a separate share of earnings, since the marketing is done by the men. A similar practice prevails in the silk-weaving industry in Kanjeevaram (Tamil Nadu) and Karnataka.

The women weavers of Assam, because they cannot market their products directly, suffer from the exploitation of intermediaries on whom they have to depend for both supply of raw materials and marketing.

Retail Trade

One of the traditional avenues of income for women was the retail trade, selling family products both agricultural and non-agricultural in daily or weekly markets. They continue to do so, and the woman vendor selling vegetables, fish gram, spices, utensils, etc., is a common sight in village markets as well as in urban areas throughout the country. In big cities, it is a common practice for women to hawk vegetables and fruits in residential areas. Many of them started with their own market gardens, but have now become dependent on buying the products from the wholesale market with a narrow margin of profits for themselves. The increasing distance of the markets from the place of production, and the need for big investment in acquiring and transporting large quantities of products inevitably leads to the exclusion of the women from their original role in the retail trade. In the coastal areas of Orissa, Goa and Tamil Nadu, the fish brought in by the men used to be sold by women. Now only a handful of them are seen actually retailing the family's catch. The main catch is captured by contractors or Government fisheries agents and transported to the bigger markets.

Most retailing done by women in urban areas is now for a very narrow margin, between wholesale and retail prices. For women living close to the cities, however, this is still an accepted avenue of income. Cities like Calcutta and Mumbai receive a daily influx of hundreds of women vendors from nearby villages, selling a variety of food products.

Food Processing

During the last decades, welfare workers and organizations, concerned by the economic hardship of women have made considerable efforts to develop self-employment in production of pickles, *papads* (a thin crisp cake which is made of many kindds of pulse, sago, potato, etc.) and various other food products. These organizations, and some individuals are found in most towns, trying to market these products by informal methods, like house to house visit or through exhibitions and fairs. The main difficulty experienced by these women is in ensuring steady and profitable sale of their products. Lack of capital prevents production on a scale sufficient to reduce costs, and their inability to market the products adequately makes returns from this occupation both meagre and uncertain.

We met several groups of women in Kerala, Bihar and other States who had started bottling pickles, jams and making variety of *papads*, *dalmot*, packets of ground spice, etc. Most of them regretted that their ventures generally face difficulties through shortage of capital and inability to market their products. We heard of several efforts which had collapsed from these difficulties. Even in urban areas these ventures face difficulties in marketing their products and are generally reduced to dependence on occasional sales and exhibitions and a limited regular clientele among friends and associates of the organizers. In villages the marketing difficulty becomes almost unsurmountable.

A few of these ventures, when backed by a well-knit organization have proved fairly successful in ensuring a modest income for the women. Amongst these we may mention the Jyoti Sangh in Ahmedabad, which we visited, the Bhagini Mandals in some towns in Maharashtra, and the All-Bengal Women's Union in Calcutta. The latter's success in sale of cooked food has enabled it to open a restaurant, for direct marketing of their products.

Problems of Self-employment

The approach to the Fifth Plan envisages expansion of self-employment in village and small industries, retail trade and services. The Committee's investigation has revealed that the most important constraints on women entrepreneurs are (a) non-availability of capital which is enhanced by the reluctance of credit institutions to advance loans for their ventures; and (b) inadequate marketing arrangements.

Without the knowledge of modern marketing methods, forward linkages with potential markets in urban areas and resources as well as techniques for sales promotion, women's efforts at self-employment or entrepreneurship are bound to languish unless they are taken in hand by some organizations with credit resources as well as techniques to organize production and marketing. A successful example of this kind is the organization of self-employed women who are being assisted by Ahmedabad Mazdoor Mahajan. The Committee on Unemployment has suggested that the Small Industries Corporations in different States should play an active role in the display and marketing of goods of small-scale units. The other suggestions are setting up of trade centres and retail outlets at important places by organizations of small entrepreneurs.

According to the Ministry of Industrial Development, assistance in the way of credit and accommodation facilities have been given to some women entrepreneurs. Their number so far is negligible. In Delhi, the number of such self-employed women is as follows:

Industry	*Number of Women*
Electronics	2
Chemicals	11
Garment making	15

Illiteracy and lack of training opportunities in different aspects of production and marketing is the biggest handicap in the way of women assuming a larger role in this field. In traditional occupations like basket-making, weaving or wood work it has become increasingly difficult for individual producers to market their goods. We had, at an earlier stage, suggested to the Government the development of training-cum-production centres in small-scale cottage type industries in both rural and urban areas for the production of processed food, ready-made garments, soap and candles, home utensils, educational equipments, toys, leather goods and other products. Such centres need to be developed on the basis of a rational programme of assistance related to the resource and market potential of the environment.

We had particularly stressed that such centres should not be designed with an urban middle class bias but should generate employment among women of low income groups in both urban and rural areas, who have suffered most because of the emergence and growth of organized industry and modern complex marketing. In our view, any programme for generating self-employment among women has to be based on an integrated network of training, production and marketing.

The organization of such a network would require a large number of educated women at all levels with information and knowledge of the changing pattern of demand for particular products and market mechanism. This calls for special attention from all agencies concerned with employment generation. Unless special attention is given to the particular problems of women, their existing handicaps, which get enhanced by the prejudices of assisting agencies will keep them out of the beneficial effects of existing programmes for generation of self-employment.

The Ministry of Industrial Development, in response to our suggestions had observed that no women candidates had been sponsored by the Small Industries Development Organizations for training in better techniques of production. While suggesting areas for training and employment opportunities for women, both the Ministry of Industrial Development and the Ministry of Labour displayed an urban bias since their list consisted of occupations like tailoring, embroidery, shorthand and typing, doll-making, pottery and novelty sales. These occupations, in our opinion, can provide opportunities for self-employment to a very small minority, only in the metropolitan cities and will not meet the employment needs of the large mass of women both in small towns and in rural areas.

It may be noted that the Report of the Inter-Regional Meeting of Experts on the Integration of Women in Development of the United Nations has also emphasised "the need to train women in all aspects of carrying on trade and small scale industry with particular reference to management, marketing, etc.". The Report also highlighted the problem of lack of access to credit and loan facilities suffered by most women in developing countries.

Four

Women in the Organized Sector

The organized sector in the Indian economy comprises of:

(a) all public sector establishments, i.e., all services under the Central, State and Local Governments and occupations in Public Undertakings in the field of industry, credit financing, public utilities, etc., and

(b) non-agricultural private sector establishments which employ 10 or more persons. This definition is important for two reasons. The Directorate General of Employment and Training, Ministry of Labour, collects detailed data regarding employment from all establishments in the organized sector, and hence data regarding this sector is much more detailed than the unorganized sector. Secondly, this sector is governed by certain laws and regulations relating to industries, services and other occupations. These provide a framework of requirements, procedures and conditions which ensure a degree of legal protection to workers in these establishments.

While the size of the organized sector has been growing steadily over the last few decades, the proportion of women employed in this sector formed only 6 per cent of the total women workers in the country in 1971, 2.7 per cent being in industry and 3.3 per cent in the tertiary sector. The changing trends in women's participation in this sector is indicated in Table 4.1. In terms of absolute numbers, women's employment in this sector has increased from 1.37 million in 1962 to 2.14 million in 1973, i.e., an increase of 56.2 per cent. The increase in the total employment during the same period was by 49.6 per cent. While the increase in the number of women has been generally somewhat faster than the total increase (with occasional fluctuations in the growth rate) their proportion in the total employment has remained practically constant at 11 per cent during this decade.

TAELE - 4.1
EMPLOYMENT OF WOMEN IN ORGANIZED SECTOR

Period	*Total*	*Women*	*% of columns*
	(figures in lakhs)		
March 1962	125.8 (+4.0)	13.7	10.8
March 1963	134.1 (+6.5)	14.9 (+8.7)	11.1
March 1964	142.3 (+6.1)	15.2 (+2.0)	10.6
March 1965	150.0 (+5.4)	16.8 (+10.5)	11.2
March 1966	154.6 (+3.1)	17.4 (+3.5)	11.2
March 1969	166.3 (+7.5)	18.5 (+0.9)	11.1
March 1970	170.4 (+2.4)	18.9 (+2.2)	11.1
March 1971	174.9 (+2.6)	19.2 (+1.5)	10.9
March 1972	179.8 (+2.2)	20.2 (+5.2)	11.2
March 1973	188.2 (+4.6)	21.4 (+5.6)	11.3

Note: Figures in parenthesis indicate growth rate.
Source: D.G.E. & T.

It should be noted that while services under Government had been governed by detailed regulations for a long time, the regulation of employment in the private sector began relatively later. Prior to independence, employment in the Government of public sector consisted mainly in the services and the number of women in these was negligible. The Constitution of independent India, however, guaranteed equality of opportunity and non-discrimination on grounds of sex. This changed the situation radically and enabled women to seek employment in the public sector.

The impact of this has influenced the role and opportunities for participation of women in the organized sector considerably. The proportion of women workers in public and private employment has been changing over the years as Table 4.2 indicates.

TABLE - 4.2
DISTRIBUTION OF WOMEN EMPLOYEES IN PUBLIC AND PRIVATE SECTORS

(Figures in lakhs)

Year	*Total*	*Public*	*Private*
1962	13.7	4.8 (35.0%)	8.9 (65.0%)
1963	14.9	5.5 (37.0%)	9.4 (63.0%)
1964	15.2	5.8 (38.2%)	9.4 (61.8%)
1965	16.8	6.4 (38.1%)	10.4 (61.9%)
1966	17.4	7.2 (41.4%)	10.3 (58.6%)
1967	18.2	7.2 (39.6%)	11.00 (60.4%)
1968	18.3	7.5 (40.7%)	10.8 (59.3%)
1969	18.4	7.7 (41.8%)	10.7 (58.2%)
1970	18.9	8.1 (42.8%)	10.8 (57.2%)
1971	19.3	8.6 (44.6%)	10.7 (55.4%)
1972	20.3	9.2 (45.3%)	11.1 (54.7%)
1973	21.4	10.1 (47.2%)	11.3 (52.8%)

Note: Figures in parenthesis indicate percentage of the total employees.
Source: D.G.E.&T.

While the number of women employed in the public sector increased by 110.4 per cent between 1962 and 1973, the increase in the private sector has been only 26.9 per cent. The proportion of women in the public sector has thus gone up from 35 per cent to 47.2 per cent of the total number of women employed in the organized sector. The share of the private sector has, however, gone down from 65 per cent to 52.8 per cent of the total. This indicates the growing importance of the public sector in the employment of women. The relatively slower increase of women's employment in the private sector, is however, a cause of some concern, and merits closer examination.

Table 4.3 indicates that the State Governments and local bodies provide bulk of the employment of women in the public sector. Next in importance are quasi-government organizations. This group consists of public undertakings in the sphere of industry, finance and public utilities, and various specialized agencies established by Government for development and research. It should be noted that the emergence of this group in the public sector is mostly a post-independence development.

Considering that, the substantial number of women employed in these bodies, and the rapid increase in their numbers during recent years is a significant trend. A substantial share of these bodies is in industry, where the general trend in women's employment which we discuss later, is rather adverse. The position in the Central Government also does not appear to be very satisfactory.

TABLE - 4.3
WOMEN EMPLOYEES IN THE ORGANIZED SECTOR ETC. 1971 TO 1973 COVERED BY THE EMPLOYMENT MARKET INFORMATION PROGRAMME OF THE D.G.E. & T.

Branch of the Public Sector	*No. of Women Employees at the end of March*			*Percentage Change*		
	1971	*1972**	*1973**	*1971/70*	*1972/71*	*1973/72*
Central Government	81.6	78.5	84.7	7.1	4.0	7.9
State Government	352.1	376.8	422.8	7.2	5.3	12.2
Quasi Government	84.4	104.4	135.7	12.9	23.5	30.1
Local Bodies	344.2	358.8	362.0	2.9	3.9	1.1
Total Public Sector	862.3	917.9	1005.2	5.9	5.6	9.5
Private Sector	1067.5	1105.3	1129.7	-1.3	3.5	2.2
Grand Total	1929.8	2023.2	2134.9	1.8	4.4	5.5

* Including Jammu & Kashmir covers all establishment in the public sector and non-agricultural establishments in the private sector, employing 10 to 24 workers.
Percentage change 1972/71 has been worked out after excluding Jammu & Kashmir figures from 1972.

Source: D.G.E. & T.

While the ratio of women to men employees in the public sector has shown a steady increase, it still remains below 10 per hundred men. In the private sector, where the ratio was much higher in the previous period, it has registered a decline during the years 1967-71. There is a slight improvement since 1972, but the ratio still remains below the '62 position. While total employment in private sector has been fluctuating during this period, the women's share has declined or remained constant. In the public sector, the steady increase in total employment is reflected in the employment of women, though the ratio has not improved appreciably. The overall share of women's employment in this sector, in relation to men, presents a poor picture. (Table 4.4)

For purposes of detailed analysis we have divided the organized sector into two parts according to the differences in the nature of the regulations and occupational requirements:

(a) Industry; and
(b) Services and Professions.

TABLE - 4.4
TRENDS IN EMPLOYMENT IN PUBLIC AND PRIVATE SECTORS — SEXWISE

(Figures in lakhs)

Year	*Public Sector*				*Private Sector*			
	Total	*Males*	*Fe-males*	*No. of Females per 100 Males*	*Total*	*Males*	*Fe-males*	*No. of Females per 100 Males*
1962	74.2 (59%)	69.4	4.8	6.9	51.6 (41%)	42.7	8.9	20.8
1963	79.5 (59.3%)	74.0	5.5	7.4	54.6 (40.7%)	45.2	9.4	20.8
1964	84.5 (59.4%)	78.7	5.8	7.3	57.8 (40.6%)	48.4	9.4	19.8
1965	89.6 (59.7%)	83.2	6.4	7.6	60.4 (40.3%)	50.0	10.4	20.8
1966	93.6 (60.5%)	86.4	7.2	8.3	61.0 (39.5%)	50.7	10.3	20.3
1967	96.3 (59.1%)	89.1	7.2	8.1	66.8 (40.9%)	55.8	11.0	19.7
1968	98.0 (60.0%)	90.5	7.5	8.2	65.3 (39.3%)	54.5	10.8	19.8
1969	100.9 (60.7%)	93.2	7.7	8.2	65.3 (39.3%)	54.6	10.7	19.6
1970	103.5 (60.7%)	95.4	8.1	8.4	66.9 (39.3%)	56.1	10.8	19.2
1971	107.1 (61.4%)	98.5	8.6	8.7	67.4 (38.6%)	56.7	10.7	18.8
1972	112.1 (62.3%)	103.0	9.1	8.8	67.7 (37.7%)	56.6	11.1	19.6
1973	122.7 (65.1%)	112.6	10.1	8.9	65.9 (34.9%)	54.6	11.3	20.6

Note: Figures in parenthesis indicate total employees.
Source: D.G.E. & T.

Industry

The first four Five-Year Plans as well as the Industrial Policy Resolution (1956) of the Government of India emphasized the need to accelerate the rate of economic growth by speeding up industrialization. "Employment was not considered an objective in itself: it was expected that the expansion of the industrial base would provide direct as well as indirect employment opportunities through the expansion of all sectors of economy".

The three main sources of employment in organized industry are factories, mines and plantations. The following tables indicate the position of women in these three groups. In the factories group (Table 4.5), the number of women employed rose steadily up to 1964, since then it has been declining with minor fluctuations. While total employment in factories has been generally increasing, though the rate of increase has slowed down in recent years, the number of women has not recovered from the position of 1964, though it has fluctuated considerably between 1965 and 1971.

The percentage of women to total employees, however, presents a very unhappy trend. Between 1951 and 1971 the women's share of total employment in factories declined from 11.43 per cent to 9.1 per cent, i.e., a decline of 20.37 per cent.

Table 4.21 indicates the trend of women's employment in the mining industry. The total employment of women in mines has declined from 1.09 lakh to .75 lakh whereas total employment in mines has increased from 5.49 lakh to 6.30 lakh. The women's share of employment in mines has declined from 20.1 per cent to 11.9 per cent, i.e., a decline of 47.4 per cent. The heaviest decline has been in coal mines from .55 lakh to .20 lakh. While the total employment in coal mines increased from 3.52 lakh to 3.82 lakh, the decline in the women's share is by 66.8 per cent. In iron-ore total employment increased from .20 lakh to .52 lakh. The number of women has increased from .07 lakh to .12 lakh. Their relative share of employment in iron ore mines has, however, declined by 36.2 per cent. In mica both total employment as well as women's employment has registered a steady and sharp decline. The women's share, however, has declined still faster by 34 per cent. In the manganese mines though the number of women has halved during these 20 years their relative share has not changed so much —declining from 43.9 per cent to 40.1 per cent, i.e., by 8.65 per cent. In all other mines total employment has increased from .69 lakh to 1.53 lakh. The number of women increased from .15 lakh to .33 lakh in 1966, but has been declining since then. Their relative share has changed from 21.8 per cent to 18.8 per cent — a decrease of over 13.7 per cent.

TABLE - 4.5
EMPLOYMENT OF WOMEN IN FACTORIES

Year	*Total Employees (1000)*	*No. of Women Employees (1000)*	*Percentage of Women to Total Employees*
1951	25,365.0	290.0	11.43
1955	2,690.4	295.1	10.96
1958	3,102.2	343.9	11.08
1960	3,367.8	367.3	10.91
1961	3,497.0	372.3	10.65
1962	3,648.6	394.1	10.80
1963	3,860.0	400.4	10.37
1964	4,024.0	409.1	10.16
1965	4,118.0	394.5	9.57
1966	4,069.0	364.7	9.96
1967	4,071.0	394.6	9.5
1968	4,067.0	346.1	9.0
1969	4,137.0	382.0	9.0
1970	4,264.0	394.0	9.0
1971	4,285.0	392.5	9.1

Source: Indian Labour Statistics and National Commission on Labour Report.

TABLE - 4.6
EMPLOYMENT OF WOMEN IN MINES

(Figures in Thousands)

Mines		*1951*	*1956*	*1961*	*1966*	*1968*	*1969*	*1970*	*1971*
Coal	T	352.0	352.4	411.3	425.5	395.4	396.4	391.5	382.2
	W	55.2	46.0	38.1	30.7	24.7	23.0	21.5	20.1
		(15.7)	(13.0)	(17.0)	(7.2)	(6.2)	(5.8)	(5.5)	(5.2)
Iron	T	20.2	37.3	54.5	60.3	52.2	48.6	51.8	52.8
Ore	W	7.7	10.7	15.3	15.7	13.0	11.4	12.4	12.9
		(38.2)	(28.8)	(28.8)	(25.9)	(24.9)	(23.4)	(23.9)	(24.4)
Mica	T	52.2	34.0	29.6	19.8	16.9	16.0	13.9	12.1
	W	7.2	2.7	2.4	1.2	1.7	1.5	1.3	1.1
		(13.8)	(7.8)	(8.1)	(6.1)	(10.1)	(9.4)	(9.3)	(9.1)
Man-	T	55.5	110.0	46.9	47.0	37.2	31.0	29.3	30.4
ganese	W	24.4	44.3	17.7	19.1	15.0	12.3	11.6	12.2
		(43.9)	(40.3)	(37.7)	(40.6)	(40.3)	(39.6)	(39.6)	(40.1)
Others	T	69.1	94.9	128.7	146.7	142.6	146.5	151.7	153.0
	W	15.1	22.0	32.8	33.9	29.9	29.9	30.4	28.9
		(21.8)	(22.1)	(25.5)	(22.9)	(20.9)	(20.3)	(20.0)	(18.8)
Total	T	549.0	628.6	671.0	699.3	644.3	638.5	638.2	630.7
	W	109.6	125.8	106.3	100.7	84.3	78.0	77.2	75.2
		(20.1)	(20.0)	(15.8)	(14.4)	(13.1)	(12.2)	(12.1)	(11.9)

T = Total average daily employment
W = Women's employment
Source: Indian Labour Statistics.

It is unfortunate that no official agency maintains comprehensive data for plantations from which a trend analysis of employment over the years could be made for the industry as a whole. Data is maintained for separate regions and separate products. Table 4.7 and 4.8 present the trend of employment in the three major plantation industries. In coffee, the number of women workers in the total labour force increased from 40.4 per cent in 1951 to 45.3 per cent in 1961 and has declined to 44 per cent in 1970. The number of women workers in coffee plantation in 1970 was 1.64 lakh. In rubber plantations their number increased from 22.1 per cent in 1951 to 35 per cent in 1970. The total number of women in that year was 8.9 lakh.

TABLE - 4.7
PERCENTAGE OF WOMEN WORKERS TO TOTAL LABOUR FORCE IN COFFEE AND RUBBER PLANTATIONS

Year	*Coffee*	*Rubber*
1951	40.4	22.1
1956	42.9	24.5
1960	38.6	22.1
1961	45.3	21.4
1970	44.0	35.0
	(1,64,000.0)	(99,000.0)

Source: *Women in Employment*, p. 15.
For 1970 D.G. E. & T.

Among all plantations tea requires the maximum amount of female labour. In the tea estates in Assam which account for the major share of production of tea, the number of women workers increased from 2.55 lakh in 1954 to 2.70 lakh in 1963, their share of total employment increasing from 46.1 per cent to 49.2 per cent during the same years. In tea estates in south India women workers represented 47.2 per cent of the total labour force in 1951 and 49 per cent in 1961.

Table 4.8(B) indicates the position of women in the tea industry as a whole in 1961 and 1970. In absolute numbers, there is an increase from 3.68 lakh to 3.76 lakh. Their percentage has increased from 44 per cent to 47 per cent. During the same years total employment in these plantations has declined from 8.22 lakh to 7.6 lakh. Plantations thus represent the only sector where women's employment has remained practically constant. The reason lies in the labour intensive nature of this industry and the accepted special aptitude of women for particular jobs like plucking. The other two sectors present a grim picture of declining numbers and proportions.

TABLE - 4.8
(A) WOMEN WORKERS IN TEA PLANTATIONS

Year	*Assam*			*Year*	*South India*
	Total	*Women*	*%age*		*%age*
1954	553,000	255,000	46.1	1951	47.2
1959	571,000	274,000	48.0	1956	49.9
1963	551,000	271,000	49.2	1959	49.4
				1961	49.1

Source: Women in Employment

(B) ALL INDIA

Year	*Total*	*Women*	*%age*
1961	822,000	368,000	44.7
1970	756,000	376,000	47.0

Source: Tea Board, Statistical Division.

The trend towards decline or stagnation in the number and proportion of women employed in industries is generally attributed to the following cases:

(i) Impact of labour laws that aim to protect health and welfare of women workers;
(ii) Impact of policies aiming at equalization of wages between men and women; and
(iii) Structural changes in industry through rationalization and modernization which leads to a general decline in employment.

Labour Laws

The beginning of legislative attempt to regulate relations between employers and labour in private industries began in the nineteenth century, but these attempts have been described as not true 'labour legislation' but at best 'legislation expressive of a foreign Government's concern with the maintenance of order and security.' The main objective of these laws was to restrict labourers from leaving their jobs, by imposing penal consequences for breaches of contract.

The use of sweated and cheap Indian labour in factories, a large proportion of whom consisted of women and children, posed serious threats to the competitive production cost of the British textile industry, and under their pressure, the Factories Act of 1881 and 1891 placed limitations on employment and working hours of women and children. The Act of 1911 limited a working day in textile factories to 12 hours.

A change of direction in the policy of regulating and improving employment and working conditions in industry began with the movement for organization of labour which received an impetus and support with the establishment of the International Labour Organization in 1919. The 1920's saw the enactment of a series of labour laws, namely, the Indian Factories Act, 1922, the Indian Mines Act 1923, the Indian Worksmen Compensation Act 1923, the Indian Trade Union Act 1926 and the Trade Dispute Act 1929.

The worldwide publicity given to labour conditions by the ILO in different countries provided a forum for discussing labour problems and aroused a degree of awareness regarding labour questions in the country. The Royal Commission on Labour (Whitely Commission) appointed in 1929 to examine the problems of workers in factories, plantations and other places recommended a number of measures which led to the enactment of further laws. Until, 1946, the Whitley Commission's recommendations provided the framework of most labour legislations. Out of 24 labour enactments passed by the Central and Provincial legislatures during the years 1932-37, 19 were based on the Commission's suggestions. These recommendations had taken into consideration the various Conventions of the ILO in this regard.

With the emergence of provincial autonomy, the popular Ministries which came into power in 1937 undertook a series of labour legislation. Attempts to consolidate and coordinate these scattered efforts had to be undertaken by the Central Government. Immediately prior to Independence, the Interim National Government drew up a 17-point Five-Year Programme for Labour. The Principles underlying this programme were incorporated in the Constitution under the Directive Principles of State Policy.

When labour legislation began in India, women constituted a sizeable proportion of workers in industry. Jute, textiles, mines, plantations were the predominant industries in the modern sector, and each of them employed a substantial number of women. The conditions of women workers, therefore, called for special attention. The ILO's special concern for protection of women workers, indicated in its various Conventions, which were supported by Indian labour representatives, and were reflected in the Indian Labour Laws.

The Directive Principles of State Policy of the Indian Constitution provide for special protection of women workers through Articles 39 and 42. Article 15(3) gives the necessary protection for such special provisions for women and children within the framework of Fundamental Rights. Article 46, which directs the State to promote with special care the educational and economic interests of the weaker sections of the people's is also regarded as a directive to improve employment opportunities and conditions of women workers'.

In line with these directives, special clauses in various labour laws provide for the protection and welfare of women workers in factories, mines, plantations and shops, and commercial establishments. These protections mainly extend to the following areas:

Regulating of Employment to Dangerous Occupations/Operations

The Factories Act 1948 prohibited women's employment in any part of a factory in which a cotton opener is at work. They are not allowed to clean, lubricate or adjust heavy machinery while it is in motion. They are not allowed to handle excessively heavy weights. Both the Factories and the Mines Act 1952, authorise the appropriate Government to fix the minimum load that can be lifted, carried or moved by women. The State Government may also prohibit or restrict women's employment in any other operations which exposes them to a serious risk of bodily injury or disease. The Mines Act prohibits employment of women underground. The Central Government is authorised 'to prohibit, restrict or regulate the employment of women in any class of mines or particular kinds of labour which are accompanied by danger to the life, safety or health of women workers'.

Prohibition of Night Work

The Factories Act, the Plantations Labour Act 1951, the Mines Act and the Bidi and Cigar Workers (Conditions of Employment) Act 1966 prohibit employment of women between 7 pm and 6 am In the case of mines and factories, the Central and the State governments respectively are authorised to relax this restriction up to 10 pm. In the case of fish canning and fish-curing factories, the State Governments are empowered to permit the employment of women during night for a period not exceeding three years at a time, if it is considered essential to prevent any damage to raw material. In plantations also they can be employed during the prohibited period with permission from the State Governments. However, in both cases, the hours of work should not exceed the prescribed period.

Maternity Relief

By far the most valued and significant of the protective measures relating to women workers are those dealing with maternity leave and payment of maternity benefits. The clauses providing for the grant of maternity leave and the payment of cash benefits are included in all the above-mentioned Acts as well as in the separate laws in the States (Women in Employment: 26). In order to bring uniformity in scope, qualifying conditions and rates of benefits, the Maternity Benefit Act 1961, was passed which applies to factories, mines and plantations except those factories or establishments which are covered by the Employees State Insurance Scheme. With the enforcement of this Act the earlier Acts stand revoked.

Welfare

(i) Creches are to be provided under the relevant Acts for use of children of the working mothers in factories/plantations/industrial premises manufacturing bidis and cigars - employing more than 50 women workers. In the case of mines creches are to be provided even if a single woman is employed.

(ii) Separate latrines and urinals are to be provided under the relevant laws for women in every factory/mine/plantation.

It should be noted that the laws for maternity protection and prohibition of night and underground work are in line with the ILO Conventions No. 103, 89 and 45 which were ratified by the Government of India.

The National Commission on Labour had observed that legal prohibition of night and underground work and employment in hazardous occupations have obviously restricted women's employment. Employers mentioned to the Committee that the ban on night work has proved to be an obstacle to employment of women since the introduction of the multiple shift system in some organized industry, since the impossibility of rotating women between different shifts gives rise to some resentment among male workers.

There are two distinct points of view in this regard. A few persons whom we met, viz., employers, experts and the representatives of the INTUC were of the view that this provision was unduly restrictive. They feel that the permission to extend the period up to 10 pm should be available to all industries. This would enable their employment on two shifts and remove the present excuse for retrenching them whenever a multiple shift system was introduced.

The other point of view, expressed by other union representatives and some labour official and experts was against the removal of the restriction. In their opinion, the employers' plea was only an excuse, since operations in which women are engaged, particularly in the textile industry, are performed during the day.

In pursuance of a decision of the Industrial Committee on Jute in 1958, a Tripartite Committee set up in West Bengal to study the decline of women in employment, observed that limitation on the load that could be carried by women was the main reason for the decline. The jute industry, which was one of the largest employers of women has been most affected by this measure. According to the present rule, women can lift a maximum weight of 65 lbs, whereas jute rolls weigh 80 to 100 lbs. The total number of labourers employed by jute mills in 1944 was 2,89,000 out of which 38,957 were women, roughly constituting almost 14 per cent of the total labour force. In 1952, i.e., 4 years after the passing of the Factories Act, the total employees in the jute industry numbered 2,92,000, out of which 32,900 (11.2 per cent) were women.

By 1962 the total employees in this industry numbered 2.4 lakh of which only 9,400 were women (3.9 per cent). In 1972 there were only 6,642 women left in the whole jute industry and these are being gradually eliminated through a process of natural wastage. One jute mill in Andhra Pradesh visited by the Committee had over 500 women workers as late as 1960. In 1973 we found only 74 engaged in hand sewing, most of whom were elderly women. Their services were being retained because they were permanent workers. In another mill in West Bengal the management was clearly opposed to any further recruitment of women and observed that their services could only be utilized in sweeping, baling and hand sewing.

Coal mines employ the largest number of women. In the past they were engaged in both underground and surface work. In 1919 women formed 38.1 per cent of the colliery labour force and for every 10 men employed underground, there were 7 women for the same job. In 1929 Government of India ordered a gradual reduction in the number of women working underground. A total ban was promulgated in 1939. The number of women consequently dropped to 11.4 per cent. The ban was lifted during the Second World War because of the need to increase production, but was reimposed in 1946. While this ban eliminated underground women workers, the subsequent decline of women in the coal mines is the result of introduction of new methods of surface screening and coal handling. In 1947 women constituted about 21 per cent of the colliery labour force. By 1951 this had come down to 16 per cent. It declined further to 9.3 per cent in 1961 and 5.5 per cent in 1970.

Apart from these provisions that aim to protect the health of women workers, the general welfare provisions regarding sanitation and health services, canteens, social insurance, etc., apply to all workers. The specific welfare measures for women in organized industry are maternity benefits and provision of creches in establishments employing 50 or more women except in mines where the provisions are obligatory irrespective of the number of women workers.

The theory that provision of maternity benefits has proved to be a deterrent to women's employment cannot be substantiated as the total expenditure on maternity benefits under the Maternity Benefits Act between 1961 and 1970 is negligible. For factories this expenditure declined from 8.2 lakh in 1961 to 5.4 lakh in 1969, for plantations from 62 lakh to 55.3 lakh, but for mines the amount increased from 5.8 lakh to 16.2 lakh. In areas covered by the Employees State Insurance maternity benefits no longer represent a burden on employers. During 1969-70, the ESI paid out a total of 61 lakh on this head. Table 4.9 indicate that as compared to the number benefitted by the ESI, only a small number of women employees received this benefit, under the Maternity Benefit Act. The average amount of maternity benefits ranges from Rs 46 to 117, since it is calculated on the basis of the daily wage, which is low for the large majority of women workers.

TABLE - 4.9
MATERNITY BENEFIT PAID UNDER MATERNITY BENEFIT ACT

Year	*Average No. of Women Employed*	*No. of Women who Claimed Maternity Benefit*	*No. of Women who were Paid Maternity Benefit*	*Total amount Paid (Rs. in lakh)*
FACTORIES				
1961	309,904	12,584	11,489	8.29
1964	358,675	18,705	14,347	11.77
1967	277,615	6,573	6,132	7.07
1970*	262,290	5,502	4,931	7.27
1971**	112,165	1,995	1,931	4.46
PLANTATIONS				
1961	302,650	74,300	70,114	62.07
1964	319,703	64,855	63,650	74.70
1967	281,687	37,724	35,337	6.60
1970	260,814	39,496	38,337	48.45
1971**	301,855	43,952	43,346	598.63
MINES				
1961	66,250	7,299	7,462	5.88
1964	43,400	7,609	7,326	14.20
1967	41,800	6,748	6,648	14.89
1970	30,424	4,444	4,420	14.01
1971**	2,631	487	495	2.47

* Including some cases pending from previous year(s)

* Incomplete Excluding Chandigarh

** Incomplete Excludes Bihar, Gujarat, Maharashtra, Mysore, Rajasthan, Tamil Nadu, Goa, Chandigarh, Manipur and Mines other than coal. Besides in Factories the figures are also exclusive of Assam.

Source: Indian Labour Statistics, 1973 Labour Bureau.

As for the other welfare provisions, e.g., creches and sanitary facilities, the expenditure involved is negligible and this cannot explain the declining trend in women's employment in organizing industry. Many employers still do not provide separate toilets or rest rooms. Where they do exist, the arrangements are inadequate, without proper service and maintenance. Creches are very often a room without proper arrangements.

TABLE - 4.10

PROGRESS OF ESI SCHEME AS ON MARCH

	1952	*1956*	*1961*	*1966*	*1967*	*1968*	*1972*	*1973*
States	2	8	14	15	16	16	18	18
Centre	2	31	120	259	273	300	318	339
Insured Women	NA	NA	1,20,750	2,13,650	2,30,750	2,51,900	2,59,650	2,75,000
Total Benefi-ciaries	1,20,000	12,90,000	38,93,000	1,21,42,650	1,30,16,600	1,37,62,550	1,67,14,550	1,75,31,700

The general view that these measures have made women workers more costly for the employers is not borne out by facts. A study conducted by the ILO (India branch) also refuted the theory. The National Commission on Labour noted that "benefits or no benefits, where women are more useful they continue to be employed. Plantations is an instance in point."

Wages

It is often claimed that equalization of wages leads to retrenchment of women workers who are usually employed because of their cheapness. The National Commission on Labour offers standardization of wages as one of the reasons for the retrenchment of workers in the textile industry. Official agencies admit however, that, "it has not been possible to make an assessment of the extent to which the equal pay principle has really resulted in the displacement of women workers."

An often-quoted example is the Mazumdar Award of 1954 for West Bengal Mining Industry which equalized wage for men and women workers. The Survey of labour conditions in Coal Mining Industry in 1966 agreed that this award 'may also be a contributory factor', to the reduction in the number of women in coal mines. According to the survey's findings however, the decline in the number of women workers in the coal industry started well before the Mazumdar Award. In 1944 "out of every four workers in the coal mines one was a woman. However, since then there has been a steady decline in the number of women workers in the industry". This makes it clear that the declining trend in women's employment in the coal mines could not have been precipitated by the equalization of wages, since the rate of decline did not increase after the award.

In our view, these types of conclusions which ignore previous trends in particular industries, and the influence of other factors are not only unscientific but also indicate a desire to arrest the movement towards equalization of wages. In reality the principle of equalization has not been seriously applied in most industries and cannot be regarded as a contributory factor to the decline of women's employment in any industry. The present wage structure in most industries, indicate that in spite of the attempts to bring about equalization of wages between men and women, most industries continue to maintain the pattern of differentials by indirect methods. The two Occupational Wage Surveys conducted in 1958-59 and 1963-65 reported differences in the minimum, maximum and average earnings of men and women in most industries.

As a result of the differences the Survey found the average daily earnings of men to be higher than those of women in all the industries except fine chemicals, whether they were in the manufacturing, mining or plantation sectors. In a few industries, viz., jute and silk textile, textile machinery, cigarette industry and tea plantations, earnings of men and women were quite closer to each other but in the remaining industry "the differences were quite substantial". The survey reported that the principle of equalization is evaded by individual establishments by not employing both men and women for the same jobs. Table 4.11 gives the Average daily wage rates for men and women in selected occupation.

It will be observed that differences in wage rates between men and women were present in both minimum and maximum rates for most occupations in different industries. There are, however, a few instances where the gaps have narrowed considerably or even become favourable to women at the level of

TABLE - 4.11
AVERAGE DAILY WAGE RATES FOR MEN AND WOMEN IN SELECTED OCCUPATION

Industry	*Minimum*		*Maximum*		*Average Daily Earnings*	
	Men	*Women*	*Men*	*Women*	*Men*	*Women*
I	*II*		*III*		*IV*	
A. Cotton Textiles :						
Head jobber	9.08	6.18	28.41	6.18	15.13	6.67
Jobber	6.60	5.11	9.59	5.39	7.97	3.30
Weaver	5.10	1.84	6.32	1.84	7.59	1.50
Drawing Tenter	5.15	4.86	5.65	5.25	5.35	4.44
Residual occupations	4.54	3.96	9.33	5.38	6.34	4.51
All occupations	4.93	4.36	7.01	5.06	6.06	4.76
B. Jute Textiles :						
Warp winder	3.17	3.08	4.17	4.60	4.77	3.97
Softener feeder	3.05	2.91	3.05	2.91	3.67	2.60
Mazdoor	3.05	2.85	3.08	2.88	3.15	2.89
Residual occupations	3.04	3.05	5.78	3.05	3.79	3.08
All occupations	3.17	3.17	4.47	4.09	3.79	3.61
C. Silk Textiles :						
Healed & Reed repairer	3.81	4.15	4.33	4.15	4.24	3.36
Warper	4.31	2.62	5.08	2.62	4.88	2.94
Asstt. Warper	3.42	1.01	3.75	1.01	3.61	1.00
Cut looker	4.38	3.84	4.55	4.11	4.51	4.00
Stentering machineman	3.96	2.39	4.71	3.46	4.33	3.04
Mazdoor	3.78	2.72	4.15	3.05	3.75	2.99
Weavers	4.08	2.08	6.69	2.95	5.42	2.50
Creel boy	3.60	1.59	3.73	1.63	3.76	1.60
Picker	1.20	1.08	1.75	1.11	2.82	1.11
Silk examiner	2.89	2.03	3.55	2.14	3.22	2.08
Cooker	2.87	1.87	2.87	1.93	4.07	1.90
Sorter	1.81	1.96	2.48	1.97	2.10	1.96
Doubler	2.09	1.28	2.48	1.38	2.31	1.62
Residual occupations	3.65	2.59	7.08	3.33	4.63	2.92
All occupations	3.90	2.11	5.87	2.34	4.84	2.38
D. Woollen Textiles :						
Darner	4.71	4.87	6.07	5.89	5.76	5.12
Mazdoor	4.25	1.19	4.86	1.43	4.45	1.25
Bobbin setter	3.98	1.01	4.59	1.01	4.12	1.00
Weaver/handloom	3.97	2.45	8.09	3.20	5.56	2.75
Reeler	4.07	3.32	5.25	3.63	4.41	3.65
Mule minder	4.51	0.98	5.47	0.98	4.74	1.00
Residual occupations	4.37	2.92	9.95	4.30	5.15	3.41
All occupations	4.30	4.03	6.70	5.21	4.89	4.37
E. Metal Extracting and Refining :						
Mazdoor	3.12	2.73	3.69	3.04	4.66	3.76

(Continued...)

(Table 4.11 Continues)

F. Rough Casting & Forging :						
Moulder and core maker	2.61	1.62	7.75	2.37	4.82	1.86
Mazdoor	2.35	1.55	3.25	1.88	3.02	1.63
G. Bolts & Nuts Manufacturing :						
Sharper	2.89	1.50	6.28	1.50	9.12	1.50
Packer	2.54	1.65	3.67	2.40	2.87	1.75
Mazdoor	2.70	2.22	2.88	2.22	4.24	2.10
Hand machine operator	2.81	2.26	4.45	2.26	5.46	2.00
H. Machine Tools :						
Machinist grade I	5.22	5.93	9.69	5.93	6.00	5.00
I. Electrical Machinery Appliances :						
Meter mechanic grade II	8.96	4.55	15.88	5.72	14.32	5.15
Mistry	6.28	6.75	11.52	10.11	10.29	8.66
Examiner grade I	5.34	4.35	7.41	5.31	6.99	4.82
Examiner grade II	4.79	5.31	7.47	5.65	7.94	5.45
Coil winder grade I	3.92	3.45	11.29	4.86	6.70	4.18
Coil winder grade II	3.58	2.94	5.32	3.65	9.20	2.29
Machine operator	4.46	3.36	8.03	5.47	8.32	4.07
Packer	4.01	2.18	5.62	2.18	6.20	1.83
Assembler	3.84	3.41	6.88	4.90	6.96	3.91
Residual occupations	3.39	2.33	8.53	5.06	9.78	2.03
All occupations	3.99	2.95	6.71	4.28	6.54	3.37
J. Paper & Paper Products :						
Finisher	4.85	3.30	7.31	3.92	6.71	3.82
Unskilled helper	2.71	1.48	3.18	1.69	3.18	1.99
Digestor operator	3.46	1.43	4.42	1.68	4.45	2.88
K. Glass :						
Cutter	2.60	1.07	4.60	1.15	3.39	1.12
Finished wheel grinding	2.04	1.41	2.93	1.83	2.68	1.72
L. Petroleum Refining :						
General workmen	5.07	4.69	6.37	5.88	6.27	4.96
M. Tea Plantations :						
Plucker	2.16	1.31	2.30	1.67	2.39	1.67
Labourers	1.55	1.38	4.67	2.41	2.17	2.26
Supervisor	2.48	2.26	3.59	3.22	3.09	2.63
N. Coffee Plantations :						
Maistry/Kangani	1.97	1.77	2.23	1.77	2.10	1.90
Labourer	1.66	1.26	1.73	1.30	1.53	1.27
O. Rubber Plantations :						
Field worker	1.89	1.42	1.90	1.42	1.98	1.48
Tapper	1.42	1.24	2.07	1.87	2.22	1.96
P. Manganese Mines :						
Ore washing operator	2.11	1.46	3.65	2.59	2.50	1.81
Mate	2.48	0.98	3.29	0.98	2.63	1.08
Loader unloader	2.03	1.43	2.27	3.28	2.29	2.27
Miner	1.50	1.28	3.21	2.81	2.81	2.12
Q. Mica :						
Dhani	1.76	1.00	1.85	1.00	1.72	1.00

minimum rates (Jute-residual occupations, Wool-darners, Electrical machinery-industries, examiners grade II, Machine Tools-machinists Grade I). Even in such cases the maximum rates for women are lower, leading to lower average earnings. The difference in wage rates of unskilled labourers or *mazdoors* and semi-skilled worker like packers, loaders and unloaders, etc., support our view that prejudices rather than skill or productivity differentials determine wage-differences between the sexes. In the plantations, the margin of difference is much smaller than in the factories and there are cases where the average earnings of women exceed that of men. These are, however, exceptions. The other significant trend is in the case of electrical and engineering industry where women are found in a few operations of highly skilled type.

The Committee's investigations confirm the continuation of these differentials in wages and daily earnings between men and women in the same industry. We cannot altogether support the findings of the Second Occupational Wage Survey that such differences do not exist within the same establishments. We have found such differentials among men and women pluckers in the same plantation. In one garden in North Bengal the daily wage for a man plucker is Rs 3.15 and that for a woman only Rs 3.00. The plantation management explained this by slight difference in the required minimum output.

Since we also found that the majority of the women were qualifying for the incentive scheme by giving a higher output than the fixed minimum, we failed to appreciate the reasons for continuing this discrepancy. Since the plantation industry, being highly female intensive, is the one which can ill-afford to dispense with the services of women, it seems to us that this unnecessary differential in minimum output and wages has been maintained purely out of deference to social prejudice. We found similar differentials in other plantations.

The other, indirect way for evading this principle is by classifying certain jobs as earmarked for women, and keeping lower wage rates for such jobs. According to the Second Occupations Wage Survey, the restriction of women to a few selected occupations is undoubtedly one of the most important factors affecting women's employment and the principle of wage equalization. Table 4.12 indicates the extremely limited number of occupations in different industries which appear to be open to women.

TABLE - 4.12
NUMBER OF OCCUPATIONS EMPLOYING WOMEN IN SELECTED INDUSTRIES

Industry Occupations in which women constitute 5% or more of total employees

	Total Number of Occupations Selected	*Number in which Women form > 5% of Employees*	*Names of Occupations in Column 3*
A. Manufacturing			
Cotton Textile	28	4	Winder, Sweeper, Winder (cray), Reeler
Jute Textile	37	6	Work winder, braker feeder hand-sewer, Reving feeder Softner`receiver, sweeper
Woollen Textile	26	6	Darner/Cloth Mender, Picker, Bobin Seeter, winder, reeler, residual occupations
Metal extracting and refining	30	1	Reza/Mazdoor
Manufacture of Machine tools	27	1	Packer
Manufacture of electrical machinery and appliances	31	6	Examiner (Mechanical) Grades I and II, Coil Winder Grades I and II, Apprentice, Assembler.
Fine Chemicals	38	10	Helpers, machine/plant operators and attendants, *Muccadam*.
B. Plantations			
Tea	7	2	Labourers (field worker, *mazdoor*/pruner/*beldar*/plucker, etc.) residual occupations
Coffee	7	2	Regular Labourer, casual labourer Tap-
Rubber	6	3	per,. field worker, residual occupations
C. Mines			
Coal	26	5	Sweeper, general mazdoor (earth cutter, stone cutter, crushing *mazdoor*) shale picking *mazdoor*, loader/unloader, miner
Iron ore	31	4	Reza/*mazdoor*, sweeper, skip loader miner.
Mica	20		Surface *mazdoor*, Reza residual occupations
Manganese	28	12	Ore washing operator, excavator, loader/unloader, *mazdoor*, digger, sweeper, carrier, open cast miner, sorter, scrooner and cleaner, dresser, miner.

Source: Second Occupational Wage Survey (1963-65).

It may be observed that in most of the older industries, the majority of the occupations employing women are mostly of an unskilled and semi-skilled nature. This enables employers to keep their wages at levels lower than the male workers. The other trend noticed in many industries is that while male workers may graduate from unskilled to semi-skilled and from the latter to the level of skilled jobs, sometimes even to jobs at supervisory levels, the female workers, by and large, tend to remain at the level where they are recruited. According to the Directorate General of Employment and Training, the occupational pattern of women employees indicates their concentration at the level of unskilled workers. In the private sector 55.3 per cent of the women employees and in the public sector 20.4 per cent of them are unskilled workers, as against 33.5 per cent and 17.4 per cent in the case of men. In both public and private sectors there is a continuous decrease of unskilled workers.

A study initiated by the Committee in 1973-74 covering a sample of 200 undertakings in the public and private sectors reveals the concentration of women at the lower levels of the production process.

Table 4.13(A) indicates that among the industries covered by the study in the private sector, all the women in cement, metallurgy and mining are unskilled workers. In textiles, light electricals, electronics and engineering industries the large concentration of women workers is at the semi-skilled level with a substantial number of unskilled workers in textiles and heavy engineering. Only in textiles and engineering do we find a significant number of women at the skilled level. Only one of the industries in the private sector has provided any opportunity for women at the supervisory level.

Even the newer industries like engineering, electronics and pharmaceuticals which are increasingly employing educated women as skilled workers tend to limit their participation to a few processes where the job involves dexterity of fingers or is repetitive and monotonous in nature. In the pharmaceutical industry in which women are said to have found 'a comfortable place', semi-skilled jobs like bottling, labelling and packing are done by women, though a few are employed as analysis and chemists.

TABLE - 4.13(A)
WOMEN EMPLOYEES ACCORDING TO DIFFERENT CATEGORIES AT PRODUCTION LEVEL IN (PRIVATE SECTOR)

Sl. No.	*Name of Under-taking*	*No. of Units Included*	*Total Women emplo-yed*	*Female Emp. at Produc-tion Level and %age to total Emp. Women*	*(1) Super-visory*	*(2) Skilled*	*(3) Semi-skilled*	*(4) Unskilled*
1.	Textiles	14	2267	1925 (84.91)	- -	370 (19.22)	1154 (59.95)	401 (20.83)
2.	Light Electricals	1	1414	1186 (83.88)	-	13 (1.10)	1161 (97.89)	12 (1.01)
3.	Electronics	8	1344	1130 (84.08)	-	95 (8.41)	980 (86.73)	55 (4.86)
4.	Engineering							
	(a) Heavy	15	575	426 (74.09)	-	17 (3.99)	290 (63.08)	119 (27.93)
	(b) Light	2	17	12 (70.59)	-	6 (50.00)	6 (50.00)	
5.	Cement	2	103	85 (82.53)	1 (1.18)	3 (3.53)	-	81 (95.29)
6.	Mining	1	661	649 (98.18)	-	5 (0.77)	1 (0.15)	643 (99.08)
7.	Metallurgy	1	34	23 (67.65)				23 (100.0)

Table 4.13(B) indicates that the situation is a little better in the public sector where a few women are found at the supervisory level in the engineering, electricals, telecommunication and other industries, with a large number of them in the mining industry. Women employed in the mining, telecommunication, simple engineering and electronics industries particularly, their distribution at all the levels of the production process indicates a very healthy trend. It would appear, therefore, that the public sector is shunning the existing prejudices against appointment of women in higher levels of the production process at a faster rate than the private sector.

The division of the labour market into a male and a female sector very often tends to control the distribution of women workers within the economy and restricts opportunities for employment, training and promotions within the industry. In a television manufacturing unit at Kanpur we found the entire assembly shop manned by women. The majority were matriculates but four had graduated from the polytechnic. Their promotions to the supervisory level as 'testers' had been conceded by the management only when they threatened to resign.

TABLE - 4.13 (B)

WOMEN EMPLOYMENT AT PRODUCTION LEVEL IN PUBLIC SECTOR

Category of Industry	*No. of Units Included*	*Total Women employed*	*Women Employees at Production Level*	*(1) Supervisory*	*(2) Skilled*	*(3) Semi-skilled*	*(4) Unskilled*
Engineering							
(a) Heavy	6	904	383 (42.37)	-	-	-	383 (100.0)
(b) Light	7	614	348 (56.68)	1 (0.29)	17 (4.89)	260 (74.71)	70 (20.11)
(c) Simple	22	1547	630 (40.72)	26 (4.13)	438 (69.52)	85 (13.49)	81 (12.86)
Electricals							
(a) Light	2	117	68 (58.12)	-	66 (97.06)	1 (1.47)	1 (1.47)
(b) Electronics	1	2750	2393 (87.02)	69 (2.88)	2309 (96.49)	3 (0.13)	12 (0.5)
(c) Heavy	7	1164	371 (31.87)	1 (0.27)	38 (10.24)	89 (23.99)	243 (65.5)
Chemicals							
(a) Fertilisers	15	739	298 (40.32)	-	-	298 (100)	-
(b) Plastics	4	248	204 (82.26)	1 (0.49)	9 (4.41)	14 (6.86)	180 (88.24)
Mining	5	33,978	16588 (48.82)	3452 (20.8)	4994 (30.11)	6258 (37.73)	1884 (11.36)
Telecommunication	1	597	222 (37.19)	10 (4.50)	112 (50.45)	53 (23.87)	47 (21.18)
Miscellaneous	7	899	85 (9.45)	3 (3.53)	45 (50.94)	1 (1.18)	36 (42.35)

Note: Figures in Parenthesis denote percentage of total of women employees.
Source: Data collected by the Committee.

In Hindustan Machine Tools at Bangalore certain operations are virtual monopolies of women because the jobs require both dexterity and patience. We were told by the management that the women had to be recruited before the age of twenty, as they cannot acquire the skill at a later age. In aptitude tests applied before recruitment, women had been found to fare better for these operations. This is one of the rare cases where we found that some scientific assessment of the relative productivity of the two sexes for a particular job had been undertaken. In the majority of concerns which we visited no such job appraisal had been made and restriction of women to particular types of jobs and their exclusion from the higher levels of the production process was merely based on prejudice and continuity of a traditional situation.

The causes for this restriction and what may be termed as feminization of particular occupations lie in the - (a) prevailing social attitudes which tend to regard women as unfit for most occupations; (b) the resistance of employers, and in some cases, of male workers to appointment of women at higher levels; (c) denial of on the job training opportunities in higher skills; and (d) the ignorance of most women regarding jobs outside the conventional classifications. Absence of any clear policy or criteria by which jobs may be classified as suitable or unsuitable for women helps to perpetuate this restrictive tendency. In our opinion, the prejudice is higher among employers, who use the resistance of men workers as a device to justify their own biases. Since men workers do not object to women supervisors in the services, we do not feel that it would be impossible to get a similar situation accepted in industry. As we have seen, women have started appearing in supervisory capacity in some of the new industries.

There is no doubt that wage discrimination is reinforced by the feminization of particular jobs, generally all lower unskilled levels of the production process, with low rates of wages. Employers confess that men would not do the same jobs at the existing wage rates. In areas where men have to be employed for the same jobs, they are usually placed in a higher category, in order to maintain the wage differential.

The ILO convention on Equal Remunerations permits wage differentials on the grounds of differences in productivity and in the nature of the jobs performed by men and women. In our opinion this is being misused to justify wage differentials and restricting women to limited occupations. In answer to our specific questions in this regard, some employers conceded that women, being more disciplined and conscientious, are more productive than men. They take less time off during work and being more conscious of their responsibility for feeding the family, work harder to increase their earnings. In spite of such concessions, we regret to find that differentials and lower wage rates for women continue to be justified on the theory of lower productivity of women. In the absence of any scientific job appraisal system, this theory cannot be accepted. Nor can we accept the tendency to restrict women to limited occupations or placing workers on the same jobs in different categories in order to maintain women's wages at a lower level.

It may be noted that the ILO has emphasized the need to pay greater attention to wage fixing procedures in industries and in areas of employment largely reserved for women. In our opinion, unless this trend of relegating women to limited fields and levels of employment is arrested, the principle of equalization of wages and opportunities for employment will remain inoperative.

Structural Changes in Industry through Rationalization and Modernization

The single-most important factor contributing towards this declining trend in women's employment in industry lies in the fact that the extent of employment in factories, of which a substantial proportion is constituted by large scale industry is largely determined by the relative degree of capital intensity and the choice of technology. These represent part of the general structural changes taking place in our economy. Technological changes in some of the urban occupations, like industry trade, commerce and in public offices not only reduce the rate of absorption of new labour but also involve the displacement of some labour, thereby increasing the number of the unemployed.

Both the National Commission on Labour and the Committee on Unemployment pointed out that a policy of heavier investment in more capital intensive industries and technology has an effect on employment and utilization of labour.

The initial adverse impact of more sophisticated technology in industry on the employment of women has been a global trend. When modern industry first started in India, the process of production included several stages of manual and semi-manual operations such as reeling, waste picking, winding and sizing in cotton and silk industries, batching, preparing, warp winding and hand sewing in jute, liming in leather tanning, etc. With increasing mechanization some of these processes became obsolete. The introduction of high speed machinery in the winding section of textile manufacturing reduced the number of workers to one-fourth or one-fifth of the original number. The introduction of automatic machinery in silk industry and the switching over to production of synthetic materials, the supply of processed yarn in 'cone' instead of 'hanks' or cakes decreased the demand for female labour who were engaged in the earlier manual processes.

There is a standard argument that women workers tend to stick to a single operation and do not want to learn new processes. Out of about 200 operations in the textile industry, women are employed only in four or five. The fundamental assumption underlying this practice is that women have limited aptitudes and are not capable of developing higher skills required for machine operations. This is not borne out by any empirical evidence. We have presented evidence of a large number of mechanical operations where women are playing their full role. Some of the new industries like electronics, telecommunication, light electricals etc., have found women capable of handling machines and prepared to acquire the skills needed for some of the sophisticated mechanized jobs.

The so-called incapacity or lack of aptitude of women results from lack of training. We have found ample evidence that in many industries women are not given any chance to acquire training when a new process or machine is introduced. In the case of men there is generally an agreement between the trade union and the management that training would be provided to prevent their being declared as surplus. It is remarkable that the need to train women workers in a similar manner is generally overlooked by both management and the unions. The main impact of modernization and new technology thus falls on the women who become dispensable. Senior executives of important industries admit practising a policy of 'replacing women by men or machines'.

Apart from the absence of training within industry, women are handicapped by lack of pre-recruitment training, particularly of the technical variety. Vocational and technical training for women is a new development and the number of women with such training is still small. The majority of the women being displaced from employment as a result of technological changes are the illiterate and semi-literate workers. Illiteracy still constitutes the biggest barrier for learning new trades, particularly those involving sophisticated methods of production.

The efforts made by the Ministry of Labour to spread education among industrial workers through the Worker's Education Programme have so far tended to ignore the needs of women. The success of this programme depends on a number of trained and competent 'worker-teacher' who are given the training in the first phase. We understand that among the workers sent for this training from industries in Bombay, the first batch of two women were admitted only in 1974.

There is a strong belief that workers in the lower income groups and women in particular are still very much under the influence of the traditional pattern of family and caste occupations. "Tradition governed jobs to a great extent and often because of this mechanical form of working, training and apprenticeship courses are held unnecessary." This is often offered as an explanation for the reluctance of women to change their occupations or to acquire new skills. The refusal of some women to change their modes of dress and ornaments in the interest of safety in factories is cited as an example of their tradition-bound attitudes.

These arguments were perhaps applicable in earlier years when factory workers were first generation migrants from the rural areas with little exposure to urban influences. In the last three decades, however, the situation has changed rapidly. The industrial workers of today are very much exposed to the rapid processes of social change that are more visible in the urban areas. Modes of dress and living are changing rapidly. Rising levels of aspirations and the increased exposure to mass media, particularly films have affected the attitudes of industrial workers and their families greatly. In a rubber factory at Pune we met semi-skilled women workers, whose mode of dress and attitude for coming to work was not different from those of white-collared workers.

In our opinion, the main obstacles to women adjusting themselves to the new methods of production are illiteracy and absence of training opportunities. The argument regarding their reluctance to learn new skills or change their ways according to job requirements represents the legacy of a period that has passed away. New industries like electronics and pharmaceuticals which have found women's productivity to be higher than that of men have not experienced any difficulty in giving them the necessary training.

The technological changes and the preference for higher investment in capital intensive technology have contributed largely to the rising level of general unemployment in the country. The increasing number of unemployed men have better access to employment information as they are relatively more literate and educated and do not suffer from the same degree of restricted mobility as the women. A large number of women who need work are handicapped by their ignorance of job opportunities. The National Employment Service, designed to provide assistance in employment information and placement has not penetrated beyond urban areas, and has proved itself to be totally inadequate in meeting the needs of women job seekers. Many women are still ignorant of the existence of employment exchanges. Even for the few who register themselves with the exchanges, the assistance provided has been negligible.

The causes of decline of the number and proportions of women in industry, therefore lie primarily in their displacement from the old industries like textile, jute and mines, a decline which has not been offset by the increase in women's employment in a few new industries . The major share of industrial development in the post-Independence period has gone to the heavy industries, which are capital intensive. Their failure to generate adequate employment opportunities has affected both men and women but women have suffered more because of their lack of competitiveness and bargaining power, which are directly linked to their illiteracy and lower social status. The solution of the problems that affect women workers in organized industry will require special attention and consideration from Government, employers and trade unions.

Five

Women in Services and Profession

Unlike the situation in non-agricultural occupations and organized industry, the services and profession have provided greater opportunities to women in the post-Independence period. Earlier, both in the public and private sectors, women's participation was practically confined to health and education, though the Second World War period ushered in a small but significant entry of women into clerical and secretarial occupations. Other services and professionals were the monopolies of the urban educated middle class, whose views about women's employment were extremely restrictive.

While the range of jobs open to educated women has widened in both public and private sectors, as has already been discussed in the preceding sections, the demand for unskilled women labour is shrinking.

Factors Responsible for Emergence of Women in Non-Traditional Fields

The immediate factors responsible for the emergence of women in non-traditional fields of employment in the post-Independence period are:

(a) the Constitutional guarantee of non-discrimination and equality of opportunity in matter of employment;

(b) development of women's education and their entry into areas of education and employment hitherto monopolized by men;

(c) an increasing tendency among the urban educated women to take up paid employment which reflected gradual ideological change in social values as well as the growing economic pressure on urban middle class families;

(d) expansion of employment opportunities in the tertiary sector, as a direct consequence of the increasing rate of development.

Emerging Factors

The Constitutional guarantee of 'equality of opportunity' and non-discrimination on grounds of sex in employment and office under the State and the specific directive 'to promote with special care the educational and economic interests of the weaker sections of the people' had a direct bearing on the employment aspirations of middle class women. The emphasis on women's equality, that emerged during the last phase of the freedom movement had influenced the attitudes of educated middle class women in a most marked manner.

The immediate expression of this in the period after independence could be found in three spheres: (i) in higher education; (ii) the employment market, particularly for jobs requiring higher education; and (iii) in politics. Women began to enter the competition for services under the Government from the very beginning, and the success of a few in these most prestigious occupations, which had hitherto been the monopoly of men, inspired others and helped them to shake off their traditional inhibitions and lack of confidence. By this they set in motion the attitudinal change of society, particularly of men in Government agencies to their unfamiliar presence in these occupations.

The rapid expansion of women's education that characterized the post-Independence period both contributed to, and gained further momentum from this process. Hitherto women's education had been seen more as a measure for promoting social justice and family welfare. The possibility of employment under Government provided the stimulus that women's education had lacked so far, particularly in the field of higher education. The demand for increasing opportunities led to increase in the number of institutions, while the demand for equality broke down the resistance of academic authorities, and opened to women training in engineering and other applied and vocational sciences which had been monopolies of men till then.

Apart from education the most important force behind this increasing entry of a new class of women, in the field of wage employment, is sometimes, described as 'emancipation born out of necessity'. With a few exceptions in the higher strata of society, the majority of women take to work for economic reasons.

This has been confirmed by several studies on women's motivation for employment among the urban middle classes. An increasing number of these women now have to support their families, both before and after marriage. Rising prices and levels of unemployment, added to the increasing costs of education and housing, and absence of social security, have increased the degree of economic pressures on the major section of this class. At the same time, for at least an important segment of this group, aspirations for a higher standard of living have increased the necessity of having more than one earner in the family.

Reasons of taking up Work among Women

According to a study undertaken by the Sriram Centre of Industrial Relations in 1972 covering a total sample of 500 respondents drawn from middle class working women, the respondents attached highest important to "reducing the economic burden of their families". In terms of specific economic advantages arising from their employment, they attached primary importance to "augmenting the education and diet of the family members — of children in particular." Next in order of importance was savings from future economic security of the family as compared to the expense on current consumption. According to

> In the scheme of thinking of the respondents, personal enjoyment, up-keep or comfort were rated very low as the end results of additional earnings from their own job. On the other hand, relatively much higher importance was attached to proper furnishing of the house and for being able to use gadgets and conveniences for facilitating the performance of their own domestic chores.

Though some of these studies have referred to non-economic motives among women of this class in taking up employment, the recent studies indicate that the importance of such factors is relatively much less significant. The study cited above found one non-economic reason to be significant among trained women. This was to utilize their education and training.

The Committee's experience during its tours as well as the results of our Survey confirms the reality of this trend. Wherever we went the most repeated demand from middle-class women in urban and rural areas was for increasing employment opportunities without which many families would be reduced to starvation. In West Bengal, a region where the taboos on women's work outside the home had been higher than in most other areas, we met with this demand from even elderly middle-class women. In their view, if their daughters and daughters-in-law did not obtain some employment then the families, particularly the dependent, old and young would face destitution.

According to our Survey, an overwhelming majority of the respondents, male and female, supported women's employment to augment the family's income. Almost half of the respondents agreed that a woman can do same work that a man can do, and 87 per cent observed that they should get the same wages as men for similar work. This response was in spite of the view of nearly half the respondents that general service conditions are unfavourable for women. Views on purpose of educating women revealed that fear of insecurity, resulting from loss of support from the bread-winners of the family caused by death or other reasons is still the most compelling force behind this change of attitude to women's employment.

The disintegration of joint families and the loss of their rural income has made many of these families totally dependent on their earnings from jobs. At the same time, the number of unmarried, widowed, divorced or separated women who can no longer expect to be fully supported by their families is on the increase.

An argument which is often raised in debates regarding women is that their employment deprives men of jobs that they need to support their families. It is assumed that all women who work are only supplementing the family income to ensure a higher standard of living. These theorists have never tried to investigate how many women who work are sole or main earners in the family. The majority of working women whom we met during our tours, were supporting either their parents and younger brothers and sisters or their own children. We came across some married women, who had continued to work after their marriage in order to support their aged parents and to educate their younger brothers and sisters. Such cases may be rare, but they are significant as they express a complete transformation in social attitudes. A few years ago, parents would have considered it highly improper to accept any support from married daughters. Even today though economic necessity has helped to erode this attitude, the women who take up such a responsibility require considerable courage, because it is generally disliked by their in-laws. The fear of loss of earnings of a daughter is becoming an important factor in deferring marriage of middle-class women in urban areas.

The last factor stems from the pattern in India's economic development in the post-Independence period and, the relatively higher rate of growth of the tertiary sector. This has opened up considerably more avenues for employment of women than in the past, both in the public and private sectors.

Occupational Distribution of Women Workers in Public and Private Sectors

The occupational distribution of women workers in public and private sectors and their proportion to total workers in each category indicated in Tables 5.1 and 5.2 yields some interesting information. In the public sector, while the number of women employees in the categories of professional, technical and related workers and primary and middle school teachers, has been continuously rising since 1960, their proportion to total employees has more or less remained constant with only minor fluctuations.

The number of women as administrative, executive and managerial workers increased from 0.10 lakh in 1960 to 0.12 lakh in 1966 but there was a downward trend in 1968. Their proportion to total workers, which was more or less constant at 3.3 per cent declined to 2.5 per cent in 1968. In the category of clerical and related workers, the number of women with the only exception of 1962, has gone up from 0.37 lakh in 1960 to 0.79 lakh in 1968. For the same period their proportion to total workers in this category has gone up from 4.2 per cent to 7.6 per cent. The number and proportion of women workers in transport and communication has remained steady, while in services, sports and recreations their number has gone up from 0.05 lakh in 1960 to 0.13 lakh in 1968. It may be noted however, that in this occupational division majority of women were working as maids, cooks, housekeepers, cleaners, sweepers and laundrers. The number of women as unskilled office workers has declined from 0.25 lakh (4.5 per cent) in 1960 to 0.16 lakh (2.9 per cent) in 1968.

TABLE - 5.1
OCCUPATIONAL-EDUCATIONAL PATTERN IN INDIA — PUBLIC SECTOR
(Figures in Lakhs)

Sl.	*Categories*		*1960*	*1962*	*1964*	*1966*	*1968*
1.	Professional,	T	5.05	6.11	7.19	7.32	8.59
	Technical	W	1.77*	2.09*	1.08	1.11	1.31
	Related Workers	%	(35.04)	(34.2)	(15.0)	(15.2)	(15.3)
2.	Primary and	T	5.77	6.19	7.52	9.72	10.79
	Middle School	W			1.44	1.81	2.13
	teachers	%			(19.1)	(18.6)	(19.7)
3.	Administrative,	T	2.76	2.93	3.17	3.59	3.87
	Executive and	W	0.10	0.09	0.11	0.12	0.10
	Managerial Workers.	%	(3.6)	(3.1)	(3.4)	(3.3)	(2.5)
4.	Clerical and Related workers including sales workers	T	8.83	8.82	9.43	9.59	10.41
		W	0.37	0.31	0.40	0.47	0.79
		%	(4.2)	(3.5)	(4.2)	(4.9)	(7.6)
5.	Workers in transport and communication occupations.	T	2.91	4.81	4.83	4.78	4.81
		W	0.04	0.06	0.05	0.06	0.07
		%	(1.14)	(1.2)	(1.0)	(1.3)	(1.40)
6.	Service, sports	T	4.54	4.90	5.36	6.00	5.53
	and recreation	W	0.05	0.09	0.10	0.11	0.13
	workers	%	(1.1)	(1.8)	(1.9)	(1.8)	(2.4)
7.	Unskilled office	T	5.59	4.71	5.12	5.14	5.55
	workers	W	0.25	0.13	0.15	0.13	0.16
		%	(4.5)	(2.7)	(2.8)	(2.5)	(2.9)

Source: Occupational - Educational Pattern in India, Public Sector, 1968.
* Includes primary and middle school teachers.

In the private sector, the categories where both the number and proportion of women to total workers has shown a steady increase are: clerical and related workers, service, sports and recreation workers and primary and middle school teachers. It may be interesting to note that there was a general slump in the employment of women in all categories in 1963 except for unskilled office workers. This decline was more marked in the administrative, executive and managerial workers and professional, technical and related workers.

TABLE - 5.2

OCCUPATIONAL-EDUCATIONAL PATTERN IN INDIA — PRIVATE SECTOR

(Figures in Lakhs)

Categories		*1961*	*1963*	*1965*	*1967*
1. Professional,	T	1.61	2.42	3.0	2.95
Technical and	W	0.55	0.31	0.75	0.01
Related workers	%	(34.2)	(12.6)	(25)	(34.3)
Primary and	T	0.20	0.51	0.33	0.48
Middle School	W	-	0.02	0.17	0.33
Teachers	%	-	(3.8)	(51.5)	(68.7)
Administrative,	T	0.44	0.56	0.60	0.56
Executive and	W	0.05	0.01	0.01	0.01
Managerial Workers	%	(11.3)	(1.8)	(1.6)	(1.8)
Clerical and	T	2.74	3.37	3.72	3.46
Related Workers	W	0.13	0.12	0.16	0.23
including sales workers	%	(4.3)	(3.5)	(4.30	(6.6)
Workers in transport	T	0.46	0.64	0.67	0.55
communication	W	0.01	0.01	0.02	0.01
and occupations.	%	(2.2)	(1.5)	(3)	(1.8)
Service, sports	T	0.35	0.49	0.54	0.56
and Recreation	W	0.04	0.05	0.07	0.08
workers	%	(11.4)	(10.2)	(13)	(14.3)
Unskilled office	T	1.74	1.10	1.14	1.09
workers	W	0.6	0.11	0.04	0.07
	%	(3.4)	(10)	(3.5)	(6.4)

Source: Occupational Pattern in India, (Private Sector), 1967, D.G. E. & T..
Note: Figures in parentheses show percentage of women to total.

Women employed in the management cadre belong generally to the upper-middle class, where no distinction is made in the education of boys and girls. These highly educated women hold degrees in specific disciplines relevant for business management. Some of the fields where they are usually employed are in public relations, advertising, market research and cottage industries. This situation derives from certain socio-psychological reasons regarding their special abilities in these fields. There is a trend to employ women more in areas where the market or clientele consists primarily of women or where the nature of the job calls for a woman manager. The expansion of the hotel industry, for example, has opened some new avenues for women in the field of marketing, personnel management, house keeping and public relations. Some illustrative examples of women in managerial positions are as follows:

The India Hotels Private Limited has a woman as the Sales Manager and Marketing Manager. Hindustan Milk Foods has a woman as Product Manager. India Tobacco Company Limited has a woman Accountant heading its Tax Department and a woman as Head of the Personnel Department of its Research Section.

TABLE - 5.3
WOMEN IN SELECTED PROFESSIONS IN PUBLIC AND PRIVATE SECTORS

Profession	*No. of Women Employed*	
	Private Sector (1967)	*Public Sector (1968)*
A. Teaching Personnel		
(i) Teachers - Middle and Primary	21,431	21,3452
(ii) Teachers - Secondary Schools	32,686	28,260
(iii) Teachers - University	18,897	4,206
B. Medical and Health Personnel		
(i) Nurses	6,845	22,727
(ii) Midwives & Health Visitors	1,196	24,318
(iii) Nursing attendants & related workers		23,881
(iv) Physicians and Surgeons	NA	3,091
(v) Ayah and nurse maids		5,675
C. Telephone Operators	1,051	5,052
D. Clerical & Related Workers		
(i) Steno	3,494	2,113
(ii) Ministerial Assistants and Clerks	6,226	67,623
(iii) Typist and Teletypist	1,643	5,852

Source: D.G.E.&T.

In some traditional industries, however, women have not yet been accepted at this level nor has industry yet developed the conditions suited to the life cycle and special requirements of women. It is for this reason that they find it more difficult to reach top level jobs. While some of the companies have opened their management cadre to women, it remains to be seen whether this will become an agent for change or whether it will terminate at an experimental stage.

The detailed statistical data needed to assess the major occupational trends, namely, the extent of women's entry into various professions and services and the levels of their employment in various collared jobs is unavailable over a period. It is, therefore, difficult to give a correctly statistical profile of the educated women workers. However, a review of the available data indicates that while a change is perceptible in the occupational pattern of women in this sector during the last two decades, two trends are clearly visible:

(a) the concentration of women in the profession of teaching and medicine; and

(b) recognition of certain low prestige jobs in the clerical services as particularly suitable for women and a consequent concentration of women in these occupations.

Women in Profession

According to an ILO study, made in 1970, only 17 per cent of the professional and technical workers were women of which three-fourths were teachers. The Directorate General of Employment and Training's data for selected professions in public and private sectors (organized) identifies teaching, medical and health, clerical and related workers and telephone operators as the four occupations, where there is the largest concentration of women workers.

The national classification of occupation adopted by the Census of India, 1971 indicates that the number of women teachers was 6 lakh, whereas their number in other professions was negligible - physicians and surgeons .2 lakhs, nursing and other medical and health technicians 2,500, lawyers 1,700 and architects, engineers and surveyors 700, accountants, etc., 2,700. Apart from persons serving as teachers, other qualified scientists, serving in professional capacity (physical scientists, life scientists, social scientists, mathematicians) add up to a total of 18,000. Of this last group, social scientists form the major section (16,000). It would thus appear that research, particularly in the field of social research and social work are emerging as new occupations where women are present in a significant number. In relation to men, their ratios in these selected occupations are given below:

Physicians and Surgeons	7.1%
Lawyers	1.2%
Teachers	30.3%
Nursing and other medical and health technicians	72.2%
Scientists	10.9%

Within teaching, primary school teaching account for about 71 per cent of the women teachers followed by secondary schools which accounts for 21 per cent.

Teachers

The heavier concentration of women professionals in teaching and medicine reflects both opportunities as well as preferences. Teaching as an occupation, particularly at the school stage, requires relatively little training beyond general education, in comparison to the professions of medicine, engineering, etc. In the prevailing social ethos, a long-term professional training for women is still accessible to a minority among the upper middle-class. The second reason for their preference is respectability attached to this profession in society, in spite of its lower salary structure. Teaching has been always accorded a high status in Indian society, though its income potential has always been limited. Middle-class families prefer to see their women in this profession more than any other. One of the reason for this is perhaps because it gives a woman comparatively more time for her household duties, as there are more vacations and limited hours of work.

Another reason for the heavy concentration of women in teaching has been suggested by sociologists, who report that the percentage of women teachers in lower age-group is much higher than the men teachers at practically all levels of teaching. Women enter the profession in substantial number but their number declines beyond the age of 30 and drastically after 35.

This may be interpreted to suggest a substantial entry of women into this profession before marriage and a tendency for some of them to leave employment with increase in their family responsibilities. In the absence of studies based on the same cohort of teachers over a time period, it is impossible to accept this explanation. An alternative explanation; and in our opinion the more valid one, is the increasing rate of expansion of employment opportunities in this profession in recent years, and the greater degree of preference for women teachers in primary and middle schools which would account for a larger number of younger women in this profession. A third possibility, which required investigation, is the relatively lower salary structure in many private schools. It is an accepted fact that it is easier to obtain the services of women for such low rates than men since women constitute a higher proportion of the educated unemployed.

Doctors

According to the manpower Survey of 1967-68, the existing medical workforce comprised 12,000 women out of a total of 1,20,000 doctors. According to 1971 Census (1 per cent sample data) however, the ratio of women physicians and surgeons is only 6.1 per hundred men — 23.8 thousand women to 336.3 thousand men. The number of qualified women doctors is however about 25 per 100 men. This may indicate both under utilization due to women doctors dropping out of the profession, or alternatively their migration to other countries for employment.

It may be noted that though medicine has been an accepted and respected profession for women for a considerable period the general tendency has been for women to concentrate in the practice of obstetrics and gynaecology. In recent years they have also entered paediatrics, surgery, medicine, pathology, radiology, anaesthesia, etc. Since the majority of their clientele continue to be women, as very few men would still consider it proper to consult a woman doctor, it is but natural that the majority of women doctors should take up specialization in women's and children's diseases. A new field for women doctors is administration in hospitals and public health. During the pre-Independence period, there was a considerable disparity between men and women medical officers in the management of hospitals. In some of the States, women doctors were not given the same status or pay scales as men. This disparity continued in Punjab until 1962, when women doctors were given the status of Civil Surgeons, after considerable struggle on their part.

One particular problem in employment of women doctors is their heavy concentration in urban areas, and the regional disparities in their utilization. Out of 23,000 employed doctors in 1971 as many as 19.5 thousand were serving in urban areas. According to the Ministry of Health and Family Planning, in large urban centres like Mumbai, Delhi and Chennai women doctors form 20-40 per cent of the total number of doctors. In relatively backward States like

Assam and Madhya Pradesh they form only 2-4 per cent while they constitute about 16 per cent in Punjab and 20 per cent in Maharashtra. Since most women doctors come from urban middle-class families, they tend to stay in urban areas, while rural areas continue to suffer from a shortage of women doctors. It would be difficult to improve their representation in rural areas unless adequate arrangements for housing and other amenities, particularly the schooling of young children are provided.

We would like to note here that as compared to the rather indifferent reception of other women workers in the rural areas, the professions of teaching and medicine have come to receive a high degree of respect and acceptance from rural society. We were informed by women in different States, that these two groups of professionals now enjoy a great deal of respect in rural areas. It should, therefore, not be difficult, in our opinion, to elicit a greater degree of public cooperation to make their stay in these areas easier.

Nurses

Regarding the other categories of medical personnel, Table 5.4 indicates the increase in the number of nurses, mid-wives and health visitors during the last two decades. Nurses and midwives constitute the largest of these three groups. According to the Census of 1971, the total number in all categories of para-medical personnel amounted to 1.55 lakh, of which .9 lakh were concentrated in urban areas, their ratio to men being 72.7 per cent. While these professions do not carry the same status as that of the doctors, nor the same pay scales, there is no doubt that their status has increased in the post-Independence period. Before independence, nursing used to be a monopoly of a few communities like Anglo-Indians and Indian Christians, viz., communities which did not impose any taboo on their women taking up this profession.

These taboos have lessened to a very great extent in most States and better training opportunities for women in Nursing schools and colleges have helped to increase the status of this category of professional workers. The expansion of health services has increased employment opportunities. In spite of this, however, the arduous nature of the duties which includes night work and the relatively low scales of pay still constitute handicaps for women in this profession. It should be noted that there has been an increase in the migration of qualified nurses from the country in recent years. Unless this trend is arrested by providing better terms of service and facilities, this trend may form one of the important elements of the 'brain-drain' from the country.

While the principle of discrimination against married women in both these professions has been formally abandoned, elements of discrimination still remain. It was brought to our notice that in the Army Medical Service, which employs a large number of women doctors and nurses, until 1972, married women had to leave the nursing service. Revision of the rules in that year has made it possible for them to continue in the service at their request, by grant of 2 years extended tenure at a time. Married women are still not recruited to the Military Nursing service, and if they marry during probation they have to leave the service. Married women may, however, be recruited on local basis on one year contract renewable annually. One glaring omission in the Army Service Regulations is the lack of provision for any paid maternity leave to both women doctors and nurses. This, in our opinion, constitutes a definite disability, and should be removed forthwith. Table 5.4 gives the number of nurses, midwives and health visitors registered during 1951 to 1970.

TABLE - 5.4
NURSES, MIDWIVES AND HEALTH VISITORS

Year	*Nurses*	*Midwives*	*Health Visitors*
1951	16,550	19,281	578
1961	35,584	41,575	1,690
1967	59,914	65,589	3,307
1970	71,199	76,293	4,283

(This table gives the actual number of nursing personnel registered with the nursing council or boards according to different categories. - Statistical Abstracts India. Figures for 1970 from Pocket Book of Health Statistics, 1973)

Lawyers

In the absence of any reliable data of case studies, it is difficult to make any observation regarding the status of women in other professions. We have, however, received complaints from women lawyers in many States regarding lack of opportunities extended to them for judicial appointment. While the number of practising lawyers has been on the increase, only one woman has, so far, been appointed a High Court Judge. In our view, a change in this trend is necessary not only in the interest of women in this profession, but also for the large number of women who find a lack of understanding of their personal difficulties in family matters from the judicial profession. The Family Courts and the Special Tribunals that we have recommended elsewhere, if accepted, should provide increasing opportunities for women trained in law.

Social Workers

A new profession which is emerging mainly after independence is social work, a field where leadership was generally assumed by women on a voluntary basis in the years before independence. The majority of professionally trained social workers today work in institutions, departments and organizations engaged in social welfare, both public and voluntary. The first school of social work in India was established by a woman. These schools offered equal opportunities to men and women from the beginning.

According to a study undertaken by the Indian Council for Social Welfare in 1968, there were about 3153 social work graduates at that time. This number is estimated to have risen to about 6000 by 1971. Out of a sample of 1107 covered by the study, 30 per cent were women. In employment opportunities, however, women were found to have obtained their first jobs earlier than men. Out of 319 women, 40 per cent found employment within one month after training, while only 29 per cent of the 732 men succeeded in doing so. 80 per cent of the women could find employment within 6 months of training, while this was true of only 53 per cent of the men in the sample.

The reasons offered for the greater ease with which women get employment in this profession are: (a) personal inclination on the basis of aptitude which makes them less selective about the type of employment; and (b) the greater difficulty for social workers obtaining employment in industrial jobs. Since men tend to specialize more in labour and industrial relations, they find it more difficult to get jobs. According to Ramachandran and Padmanabhan (1969) "On the contrary, the women who normally tend to specialise in primary social work and community organization, have less difficulty in getting absorbed in the related settings."

19 per cent of the women, however, complained of poor services and working conditions as a discouraging trend in the employment of social workers. The salaries for this occupation in both voluntary as well as private sector generally ranges between Rs 200 and Rs 800. According to Sita Basu (1973):

> This is not true of the few who today hold high positions both in government departments as heads of educational institutions or other capacities, who draw a fairly large salary in keeping with the positions held, but they are a very small minority. Academic institutions such as schools of social work and industrial establishments offer better salaries, service and working conditions and opportunities for professional growth, than the primary social work fields.

Positions held by the majority of women in this profession are generally in the middle and the lower category with very few holding key posts. Only two schools of social work are headed by women and very few heads of departments dealing with social welfare or related subjects at the Central and State levels are professionally qualified women.

Concentration of Women in Low Level Jobs in Clerical and Related Services

Registers of Employment Exchanges and the views expressed by various employers both in public and private sectors, make it clear that jobs of receptionists, clerks, stenographers and typists are absorbing more and more educated women. Out of 9.18 lakh of women work seekers registered with the employment exchanges at the end of 1973, as many as 69,355 were seeking clerical and related jobs. The concentration in particular fields is indicated below:

Typists	50,448
Stenographers	7,080
Clerks	2,800
Key Punch Operators	2,592
Telephone Operators	1,392
Middle School teachers	27,525
Primary School teachers	26,100
Secondary School teachers	24,163
Manual Training teachers	6,885

Nursing attendants	5,926
Midwives	2,555
General Nurses	2,058

Source: Directorate General of Employment and Training.

The demand for unskilled women labour is shrinking both in public and private sectors and the growth in the numbers of women in white collared jobs is definitely on the increase but predominantly in the low prestige occupations.

A sample survey of the pattern of graduate employment in the country undertaken by the Directorate General of Employment and Training towards the beginning of 1960 also found that the second highest percentage of employed women graduates were engaged in clerical and related work in the Central Government. About three-fourths of the employed women were earning below Rs. 300 per month and only 6% had a monthly income of Rs. 300 and above.

The Committee obtained information from various Ministries and Agencies of the Central Government regarding the number of women employees at different levels. The data presented in Table 5.5 indicate that the largest numbers are concentrated in Class III, i.e., ministerial and related staff. The expansion at this level has been much faster than that at the other levels, increasing from 720 in 1961 to 4175 in 1971. As compared to this, the number of women in Class II services has increased from 231 to 269 and that in Class I from 42 to 251. The number of Class IV employees increased from 10 to 84. The percentage increase of employees in this limited group of Central Government agencies indicates a faster rate of growth of women employees than the total. A detailed analysis shows that the highest number of Women Class I officers is to be found in the Department of Atomic Energy (121). Other Ministries with a relatively higher number of women at this level are the Ministry of Education and Social Welfare, External Affairs and Tourism and Civil Aviation. Their numbers in the other Ministries are negligible. In Class II, the highest numbers are found in Tourism and Civil Aviation (626), Education and Social Welfare (65) and Atomic Energy (48). In Class III the largest concentration is again in Atomic Energy (1092), Defence (652), Supply and Rehabilitation (637), Educational and Social Welfare (628), Tourism and Civil

Aviation (206), Irrigation and Power (195), Commerce (148), Shipping and Transport (131). This indicates that only a few Ministries have shown themselves particularly friendly to receiving women on their staff. The new Department of Science and Technology would also come within this group 11 women in Class I, 14 in Class II, 99 in Class III. While we regret our inability to make this study comprehensive, our failure to obtain similar information from the other Ministries confirms our belief based on unofficial information, that certain Ministries and agencies of the Government of India are practising a subtle form of discrimination by resting the posting of women on their staff. Another inference that may be drawn from this data is that the discrimination against women is considerably less in agencies which employ a larger proportion of scientists and other professionals. The case of Atomic Energy, Education and Social Welfare and Science and Technology provide distinct evidence of this. Since these are relatively lower staffed agencies, their impact on the total employment of women in Central Government agencies can be only marginal.

TABLE - 5.5

WOMEN EMPLOYED IN CENTRAL GOVERNMENT AT DIFFERENT LEVELS

Total	*Class I*		*Class II*		*Class III*		*Class IV*	
	1961	*1971*	*1961*	*1971*	*1961*	*1971*	*1961*	*1971*
Females	42	251	231	269	720	4175	10	84
	(100)	(100)	(100)	(100)	(100)	(100)	(100)	(100)
General	29	176	267	785	549	2959	5	68
	(69)	(70)	(95)	(90)	(76)	(71)	(50)	(81)
Technical	7	29	13	61	109	902	2	8
	(17)	(12)	(4)	(7)	(15)	(22)	(20)	(10)
Professional	6	46	1	23	62	314	3	8
	(14)	(18)	(1)	(3)	(9)	(8)	(30)	(10)

Figures in brackets denote percentage.

We tried to obtain similar data regarding the employment of women at different levels from various public and private undertakings. Information was obtained from 137 public undertakings and 72 private ones. Table 5.6 indicates the distribution of women employees at the level of management, executives and clerical staff. The trend is clear regarding their concentration at the clerical level, both in public and private sectors.

TABLE - 5.6
DISTRIBUTION OF WOMEN EMPLOYEES IN DIFFERENT CATEGORIES IN PUBLIC AND PRIVATE SECTOR

Undertaking	*No. of Units*		*Total Women Employees*		*Managerial Level*		*Officers Level*		*Clerical Level*	
	Public	*Private*	*Public*	*Private*	*Public*	*Private*	*Public*	*Private*	*Public*	*Private*
1. Engineering										
Heavy	6	15	964	575	18	—	35	3	436	135
					(1.99)		(3.87)	(0.52)	(48.33)	(23.48)
Light	7	2	614	17	1	—	13	1	210	4
					(0.16)		(2.12)	(5.88)	(34.20)	(23.53)
Simple	22	-	1547	-	3		27	-	816	-
					(0.19)		(1.75)	—	(52.75)	
2. Electricals										
Light	2	1	117	1414	-	44	2	-	47	18
						(3.11)	(1.71)		(40.17)	(13.01)
Electronics	1	8	2750	1344	-	-	12	11	328	187
							(0.44)	(0.82)	(11.93)	(13.91)
Heavy	7	-	1164	-	-	-	38	-	702	-
							(3.26)		(60.31)	
3. Chemicals							10	1	389	98
Fertiliser	15	5	739	122	-	-	(1.74)		(52.64)	(80.33)
Plastics	4		248		-	-	1		43	
							(0.40)		(17.34)	
4. Finance, Banking & Insurance	30	1	3332	3	11	-	58		3126	
					(0.30)		(1.74)		(93.28)	
5. Tele-Com munication:	1	-	597	-	-	-	13	-	359	
6. Advertising	-	7	-	157	-	3	-	36	-	103
						(1.91)		(22.93)		(65.61)
7. Textile	1	14	12	2267	-	-	-	11	11	174
								(0.49)	(91.67)	(7.68)
8. Mining	5	1	33978	661	-	-	43	-	974	12
							(0.12)		(2.87)	(1.82)
9. Steel	5	1	532	22	-	-	28	2	504	20
							(5.26)	(9.09)	(94.74)	(90.91)
10. Oil	4	-	355	-	-	-	10	-	332	-
							(2.82)		(93.78)	
11. Research & Development	2	-	465	-	-	-	1	-	464	-
									(99.78)	
12. Planning & Construction	8	-	167	-	1	-	-	7	-	158
					(0.60)			(4.19)		(94.61)
13. Others	7	13	899	305	-	2	51	23	763	230
						(0.66)	(5.671)	(7.54)	(84.67)	(76.41)

N.B. Figures within brackets denote percentages to total Women Employment.

The greater percentage of women employees is found in the production level with the exception of fertilizers, advertising and steel. In the public sector it is remarkable that their proportion in clerical work outstrips their proportion in the production level (Simple engineering, heavy electricals, fertilizers, textiles, steel and oil). At the level of executives only the advertising industry in the private sector seems to have accommodated a few women. In the public sector, while finance, banking and insurance, steel, heavy engineering and heavy electricals have a certain number of women their proportion is exceedingly small. The number of women at the managerial level is negligible except in light electricals in the private sector.

The distribution of women clerical staff at the levels of supervisors, assistants and lower grade employees indicates the same pattern (Table 5.7 (A) and (B). The concentration is generally in the ranks of typists, stenographers and receptionists except in mining and steel, heavy electricals and tele-communication.

TABLE - 5.7(A)
WOMAN EMPLOYEES AT CLERICAL LEVEL IN PUBLIC SECTOR
(Clerical & Related Workers)

Sl. No.	*Name*	*Total Women Emp-loyees*	*Total Clerical & their % to Total Women Employees*		*Super-visory*	*Assis-tant*	*Typist/ Steno/ Recep-tionist*
1.	Eng.						
	(a) Heavy	904	436	(48.23)	14	30	392
	(b) Light	614	210	(34.20)	14	26	170
	(c) Simple	1547	816	(52.75)	16	771	29
2.	Electricals						
	(a) Light	2750	328	(11.93)	30	164	134
	(b) Heavy	1164	702	(6.31)	19	459	224
3.	Chemicals Fertilisers	739	389	(52.64)	4	33	352
4.	Finance, Banking & Insurance:	3332	3126	(93.82)	6	207	2913
5.	Planning & Construction	167	158	(94.61)	6	42	110
6.	Oil	355	332	(93.52)	3	95	234
7.	Mining	33,978	974	(2.87)	380	268	326
8.	Steel	532	504	(94.74)	6	347	151
9.	Research & Development	465	464	(99.78)		1	463
10.	Food Processing/ preservation	91	86	(97.80)	3	10	73
11.	Telecommunication	597	359	(60.13)	79	127	153
12.	Miscellaneous	899	763	(84.87)	375	11	377

TABLE - 5.7(B)
WOMEN EMPLOYEES AT CLERICAL LEVEL — PRIVATE SECTOR

Sl. No.		Total Women Employees	Clerical Level	Supervisory	Assistant	Typist/Steno/ Tel. Operator
1.	Electricals					
	A. Light	1414	184 (13.01)	-	15	169
	B. Electronics	1344	183 (13.91)	-	84	99
2.	Engineering					
	A. Heavy	575	135 (23.48)	2	19	114
3.	Chemicals	1122	98 (80.33)	-	2	96
4.	Advertising	157	103 (65.81)	-	7	96
5.	Textiles	2267	174 (7.68)	2	-	172
6.	Steel	22	20 (90.91)	-	-	20
7.	Miscellaneous	305	230 (75.41)	-	15	215

Data supplied by the Union Public Service Commission also indicates an increase in the number of women being recruited as stenographers and assistants in the Central Services as indicated by Table 5.8. Their ratio to men has shown a steady improvement during the last decade.

TABLE - 5.8
STENOGRAPHERS AND ASSISTANTS AS RECOMMENDED BY THE UNION PUBLIC SERVICE COMMISSION

Name of the Examination and Year	No. of Candidates Appeared			No. of Candidates Recommended			Ratio of Women to Men
	Total	Men	Women	Total	Men	Women	
Stenographers							
1. 1963	1944	1913	31	457	454	3	1 : 151.3
2. 1966	1747	1676	71	219	212	7	1 : 30.3
3. 1969	2038	1897	141	280	264	16	1 : 16.5
4. 1971	2366	2077	289	129	113	16	1 : 7.1
5. 1973	1729	1481	248	200	180	21	1 : 8.6
Assistant Grade Examination							
1. 1963	3063	3036	27	197	195	2	1 : 97.5
2. 1965	1901	1867	34	92	91	1	1 : 91
3. 1969	2891	2779	112	353	397	16	1 : 24.8
4. 1971	7889	7229	460	362	350	12	1 : 29.2
5. 1973	8096	7347	749	374	352	22	1 : 16

The Central Services which threw open their ranks to open competitions, giving equal opportunities for women, since 1948 show a slow but steady increase in the number of candidates as well as successful entrants (Table 5.9). In the IAS/IFS/IPS examination the ratio of women to men recommended for appointment has improved from 1 : 65.6 in 1960 to 1 : 7.6 in 1972. In the other services, however, e.g. the Indian Economic Service, the Statistical Service and the Engineering Service their proportion still remains low, though in the Electrical Engineering Service their position is relatively better as also in the ranks of Geologists. The Forest Service has received no women even though women have been appearing in these examinations, though in very small numbers. It should be noted that the Indian Police Service, which had refused to accept any woman earlier, withdrew its resistance after a representation from some women candidates.

TABLE - 5.9
NUMBER OF MEN AND WOMEN APPEARING/RECOMMENDED IN THE ALLIED SERVICES

Name of the Examination and Year	*No. of Candidates Appeared*			*No. of Candidates Recommended*			*Ratio of Women to Men (Recommended for Appointment)*
	Total	*Men*	*Women*	*Total*	*Men*	*Women*	
I.F.S., I.A.S., I.P.S., etc.							
1. 1960	5873	*	*	333	328	5	1 : 65.6
2. 1963	4282	*	*	417	400	17	1 : 23.5
3. 1966	5040	*	*	426	385	41	1 : 9.4
4. 1969	6516	6153	363	378	337	41	1 : 8.2
5. 1972	8424	7800	624	549	485	64	1 : 7.6
Indian Forest Service							
1. 1967	1338	1335	3	54	54	—	
2. 1969	949	947	2	16	16	—	
3. 1971	1510	1504	6	11	11	—	
4. 1973	2439	2420	19	26	26	—	
IES/ISS							
1. 1967	2386	*	*	45			
2. 1969	1892	*	*	48			
3. 1971	572	*	*	25			
4. 1973	304	260	44	13	13	—	
Eng. Services							
(1960-66 no women candidates recommended for Eng. Service)							
1. 1969	2105	2104	1	235	235	—	
2. 1970	2105	2100	5	277	276	1	1: 276
3. 1971	1883	1877	6	321	321	—	
4. 1972	2745	2739	6	453	452	1	1: 452
Eng. Service (Elect.)							
1. 1971	315	307	8	89	87	2	1 : 43.5
2. 1972	516	509	7	250	248	2	1 :124
3. 1973	879	862	17	85	83	2	1 : 41.5
Geologists Exam.							
1. 1969	239	238	1	42	42	—	
2. 1972	322	314	8	100	99	1	1 : 99
3. 1973	332	325	7	137	134	3	1 : 44.7

Source: U.P.S.C.

While we regret that we did not get any response from the Ministry of Railways to our request for information, we have been unofficially informed that of the 10 Services under the Railways, women have been accepted at the Class I level only in two viz., Accounts and Medical. Certain candidates who have sought admission to the Traffic Service, were denied the opportunity and persuaded to opt for Accounts. We have also been informed that the Railway Board has resisted the posting of Class I women officers on the staff of the Board.

The important issue concerning women in the Central Services that received considerable public attention recently was regarding the constitutional validity of Rule 5(3) of the IAS Recruitment Rules 1954. According to this Rule, when an unmarried woman officer married "the Central Government may, if the maintenance of the efficiency of the service so requires, call upon her to resign". This rule had been cited in a case which came up for consideration before the Supreme Court under the Industrial Disputes Act, 1967. In this case, the legality of a service rule adopted by the respondant concern, (International Franchise (Pvt.) Ltd.), by which the services of a woman worker were automatically terminated on marriage, was sought to be defended on the analogy of Rule 5(3) of the IAS Recruitment Rules. The Court, while striking down the said rule in the respondent concern in the interests of social justice, observed as follows:

> It will be seen that this rule for the Indian Administrative Service is not unqualified like the rule in force in the respondent concern. It only lays down that where an unmarried woman married subsequently, the Central Government may, if the maintenance of the efficiency of the Service so requires, call upon her to resign. Therefore, this rule does not compel unmarried women to resign on marriage as a matter of course, as is the case in the respondent concern. It is only when the Central Government considers that marriage has impaired the efficiency of the women concerned that the Central Government may call upon her to resign. The rule which is in force in the respondent concern however assumes that merely by marriage the efficiency of the women employee is impaired and such an assumption in our opinion is not justified.

Though Rule 5(3) was upheld by the Supreme Court, we are happy to note that it was deleted from the IAS Recruitment Rules in 1972, after an assurance given by the Prime Minister in Parliament, since it amounted to discrimination against married women.

The low proportion of women in the higher ranks may be a reflection either of prejudices and discriminatory recruitment policies or lack of career orientation and career commitment on the part of women. Disparities in the proportion of men and women at different levels of responsibility are important indicators of the unequal employment status and opportunity for men and women which are the direct result of a combination of factors, i.e., the educational system, training, job orientation and culture conditioning. Many private concerns do not recruit women into their managerial cadre as a matter of policy as they believe that women cannot exercise supervision and control and they are weeded out in promotion. Such prejudices tend to persist and are difficult to break down. In response to our request for information regarding policy in regard to recruitment of women, one nationalized undertaking (A Unit of LIC India) observed:

> Our general policy has been to avoid, as far as possible, appointment of female employees in the Organization. Lack of education among womenfolk, socio-economic backwardness of the State, have been largely responsible for creating an atmosphere which has been discouraging to women's employment. Amidst these conditions, while very few women candidates were coming forward for jobs in our organization, we were reluctant to appoint them lest it may create administrative problems. Besides, as a private business organization prior to nationalisation, we gave due consideration to efficiency discipline, administrative ability, hard work and in our opinion women candidates in general were not upto the mark.

The ILO report on "Women Workers in a Changing World" noted that "while formal discrimination in employment based on sex is tending to disappear, informal policies and practices are tending to persist. The residual forms of discrimination tend to operate, formally and informally at a higher level in the occupational pyramid, often blocking the advancement of women on the ground of their individual merit irrespective of sex."

In spite of these limitations, an overview of the trends during the last three decades reveals that the contribution and achievement of women in this has been significant. The number of women working as lawyers, engineers, technologists, scientists, accountants, auditors, journalists, business managers and executives, may be small but they indicate a qualitative change.

While the overall increase in the number of women in these occupations indicate a relatively widening field for employment of educated women, this should not be given undue importance. We did not attempt any definition of the type of work or of the sections of workers employed in this sector since it was neither possible nor necessary. Broadly, the tertiary sector constitutes that sector of the economy in which no production of material goods take place.

In this sense, all work in the tertiary is unproductive. In an economy like ours, where an unusually high proportion of total capital is invested in trade and commerce or where because of social and political considerations, allocation of resources for defence, maintenance of law and order and certain social services like education and health are high, the tertiary sector is somewhat bigger in volume than in other developing countries. As a result of this, employment in the tertiary sector in general and in the public sector in particular has increased at an exceedingly fast rate. The expanded role of Government at all levels of the development process has been one of the greatest contributory factors towards this.

As compared to this, the actual production of goods has not increased at the same pace. It has been increasingly realized that a developing economy cannot bear the weight of this very heavy tertiary sector, with the increasing constraints on resources available for development and inflationary tendencies. The increasing financial crisis has already imposed severe constraints on public resources and calls for reduction in public expenditure and non-productive expenditure in the economy as a whole. The major impact of these demands are bound to be on these sectors where we have noticed a concentration of a larger proportion of women's employment, viz., education, health and other social services. It is an established fact that this is the sector which receives the first impact of an economy drive, both in the public and in the private sector. We may, therefore, anticipate a slowing down, if not an actual reduction in the opportunities for women's employment in these services and professions.

The overriding inference from the existing trends in different sectors of the economy suggests, that without increasing opportunity for women's employment in the productive sectors, it will not be possible to arrest the established trend of decline in women's economic participation that we have pointed out earlier. The marginal contribution that the tertiary sector can make to the employment situation as a whole is negligible, and in the interest of economic development of the country as a whole, attempts are bound to be made in the near future to reduce the present imbalance between the production and the tertiary sectors. This points to the imperative need to increase opportunities for women in the former.

Infrastructure for Women's Participation in a Modernizing Economy

The sectorwise examination of women's rights and opportunities for economic participation, indicates that the major forces affecting women's employment, stem from structural changes within the economy — in agriculture, industry, and the economy as a whole. The change from traditional to a modern market economy, from laissez-faire to deliberate planned development, from unorganized to organized production, from unregulated to regulated relations of production, from labour to capital intensive technology, and the intensification of socio-economic inequalities, all have had an impact on the employment situation. Women being a vulnerable group with fewer avenues open to them, have been affected more adversely than men.

Six

Development of Women after Independence

Modern methods of production, marketing and planning call for a higher level of knowledge and those skills than required by a traditional economy. The increasing complexity and inter-relationship among production, investment and the process of competitive selection, increases the importance of education and dissemination of information.

Though educational opportunities did expand in the post-Independence period, it was relatively slower among women, particularly at the primary and secondary levels. The rate of expansion was much faster at the level of higher education, and was the virtual monopoly of the middle-class. In the case of women, both secondary and higher education was practically confined to the urban middle-class. On the other hand, the number of illiterates, who remained outside the reach of the educational system also increased — the women outnumbering the men. This pattern of educational development, coupled with the changes in the economy, has, inevitably affected the economic opportunities of women.

The work participation rate by educational level shows that while employment opportunities for educated women have increased, there has been a negative trend in the participation rate of illiterate and semi-literate women, whose share in employment has declined.

During 1961-71 the participation rate for illiterate women declined substantially from 81.1 per cent to 65.8 per cent in urban areas, but showed marginal variations in rural areas [Tables 6.1(A) & (B)]. As pointed out in section II B and III A, the employment of women has declined significantly both in unorganized non-agricultural occupations and in organized industry. Our review indicates that there is a large-scale displacement of illiterate and semiliterate women workers from organized industry and non-agricultural occupations in the unorganized sector. This is also evident from the fact that the drop has been more marked in the urban areas. A superficial conclusion that could be drawn from this data, is that the decline in the numbers of illiterate or semi-literate women workers, indicates a rising level of education.

TABLE - 6.1(A)

EDUCATIONAL STATUS OF WORKERS URBAN 1961 AND 1971

Sl. No.	*Educational Level*	*1961*				*1971*			
		Total Workers		*% workers to total M & F*		*Total Workers*		*% workers to total M & F*	
		Males	*Females*	*M*	*F*	*Males*	*Females*	*M*	*F*
1.	Total	22419892	4010042			28554300	3285700		
2.	Illiterate	7895414	3253237	35.2	81.1	9129500	2165400	31.9	65.8
3.	Literate without educational level	6792861	321460	30.2	8.0	3295100	165300	11.5	5.0
4.	Primary or junior basic	4449714	209167	19.8	5.2	5260000	208100	18.4	6.2
5.	Matriculation or Higher Secondary	2330992	143113	10.4	3.5	4368300	149500	15.1	4.4
6.	Technical diploma not equal to degree	67116	6914	0.3	0.1	4759000	371200	16.6	11.3
7.	Non-technical diploma not equal to degee	110385	11957	0.4	0.2	42000	5800	0.1	0.1
8.	Graduate or postgraduate	599707	36370	2.6	0.8	132600	27200	0.4	0.8
9.	Technical degree or diploma equal to degree or post-graduate degree	173703	27824	0.7	0.6	983300	87300	3.4	2.3
10.	Engineering	42831	116	0.1	0.0	305800	49800	1.0	1.4
11.	Medicine	36849	5713	0.1	0.1	278700	56100	0.9	1.3
12.	Agriculture	4992	28	0.0	0.0	132600	1400	0.4	0.0
13.	Veterinary and dairying	2170	10	0.0	0.0	67900	15100	0.2	0.3
14.	Technology	2744	30	0.0	0.0	11900	200	0.0	0.0
15.	Teaching	42487	114470	0.1	0.4	57000	38100	0.1	1.1
16.	Others	41610	2457	0.1	0.0	9300	1300	0.0	0.0
				100.0	100.0			100.0	100.0

The pattern of women's educational development in the years since independence, however, indicates that it has failed to penetrate, in any significant manner, the large mass of illiterate adult women, whose numbers have increased over the years. Since they also come from the poorest section of the population, where employment is a dire necessity, this change in the composition of the women workforce has to be regarded as an indicator of the displacement of this section of women from the workforce, a consequence of the changing levels of technology, and methods of business organization. The increase in the participation rate of the technical diploma holders from 0.6 per cent to 2.3 per cent, indicates the operation of the growing demand for modern technical skills in new industries like electronics, pharmaceuticals, electricals, etc., and in new services for technical personnel. The distribution of degree holders and technical female personnel by labour-force status and level of education indicates that the majority of them were employees and only 2.1 per cent being self-employed (Table 6.2).

TABLE - 6.1(B)
EDUCATIONAL STATUS OF WORKERS IN RURAL INDIA. 1961 &1971

Sl. No.	*Educational Level*	*1961*				*1971*			
		Total Workers		*% workers to total M & F*		*Total Workers*		*% workers to total M & F*	
		Males	*Females*	*M*	*F*	*Males*	*Females*	*M*	*F*
1.	Total	106750873	55494693			119791400	27712600		
2.	Illiterate	73244022	53078059	69.5	95.6	77887100	25527400	65.1	92.1
3.	Literate (without educational level)	23403673	1772430	21.0	3.2	14857100	893300	12.4	3.3
4.	Primary	8512723	578515	8.1	1.1	15382000	842000	12.9	3.0
5	*Middle	—	—			7286900	241300	6.1	0.8
6.	**Matriculation and above	1590185	65689	1.4	0.1	4378300	208600	3.7	0.7
7.	Matriculation or Higher Secondary					3645400	138100	3.1	0.4
8.	Non-Tech. diploma or certificate not equal to degree					55300	7400	0.0	0.0
9.	Technical diploma or certificate not equal to degree					109900	36700	0.0	0.1
10.	Graduate and above					567700	26400	0.4	0.0

* The educational category as 'middle' given separately is applicable only to 1971 figures whereas for 1961 it is included in the category of 'primary'.

** Classification of educational level in 1961 is made only up to 'Matriculation and above' whereas that of 1971 is up to Graduate and above and is in the table. The figures in the 1971 column against the educational category of Matriculation and above are given to facilitate comparison. These figures represent the total sum of all educational categories, commencing from Serial Nos. 7 to 10.

Source: 1961 figures : Part II B (i) General Economic Tables; and 1971 figures : Paper 3 of 1972 Economic characteristics of population.

TABLE - 6.2

DISTRIBUTION OF DEGREE HOLDERS AND TECHNICAL FEMALE PERSONNEL BY STATUS AND LEVEL OF EDUCATION, 1971

(Selected Categories)

Labour Force Status	*Doctorate*		*Master Post-graduate*		*Bachelor*	*Equivalent*	*Diploma*	*Certificate*	*Total*
	No.	*%*	*No.*	*%*					
A. 1. Employee	1373	70.8	40302	48.1	99344	32.0	6599	55.0	147618 (36.1)
2. Self-Employed	51	2.6	1700	2.0	5982	1.9	950	7.9	8683 (2.1)
3. Unemployed trying for jobs	243	12.5	15376	18.4	62126	20.0	2061	17.2	79804 (19.5)
B. 4. Student trainees	84	0.2	326	0.4	3424	1.1	159	1.3	3913 (1.0)
5. Apprentice	—	-	33	Neg.	394	0.2	65	0.5	492 (0.1)
C. 6. Unemployed and not trying for job	135	7.1	15192	18.2	73721	23.7	1107	9.3	90155 (22.1)

Compiled from Census of India 1971, G. Series Table (National level) Degree holders and Technical Personnel (P), Office of the R.G. India.

Among the educated women, the worker rates for women who have received a technical degree and diploma (mainly in teaching and medicine) were substantially higher than those who had received non-technical degree or diplomas or had studied up to the Higher Secondary level. The differential according to fields of specialization of technical degree and diploma holders are smaller among males than among females. The distribution of women degree holders and technical personnel by sector of employment show that 58 per cent are employed in the public sector, 36.6 per cent in the private sector and 5.4 per cent are self-employed. (Table 6.3)

The extent to which persons of different educational levels undertake productive roles in the economy is an indicator of the nature of utilization of the investment in their education. Women with degree or diploma in medicine and teaching generally pursue a career. The differential in participation rate between such women and their male counterparts in not more than 20 per cent.

The Table 6.4 gives the proportion of formally trained men and women in selected occupational categories indicating that employed women by and large are better equipped than men in most of the occupations.

TABLE - 6.3
DISTRIBUTION OF WOMEN DEGREE-HOLDERS AND TECHNICAL PERSONNEL BY SECTOR EMPLOYMENT

Level of Education	*Total*	%	*Sector of Employment*					
			Public	%	*Private*	%	*Self-Employed*	
Doctorate	1380		1005	1.2	328		47	
	(100.0)	0.9	(72.8)		(23.8)	0.6	(3.4)	0.6
Master/Post-	40081		22507		16015		1559	19.3
graduate	(100.0)	26.8	(56.2)	26.0	(40.0)	29.3	(3.8)	
Bachelor/	100605		58231		36798		5576	
Equivalent	(100.0)	67.3	(57.9)	67.1	(36.6)	67.3	(5.5)	69.0
Diploma/	7444		4980		2565		899	
Certificate	(100.0)	5.0	(66.9)	5.7	(21.0)	2.8	(12.1)	11.1
All levels of	149510		86723		54706		8081	
Education	(100.0)	100.0	(58.0)	100.0	(36.6)	100.0	(5.4)	100.0

Source: Census of India 1971, G-Series Table (National Level), Degree holders and Technical Personnel (Provisional), Office of the Registrar General, India, Ministry of Home Affairs, New Delhi.

TABLE - 6.4
PERCENTAGE OF FORMALLY TRAINED * MEN AND WOMEN IN SELECTED OCCUPATIONAL CATEGORIES

		Men	*Women*
(i)	University teachers	49.4	37.9
(ii)	Secondary teachers	63.7	77.8
(iii)	Primary & Middle teachers	77.0	81.6
(iv)	Labour and Social Welfare	21.2	35.2
(v)	Librarians & Archivists	53.8	72.5
(vi)	Village Officials	27.8	35.5
(vii)	Allopathic physicians and surgeons	96.1	100.0

* Holding degrees, diplomas, certificate in profession concerned.
Source: Occupational-Educational Pattern in India (Public Sector) 1968.

The rising participation rate of educated women is also witnessed by the Employment Exchange statistics. Since 1963 the number of female job seekers with matriculation as well as higher education on the live Register has increased more rapidly than for males. Between 1964-68 the number of female job seekers registered with Employment Exchange increased by about 81 per cent while that of male job seekers increased by only 14 per cent. For matriculates and higher educated job seekers the corresponding increases were 72 per cent and 116 per cent for males and females respectively (Visaria, 1971). In 1973 the percentage increase of women work seekers over the previous year was 25.7 per cent for those with qualification below middle school, 39 per cent for matriculates and undergraduates and 95.4 per cent for graduates and postgraduates. This phenomenon assumes importance in view of the relatively rapid spread of women's education in urban India and the paucity of employment opportunities. Taking different subject fields together, the average duration of unemployment is higher for women than for men, as indicated in the Table 6.5.

TABLE - 6.5

AVERAGE (MEDIAN) DURATION OF UNEMPLOYMENT AMONG GRADUATES AND TECHNICAL PERSONNEL BY SEX LEVEL OF EDUCATION

	Male	*Female*
All levels of Education	12.9	14.8
Doctorates	12.0	15.1
Master/Postgraduate	13.1	16.9
Bachelor/Equivalent	12.7	14.2
Diploma	16.7	17.4
Certificate	20.8	24.0

* 1971 Census special enumeration.

According to the Census of 1971, the average waiting period for a male graduate before getting employment was 12.9 as against 14.8 months for a woman graduate. The only exception to this in the field of medicine and nursing where the average waiting period for men with postgraduate qualification and with doctorate is higher than for women. This sometimes acts as a strong deterrent for many a woman without specialization from seeking employment.

The total stock of degree holders and technical personnel by subject field, level of education and sex, and the distribution of degree holders and technical personnel who were found unemployed, was obtained by CSIR on individual enumeration slip in 1971. The study revealed that out of 4 lakh women degree holders only one and a half lakh were employed which is only 4 per cent of the total working women is the country. Of these employed women, 62 per cent earned less than Rs. 500 and 17 per cent earned between Rs. 500 and Rs. 1000. Of total number of unemployed women graduates only 110,000 women were seeking jobs and the largest number of this component were holding degree in Arts and Humanities and the next were those holding degrees in Science. Of the women who were not seeking employment, 55 per cent had degrees in Arts and humanities, 50 per cent in Science, 18 per cent in technical or engineering and 9 per cent in vocational courses.

The Dilemma of Idleness among Educated Women

The paradox of women's employment is that while illiteracy drives many out of employment, education does not necessarily lead to their employment.

> That participation ratios are not higher has at least as much to do with considerations of status and prestige as with the absence of jobs for those who seek but cannot find them. It is of course conceivable that a more progressive and expanding society could elevate the position of women and change attitudes towards female work. But an economy whose capacity to absorb men of working age is strained, does not encourage the elimination of traditional forms of discriminations against economic activity by women. G. Myrdal (*Asian Drama*).

Idleness can both be voluntary and involuntary. Since our labour market does not provide full, productive and freely chosen employment and jobs are at a premium, many women prefer to avoid the competitive pressures. Utilization of labour in any society depends to a certain extent on social institutions, taboos and inhibitions related to status and work which affect women more than men. These attitudes are reflected in social institutions, and the relationship between institutions and attitudes is mutually reinforcing.

The development of education has been mainly confined to middle-class families, among whom the attitude to women's employment outside the home had been most restrictive. This attitude however has been changing rapidly under economic pressure and the changing social scene. The real difficulty lies in the failure of the economy to absorb all its labour power and to appreciate the need for an institutionalized pattern of labour utilization that takes note of women's roles as housewives and mothers. So far, in spite of occasional lip service to the idealised image of women in these roles, little attempt has been made to assess its productive value. Still less attention has been given to providing the necessary infrastructure to remove women's disabilities in the labour market. Education alone cannot remove these disabilities.

Vocational and Technical Training

The need to relate education and particularly vocational training to actual employment opportunities has been repeatedly emphasized by various expert bodies like the ILO, the National Commission on Labour, the All-India Council for Technical Education, the Institute of Applied Manpower Research and the University Grants Commission, Committee on Coordination of University Education with Manpower Requirements (1967).

In view of the current social prejudices against employment of women and their large-scale displacement from employment as a result of structural and technological changes taking place in the economy, vocational training for women requires special attention and priority. This has been emphasized by the International Labour Conference in 1965 and the UN Commission on the Status of Women in each of its reports. In India, the National Committee on Women's Education, had pleaded strongly for better and more extensive facilities for vocational training for women particularly since the general educational system paid little regard to the needs of industry and commerce.

The inadequacy of vocational training opportunities for women, widens the productivity gap between men and women at all levels and makes them unwanted by the economy. Training facilities when they are provided, display the existing social bias regarding the suitability of particular occupations for women which leads to overconcentration in a limited group of subjects.

Our examination of opportunities for vocational and technical education for women is based on the following: (a) on the job training; (b) pre-employment training-technical and professional; (c) training programmes undertaken by different Government

Departments and Voluntary Organizations for developing skills and human resources. We have not included professional training at the university level because, as will be discussed in the next chapter, there is no real evidence of discrimination or any substantial wastage of training at this level.

On the Job Training

The major factor limiting women's contribution to the modern industrial sector is lack of adequate opportunities for on-the-job-training. We have already pointed out that women have been greater victims of rationalization and modernization in industry. Some of the new industries like electronics, simple engineering, telecommunications etc provided in-service-training to women with comparatively higher educational qualifications. In spite of opportunities provided by these few industries, however, the disparity in opportunities available to men and women is glaring. Under the Apprentices Act, 1961, 161 trades with 87,000 places have been located for apprentices in 101 industries. 52,500 apprentices have actually been engaged against these places of which only 104 are women whose distribution in different trades may be seen in Table 6.6. The bias for confining women trainees to limited group of trades is clearly visible here.

TABLE - 6.6

STATEMENT INDICATING THE NUMBER OF WOMEN APPRENTICES UNDER TRAINING, UNDER THE APPRENTICES ACT-1961 (AS ON 31.3.74)

S.No.	*Designated Trade*	*No. of Apprentices*
1.	Book Binder	41
2.	Compositor Hand	21
3.	Clerk General	16
4.	Book Keeping & Accountancy	1
5.	Sales Assistant	6
6.	Hotel Clerk/Receptionists	2 + 2
7.	House Keeper	6
8.	Laboratory Assistant	1
9.	Sheet Metal Worker	3
10.	Grinder	1
11.	Draughtsman Civil	3
12.	Others	1
	Total :	104

Representatives of trade unions informed us that the training provided to workers for handling new machinery in different industries, seldom extends to women except in the few specific industries like machine tools, telecommunications and electronics in which women's greater aptitude for particular operation has already been recognized.

Pre-employment Training

In the non-engineering trades where women constitute 44.97 per cent of the total number of trainees, the most popular, trades are cutting and tailoring, embroidery and needle work, knitting, and stenography. Of these, the first two are completely monopolized by women even in co-educational institutions. The situation is very different in the engineering trades where they form a mere 0.27 per cent of the total trainees. The most popular courses are for draftsman, instrument, mechanics, radio and T.V. mechanics, electronics, surveyors, carpenters and painters.

On the recommendation of the National Committee on Women's Education, the Ministry of Education took up a scheme to establish 24 women polytechnics for post-matriculation training in various skills in industrial, commercial and public service occupations 'in accordance with developing needs of the national economy' and to 'promote awareness of new opportunities and needs for women workers in such fields as social welfare, nursing, chemical and pharmaceutical industries, etc., in which women could be gainfully employed'. The total admission capacity of all these polytechnics is over 2000 for courses which require 2 to 3 years for completion. According to the Ministry of Education in commercial practice, stenography, catering and food technology, the admissions exceed the sanctioned capacity, while in other trades they fall short of the available number of seats. The out-turn for all the courses is considerably lower than the admissions. The total out-turn during 1973 amounted to only 822 against an admission figure of 2143, i.e., 38.3 per cent. This points to both wastage of available facilities as well as a failure in the realization of the objectives of this scheme. In the absence of inadequate assistance in placement, quite a few women on completion of these courses remain unemployed. The second reason for this is that the courses are not designed with any particular consideration for the employment potential of the locality. For example, during the Committee's tour of Andhra Pradesh we were informed by officials of the Industries Department that though there was an increasing demand for women in the telecommunication and electronic industries, none of the women's polytechnics in the State were providing training in these subjects. On our asking why nothing been done, the officials replied that the control of polytechnics rested with the Department of Education and not Industries. In Himachal Pradesh we received a number of requests from women's groups for training in food technology so that the products of their orchards are not wasted but no training facilities of this type exist in that State. Courses introduced are not always in relation to the demands of the region, e.g., dress and costume designing, a significant avenue for employment of women in bigger cities, hardly constitutes an important or a significant source of employment in the interior of the country. A heavy concentration on the same course, e.g., tailoring, also leads to minimization of job opportunities.

In 1968-69 the All India Council for Technical Education reviewed the functioning of women's polytechnics and came to the conclusion:

1. A direct relationship should be established between course of training provided and employment opportunities available. For this purpose, for each polytechnic, there should be an advisory Committee including representative of employing organizations. Before any new course is started, close consultation should be held with the prospective employers to determine available job opportunities.
2. Each polytechnic should establish a production centre in the relevant field to provide practical training and improve standards and content of the courses. Such production centres might be started with the assistance of small-scale industries departments of the State concerned.
3. Polytechnics should offer short term job-oriented courses in selected fields where employment opportunities exist.
4. Start an employment advisory service for its students.
5. Service units should be established in these institutions to

cater to the needs of the local public in such matters as providing practical, services blue prints, model estimates, etc.

Earlier 75 per cent of the non-recurring expenditure and 75 per cent of the recurring expenditure was borne by the Central Government. Since the commencement of the 4th Plan the Central Government stopped direct financial assistance for implementing specific development programme and now it is for the State Government to implement these recommendations.

Unfortunately while the Ministry of Education supplied information regarding the list of sanctioned courses and admission capacity in each of the 24 polytechnics, we were unable to obtain actual information regarding the teaching facilities available in the different institutions. Unofficially information received from different sources suggests that in many of the institutions some of the courses exist only on paper, particularly since the stoppage of central grants. Many of the State Governments find it difficult to provide adequate support to these institutions for their general maintenance. This could account for the very poor number of admissions against the courses for the country as whole. The second reason is the failure to implement the recommendations of the All India Council for Technical Education regarding the opening of production centres and provision of employment advisory service. Technical training for women is a relatively new field in India. In the absence of greater assistance in the placement of successful trainees, parents will be reluctant to send them to these institutions.

It is to be noted that some private institutions providing similar types of training to young women in the large cities, including a placement services, which connect training to the actual employment potential of the area, have proved to be highly successful. Mention may be made here of two institutions in Delhi. The Secretarial Training School, started by the Young Women's Christian Association some years ago, has proved to be so successful as to justify its expansion to other types of vocational courses during the last few years. A similar unit started by St. Thomas Girls' Higher Secondary School has also expanded rapidly, and is attracting students with even university degrees. Their success lies in their placement assistance and in the liaison that they maintain with employing agencies.

In the present socio-economic set up, self-employment of women requires much more than training in a particular productive trade. Without knowledge of the market mechanism, and capital resources, training alone cannot help women to face the competition. The production centres recommended by the All India Council for Technical Education as a part of polytechnic training have remained conspicuous by their absence. In our view, without supportive assistance in the way of training in organization of production and marketing and in procuring capital and raw materials, it will not be possible for the majority of these young trainees to utilize their training in self-employment.

The officials of the Industries Department in Andhra Pradesh informed us that in spite of the existence of a Government scheme to provide financial assistance for generating self-employment, the Department has been unable to assist many women to obtain the required help from banks. Even when such projects are sanctioned by Government, banks hesitate to provide the loans as they feel that the life of the projects may terminate when these young women get married.

Training Programmes Undertaken by Different Agencies in Charge of Development

Unlike the more formal programmes of pre-employment training, in the sphere of informal training programmes, a great deal of emphasis has been given to training women by various agencies in charge of development and welfare. All agencies specifically concerned with women's welfare and development, both government and voluntary, have always attached the highest priority to improving women's earning capacity.

Training Schemes to Improve the Earning Capacity of Women

Programmes have been developed to solve the economic needs of women hard-pressed by the processes of social change and break-down of familiar obligations to support needy women-widows, deserted and aged women as well as women from lower income groups.

(i) The Central Social Welfare Board is the most important agency providing assistance for these programmes operated by autonomous and voluntary organizations. It provides financial assistance for setting up production units in small-scale industries, handicrafts and ancillary units for larger industrial undertakings. In 1972-73, 24 handicraft units were functioning with an employment potential of 975. Apart from this, 21 handloom training-cum-production centres are being assisted by the Board. Some training centres have also been set up in association with the All-India Handicrafts Board. There are 21 institutions running production units for handlooms under this programme in various States with an employment potential of 790. According to information available, a total of 140 units are in existence under this programmes providing employment to 4,235 workers.

(ii) Training of development cadres: Under the insistence of various developmental agencies, particularly the Central Social Welfare Board, training courses have been developed for village level workers (Gramsevikas, Gramlakshmis, Mukhya Sevikas, Bal-sevikas, etc., by agencies like the Kasturba Memorial Trust, Visva Bharati, Jamia Milia and various schools of social work. They are mostly pre-service or in-service training for these cadres, fully financed by Government.

(iii) The programmes by the Kasturba Memorial Trust, Visva Bharati and Jamia Milia, have displayed considerable innovative acumen in developing new types of cadres for working in rural areas.

(iv) The Indian Council for Child Welfare also runs 27 centres in different parts of the country for pre-service and in-service training for Bal-sevikas. The training is financed by the Government.

(v) The Ministry of Health has training programmes for Health Visitors and auxiliary nurse midwife for developing health services in both rural and urban areas.

The Ministry of Food and Agriculture has also organized 22 community canning and food preservation centres. There are four institutes of catering technology and applied nutrition in the country. Though not exclusively for women, they train some women. Under the co-ordinated programme for community development, training is given in selected productive activities like kitchen-gardening, poultry keeping, dairy science, etc.

The Ministry of Home Affairs has a scheme for training of women and children of Central Government employees belonging to the low income groups. There are 62 centres under this scheme. Training is provided in cutting, tailoring and embroidery. Students are recommended as private candidates for the diploma courses of the Industrial Training Institutes. Some home employment is provided to these women through Government contracts.

Similar programmes have been initiated in few of the States by the Department of Welfare, Labour, Industry and Education for training mainly in sewing, embroidery, handicrafts and tailoring.

We visited a number of these training centres. In our view, much of this well-meant effort ends in futility, because they are not linked to production and marketing. The bias for traditional or home crafts limits their scope since the indigenous markets for these products are now on the decline, and marketing, both internal and for export, is mainly in the hands of intermediaries. Strangely even the Government Emporiums are also dealing through middlemen and do not buy directly through the production centres, even though the latter are financed by Government. Even without these handicaps, the scope of the programmes are so limited that they can only make a marginal impact on the employment needs of women. Another difficulty lies in the multiplicity of agencies engaged in this work, leading often to duplication and over-concentration in a few areas, leaving the large areas of the country completely untouched.

It is unfortunate that though the training programmes developed by welfare and other developing agencies have shown greater understanding of the employment needs of women, their efforts suffer from lack of adequate resources and coordination. In our view, better degree of planning, coordination and redistribution of responsibilities in these fields would prevent considerable wastage of resources and instil a greater sense of urgency and productivity in these schemes for improving women's earning power.

Seven

Problems of Working Women

Part-time Employment

While part-time employment presents a partial solution of the employment needs of many women, there is no generally accepted definition of such types of employment in terms of hours, remuneration and other facilities. The ILO described two occupational categories which employ the largest number of part-time workers in both developing and developed countries, cleaning and related work—both in private households and institutions, and professional and technical services. Other areas where part-time work is common are agriculture and commerce and manufacturing. Particularly in consumer goods industries. The available statistical data does not make it possible to obtain an accurate picture. Since the arrangements for part-time employment are largely determined by the nature and pressure of work, it can only be conceived within the framework of the broader policies guiding and governing the integration of women in economic life.

In response to the ILO's enquiry regarding the possibility of providing part-time employment to women with family responsibilities, many governments expressed their reservation. They felt that providing such employment to women only may adversely affect full-time employment opportunities, or may result in discrimination and exploitation in respect of employment and promotion. It was stated that part-time employment should not be imposed on women with family responsibilities who, if given suitable child-care services, would prefer full-time employment.

Such views ignore the repeated advice of expert bodies like the ILO or the National Committee on Women's Education in India and reflect the attitude of employers and workers who fear the invasion of the labour market by part-time workers. Part of this apprehension is also due to the difficulties in making administrative arrangements for such workers. It should be noted that this kind of resistance is found mainly in the organized sector whose wide structure, labour policy and legal provisions are geared to the needs of full-time workers only. In the unorganized sector, part-time employment is very much of a reality. As we have pointed out earlier, very little is known about dimensions of this group either in numbers or in the nature of their problems. The studies conducted by the ILO in 1952 and 1962, referred to the serious gaps in national information regarding employment opportunities, number and characteristics of persons engaged in or seeking part-time employment. The International Labour Conference recommended that surveys need to be conducted in cooperation with employers and workers, regarding the scope of part-time employment.

The International Labour Conference resolution concerning part-time employment and the employment of older women, adopted at the 38th session in 1955, drew attention to the basic principles that it should not adversely affect full time employment and general level of wages, contrary to the provision of the Convention on Equal Remuneration. It further mentioned that adequate attention should be paid to the conditions of employment. With particular reference to the need of equality of opportunity and treatment with full-time workers, equality of remuneration and rights in respect of holidays with pay, sick leave and maternity leave, and adequate social security protection. Obviously these points raise many problems in practice, because of adequate information relating to the demand and the opportunities for part-time work, needs and preferences for such work and the size and characteristics of part-time workers.

While empirical investigations are necessary to assess the need, scope as well as problems of part-time employment, conducting such enquiries among women already in full-time employment can yield misleading results. A pilot study conducted by the Tata Institute of Social Sciences and the Delhi School of Social Works found 74 per cent of the women reluctant to accept part-time employment because of its low remuneration. Such responses are obvious when it is noted that one-third of the respondents earned 50 per cent of their family income. Some were either the major or the only source of income of their respective families.

For women who need employment to augment the families income, and whose inability to arrange child care or home responsibilities, make full-time employment a burden on their physical and mental resources, part-time employment could be a boon provided it carried adequate remuneration and greater security and protection than it does at present. The first step to provide support to such women is to investigate the existing models of part-time employment prevalent in the unorganized sector and to provide legal and social support against their exploitation. We have been informed that the National Labour Institute proposes to initiate some experiments in offering part-time employment to women workers.

We suggest that an all-India survey should be undertaken to investigate in which areas and in what manner part-time employment of women, is possible, keeping in view their special problems. Availability of this data will help in adopting legal measures which will provide security of some employment benefits.

Problem of Re-entry

The ILO has drawn attention to the problem of re-entry into employment after a lengthy absence mainly caused by family reasons. Some countries have already provided safeguards for working mothers protecting their right to employment in jobs previously held or comparable ones, for a stipulated period of absence on prolonged maternity leave.

The ILO's questionnaire regarding adoption of an international instrument on this issue "evoked high proportion of negative replies, and of replies giving strictly qualified agreement". Most countries felt that in the early stages of social and economic development, an absolute commitment of this kind would not be justified as it may affect women's employment opportunities in an adverse manner, more so in the case of labour surplus economies, where law of supply and demand plays a decisive role. The general reaction from most Governments suggests that there would be considerable resistance to any uniform measure on this issue. Labour shortage economies may find it necessary to attract women into industries. But most countries believe that any such pressure may create resentment in the male labour force as discrimination.

The Government of India while supporting such policies as an ultimate objective felt that "in developing countries the more pressing problem is the expansion of employment opportunities for the vast numbers of the unemployed and the under employed. This must inevitably be a prior pre-occupation of all policies in these countries."

Re-entry after a prolonged absence caused by definite withdrawal from employment for family reasons may pose a greater problem, particularly in white-collared jobs and professions. Technological, scientific and organizational development during the period of their absence tends to make the previous experience of such women obsolete.

It should be noted that this type of withdrawal and return to employment is found mainly among middle and upper class women. Working class women, whose survival depends on their earnings cannot afford such behaviour. With greater acceptance of small family norms and higher cost of living, the need for such return to active economic participation will increase for both economic and social reasons. In our opinion, provision for part-time employment will reduce the problem of lack of continuity in such cases.

Problem of Late Entry

Such measures, however, cannot solve the problems of women who seek employment at a later age without previous experience, primarily for economic reasons. Loss of financial support, due to widowhood or separation from husbands make their need for employment more acute. In many cases such women also lack educational qualifications. The condensed courses have tried to meet their educational problems to a certain extent, but unless the age limit for recruitment for this group is realized, it would be difficult to solve their employment problems.

A great necessity for all these groups is assistance and counselling for placement and training. The present employment service is ill-equipped for such assistance. Special efforts will have to be made to provide adequate information and assistance to such women seeking work. It will also necessarily combat existing prejudices among employers and workers against them.

Child Care Services

The need for child care services for employed women has already been accepted though legal provision for it has been made only for women in organized industry. No such arrangements are available for women working in offices or the vast mass of women employed in the unorganized sector.

During our tours, groups of working women, particularly in the urban areas, referred to the great difficulty which they experienced in the absence of creches or day nurseries for their children. Women office workers in the urban areas, do not enjoy any facilities of this kind for the care of their children during their working hours. The few private creches or nurseries, being operated by voluntary organizations or individuals, are highly inadequate and generally, too expensive for women who need them most. A suggestion that was made to us by many office workers was to provide a room in offices where children could be looked after. Many of them were even prepared to make necessary arrangements to provide an attendant out of their own resources.

In big cities, where the problem of distance and overcrowding on public transports makes it difficult for women to carry their children to their place of work, the best solution lies in community or neighbourhood creches in the residential areas. The urgency of providing these institutions have been repeatedly emphasized by all expert bodies studying problems of women's employment. The ILO has suggested that governments should take steps to coordinate the provision of these facilities by employers, voluntary agencies and community effort to ensure their even distribution and at least minimum standards of services.

Accommodation and Security

The problem of accommodation has become acute for working women both in urban as well as rural areas. This was emphasized in a National Seminar on Social Problems of Working Women in 1973. Educated women are reluctant to go and work in rural areas because of accommodation difficulties, though efforts are being made by Government to provide accommodation to Government functionaries in education, health and other developmental services. These efforts have not, however, always taken into consideration the questions of security and distance from place. The problem is acute for both single women who are not fully accepted by rural society, and for married women with families.

In urban areas, working women living in slums face high incidence of disease and socially deviant behaviour, the primary cause of which lies in bad housing. The employers' responsibility for providing adequate housing is generally not fulfilled. For unmarried working women some efforts have been made during the last two decades to provide hostels with the aid of voluntary agencies. The Central Social Welfare Board's programme in this connection is being supported by the Department of Social Welfare, with building grants for such hostels. Their numbers are, however, still very limited, and they can cater to the needs only of middle-class working women. The problem needs to be solved by co-ordinating efforts of Government, employers and voluntary agencies.

The problem of security to which women workers, particularly young ones, are exposed, has been pointed out in the reports of certain Committees of the Government and Social Welfare Organizations. A Committee of the Maharashtra Government examined the difficulties that women government functionaries have to face, particularly in rural areas, and recommended that women functionaries posted in rural areas should be of a more advanced age. A similar Committee, appointed by the Government of Karnataka, recommended posting older women as supervisory staff and involvement of senior local women, including wives of senor official. The Committee of the Maharashtra Government also advised setting up of enquiry committees at divisional headquarters for such grievances of women officials on a priority basis.

While we realize that these problems are essentially related to the transitional state of our society, some supportive measures to look into these difficulties and to provide assistance, is a necessity at present.

Service Conditions

Both the Committees of Maharashtra and Karnataka, referred to above, recommended changes in the cadre and recruitment rules for various categories of women workers needed for developmental activities. The existing rules, in their opinion, kept out "really qualified and experienced women from the purview of these posts." The Maharashtra Government has relaxed the maximum age limit for recruitment with a view to recruiting women of greater experience for work in rural areas. Possibilities for similar relaxation in other states need to be examined. In Uttar Pradesh, local women are trained and posted to their own villages to ensure greater acceptance by the society.

During our tours, we received complaints from various categories of women employees regarding service conditions. Many of these cadres are working on an ad hoc basis from plan to plan or sometimes even on annual extension of their services. They are denied promotion opportunities and adequate pay scales. This is particularly the case with women recruited for the rural development programmes of the Central Welfare Board and Department of Community Development. Similar complaints of lack of promotion opportunities were made by telephone operators, clerks, typists and stenographers. The representatives of the Trained Nurses Association pointed out the absence of gazetted posts in their profession. Nurses we met during our tours also complained of overcrowding in hospitals, long hours of duty, and lack of accommodation for married nurses. The Auxiliary Nurse Midwives posted in rural areas face an additional problem of transport and security in case of night calls.

There is a general feeling among many of these women workers that even where promotional possibilities exist. The claims of the women are discriminated against not only by private employers but even by the Government.

A major problem repeatedly brought to our notice was on the question of transfers. Though most of the State Governments have adopted conventions, to post husband and wife to the same place, if they are both in Government service, this has not always been possible. This convention has sometimes resulted in single women being subjected to frequent transfers causing great hardship. While we appreciate the administrative difficulties of fulfilling such a convention, frequent transfers of low paid women employees should be avoided as they cause innumerable difficulties.

Some consideration is also needed for provision of adequate transport or transport allowance to women who have to carry out touring duties. The inadequacy of this provision often results in inefficiency. The assistance of local authorities, including local self-governing bodies, could be obtained to provide suitable accommodation during night halts for these touring officials.

While we realize that many of these difficulties may be inevitable in a transitional situation, it is our belief that a commitment to the national objective of integrating women into the process of development at all levels can help to solve them in due course. The constitutional guarantees and the objectives of the nation, require acceptance by the society of the multiple roles of women as home makers and mothers as socially and economically productive in the same manner as direct participation in the economic process. It is, therefore, imperative that society in general, and the State in particular, provide the necessary conditions and support to enable women to perform their various roles successfully. As citizens they deserve the protection of society. Marriage and motherhood, which contributes to the continuation of the nation should not become disabilities in the gainful participation of women in the economic process. Without the type of supportive services and institutionalized aids suggested above these dual roles will continue to impose a tremendous strain on the physical and mental resources of women. It will also affect the welfare and development of the future generation through inadequate care in childhood.

Conclusion and Recommendations

The Indian Constitution guarantees equality of opportunity in matters relating to employment and directs the State to secure equal rights to an adequate means of livelihood, equal pay from equal work, and just and humane conditions of work. Our Labour Laws concerning women reflect the attitude of protection and welfare through provision of maternity benefits, creches and restriction on types of work that are considered unsuitable to their health. Though the Government of India ratified the ILO Conventions regarding equal remunerations and against discrimination, this shifting emphasis towards equality and greater employment opportunities has not as yet found reflection in Indian laws. Executive actions initiated in this direction, have made some impact in the organized sector, but in the vast unorganized sector no impact of these measures have been felt either in conditions of work, wages, or opportunities.

The impact of transition to a modern economy has meant exclusion of an increasing number and proportion of women from active participation in the productive process. A considerable number continue to participate for no returns and no recognition. The majority of those who do participate fully are on sufferance, without equal treatment, security of employment and humane conditions of work. A very large number of them are subject to exploitation of various kinds with no protection from society or the State.

Adequate means for livelihood or employment is the chief objective of development. There has been little progress in the achievement of this right for both men and women, but estimates of employment and underemployment clearly indicate that the position is worse for women. While the Constitution has guaranteed equal rights, the measures initiated since independence to remove women's disabilities and handicaps, particularly in the field of economic participation, have proved to be extremely inadequate.

While the draft Fifth Five-Year Plan emphasizes the need to utilize all idle manpower to speed up the process of development, its priorities for women's development omits employment generation as a specific objective. It is assumed that the ratio of females to males in the labour force will remain constant at 16 per cent for the next years, visualizing no structural changes by which a greater participation of women in the productive process can be ensured.

The experience of some countries has shown, that it is possible by public policy to accelerate women's employment in new areas of work, by finding solutions to their problems of family life and child care. These countries see no necessary contradiction between encouraging women's work at all levels and maintaining laws protecting women's health and welfare, in view of their role as mothers. What is more distinctive about socialist countries is the effective institutionalization of the rights of a working mother by protecting her right to return to her job.

While several factors have handicapped Indian women from being effectively integrated into the process of development, the lack of a well-defined policy indicating areas where they require special assistance and protection leave them without access to knowledge, skills and employment. The replies received to our question regarding the policy followed in employing women in various concerns, indicate the continuation of old prejudices regarding women's efficiency, productivity, capacity for skills, and suitability that debar them from employment in many areas. Wage discrimination is the result of this restrictive confinement of women to limited types of work. The replies clearly indicate that while there is a definite policy for excluding women from various types of jobs, the criteria for determining their unsuitability are not clear or uniform. Certain industries declare them to be unsuitable for technical as well as manual jobs, others declare them to be unsuitable for managerial and administrative jobs as well as unskilled work, yet another group finds them unsuitable for field duties. The general tendency appears to be, to find them unsuitable for all jobs other than clerical. The West Bengal Public Service Commission even finds them unsuitable for certain teaching posts, though teaching is generally accepted as the most suitable profession for women. The Defence Forces find them unsuitable even for posts of legal officers in the office of the Judge, Advocate General which involves no combatant duties. We have pointed out many industries and administrative agencies where women have been found to be suitable for all these types of work.

The objective of a labour market policy is full, productive and freely chosen employment. Recasting the employment policies for women requires re-examination of existing theories regarding their suitability for different types of work on scientific lines, and a deliberate effort to promote equality of opportunity by special attention to women's disabilities and handicaps. The recommendations that we make are directed towards making the Constitutional guarantees meaningful and for arresting the trend towards gradual exclusion of women from their right to a fuller participation in the economic process.

We therefore recommend:

(i) The adoption of a well-defined policy to fulfil the

Constitutional directives and Government's long term objective of total involvement of women in national development. Such a policy should be framed by a government resolution.

This policy will need to be implemented carefully to avoid evasion by direct or indirect methods. Apart from specific occupations from which women are debarred by law, employers should not be permitted to exclude them from any occupation unless the basis for unsuitability is clearly specified.

(ii) The creation of a cell within the Ministry of Labour and Employment at both Central and State levels under the direction of a Senior Officer to deal with problems of women.

(iii) We further recommend the following changes in the existing laws:

A Maternity Benefits Act 1961

(i) This Act should be extended to all industries not covered by the Act at present and the provision of maternity relief ensured by the creation of a Central Fund by levying contributions from employers. The administration of the Fund should follow the pattern already established by the Employees State Insurance Corporation.

(ii) The Act should also cover agricultural labourers in the same manner as suggested for other industries. To facilitate its implementation, the Central Fund should also include a levy on agricultural farms employing hired labour, the quantum depending upon the size of the holding as recommended for the Agricultural Holding Tax by the Committee on Taxation of Agricultural Wealth and Income.

(iii) The anti-retrenchment clause already included in the Employees State Insurance Act 1948 should be incorporated in the Maternity Benefits Act.

(iv) For women retrenched for short period and re-employed on the same jobs, the period of unemployment should not be treated as discontinuation of service for their eligibility for this benefit. For casual labour, a minimum of 3 months of service should considered as qualifying them for this benefit.

(v) As decided by the Supreme Court in the case of bidi workers, the provision of maternity benefits should be extended to home workers in all other industries.

(vi) In order to eliminate unjust denial of maternity benefits, scrutiny of applications should be done by Committee of the management and trade union representatives. The latter should preferably include a woman. This will provide greater incentive to women workers to participate in trade activities.

(vii) The penalties for evasion of this law should be made more stringent.

(vii) The system of paying cash benefits in a lump-sum sometimes give rise to inadequate attention to the nutritional needs of the mother and the child. Payment of maternity benefits should be made in two instalments, before and after confinement, as already prevalent in many industries.

Provision of Creches

(i) The present limit of 50 women workers for the application of this provision under the Factories Act should be reduced to 20.

(ii) Women employed as casual labour or as contract labour should be entitled to share this benefit.

(iii) Wherever there is a demand, a day-centre should be provided for keeping small children for other groups of women workers, e.g., workers in offices, hospitals, shops and commercial establishment.

(iv) As far as possible, creches should be established near the residence of women workers rather than the place of work. The ideal arrangement, in our view, would be neighbourhood creches. This will benefit women in all occupations, both in the organized and unorganized sector.

Working Time

Permission to work up to 10 pm should be granted provided arrangements for transport and security are made.

We further recommend effective implementation of the Maternity Benefits Act in all States, and the extension of the Employees State Insurance Scheme to those areas which are not covered by it at present.

Equalization of Wages

(i) We recommend legislative enactment of Article 39 (d) of the Constitution — equal pay for equal work — to add the weight of legal sanction to what is only a policy at present.

(ii) We further recommend incorporation of this principle in the Minimum Wages Act.

Integrated Development of Training and Employment

(i) We recommend reservation of a definite quota for women for training within the industry in order to arrest their retrenchment as a consequence of modernization.

(ii) A similar quota should be reserved for women for training of apprentices under the National Apprentices Act.

(iii) We further recommend developing programmes of vocational training in close relationship with industries and resources located in the area. Links with possible employing agencies have to be developed from the beginning so that the training does not end in futility.

(iv) As recommended by the Committee of the All India Council for Technical Education, Polytechnics for women should include a production centre with assistance from the Small Scale Industries Department of the State concerned.

(v) Development of training programmes in production and market organization to develop self-employment.

(vi) Special efforts have to be made to develop vocational training for both illiterate and semi-literate women workers.

(vii) We further recommend development of training-cum-production centres in small scale or cottage industries in both rural and urban areas to provide employment to women near their homes.

Part-time Employment

We recommend specific provisions for part-time employment of women by suitable revisions in recruitment rules and service conditions. We also recommend detailed investigation of areas where part-time employment could be generated by agencies like the Directorate General of Employment and Training, the Institute of Applied Manpower Research, the National Council of Applied

Economic Research, etc. Such studies should include examination of existing avenues for part-time employment, viz., in the unorganized industries and occupations.

Employment Information

We recommend expansion of the national employment service, particularly in rural areas, and the development of a women's cadre in the service to provide employment information and assistance to women.

Provision for Re-entry

We recommend that provision for special leave without pay, subject to a maximum of 5 years during service, should be made in all occupations, in order to enable women to devote full-time for the care of their families. Their lien should be protected.

Enforcement of Laws Protecting Women Workers

We recommend increase in the number of women on the inspectorate of different labour Departments as well as provision for women welfare officers wherever women are employed.

We further recommend:

(i) That trade unionists and labour leaders should take steps to organize labour unions in the field of agriculture and other industries where such organizations do not exist at present.

(ii) Formation of women's wings in all trade unions, to look after the problems of women workers and to improve women's participation in trade union activities.

Rural Development and Agriculture

In India, rural women constitute nearly 80 per cent of the female population. They contribute largely to the country's economy which is mainly agriculture based. Although distributive justice has been categorically underlined in all the development plans, the needs of women have not been adequately addressed. While laying emphasis on enhanced agriculture production in which the involvement of women is high, the plans have fostered a target group and area oriented approach to reduce regional and ecological imbalances disregarding women's equality as embodied in the Constitution. Rural development programmes for women have only in recent decades recognized the crucial role of organization and mobilization as strategies for women's empowerment and development. Rural women's organizations are also mechanisms for restructuring and redistributing power and have been utilized pressure groups that influence and/or bargain on behalf of rural women.

Situational Analysis

The launching of the Community Development Programme in 1952 was a landmark in the history of India and ushered in an era of development with the participation of the people. The Community Development Programme adopted a systematic integrated approach to rural development with a hierarchy of village level workers and block level workers drawn from various fields to enrich rural life. Agriculture, animal husbandry, public health, women's development, rural industries, etc., found a special niche in the framework cast for this purpose. Five thousand National Extension Service Blocks were created under the Community Development Programmes by the end of the Second Five-Year Plan. During the Third Five-Year Plan the momentum was maintained through a series of developmental schemes though allocations under the NES programme tapered. This was succeeded by the Small Farmers Development Agencies, Crash Schemes for Rural Employment, Food for Work Programme, Drought Development Programme and Desert Development Programme in the early seventies. The contents of all these programmes were to strengthen the rural base of the economy, specifically the primary sector comprising agriculture, animal husbandry, etc., and employment through labour intensive works that would create the infrastructure of roads and other community assets for the benefit of the rural people.

It was recognized that the skewed pattern of landholdings stood in the way of creating an egalitarian society and obstructed modernization and intensification of agriculture. Land reform measures for abolition of intermediary tenures, tenancy reforms, imposition of land ceiling on agricultural holdings, distribution of surplus land to the landless agricultural workers and consolidation of land holdings were introduced through a series of State Legislations under Central guidelines.

Certain areas of the country are characterized by soil erosion, water stress and environmental degradation. The Drought Prone Areas Programme was started in 1973 aiming at an integrated area development for optimum utilization of land, water, livestock and human resources through a watershed management approach to mitigate the effects of drought. A few years later the Desert Development Programme a wholly centrally funded scheme, specifically to cover extremely arid areas for controlling desertification and restoration of ecological balance, was also started.

The emphasis shifted to fulfilling minimum needs of the people during the Fifth Five-Year Plan.

A systematic analysis and examination of the status and role of women within the agriculture and rural development strategies in India started with the National Plan of Action (NPA) for women which followed the report of the Committee on the Status of Women in India (CSWI). Subsequently, efforts of women activists, social science institutions and researchers produced enough documentary support to persuade the Sixth Plan document to include a chapter on 'Women and Development' for the first time in the country's history of planned development.

A strategy of direct attack on poverty was adopted in the Sixth Plan as the theory of trickle down benefits of general development programmes had not proved as a successful strategy for the removal of poverty. Forty-eight per cent of the population were found to be living below the poverty line at the beginning of the Sixth Five-Year Plan.

One positive outcome of these developments has been the recognition that rural women are not a homogeneous group to justify a uniform development strategy. The development plans in the case of women must be based on the assessment of their actual role and participation in socio-economic activities.

Women's employment has been recognized as the 'critical entry point' for women's integration in mainstream development. The low and deteriorating status of rural women is attributed to their declining economic participation and other factors like the modernization of the agricultural sector. The need for giving a better deal to the rural women is beginning to be widely recognized. It is now accepted that the participation of women themselves in development activities is the most effective tool for the promotion of the access of women to the benefits of development. A working group set up by the Deptt. of Rural Development, Ministry of Agriculture and Rural Development in 1978 recommended that the major objectives of the development plan for rural women should be (i) The improvement of their economic status; and (ii) The promotion of women's organization to have the collective strength to articulate their needs and promote their participation in the development process.

The Integrated Rural Development Programme initiated in 1978-79 and extended to all the development blocks in the country in 1980-81 was conceived as one of the instruments for a direct attack on poverty. It dealt with individual rural families below the poverty line. Credit from banking institutions and subsidy from the Government were given to the families for self-employment and income generation. Under IRDP, a special place was accorded for training rural unemployed youth for employment with the introduction of TRYSEM. An extensive scheme for the social and economic uplift of women belonging to families below the poverty line, DWCRA (Development of Women and Children in Rural Areas) was launched in 1982 as a subcomponent in IRDP.

The Sixth Plan accepted poor rural women to be targets of rural development strategies. The specific problems identified concerning rural poor women were (i) marginality of attention and services to them in rural and agricultural development (ii) special constraints that obstruct their access to available assistance and services such as, lack of training to develop their awareness and skills; lack of information and lack of bargaining power; (iii) low productivity and narrow occupational choices; (iv) low level of participation in decision-making; (v) inadequate finance and expert guidance for promoting socio-economic activity of rural women and their participation; (vi) inadequate monitoring of women's participation in different sectors; (vii) wage discrimination; (viii) inadequate application of science and technology to remove drudgery; and (ix) low health and nutrition status.

The Sixth Plan document stated that one of the most important means of achieving improvement in the status of women would be to secure for them a fair share of employment opportunities, to earmark a percentage of allocation for women, and to fix for them a quota in all the poverty alleviation programmes. The Seventh Plan reiterated the strategies suggested in the Sixth Plan with a sharper focus on the increased coverage of women in various rural development programmes.

Simultaneously, the National Rural Employment Programme (NREP), assuring wage employment to the unemployed rural population was introduced in 1980. Subsequently, concentration on the rural landless was attempted to the introduction of the Rural Landless Employment Guarantee Programme (RLEGP) in 1983. The Indira Awas Yojana was added as an important component of the programme in the Seventh Plan for constructing houses for SC/STs and freed bonded labourers. Social Forestry was added as another component of the RLEGP with national emphasis on greening fuel and fodder.

The establishment of the Technology Mission on Drinking Water and Related Water Management gave a new thrust to the Rural Water Supply Programme. Safe and adequate drinking water is to be provided to the entire rural population by the end of the Seventh Five-Year Plan.

The impact of the poverty alleviation programmes coupled with the development in various sectors reduced the rural population below the poverty line to 37 per cent by the beginning of the Seventh Plan. The target is to bring this down to 28 per cent by the end of the Seventh Plan Period.

Agriculture and allied fields provide the largest sector to women's employment. It largely determines the rural women's socio-economic status. This is the sector where women's role as unpaid labour in productive activities is most prominent and is responsible for conferring women a non-working status. In case of both agriculture and animal husbandry, development strategies have provided very little attention to women in comparison to their active involvement in both the sectors. Some training is imparted to women in agriculture and animal husbandry under the programmes for Farmers' Training and Krishi Vigyan Kendras.

But the Farmers Training Programme has lost much of its importance after the introduction of the new extension system of Training and Visit (T&V). Though women constitute a major work force in agriculture which with regional variation is estimated to be around 60 per cent, they are invisible in the T & V system. Currently there is one major extension programme for women in Karnataka and 2-3 such programmes on the anvil in other States. There is an inbuilt resistance observed in them in viewing women within their home making role. Even the visual presentations (slides, filmstrips and films) which are used for the orientation of the functionaries often depict the women in the field and the extension agent talking to the contact farmer on the field, fail to project the full dimension of women's role.

While rural women have become marginally visible in the anti-poverty programmes, they have not been adequately recognized in agricultural development, land reform, or rural industrialization. Non-recognition of women in agriculture has many implications. Intensive agriculture and the green revolution have reduced women's participation in on-farm activities but the work load related to the home based farm activities has increased considerably. That has only reduced them from the 'working' to a 'non-working' status. Limited employment opportunities created by technology resulting in the means of production being concentrated in the hands of a few, and increased landlessness for the poor led to men replacing women in many of their traditional areas of employment. But women have had to work and survive. They are thus found gradually moving to the non-traditional sectors seeking employment for survival.

Following the Sixth and Seventh Plans, the Department of Rural Development issued directives to the State Governments to give priority to women headed households, enhance the share of women under the anti-poverty programme (IRDP), and the programme of Training and Self-Employment (TRYSEM). Guidelines for NREP and RLEGP envisage increasing participation of women in wage employment and creation of assets specific to the needs of women's groups. At present the share of employment generated under NREP for women is approximately 20 per cent. A special programme for women entitled Development of Women and Children in Rural Areas (DWCRA) was also introduced in 1982, as a sub-component of IRDP to accelerate the process of integration of women in the rural development programmes. Up to 1987, 11,533 groups are reported to have been organized in 106 districts under this scheme.

The Integrated Rural Development Programme meant for the poorest in the rural areas has been formulated for creating assets with a view to increasing the productivity and income generation abilities of the beneficiaries. Efforts have been made under this programme to select female headed households. The scheme of DWCRA could be strengthened and modified in order to ensure that the benefits reach more target groups. The National Rural Employment Programme (NREP) and Rural Landless Employment Guarantee Programme (RLEGP) would generate additional employment to women in the lean season. Under Training of Rural Youth in Self-Employment (TRYSEM), one-third of the beneficiaries were expected to be women and special attention was to be given to improve existing skills of women and imparting to them new skills under the programmes of farmers training, fodder production, post harvest technology, application of pesticide, budding and grafting, training in horticulture, fisheries, poultry, dairy and social forestry, etc. The training of women under TRYSEM has exceeded the target to 44 per cent as of January 1988. Out of a total of 37.23 lakh families which received benefits under the IRDP during 1986-87, the number of women headed families was 5.67 lakh which amounts to only 15.23 per cent as against the target of 30 per cent. On assessment of the programmes, it is observed that considerable efforts are required to elicit the participation of women in these activities. The training provided under TRYSEM and DWCRA is not always viable and there is a tendency to limit to a few traditional crafts, though the Department of Rural Development is laying greater stress on taking up innovative activities too. Therefore, a fresh look is needed to be given to identification of trades and activities which may gainfully be taken up by women. Many income generating programmes have not succeeded due to full thought not being given to the input availability, training and marketing of products.

Special development projects linked to certain ongoing

activities need to be taken up on a project basis to improve the effectiveness of the programmes related to women. Specific projects such as sericulture for tribals in certain states like Bihar and Orissa, development of dairy units linked to Operation Flood areas, fruits and vegetables cultivation linked to marketing through Mother dairy, prawn farming and fishing in the coastal region were commended. Agro-based industry schemes, etc., are essential.

The scheme of Training of Rural Youth for Self-Employment (TRYSEM) should be revamped with a view to organizing training in trades with assured employment potential to women in rural areas, as well as for wage employment in peripheral metropolitan and urban areas. State Emporia, marketing channels of KVSIC, etc., should be tapped to ensure elimination of middlemen and better process.

The Accelerated Rural Water Supply Programme (ARWSP) and the Minimum Needs Programme (MNP) are of special significance to rural women who are the victims of drudgery, such as fetching water from distant locations. The Technology Mission on Drinking Water and Related Water Management lays emphasis on purification of water to make it potable, training in the use of water and maintenance of water sources. Women are the target of the awareness creation programmes as well as agents for creating awareness in conservation of water and maintenance of water sources. The low cost sanitation programme is also of great importance to women, who are otherwise subjected to a lot of privation due to lack of appropriate sanitation facilities. Rural Technologies and innovation promoted by CAPART aim at relieving the drudgery to women in several areas of their households and economic activities. They include the improved varieties of stone grinder, wheel barrow, ball-bearing pulley, ground nut sheller and smokeless *chulhas*.

The limited performance of the programmes introduced to achieve the integration of women in the development process suggests that only policy directives do not achieve the desired objectives. Programmes do not get implemented due to the lack of comprehension of the relevance of women's contribution to national development. Although the concern for development of women is well articulated at the central policy making level, an ambivalence is observed at the implementation level. The policy directives issued by the Government of India for the increased share for women in the development programmes and the promotion of a participatory approach, do not provide for corresponding development in the infrastructure, extension, training information support and a strong monitoring system which is particularly lacking at the State level. The programmes for rural women still continue as a separate exercise within the sectoral programmes with marginal attention, resources and inadequate monitoring.

The major shortcomings noticed in the implementation of the programmes for women with development objectives are: (i) Perpetuation of the concept that women need only welfare services; (ii) That the developmental benefits will automatically accrue to the women as a result of economic development of the family; (iii) Inadequate knowledge and skills for designing socio-economic activities for women and in group organizations; (iv) lack of supportive services such as credit, child care, marketing, training and technology for reducing the drudgery.

Methodological Issues

The approaches used for integrating women in the mainstream of development have raised some methodological issues. These relate particularly to the organization of groups, involvement of the voluntary sector, and the household approach in development programmes for rural women.

The organization of women's groups is considered to be one of the most effective tools for integrating women in the development process. Yet it has raised several issues which are not fully resolved. Some of the questions which are being asked repeatedly are:

(i) Who will organize the groups (the role of intermediaries)?
(ii) What will be the size, structure and status of groups - formal or informal?
(iii) Should the groups be organized first and the choice of activities to be undertaken by the groups come next?
(iv) Should women be assisted individually under the IRDP, etc., or be formed into groups.

Apart from these unresolved issues, there are problems in selecting and working out economically viable group projects. Women activists argue against giving individual projects to be carried out within the household as it would only perpetuate their subordination in the household hierarchy. They claim that assistance to the voluntary agencies, which was expected to provide grass-roots structural support in this regard, is either not forthcoming or has not been sought.

It is logical that the size of the group to be mobilized should be such as to enable close interaction amongst the members which is only possible when they come from the same background and from one cluster of villages. It is also evident that poor women acquire confidence when they get organized. The delivery system will respond positively even if they are informally grouped. But in the interest of economic viability, and to strengthen their earning capacity, it is desirable for the group to be formalized. It is however, not possible or advisable to suggest one organizational model for all situations. The experience by and large is that the organization based on personal interface and on localized issues is more effective, more flexible and functional than the highly structured and impersonal form of organization.

Some of the processes under IRDP, such as identification of beneficiaries/productive activities, preparation of loan application, sanction of the same and procurement of assets have not been given much attention in terms of proper planning, particularly of the linkage required after the asset is given, to make the same optimally productive. Such linkages include most critically the supply of raw materials and facilities for marketing. These processes and linkages are more effective when implemented through the group approach.

The crucial question in the field of land reforms is how rural poor women should get land and have access to land. Power structures in the villages are dominated by the relatively better off classes. Considering that implementation of land reform measures leaves much to be desired, there is an urgent need for people's participation more specifically of the women, by promoting their groups organizations and through Panchayati Raj institutions. Each village should have a village plan which should include land use for cultivable lands, *gochar* lands and forest lands with clearly demarcated boundaries.

The involvement of intermediaries in development programmes for rural women has been considered vital, particularly in demonstrating and promoting the participatory model and to provide support to the grassroots structure. Here too, there are basic issues which need to be carefully resolved. Among others, it is queried whether the role of the intermediary organizations has been understood by the Government, or whether it is feasible for the voluntary organizations to function in partnership with the government, given the differences in approach.

There is no uniform understanding and acceptance of the role of the voluntary agencies in the States. In some cases, there is a complete lack of rapport between the Government and voluntary agencies. In others, there is the tendency of associating the women's programmes entirely with voluntary action, showing a lack of initiative on the part of the Government. There is little doubt that the voluntary agencies are committed to the cause of women and have expressed a real concern for the enhancement of women's status. They have also demonstrated skills for mobilizing women, and in trying innovative projects. In view of this, the association of the voluntary agencies with the programmes is bound to enrich the programmes as well as the delivery mechanisms. Yet, they cannot be a substitute for Governmental action. To end women's isolation from rural development, the Government must work in partnership with voluntary agencies.

Currently debated issues in the context of women in rural development and in the anti-poverty programmes, is the household versus group approach; some argue in favour of ensuring a share of developmental resources and benefits to women in all sectoral programmes, while others argue in favour of having separate investments for women.

In India, the family is hierarchical, traditional and the status in the family is determined by sex and age. In the patriarchal society, it is the man who holds the position of the head of the family and the bread winner. Therefore, it is the man who gets attention in the investment of developmental resources, training, extension and other supports. Women's contribution to the family's earnings goes unrecognized. This bias, in fact, is responsible for the earlier programmes not taking note of women headed households whose number is currently estimated at 30-35 per cent of all rural households. In mounting pressure on the government to give priority to this group, it has been convincingly argued that an improvement in the income of the household does not necessarily mean development for women. The household approach instead of creating equitable conditions, perpetuates the subordination of women and limits their opportunities for self-growth and self-expression.

Having a special component within sectoral plans can stimulate action for women provided the components are monitored separately. The introduction of the scheme of DWCRA within the programme of IRDP was aimed at stimulating the response of the State Governments to integrating women into anti-poverty programmes. Therefore, in case of women, it can be contended that a combined approach is desirable. This would allow women to be adopted as a target in all sectoral programmes, with earmarked resources along with special component plans aimed exclusively at women. Such dual approaches can be continued until women acquire sufficient power to articulate their needs and demands and until such time as women's concerns get to be internalized in the planning and administrative structures.

Women Access to Land: Inheritance and Ownership Patterns

In the economic sphere and in particular in the rural sector, the 'empowerment' of women relates mainly to their access to means of production and control over the fruits of their labour. The access to the means of production implies ownership of land, other productive assets, access to capital and access to technology and acquisition of various skills required to make labour power more productive.

The aspect of ownership of land relates to rights of inheritance which are governed by personal laws of different communities. These personal laws at present are discriminatory against women and have a bias in favour of the male heirs. The State Governments of Kerala and Andhra Pradesh have sought to remove some of these discriminations with a view to give daughters in the family, co-parcenary ownership in the family property on the same level as the sons. But even these changes do not go far enough and still discriminate against a married daughter and a widow and do not apply equally to the separate properties of the father in the Hindu customary Law. There is discrimination against women of different types in the personal laws of other communities also. In the customary law of certain tribes, only male agnates in the male line are recognized as valid heirs and an unmarried daughter is only entitled to usufructuary maintenance. It would be necessary to introduce correctives to overcome the discrimination in order that the gap between the State's proclamation to achieve equality of the sexes and its laws which deny it, is bridged. Women's undiluted access to land, the most productive resource, would undoubtedly bestow on her necessary economic independence and power and would improve her social position in the family as well.

Regarding access of women to land, the land records do not incorporate the rights of women in the landed porperty shown in the name of the husband or the father. Only where a woman is a widow and happens to be the '*karta*' of the family, her name may figure in the record of rights as the owner of property.

Co-ownership of property by women, should not merely be confined to land but also to other productive assets like house, family wealth, shops, factory or any other income generating establishment or asset. This would provide sufficient conditions for women to participate in and influence the decision concerning the use and disposal of such properties.

As regards access to capital, there is a general reluctance on the part of the public financial institutions to extend credit to women independently of the male head or guardian of the family.

The existing land ownership pattern in India is largely male oriented except in some areas of the north-east and a few other places where matrilineal system is in operation and inheritance of property passes through the institution of the mother. The land records, to the extent they reflect the ownership and other interests in land, only record the names of men. Similarly, where shareholders of such lands are recorded, it is usually the male shareholder who finds mention in the land records. The processes of preparation of land records, i.e., the survey and recording of rights also deal with such male holders of interests in land. The only exception would be in such cases where a widow with no other male person, manages the land. Her name is recorded as the owner and manager of land. Land reform measures have also not taken into cognizance interests of women as co-owners or cultivators of land, and to this extent land reform measures seem to have by-passed the women. The most prominent example where this inherent discrimination in land reforms has been noticed is the case of ceiling laws where most State laws have provided for a separate unit of ceiling for major sons in the family but not major daughters married or unmarried. Although from the point of view of implementation of such ceiling laws, addition of yet another unit in the name of major daughters would have further defeated its objectives, nonetheless, the discrimination cannot be denied. Further, in the matter of distribution and allotment of various lands, it is usually the male head of the family who gets the *patta* in his name. Recently, of course instructions have been issued to give joint *patta* in the name of both husband and wife while allotting land and house-sites. Similarly, in the matter of collection of minor forest produce and enjoyment of rights over common property resources, the rights of women are not focused, even though it is the women who have to collect fuel-wood and fodder and minor forest produce from such lands.

Tribal social structures are more egalitarian and open and less stratified than social structures of larger and more advanced communities in India. The status and position enjoyed by tribal women in society, is therefore, in certain tribes, much better than their counterparts in other communities. This is on account of many reasons. Tribal society has a tradition of both men and women working on an equal footing whether in agriculture or in other vocations. Thus tribal women have access to income and are therefore, economically independent. There are also no restrictions on women going out for work independent of men, and not necessarily along with them. Usually tribal women go out for work in large groups. In social matters and family life also tribal women are far more emancipated. They have a much greater say in the decision making in family and community matters and are not subjected to the same degree of social control by male members of the family as women in other communities are.

Despite this, in matters of inheritance of father's/ husband's property and in access to land, there is a certain built-in discrimination against women in some tribal communities. The customary law of some tribal communities excludes women from inheritance rights, such inheritance rights being restricted to "male heirs in the male line". These customs are even enshrined in tenancy laws wherever enacted and applicable to these communities. This discrimination against women has a harmful effect on their lives, rendering them economically and socially powerless and driving large numbers of them into destitution. In fact, in certain tribal communities, for example, the Ho Tribe in Singhbhum district of Bihar, a large number of women remain unmarried so as to ensure to themselves usufructuary rights available to them as unmarried daughters. Many of them are harassed by their husband's and father's male agnates who wish to deprive them even of this usufructuary right. A number of women are forced to migrate in order to earn their livelihood, since their hold over the family land is so insecure and dependent on the attitude of their male relatives even though these women do the bulk of agricultural work. Sometimes, the women are declared witches, the concealed motive being to drive them out of the village or even to kill them in order to usurp the family property.

The married women also enjoy limited usufructuary rights in the deceased husbands' property. Even these usufructuary rights cannot be freely exercised by them since the husbands male agnates often harass them and try to get rid of them in the hope of asserting their inheritance claims to the land. If the married women has a son, he inherits the land from his father, and she has no legal claim to it. If the husband has one or two or more wives, the sons of other wives have inheritance rights to the land, and she is dependent on them for maintenance. In case, the marriage breaks up, or a man remarries or deserts his first wife, the woman is absolutely without land rights, since she has, by marriage, lost the usufructuary rights in her father's house, and she is also deprived of rights in her matrimonial home. Since tribal communities have their customary laws, the Hindu Succession Act, the Indian Succession Act, or any other succession Act do no apply to them.

The discrimination against women in the customary law of tribal communities, historically speaking, may have evolved with a view to preserve the integrity of the tribe and to prevent land passing from the tribal to persons outside the tribe which would have the effect of disintegrating the tribal society. While, it is necessary to preserve the integrity of the tribe and to protect the interest of tribals in land against any encroachment by non-tribals, it is also necessary to protect the interest of tribal women in land by giving them rights to inheritance in father's and husband's property. But safeguards will have to be provided in the event of marriages outside the tribe.

Therefore, provision in law and customary practices which discriminate against women in matters of inheritance of property and restrict such inheritance to male agnates in male line should be changed while at the same time preserving the integrity of the tribe and preventing alienation of tribal land to non-tribals.

Women, especially tribals, migrate in search of work. They are employed in large numbers in the unorganized sector like brick-kiln, road construction, irrigation works, agricultural operations, forestry operations, stone-cutting, domestic labour, etc. They are subjected to brutal exploitation at places of work by contractors and the middlemen who recruit them. The exploitation is not merely confined to payment of low wages, long hours of arduous work and other dismal working conditions. They are also subjected to sexual exploitation. It is necessary, that for each category of employment in the unorganized sector, specific institutional mechanisms be built-in to protect women's interests.

Perspective for 2000 A.D.

The Seventh Plan is set within a 15 years' perspective in which poverty alleviation in the rural sector remains central. It is targeted to bring down the percentage of rural poor below 10 per cent by 2000 A.D. The Department of Rural Development has already suggested that in case of women, poverty alleviation goals for 2000 A.D. should be to:

(i) Bring all women- headed households (estimated to be 30-35 per cent) above the poverty line; and

(ii) Attain the target of having women constitute 30 per cent of all beneficiaries to be assisted under IRDP.

In addition, the endeavour should be to bring in the women's development dimension into sectors which have hitherto not responded adequately to women's needs. Women's access to productive resources must also be ensured.

Political power and access to positions of decision making and authority are critical prerequisites for women's equality in the processes of nation building. Hence it is crucial that the representation of women in local bodies up to the district level be ensured.

Recommendations

1. In view of the inter-linkages of the economic and the social sectors and their supportive role in strengthening each other, the rural development agencies should function in the direction of convergence of the services of education, health, child care technology and other developmental measures. For maximizing impact wherever possible programmes must adopt the group approach to mobilization of women.

2. The Minimum Needs Programmes should be strengthened and expanded. Efforts should be made to achieve the objective of water for all by the neginning of twenty-first century. Increasing involvement of women in the selection of sites for the installation of water sources, maintenance, utilization, etc., should be aimed at. Fuel, fodder, creche, sanitation should also be included in the Minimum Needs Programme.

3. Emphasis should be given to higher growth rate of industry in rural areas and expansion of housing programmes to generate a large volume of employment in the non-agricultural sector.

4. Land reform and redistribution are basic prerequisites for increased economic outputs and gains. Women's access to productive resources such as land for cultivation and credit inputs must be ensured.

5. Regarding access of women to land, the land records do not incorporate the rights of women in the landed property shown in the name of the husband or the father. Only where a woman is a widow and happens to be the *karta* of the family, her name may figure in the record of rights as the owner of property. Therefore, in order to give the women genuine economic power through access to land, the following steps are necessary:

(a) Where a woman has brought some property to the family through marriage, this property must be exclusively recorded in her name.

(b) Property which is acquired during the subsistence of marriage should be recorded in their joint names.

6. Regarding women as co-owners of property should not merely be confined to land but also to other productive assets like trees, animals, house, family wealth, shops or any other income generating establishment or asset. This would instill confidence in women to participate in and influence the decision concerning the use and disposal of such properties.

7. Wherever shareholders in land and other assets are recorded in the record of rights, the shareholding must necessarily record the shares of female right holders also as per their entitlement. Existing records need to be reviewed and methods to revise entries to indicate joint ownership evolved.

8. Wherever other interests in land like cultivating possession, share-cropping, tenancy rights, rights in common property resources, rights of collection of minor forest produce, grazing and unsurfructuary rights, etc., are recorded, such rights must be recorded in respect of both male as well as female spouse.

9. The allotment of Government wastelands, village common land, developed house-sites, allotment of Indira Awas Tenaments should invariably be done in the joint names of the husband and wife or single title of ownership given to women heads of house-holds, tribal women and Scheduled Caste, particularly those who are widows, unmarried or victims of harassment.

10. There is no reason why land, house sites, dwelling units should not be allotted exclusively to 'women' as eligible categories. This will give greater strength and confidence to women and will prevent men from disposing of the land without her consent. In future, as a matter of policy in the allotment of Government land and surplus ceiling land and house sites, at least 40 per cent women members of the eligible categories may be given *pattas*.

11. Apart from ownership, certain interests in land are heritable, as for example rights of share-cropping and cultivation on certain lands. This heritability does not usually devolve on the female spouse after the death of the husband but gets shifted to

the male agnates of the family: The recording of joint interests should ensure that the female co-owner of such holdings inherits the interest after her husband dies.

12. Personal laws of many communities discriminate against female members, particularly married daughters in regard to share in the father's property. A review of property laws is essential to extend the principles of inheritance to women as they are applicable to men.

13. In customary laws of many tribal communities, women do not have any right of inheritance in father's or husband's property, although they are entitled to maintenance during their lifetime. This discrimination should be ended and safeguards should be provided that this process should not lead to non-tribals usurping tribal landed property.

14. Tree 'pattas' should be issued in the name of women as a matter of preference. Social forestry schemes on Government or village common and forest lands should be allotted exclusively to women's groups. This is particularly applicable to tribal and Scheduled Caste women.

15. Productive assets under Integrated Rural Development Programme such as ploughs, bullocks, hand pumps, etc., should be issued in the name of husband and wife and, in the case of women headed households, to the women exclusively.

16. In dairy cooperatives or similar activities, the name of the female spouse should also be recorded as a shareholder along with her husband.

17. An effective support mechanism is a watchdog committee at village/panchayat, tahsil level to ensure that rights admissible to women are not deprived to them by members of the family and other vested interests should be developed so that their assistance can be taken by women in distress.

18. In implementation of land reform measures, potential women beneficiaries should be associated with any committee or representative groups set up to aid and advice the implementation machinery. The enforcement machinery for implementing land reforms needs to be made more effective.

19. In some communities, there are customs whereby if a tribal woman is raped by a non-tribal or lives with a non-tribal,

she becomes automatically outcast from the tribal society and even deprived of the minimal usufructuary rights in land available to other women. It is necessary to make appropriate changes wherever such practices exist, and provisions under the customary law for their maintenance should be made available to them.

20. Tribal women who are accused of witchcraft should be given legal, social and economic protection.

21. The rights of collection of minor forest produce by tribal women should be specifically recorded in the record of rights, along with their rights to collect fuel-wood, fodder and raw material for their employment from the forest.

22. The migration of women labour needs to be regulated to protect their interest by effective enforcement of existing legislation and other administrative measures wherever possible, rural development programmes for women must recognize seasonal migrant labourers as a special category.

23. Mining leases for such activities as brick-kilns, stone crushing, contracts for road construction, etc., where women are employed in large numbers, should be issued in the name of women applicants.

24. Programmes of creating awareness, organizing of labour camps, helping tribal women to organize themselves into collective groups for better bargaining and improving their skills should be the key to the future strategy of their development and physical and social protection. This training should also teach them how to cope with various exploitative situations including those of the marketing. Support systems should be built up with the help of traditional tribal community organizations. Legal aid, para legal training to educate tribal women and spread of legal literacy, among tribal women in general and migrant labourers in particular, should be important components of the support structure.

25. Women members of households should be entitled to credit, independent of the male head of the family or without his endorsement, where no mortgage of his property or joint property is required.

26. Since women constitute a substantial proportion of the self-employed categories, requiring, credit assistance, credit societies exclusively for women members need to be organized.

27. In terms of credit as a development input, the banking

system is not sufficiently responsive to social banking needs and has not been able to deal with barriers that hinder women from using or gaining access to credit. Priority sector lending of banks must be extended to women as a group. Special counters for women in banks may also be initiated. Particular emphasis should be placed on institutional credit mechanisms at differential rates of interest for women in the unorganized sector.

28. Women's Development Corporations should be established in all States. They should obtain banking support to provide credit at national and local levels. The National, Commission on Self-Employed Women has in its recommendations also suggested that the terms of reference of Women's Development Corporations be expanded to play an effective role.

29. A number of existing models in the voluntary sector provide examples of alternate strategies for providing credit to women in the unorganized sector coupled with effective interventions required to utilize the credit, which can be replicated on a large scale. In this context, it is recommended that the DWCRA programme that has been modelled on voluntary approaches should be extended to all districts. It should also be expanded during implementation to encompass adolescent girls.

30. In selection of income generating activities, both under IRDP and TRYSEM, the banks and the rural development agencies should have committed involvement in helping and guiding the women in the selection of viable activities with local markets.

31. National Wasteland Development Programmes of social and agro-forestry must become more women oriented in their priorities and implementing strategies. Social Forestry Schemes formulated by the Women's Development Corporations should have a built-in provision for employing and training women extension workers.

32. The training of women members of panchayats should be undertaken to enable them to understand their role and responsibilities and to equip them with information on their rights. Women's concerns should be included in the training programmes for male panchayat members as well. A committee including the district coordinator for women's programmes (proposed) should be formed to look into the training needs of men and women panchayat members, and to help in designing the training

programmes. The proposed, Resource Centre could assist in evolving suitable training modules.

33. Provisions and infrastructures created under NREP and RLEGP should be closely linked so as to optimize their impact on rural women's development. The linkages with the funds and other infrastructural facilities available for the line departments is to be ensured in this regard. The plans for the creation of infrastructural facilities should be devised locally, in consultation with the women, instead of waiting for a centrally prepared blue-print. The appointment of district coordinators for women's programmes would expedite this process.

34. The Agricultural Extension System (T&V) should include women that work on family farm within its purview. Food production, nutrition, population education, etc., should form the extension service package for women. Simultaneously, agriculture extension programmes for women must be initiated in all States.

35. An impact study of the Farmers' Training Programmes and Krishi Vigyan Kendras should be routinely made. The syllabii of these institutions should be geared to the productivity role of women. They should collect area specific information on women's activities, assess the training and information needs of women, as well as provide feedback to the media for dissemination of information on women's role in agriculture and allied activities. The Kendras need to be extended to all districts.

36. Women's role in animal husbandry should be approached in a more pragmatic way. They should be trained in the management of cattle, veterinary care and fodder production. Production of fodder, collectively or individually, by women is to be included as a must in self-employment projects in animal husbandry. A cadre of para veterinarians from among the beneficiaries should be created.

37. Efforts for increasing the membership of women in existing dairy cooperatives, training of women for taking up managerial responsibilities, and separate cooperatives for women should be aimed at.

38. Voluntary organizations and educational institutions should be increasingly motivated to take up micro studies and action programmes in mobilizing and organizing women, and encouraging them to avail of the provisions of various programmes.

39. There is need to organize and conscientize the women under DWCRA, TRYSEM, STEP, etc., in order to get higher benefits from these schemes. The TRYSEM schemes should recognize literacy as a skill since it is an essential input for participation in various schemes. The 30 per cent target stipulated for women in various schemes should be strictly met by the officials.

40. There should be proper publicity about various programmes meant for rural women. Awareness camps should be organized in order to make rural women aware about the various schemes and programmes by voluntary and government organizations.

Employment and Training

The vital role of women in the Indian labour force and their contribution to the national economy has been established beyond doubt. Women engage in a wide variety of occupations, especially in the unorganized sector. In the rural unorganized sector, women care for cattle, sow, transplant and harvest, weave and work on handlooms and produce handicrafts mostly as low paid wage earners, or as unpaid family workers.

In the urban informal sector, women work as petty traders and producers selling and producing a wide variety of goods, such as vegetables, fruits, flowers, cooked food, groceries, etc., or work as domestic workers. In both the rural and urban areas, they are engaged as construction workers. In addition, women spend on an average. 7-10 hours a day on domestic chores as well as collection of fuel, fodder and water, and child care. The large amounts of time and energy expanded on these domestic chores, however, remain invisible as no productive economic value is attached to these tasks. Nor has any major effort been made to improve women's access to technology aimed at reducing drudgery in the domestic chores performed by them.

Situational Analysis

Estimate and Nature of Work

Accurate data on the extent and nature of women's work is an essential pre-requisite in the development of employment policies and programmes. Data relating to the employment of women in India is currently available from six major sources. These are: (i) the decennial population census; (ii) Surveys undertaken by the National Sample Survey Organization (NSSO); (iii) Studies conducted by the Directorate General of Employment and Training (DGE&T) and Labour Bureau; (iv) Annual surveys of industries compiled by the Central Statistical Office (CSO); (v) Periodical reports from the State Governments; and (vi) Individual studies conducted by the Central and State Governments, universities and research organizations.

The decennial population census provides valuable information on important aspects such as work participation rates by age, sex and occupation for both rural and urban areas. These data, are available on as All India basis and for individual States up to the village level. The Census also provides information on the levels of employment and other work related aspects. NSSO produces comprehensive and detailed data on structure and changes in the labour force by relevant socio-demographic variables through a series of quinquennial surveys from 1972-73 onwards. The Thirty-second (1977-78) and Thirty-eighth (1983) rounds have collected valuable data on the attitudes of women towards work and other related aspects. The DGE&T and the Labour Bureau have continuously collected vital information related to the organized sector and the implementation of labour laws. The latter also conducts occasional field studies on selected topics of national importance. The Labour Bureau has brought out a useful reference document entitled "Statistical Profile on Women Labour". It gives details regarding the population of workers, their average daily employment, sex-wise employment in factories by special/normal weekly hours, live register and placement data, minimum and maximum wage rates for workers by sex and age based on occupational wage surveys, statistics on social security and information on factories providing creche facilities. The annual survey of industries (CSO) gives information on employment by sex and data on emoluments with respect to large factories. Some Organizations under Central or State Governments, universities, research organizations and individual scholars have also been conducting micro studies concerning the socio-economic characteristics of workers and other problems.

The comparability of data on employment from these sources is, however, limited due to conceptual differences in the definition of workers and lack of uniformity in classification of workers by educational level, sex, etc. The workforce participation rates given in successive census are not comparable either as the definition adopted in each census has been changing. In the 1961 census, any person engaged in gainful work for even an hour per day of the greater part of the working season was counted as worker, whereas in 1971, the person was asked as to what his/her main activity was and he/she was classified as worker or non-worker accordingly. This main activity concept of workers brought down substantially the participation rate of females. In 1981, the concepts of 'main worker' and 'marginal worker' were adopted. According to the 1981 census, the 'main worker' has been defined as a worker who has worked for the major part of the reference period, and the 'marginal worker' was one who had worked not for the major period but nevertheless had done some work during the reference period.

The standard definition used by the NSS provides figures for 'usual status,' 'weekly status', unemployed. 'Usual status' measures the usual activity status-employed or unemployed or outside the labour force of those covered by the survey. Thus the activity status is determined with reference to a longer period than a day or a week. 'Weekly status' is determined with reference to a period of preceding seven days. A person who reports having worked at least for one hour on any day during the reference period of one week while pursuing a gainful occupation was deemed to be employed. A person who did not work even for one hour during the reference period but was seeking or available for work has deemed to be unemployed. In 'daily status', activity of a person for each day of the preceding seven days is recorded. A person who worked at least for one hour but less than four hours was considered as employed for half a day. If the person worked for four hours or more during a day, he/she was considered as employed for the whole day. Those with jobs for less than half the days in the preceding 365 days are considered unemployed with 'usual status'. The 'weekly' employed are those with less than one day's job in the preceding seven days and the 'daily' unemployed with less than half a day's work in the week preceding the survey.

The employment of women is generally underestimated in many of these sources. Often women themselves would report unemployed if they were not cash wage earners. The manner in which women's productivity is interpreted is also responsible for under enumeration of the female workforce participation. In quantifying labour days of employment, female and child labour are often converted into equivalent adult man days, though the converse factors vary from source to source and region to region. Such an assumption is totally untenable. A woman often earns half the wage earned by a man for an equivalent of a day's work, but not because her productivity is less. The wages paid to women is determined not by economic criteria but is a result of the cultural attitudes, social practices and power structures in society. Some review of the relative evaluation of various operations in any sector is called for to redefine equal remuneration for work of equal value.

Eight

Women's Employment Status and Work Participation

It would be important to analyse the changes in female work participation rates over a period of time so as to assess the impact of various programmes on female employment. The main limitations in such comparison is on account of the changes in the definition of employment. General inferences may be drawn from Table 8.1 below keeping in view the conceptual limitations.

TABLE - 8.1
CRUDE WORK PARTICIPATION RATES, ALL INDIA 1971 TO 1981
(Furnished by Census & NSS)

	Rural		*Urban*	
	Male	*Female*	*Male*	*Female*
Main Activity				
1971 Census	53.62	13.36	48.80	6.65
1981 Census	52.62	16.00	48.54	7.28
1977-78 NSS	62.25	28.82	56.29	13.81
Modified main activity				
(Including Marginal Workers)				
1972-73 NSS	63.84	35.53	57.09	15.53
1977-78 NSS	64.06	38.48	57.48	17.80
1981 NSS	53.80	23.18	49.07	8.32
1983 NSS	63.23	38.74	57.71	17.13

Sources: (i) Census of India, 1981, Series 1, India, Primary Census Abstract Delhi 1983.
(ii) NSS, Sarvekshana, April, 1986 page S-III.

On the basis of 'main' activity, the participation rates for rural females in 1981 are noticeably higher than in 1971, whereas only a marginal increase is evident with respect to urban females. The NSS work participation rates for females show much higher participation rates than the census for both rural and urban females. This is due to differential base figures used in the calculations. The NSS data employing the concept of modified main activity (including marginal workers) shows an upward trend in the work participation rates between the periods 1972-73 and 1977-78. The work participation rate of 1977-78 is roughly approximated in 1983 even after recording a steep decline in 1981. Table 8.2 gives the Age specific worker participation rates during 1971 and 1981.

TABLE - 8.2
AGE SPECIFIC WORKER PARTICIPATION RATES CENSUS MAIN ACTIVITY, 1971 AND 1981

(Per cent)

Age Group	*Rural Males*		*Rural Females*		*Urban Males*		*Urban Females*	
	1971	*1981*	*1971*	*1981*	*1971*	*1981*	*1971*	*1981*
0-11	7.56	6.30	3.05	3.53	2.75	2.46	0.82	0.88
15-19	62.31	58.19	18.80	22.77	28.32	31.54	5.51	6.19
20-24	86.56	82.71	20.58	24.29	67.49	63.35	9.54	9.29
25-29	95.45	92.79	22.16	26.14	90.54	86.78	11.68	12.17
30-39	97.61	96.71	23.78	28.45	95.45	94.93	13.11	15.14
40-49	97.62	97.25	24.43	28.90	95.15	95.40	14.53	15.34
50-59	95.50	94.08	21.08	23.94	87.85	86.86	12.71	12.42
60+	77.52	67.59	11.19	11.29	55.35	47.49	6.46	5.75
All ages	53.62	52.62	13.36	16.00	48.80	48.54	6.65	7.28

Source: Census of India, 1981, Series 1, Paper 2, of 1983, Key Population Statistics Based on 5 per cent Sample Data, Delhi, 1983, Table 15.

The sex-wise distribution of workers by type of employment is given in Table 8.3.

TABLE - 8.3
SEX-WISE DISTRIBUTION OF WORKERS BY TYPE OF EMPLOYMENT

	Male			*Female*		
	1972-73	*1977-78*	*1983*	*1972-73*	*1977-78*	*1983*
1. Self-Employment	65.90	62.77	60.40	64.48	62.10	62.21
2. Regular Salary/ Wage work	12.06	10.57	10.77	4.08	2.84	3.10
3. Casual Labour	22.04	26.66	28.83	31.44	35.06	34.69

Source: NSS, Sarvekshna, Vol. IX, No. 4, April, 1986

There is a decline in the self-employed category and an increase in casual labour for both male and female workers except for a slight decrease in 1983 for female casual worker category. The Regular Salary and Wage Work categories, however, declined substantially for women in 1977-78 but has since shown an increase in 1983.

According to Census data, age specific participation rates (Table 8.2) reveals that women's participation increased for all age groups except 60+, and the increase was marked in the age group 30-39 and 40-49 for rural females. The NSS data show enhanced participation of women in all age groups, but unlike the census, do not suggest a special increase with respect to the two age groups. The Census trend data reveal that more and more women are taking up employment after completing the child bearing age. This may imply greater reliance by working mothers on older children to help raise younger children and points to the urgency of providing supportive services to working women.

Size and Composition of Female Labour Force

The size and composition of the female labour force are a reflection of their overall submerged socio-economic status. In absolute terms, the female labour force has grown from an estimated 78.6 million in 1973 to 88.9 million in 1978 and 99.4 million in 1983 or an average annual addition of 2.1 million. In proportional terms, however, their participation rate has declined dramatically from 33.7 per cent in the 1911 Census to 20 per cent in the 1961 Census. Even following the new and broader definition of work, the female participation rate between 1971 and 1981 has registered only a marginal improvement from 12.06 per cent to 13.99 per cent.

The size of women's representation in the total labour force has also shrunk from 34.4 per cent in 1911 to 31.53 per cent in 1961, and 17.35 per cent in 1971. Sectorwise composition of women workers reveals an ever increasing process of marginalization of women, with agriculture accounting for 80 per cent of the employment in 1971 as against 73.9 per cent in 1911 and 79.6 per cent in 1961. Women workers in industry declined from 14.7 per cent (1911) to 10.5 per cent (1971) and in the service sector from 11.4 per cent to 9.4 per cent between 1911 and 1971.

In the decade 1971-81, some marginal improvement has been recorded in the ratio of female to male workers. The comparative participation rate of males and females in the primary, secondary and tertiary sectors in 1971 and 1981 reveals that the percentage of female workers to total workers increased in each of these sectors during the decade 1971-81. Among females, the proportion of those engaged in the primary sector decreased by 1.4 per cent, whereas it increased by 1.2 and 0.2 per cent respectively in the secondary and tertiary sectors. The percentage increase in employment in secondary and tertiary sectors in case of females nevertheless has been less than that of males.

The organized sector in India (which consists of public sector and non-agricultural private sector establishments) absorbs less than one-eighth of the actual workforce of the country. Of this, the share of women as of 1978 was 12.4 per cent. Women's employment in the organized sector grew from 19.30 lakh in 1971 to an estimated 33.41 lakh in 1986. Whereas the growth rate of women's employment in the organized sector has shown a steady increase, their proportion in the total public sector workforce has remained roughly constant.

Within the organized sector, female employment in the public sector increased steeply from 8.62 lakh in 1971 to 19.50 lakh during 1986. In the private sector too, women's employment improved, although at a slower rate (from 10.67 lakh in 1971 to 13.07 lakh in 1986). The number of women job seekers through employment exchanges rose from 11.25 lakh in 1975 to 50.98 lakh in 1986. The percentage of placements, on the other hand, increased from 1975-82, but declined in the subsequent years, i.e., 1983-86.

Women in the Unorganized Sector

A majority of women are to be found in the vast rural and urban unorganized sector. According to an estimate by the National Commission on Self-Employed Women, 94 per cent of the total female workforce operates within this highly exploited sector. Employment in this sector is characterized by low pay, long hours of work, low productivity, low skills and lack of job security. There are few labour or trade unions/organizations to facilitate the mobilization of women workers and knit them into a conscious workforce. This is also due to the varied nature of occupation in this sector, inadequate legislation and ineffective enforcement of legal safeguards to protect these workers, particularly, in regulating their work conditions. Traditional socio-economic relations that operate in this sector defy categorization into 'employer', 'employee', 'labour', 'capital', 'rent', and 'interest' relationships.

One of the major reasons for women's work becoming increasingly limited to the unorganized sector is that women lack the opportunity to acquire skills and training which could facilitate occupational shifts. This is related to the prevailing social relations between men and women as well as the structure of the economy. Since women have to bear the major burden of domestic chores, which in a poor household is time consuming and labour intensive, they do not have the time and opportunity to acquire skills and training for better jobs. Low skill attainment among women and their consequent relegation to jobs which are labour intensive, time consuming and arduous, is perpetuated by their unequal access to technology.

A large share of employment in the rural unorganized sector is held by women. Employment of women in the rural unorganized sector is principally, traced to nine employment systems. These are agriculture, dairying, small animal husbandry, fisheries, social and agro-forestry, khadi and village industries, handlooms, handicrafts and sericulture. The first five sectors are broadly classified as agriculture and allied occupations; the last four are categorized as village and small industries sector. The sex-wise break up of employment in eight of these systems for which data is available is given in Table 8.4.

TABLE - 8.4
NUMBER EMPLOYED IN THE LARGE EMPLOYMENT SYSTEMS

(Lakhs)

	Women	*Men*
Agriculture	18.70	754.70
Dairying	750.00	50.00
Fisheries	10.00	18.00
Small Animal Husbandry	150.00	20.00
Khadi & Village Industries	17.00	19.90
Handicrafts	5.40	22.00
Sericulture	8.00	12.00
Handlooms	29.80	44.80

Source: Various Departments of the Government of India.

Although investment outlays in these sectors command high priority, and several government programmes exist to boost the productivity of these sectors, most endeavours are focused on men and male producer organizations. The programmes themselves are executed largely by male bureaucrats and male extension workers. Women are viewed as indirect beneficiaries through the male members of their households, and not as participants and target groups. Most of the jobs in these sectors are low paid and performed by women. It is also a recognized fact that women are gradually being displaced from some of these sectors. Structural problems have risen in the rural unorganized sector as a result of the hierarchical pattern of land ownership, the nature of land relations, and gender division of labour and the credit system. There is a strong class-caste relationship in the ownership of land which works to the disadvantage of the economically weaker sections and particularly against women.

Construction labour is a fairly large sector of casual work, employing women in substantial numbers. Though the construction labourers are engaged on a casual basis (daily or piece rate), many of them have long years of experience in this area of work. Quite a few are initiated as youngsters, moving from one project to another, often migrating to distant and alien places, constantly dependent on the contractors to hire them. The use of contractors to mobilize labour for this sector has perpetuated the age old method of recruiting by "credit tying" and "loan bondage" methods that are routinely used to mobilize migrant labour for the seasonal harvesting operation in high growth areas. The exploitation of these workers thus begins with the methods of their recruitment. Their services are hired by sub-contractors who most often obtain their labour from backward rural areas where unemployment is high. Sub-contractors obtain work from the main contractors on a piece-rate basis but make payments to the labourers on a daily basis. This enables them to keep their profit margins high at the expense of labour. Ideally, construction workers should be recruited through a workers' board or social work organizations and trade unions. There is a need to create such unions or bodies that could organize groups of migrant workers to press for enforcement of minimum work conditions like proper wages, maternity benefits, medical facilities, creches, etc.

Domestic work offers another major avenue to employment

for women and girls. It is the most accessible avenue of employment for female migrants and urban poor women. This section of workers, as others in the unorganized sector, has remained grossly unrepresented in the national data systems. Of all the services in India, domestic service is the most unregulated and disorganized. The major constraints are an absence of a written contract for work and protective regulations. The highly personalized nature of the work further complicates the situation. The percentage of young unmarried girls as domestic workers, many under the age of ten, who are initiated mainly as a help to the mother has increased sharply. An estimate in 1977-78 (Sarvekshana, 1987) reported 1.68 million female domestic workers as opposed to 0.62 million male workers. The spreadover of working hours for full time living in domestic workers is reputed to be 12 to 16 hours. The immediate task is that of ensuring them dignity and security at work and regulating work conditions through organization and protective legislation. Simultaneously, they must be provided with opportunities to seek alternate employment through skill training and education.

The National Commission on Self-Employed Women in the Informal Sector has recently generated exhaustive data and analysis on these sections of women workers including specific groups such as women in the primary sector in mining, tobacco and beedi work; handlooms, handicrafts and garments; women vendors and hawkers, construction workers, and domestic workers, etc. While analysing the status of these group of workers in the framework of existing macro policies and existing legislation, the National Commission makes various recommendations for their protection and empowerment.

Women in the Organized Sector

The organized sector accounts for approximately 10 per cent of the female labour force. Employment opportunities in the governmental and public sectors and the private corporate sector are limited in view of the general constraints on resources for major expansion and dependence on the dictates of market mechanisms which are prejudical to women. Given these realities and based on the performance in previous decades, it is unlikely that this sector can offer much relief by way of expanded employment potential to women.

Constraints

Whether in the unorganized or the organized sector, women workers face several constraints which account for their low status as workers. Their lack of access to productive inputs such as raw material, credit, technology, training and markets are major impediments. Despite legislation, women's right to land deeds and *pattas* continue to be ignored contributing to their marginalization. As a result, women are increasingly compelled to migrate both, rural as well as urban areas on a temporary, seasonal or permanent basis. In addition to their lack of adequate skills and resources they may face severe adjustment problems due to differences in religion, language and socialization as well as separation from their families. The situation of migrant women needs attention.

In the Indian economy, women are concentrated in occupations which are usually at the lowest rung of the ladder. In most occupations they are engaged in the more arduous and less skilled areas of work. For example, in the construction industry men do bricklaying while women carry bricks and mortar; women carry soil while men do the digging; women transplant paddy, weed, reap, pluck vegetables and bundle the harvest produce while men plough and sow the seeds. In terms of access to skills, women continue to be employed in monotonous, low skilled and low wage sectors. In terms of access to credit, while low interest credit under the Differential Rate of Interest (DRI) scheme is available to women. In reality, the need for collateral, cultural and other constraints faced by women in dealing with bank staff, low priority for small loans in banks, etc., have led to a very low rate of utilization of this type of institutional credit by women workers. Unfortunately, gender differentiated data on women's use of bank credit is unavailable nationally which could yield a more precise picture.

Absence or lack of enforcement of social and labour legislation hampers women's access to basic employment benefits. Women are denied rights such as minimum hours and minimum wages, and access to maternity benefits, maternal health care, day care and legal aid. There are a number of areas in which women receive no social security benefits. These factors together contribute to the insecurity of women and reinforce their inferior status as workers.

Factors Affecting Women's Employment Status

A combination of social and economic factors are responsible for the low participation rate of women. The most critical are:

(i) Segmentation in the labour market which works against women;
(ii) Adverse implications of technological growth for women;
(iii) Lack of unionization of female workers;
(iv) Absence of a purposeful human resource development policy aimed at improving women's employability and productivity through training; and
(v) Conceptual ambiguities and lack of a National Labour Policy encompassing workers in the unorganized sector.

Segmentation of the Labour Market

Segmentation in the labour market leads to two major types of discrimination, viz., (i) Wage differentials between men and women; (ii) Discrimination in terms of concentration of women in particular sectors (primary sector) and in certain types of jobs or operations. In the agricultural sector, for instance, the majority of women are found to be concentrated in lower paying operations. In the informal sector, women almost uniformly get lower wages than men. In the organized sector, about 90 per cent of women are known to be engaged in unskilled or semi-skilled jobs.

A fundamental economic force that keeps women's wages low is the gap between supply and demand for female labour. In the past two decades, India's overall growth rate of 3.5 per cent per annum has not been high enough to generate sufficient demand for labour (particularly female labour) and to provide productive employment to a labour force which is growing at over 25 per cent per annum. Further, the capital intensive organized sector has been heavily male oriented, while many of the traditional activities which suffered from competition offered by the modern sector were those which engaged female workers.

Impact of Technology

Technological modernization has further eliminated the traditional employment activity and adversely affected women. Instances of technological modernization eliminating traditional activities are well known. Powerlooms have put about 84,000 women handloom weavers out of work in five States between 1961-71. Modern herbicides and rice mills displaced women and eliminated their traditional incomes from weeding and milling. Apart from straight displacement of labour in the short run, there are a number of other mechanisms through which technological progress have adversely affected female incomes and opportunities. The demand from modern industry, for instance, pushes the price for raw materials beyond what traditional workers can afford (as in the case of bamboo basket weavers). Mechanized fishing displaced whole fishing communities. The rise in the water table due to increased irrigation leads to increased salinity of drinking water necessitating long trips to fetch drinking water. Conversely, increased pumping of ground water may lower the water table to such an extent that traditional wells fall dry. Increasing deforestation, linked to 'development', has often meant much longer trips for women to collect fuel, water and fodder. Reforestation has itself tended to favour cash crops over fuel and fodder and trees, entailing further hardship for women. Finally, adoption of new farming technology has significantly downgraded the input of women, largely on account of their limited education. It is therefore essential to analyse technology/industrial/agricultural/environmental, policy to assess the status of women workers.

Lack of Mobilization

In all this, the lack of organization and unionization hampers the bargaining position of women, especially in the unorganized sector, which denies women all the benefits of collective action. Dispersed, unorganized and atomized they have no political power and no bargaining strength. The unorganized sector presents a number of difficulties in implementing protective labour laws relating to wages, conditions of work, insurance, provident fund, maternity leave, creche facilities, etc. The exploitation in this sector is only marginally under the purview of laws. Hours of work are long, wages are poor, conditions are hazardous, benefits are non-existent and wages are below survival needs. Channelling inputs such as literacy, health family welfare services, etc., is also difficult in this sector. As a result, there are marked disparities between women in the organized and unorganized sectors of industry. Besides, inter-state, inter-urban disparity in the nature and structure of wages and other benefits are considerable and favour the 10 per cent in the organized sector as against the 90 per cent women workers in the unorganized sector. Investment policies too continue to award low priority to the unorganized sector.

Absence of a Systematic Training and Human Resource Development Policy

One of the major hurdles to the development of employment opportunities for women is the lack of adequate training. The purpose of training is to develop employable skills that can generate better income and improve the status of women workers. At present in most of the occupations where women are employed in large numbers, such as agriculture and construction they work as low paid unskilled labourers with little training facilities available to upgrade there skills. The existing training programmes are primarily aimed at men creating further imbalances. Though certain facilities to train women in various skills through the industrial training institutes or polytechnics and apprenticeship training under the Apprentice Act are available, there is no special focus on the training of women which is packaged along with other inputs such as credit and marketing support. Moreover, the existing facilities largely cater to urban rather than rural areas.

Currently, the nodal department for women's development in the Government of India is the Department of Women and Child Development. While it has a number of schemes such as short stay homes, working's hostels, women's development corporations, it has no national programme for women's training. Further, it is evident that the mixed programs such as the TRYSEM have not reached women as effectively as visualized. Currently, there are at least 45 schemes in 17 departments/ ministries of the Government of India catering to training of women but they do not present a systematic integrated approach to women's training. It is essential that such an approach be fostered. The focus of such training should be at those who are presently the most disadvantaged, i.e., the vast majority of women engaged in the informal or unorganized sector and forming 90 per cent of the total female labour force. It should provide training to improve productivity as well as explore new avenues of employment to facilitate occupational shifts wherever possible.

Conceptual Ambiguity

Although the constraints are multifarious and real, there is difficulty in clearly understanding the problems at hand, mainly due to the invisibility and underrecording of work done by women. In evolving suitable employment promotion interventions, a crucial issue has been the invisibility of women's work as well as lack of comprehension and value added to numerous tasks they perform for family survival. A conceptual framework for computing the value of such tasks is necessary. The poor data base of the extent and nature of employment of women on the one hand, and the absence of clarity on what constitutes work on the other, pose definite impediments in assessing women's actual productive participation in the economy. The low visibility of their productive worth is illustrated by the fact that only 14 per cent of the total female population in the country fell into the category of workers as per the 1981 census. Both the Sixth and Seventh Plan documents clearly attest that there are large numbers of women whose work continues to be unreported and invisible. It is this lack of adequate and accurate data which is one of the impediments to the formulation of informed policies for improving the employment status of women.

Conceptual ambiguity in assessing the employment status of women becomes a basis for a lack of appreciation of and sensitivity to the problems which women face, particularly in the vast unorganized employment sector. This, in turn, leads to the virtual absence of strategies for improving conditions in this sector. Presently, support structures, for employment such as training, mobilization of workers, legal safeguards, as well as the institutional base for identifying new avenues of employment and enhanced productivity for women are lacking.

Corrective Strategies

The corrective strategies are to be viewed holistically and not as isolated piecemeal actions. In order to truly be effective, the overall employment strategy for women should be viewed as a package comprising employment opportunities, legal safeguards, training support and social services, awareness generation and mobilization. Only then will a purposeful synergy be achieved.

The corrective strategies are broadly addressed to the factors which have been reviewed earlier as constraints. Those strategies must aim to create new avenues for employment of women, upgrade their existing employment conditions as well as productivity and employment potential, make them a more articulate and conscious workforce, and assure them better status and recognition as workers.

New Avenues for Employment

In the organized sector, the employment potential for women is likely to grow very slowly. On the other hand, there is a considerable scope for employment in the agricultural and service sectors. Diversification in agriculture and in the other major sectors of rural employment offers enormous potential for employment. Horticulture, commercial vegetable growing, food processing, fisheries and poultry, agro industry offer ample opportunities to rural women. Unemployed young women could be trained in extension work for imparting the necessary skills in these activities. Besides, a variety of new occupations could be created for women workers in the areas of agro-based industry weaving, textile printing, ready-made garments, production of stationery and preparation of indigenous herbal medicines and packaging, etc.

Expansion of the service sector in the rural areas is a need and reality offering scope for local women to be absorbed with the minimum training being provided. Nurseries, creches and *anganwadis* also offer employment opportunities for a large number of women. The areas of simple health care like immunization, diagnostic screening (testing of blood, etc.) and other health functions could be opened to intermediary levels without affecting the overall standards. These facilities are not currently available to poor families particularly in the rural areas. Middle level workers could be trained for employment in the provision of these services.

There is an immediate need to diversify the prevailing occupational base so as to promote skilled employment on a wider scale. Currently, training is imparted in traditional occupations like carpentry, welding, smithing, tailoring, book binding, etc., which is also male oriented. It is now necessary to provide training to women in such non-traditional fields as well. An area based identification of potential occupational clusters would have to be undertaken systematically in different regions of the country in order to determine the nature and size of opportunities that could be made available.

Effective linkages between metropolitan and large urban areas with the surrounding hinterlands is another modality with considerable potential for employment generation. The demand from these urban and metropolitan centres in the fields of food processing, packaging, transportation, storage and other services could open up large areas for production, processing and marketing, thereby providing employment opportunities in such areas on a sizeable scale.

Expansion of small-scale industries is widely recognized as a means of creating potential for employment. Suitable institutional mechanisms for the promotion of small-scale industry need to be developed to assist in the provision of credit, supply of raw materials, organization of marketing and creation of skills necessary for these enterprises. Two of the important areas requiring urgent attention for the expansion of cottage industries are: (i) upgradation of skills in order to raise the status of workers to that of artisans and improve the quality of products; and (ii) education, training and organizations of workers for collective action on various issues.

Appropriate technologies and modernization of their occupations would have to be inducted to increase their income potential. The role of middlemen who have been getting sizeable benefits disproportionate to their investment and efforts has to be reduced. Producer Co-operatives are one such strategy to reduce dependence.

An appraisal is necessary to examine the viability/ marketability of the trades for which training and assistance is being provided by the government. The Central Social Welfare Board (CSWB) is implementing some employment generation schemes under which voluntary agencies in the country have been availing of financial assistance. Training is also given under TRYSEM, etc., and socio-economic schemes are undertaken under DWCRA, IRDP and the Training-cum-production scheme of the Deptt. of Women and Child development, etc. An attempt should be made to expand the categories to encompass new and viable trades and create necessary linkages.

Training

A systematic human resource development strategy focused on women is essential. Three levels of training are envisage, viz., (i) The grass roots level; (ii) The middle level; and (iii) The policy and planning level. The content of a training strategy should encompass five principal components as follows:

* Organizational and extension training
* Skill training
* Management and entrepreneurial training
* Sensitization of administrators/ implementors to women in development issues and
* Training of trainers

Organizational and Extension Training

This component of training is to be geared to functionaries, catalysts, extension workers at the grassroots, middle and supervisory level personnel, teachers, organizers of cooperatives, etc. It should aim at conscientization on legislation, environmental health, nutrition and sanitation, education functional literacy, paralegal training and related aspects. Effective group mobilization, communication skills, skills needed for organization and management will be emphasized in this training along with functional knowledge. Particular attention will be paid to attitudinal/behavioural component essential for reaching programmes for women at the grassroots.

Skill Training

This refers to skill training with special emphasis on the nine major sectors of women's employment, i.e., agriculture, dairying, fisheries, small animal husbandry, khadi and village industries, handlooms, handicrafts, sericulture and social forestry. This type of training will entail upgrading existing skills in these areas as well as training of women in appropriate technologies. It will be aimed at programme beneficiaries as well as catalysts/ functionaries, extension and supervisory workers. These skills need to be imparted on the widest scale to rural women in order to encourage them to achieve household self-sufficiency as well as supplementary income. Also included will be the skill training in the urban/ modern sector with regard to assembly, manufacturing and processing for larger industries as well as small-scale firms. Wherever possible women's employability has to be increased in the organized sector as the employment conditions in the unorganized sector indicate the need for a shift in the occupational structure. In generating such skills, care will be taken to ensure that the training imparted does not push women into sectors where mobility is limited, wages are low, health hazards are high, and worker benefits are not enforced.

Management Training

This refers to training in project formulation, monitoring, evaluation, information systems, credit/ marketing management, and other skills required to administer and manage projects, as well as supervisory and entrepreneurial skills. Such training could be provided with the help of technical institutes (ITIs, Polytechnics, etc.) where special courses for training of women workers and entrepreneurs could be started. In conducting such courses, banks, voluntary organizations, and private and public sector industries could be effectively utilized to help formulate viable entrepreneurial projects for the trainees. Special training programmes to promote rural entrepreneurship in particular would need to be designed.

Sensitization of Administrators/Implementors

This type of training should seek to achieve sensitization of bureaucrats to the critical need to integrate women in development. The objective will be to develop appropriate attitudes and knowledge for planning/monitoring/implementing programmes and policies for women. Such training needs to be imparted through the training programmes of the Department of Personnel as well as other governmental and non-governmental agencies. A particular emphasis in this category of training must be to train the officers in charge of enforcement machineries at the Central and State levels, workers of quasi-governmental bodies, and voluntary agencies. The Women's Division at NIPCCD is already undertaking sensitization programmes for police officers/judiciary to the issue of crimes against women.

Training of Trainers

In addition to the training of trainers within the existing institutions and infrastructures, a special effort should be made to train rural women as organizers and instructors in different sectors and trades so that they could train more women and achieve a multiple effect.

In view of the criticality of training for the development of women, setting up of a National Resource Centre for Women is imperative. By playing a coordinating/interventionist role it would identify and strengthen existing governmental and non-governmental agencies to carry out training policy and programme research and information dissemination. The Resource Centre would provide a new thrust for training and work towards translating national developmental goals into a systematic grid of programmes and schemes for training in skill/knowledge/ attitudes at different levels.

As a preparatory step, it would be essential to identify and classify the various types of training institutions in the country. Examples of such institutions are agriculture and rural home science centres; schools of social services, khadi and village industries, as well as vocational training centres; universities, ITIs, polytechnics, agriculture and veterinary schools, engineering colleges, krishi vigyan kendras, etc. At present, they have no special focus on training only for women, but these should take up new courses under a coordinated effort, monitored and planned by the resource centre. In addition, newly established training and extension departments, as well as existing training institutions, agencies, management bodies, and grassroots organizations should be involved in imparting training to women.

Recommendations

1. It will be necessary to formulate a well articulated employment generation and training policy aimed at more productive participation by women, at the same time assuring them greater employment benefits, social security and better working conditions.

2. The formulation of a National Labour Policy must receive immediate attention. The National Commission of Rural Labour set up by the Department of Labour must include in its terms of reference issues pertaining to women workers in rural areas including those in the unorganized workforce. The analysis and recommendations of the National Commission on Self-Employed Women must also be given due consideration in the formulation of such a policy.

3. The agricultural extension system currently reaches only a minimal number of women in agriculture. Special extension programmes must be evolved to create awareness and skills among women in the field of agriculture, animal husbandry and other related employment sectors.

4. Rural employment programmes and employment guarantee schemes like that in Maharashtra should be strengthened and expanded by public works programme along with the provision of social inputs such as creches, drinking water, and covered shelters at work sites.

5. The nine major rural employment sectors have high participation of women, i.e., agriculture, animal husbandry, khadi and village industries, handicrafts, handlooms, sericulture, fisheries, forestry, etc., and have large resource allocations. The mainstream sectors must integrate a woman's component into the sectoral programmes. This would need 'earmarking' programmes for the development of women along with support measures and training in these sectors.

6. Though preferential emphasis should be in favour of the unprotected women workers in the unorganized sector, keeping in view the quantum of female labour force in this sector as well as the problems and constraints, wherever possible women's employability should be increased by diversification or provision of skill training in new or non-traditional employment in the organized sector.

7. It is expected that the next two development plans would be expanding the provision of basic services. Women should be enabled to take advantage of these opportunities for gainful employment arising from provision of basic services and to work as *anganwadi* workers/group organizers ANMs/LHVS, etc. The critical enabling mechanism will be requisite training and upgradation of skills.

8. While planning employment programmes, it is essential to keep in view the demand projection of employment, expansion and production projections created by different government programmes. It should, therefore, be possible to monitor the needs of the various ministries as regards women's employment and plan potential personnel needs. Similarly, income generation skills could be related to the demand created by Government programmes for specific goods. For instance, the NPE in its "Operation Blackboard" has visualized the need for teaching aids. This would be a continuous requirement for more than two decades. Similarly the supplementary nutrition need of the primary schools and *anganwadis* could be interlinked and provide jobs to local women that could prepare the nutrition supplement. One of the function of the District Employment Committee will be to match demand with supply and link potential areas of employment with women needing employment.

9. Employment for women should also mean household self-sufficiency with reference to nutritional and economic needs of the household as in the instance of backyard poultry, social forestry, small husbandry, etc. For example, in the social forestry programmes, certain basic types of trees rich in nutrition such as papaya, banana, drumstick, curry patta, etc., should be promoted. Depletion of local food resources due to food processing for export purposes must be checked at all costs.

10. Displacement of women from traditional sectors due to modernization and technology is well known, particularly in the agriculture, fisheries, textile and handloom sectors. It is essential to provide alternate skills for women displaced by new technologies. Qualitative studies of every new technology and its adverse impact on women must be undertaken before introduction of technology and formulation of policy thereof.

11. Promotion of petty trading/manufacturing/processive small industry, employment among women should be encouraged by ensuring a reasonable share of credit and other inputs. These micro-entrepreneurs should be organized into cooperatives and other types of specialized collective agencies.

12. In the sector of wage employment, women's participation in trade union activities should be encouraged. Creation of organizations for increasing their bargaining power could be stimulated through specific programmes and schemes. In this context the recommendations of the report of the National Commission on Self-Employed Women and women in the unorganized sector must receive serious attention.

13. Organization and mobilization are critical for women to perceive themselves as 'workers' and productive contributors, not merely as 'housewives'. Special programmes for non-formal education and awareness generation of women workers should be strengthened and expanded on a national scale. For instance, the Nehru Yuvak Kendras (NYKs) provide an existing avenue to support awareness and employment generation programmes. It is urged that at least one woman NSS Volunteer by employed by every NYK to assist this process. Special attention may be paid to raising employability of adolescent girls so as to provide them with alternative options to early marriage. A national programme of legal awareness for both girls and women be initiated.

14. In the organized sector, the maximum age of entry of women in employment should be increased to 35 years, with provision for job sharing, part time work and re-entry into the employment stream at a later stage. Relaxation of educational qualifications for women in specific areas of employment may be considered.

15. In the organized sector emphasis will have to be placed on the expansion of insurance cover, maternity and other benefits.

16. A Central maternity benefit fund should be set up out of the contribution made by the employers, workers and Government in order to reduce the burden on the individual employers in respect of women workers.

17. Extending paternity leave benefits require serious consideration.

18. Special incentives should be given to entrepreneurs who employ more than a certain percentage of women particularly in labour intensive industries. Recognition and incentives should also be offered to employers who appreciably increase the employment of women and take up programmes for imparting functional education.

19. Avenues for part-time employment should be explored, to improve women's earning capacities; additional employment throughout the year must be available by targeting a percentage of employment in rural works for women.

20. Women should be adequately represented on all decision making bodies concerned with personnel planning and economic development like the Planning Commission, State Planning Boards and Financial Institutions such as IDBI, IFC, LIC and NDDB, KVIC, Silk Board, etc. Mahila Mandals and other local women's organizations should be strengthened and sensitized. The local level organizations should be involved in designing suitable income generating projects depending on local resources and skills. They should be represented on the District Employment Committees recommended at point 29 here.

21. The Ministry of Labour should set up a standing committee especially for unorganized labour to promote and develop a strong organizational base to improve their working conditions.

22. In the formulation of the employment strategy, a key role has to be given to agriculture through expansion of irrigation, cropping intensity and extension of new technologies. Though the rate of industrial growth must be accelerated, it must be recognized that even a higher rate cannot guarantee a larger volume of employment for women. Therefore, massive programmes of rural development will be needed to provide larger employment. In this context, the none major rural employment sectors which have a high participation of women must incorporate a specific women's component into their sectoral programmes. This does not necessarily imply seeking higher outlays but earmarking funds and ensuring a special component for employment generation programmes for women as well as support measures, and skill training in these sectors.

23. Women should have access to productive resources such as land, buildings credit, housing and skill training. The existing loopholes in the property laws which deny women access to ownership of land should be removed.

24. Special interventions are needed to provide credit to women for production and marketing activities. Women's development banks should be encouraged at the national and local levels to provide credit, marketing and other supportive services to women's groups. Marketing is a major problem for women producers. Local producers' organizations should seek to protect their interests. In addition, marketing support for home based producers should be provided. Women's Development Corporation must play an active role in this area and the Government departments should make provision to purchase goods from organizations of women producers on a preferential basis.

25. Separate machineries at the National and State levels should be set up which can play a coordinating and catalytic role in the framing of employment policies and programmes for women. Special reinforcing cells or units in sectoral Ministries should be created to enforce and monitor the policies. Annual reports of the ministries and agencies at the Central and State levels should document and review the achievements concerning the employment status of women. A special focus of such monitoring should be the enforcement of equal pay for equal work, job security and fair working conditions for women workers. There aspects should be studied in depth by the National Commission on Rural Labour.

26. Employment Exchanges must maintain separate lists for women. Every list sent to organizations/employers by the Employment Exchange should have at least 30 per cent women candidates.

27. The largest number of women work as casual labourers. They are both underpaid and underemployed. Information on employment opportunities should be widely disseminated among these groups. Avenues for part-time employment should be explored to improve the earning capacities. Additional employment throughout the year must be made available to them by reserving a certain percentage of employment in rural works.

28. Every selection board must have women in it.

29. District level Employment Committees be set up to plan, coordinate the demand/potential of employment programmes. Line agencies, women's groups, small-scale industries be given sufficient representation. These committees should ensure 30 per cent employment for women, monitor employment opportunities, and rural training schemes, and their accessibility for women. These should become part of the agenda for the committees.

30. The National Commission on Self-Employed Women has also recommended that an advisory committee with some power of veto must be set up at the Central Government level to monitor the impact of technology on women and to identify and promote areas for research and development of pro-women technologies.

31. A small group may be set up by the Technology Policy Cell to design a format for evaluation of all proposals of technology transfer and automation in industries so that a view can be taken with reference to women's opportunities for employment.

32. It has been observed that after marriage a large number of women are forced to drop out of employment, in spite of their high qualifications and engage in household chores only. Such "post marriage brain-drain" should be stopped. Appropriate alternative measures such as part-time employment, job sharing, etc., should be accessible to these women.

33. Women workers employed in free trade zones comprise a particularly vulnerable group due to the differentials in application of labour legislation in these zones. Hence women's interests need to be protected in this area and support services provided.

Training

34. Recognition of the critical role of training in increasing and strengthening of women's productive employment is essential.

35. A National Resource Centre for Women to provide a new thrust to training and dissemination of information backed by research, data and documentation is an urgent need. It would coordinate training efforts and identify and strengthen existing governmental and non-governmental agencies and academic institutions with resource and technical support.

36. Women must be given increased access to training in skills, management, entrepreneurship, particularly in non-traditional trades. Care should be taken to ensure that women are not pushed into low paying, monotonous and hazardous jobs where mobility is also limited.

37. Training in the nine sectors of women's employment, viz., agriculture, dairying, fisheries, small animal husbandry, khadi and village industries, forestry, handlooms handicrafts, sericulture must receive priority attention.

38. Special training programmes to promote rural entrepreneurship should be designed. New areas of employment should be explored for training and absorption of women workers in these rural small-scale industrial ventures.

39. Training personnel must be sensitized to local women's issues, employment needs and trades.

40. Women displaced by introduction of modern technologies must be equipped with alternative skills and employment possibilities at the same level.

41. Facilities and incentives must be provided and increased for the enrolment of women in all training institutes, polytechnics, etc.

42. Special, condensed, job-oriented training courses must be organized for women through ITIs, polytechnics, etc., utilizing existing infrastructures. Hostels for girls should be provided in existing polytechnics, ITIs so that girls can avail training.

43. There should be a separate quota for women's apprenticeship training in non-traditional skills which should be non-transferable so that women are assured entry into such programmes.

44. Planning of training programmes for women must keep in view the demands of new Governmental programmes and maximize opportunities for women, e.g., the demand for physical education instructors, expansion of social forestry programmes, etc.

45. Training of trainers must lay special emphasis on group mobilization/skills inter-personal and managerial skills, etc., as well as sensitization to local women's issues, employment needs and trades.

46. Training for management of cooperatives organizing and mobilizing women's groups is essential. Training women for participation in trade unions is also critical.

47. Schemes for diversification and expansion of education and skill training opportunities for women should be given the highest priority. Special training programmes should be designed to train displaced women due to modernization or introduction of technologies.

48. One diversified vocational training institution for every four or five blocks should be set up for imparting sectoral and other skills to rural women.

49. Special programmes for education (entailing functional and legal literacy and family life education) of women workers have to be evolved.

50. A nodal point should be identified to design and impart paralegal training to women workers. Legal literacy particularly in respect of labour laws and employment benefits must be engendered widely. In this effort, CILAS (Committee for Implementation of Legal Aid Services) and similar structures should be closely involved.

51. The training programmes for rural women should be created taking into consideration their educational and literacy levels and local demands. Rural women's need for vocational training should not result in hasty attempts to extend training in a limited range of crafts, sectors and occupations considered 'suitable' for women, that have seldom resulted in providing an adequate livelihood for rural women in the past. Vocational training must cover managerial and organizational as well as productive skills.

52. The agricultural extension system (T&V) should take the women of farm families in its purview to provide the necessary information and training support. Food production, nutrition and population education should be included in the package of extension services for women. Agriculture extension for women must be expanded as a concept to truly encompass other allied fields. The system should be strengthened with adequate number of personnel at least at the rate of five per block with corresponding strengthening at the supervisory and planning levels.

53. Women's role in animal husbandry should be approached

in a more pragmatic way. They should be trained in management of cattle, veterinary care and fodder production. Production of fodder collectively or individually by women is to be included as an essential ingredient in employment projects and animal husbandry. Creation of a cadre of para veterinarians from the beneficiaries themselves should be aimed at.

54. Efforts for increasing the membership of women in existing dairy cooperatives and training and other provisions to enable women to take up managerial responsibilities must be a priority. Separate cooperatives for women should be aimed at. Cooperative training institutions must provide special inputs for women.

55. Training institutions in the sectors of sericulture, KVIC, handicrafts, etc., should recognize the contribution of women to these sectors and incorporate training needs of women beneficiaries and functionaries.

56. Special efforts should be made for improving the in-service training facilities for women.

57. In case of apprenticeship, incentives should be given to employers for training of women.

Supportive Services

58. The vital role of supportive services in enhancing productive employment should be recognized. It is essential to ensure that the drudgery of the rural women on tedious chores such as fodder/fuel and water collection, cooking, child care, etc., be alleviated.

59. Appropriate technology for reducing drudgery and enhancing productivity should be designed in close consultation with the local women. The possibility of harnessing non-conventional sources of energy such as solar, bio-gas, wind, etc., to decrease possibilities of environmental degradation and at the same time, ensure women easier access to fuel and other efficient systems of energy should be explored and pursued.

60. Besides the overall trends of economic development it will also be necessary to devise supplementary programmes to promote and strengthen employment among women in specific backward groups.

61. Greater emphasis should be placed on the provision of

creche/day-care centre facilities as a support service. It is, therefore, recommended that it be made mandatory for every work site employing over 30 persons to provide for a creche facility.

62. Maternity leave benefits and family planning incentives should also be available uniformly to all sectors.

63. A maternity benefit fund should be set up, out of the contributions made by the employers, workers and Government in respect of women workers. The present obligation of employers in the formal sector to provide creche/day-care centre facilities should be replaced by a contribution of employers to a common fund to be operated at the State level.

64. Women should have access to infrastructural facilities like transport, storage, raw material and other productive material such as land, worksheds, technology, etc.

65. Supportive services like creches, child-care centres, supply of firewood, etc., which indirectly increase women's employability should be developed jointly by the Government, the private sector and the voluntary sector.

66. In the organized sector, emphasis will have to be placed on the expansion of insurance cover, maternity and other benefits such as, creches. Universalization of creche services to reach all work sites with over 30 working people is critical.

Enforcement and Legal Safeguards

67. Special cells/mechanisms must be created to cater to women's needs and enforce legislation on equal work, job security and working conditions.

68. Criteria for fixation and revision of minimum wage should be evolved without impinging on the right of parties to negotiate wage agreements.

69. Legal safeguards/facilities available under various existing laws, such as the Minimum Wages Act, Equal Remuneration Act, Employees State Insurance Act, Provident Fund Act, and Maternity Benefits Act are not extended to the unorganized sectors. The possibility of extending these laws to cover the unorganized sector must be examined. The National Commission on Self-Employed Women has made specific recommendations in this regard. Trade unions and other organizations should emerge

to undertake the development of consciousness among women workers about these legislative provisions. Legal aid centres, Lok Adalats should also help workers in sorting out their problems in this context.

70. There is a strong need to eliminate all forms of discriminations in employment through legislative measures, especially to eliminate wage differentials between women and men. Review of the relative evaluation of various operations in any job is called for to redefine equal remuneration for work of equal value.

71. Working conditions should be improved in both formal and informal sectors. Protective measures against work-related health hazards should be effectively implemented. Employment of women in hazardous jobs should be forbidden and suitable steps should be taken through legislative measures.

72. The Government of India is the largest employer of women. It should ensure that regulations regarding maternity benefits, provision of creches at its work sites and wage fixations are adhered to.

73. Policies should be framed to encourage women to enter managerial levels.

Awareness and Conscientization

74. Conscientization is an integral part of organization. Presently, there is near total ignorance among women particularly at the grassroots about the various labour laws and their entitlements as well as discriminatory provisions perpetuated under these laws. Nor are they aware of the productive and social worth of their labour. Legal literacy particularly in respect of labour legislation should be widely generated. Both the Government and the voluntary as well as the private sector should come forward for setting up legal aid centres at local levels so as to develop an informed and aware female labour force. In this endeavour, effective networking with existing structures such as CILAS (Committee for Implementing Legal Aid Service) is recommended.

75. There is a need for collective action, for which purpose, organization of women need to be promoted and funded especially

in the unorganized sector. Such organizations should be capable for exercising the required pressure for furthering and protecting the interest of members.

76. Although the Government has limitations in direct involvement in unionizing or organizing the female labourers, it can facilitate voluntary organizations in this task. Organization of trade unions in both the organized and unorganized sectors where such organizations do not exist at present is critical. Further to look after the problems of women workers and to improve women's participation in trade union activities, the formation of women's wings in all trade unions should be made essential.

77. Voluntary organizations, should be encouraged by Government to undertake programmes for creating awareness about the existing exploitative structures and procedures in employment concerning women.

78. Mechanisms for conscientizing producers' and workers' groups on a regular basis should be thought of.

79. Wide publicity should be given to training programmes and training materials focusing on women. Brochures listing crafts and other cottage and small-scale industries with potential for expanding women's participation and productivity should be prepared and made available at each district headquarters and to lead institutions for training. These brochures should also contain information on the skills and knowledge to be acquired, availability of credit, marketing facilities, raw materials, etc. The All India Handicrafts Board, Silk Board, and other agencies should have special units for dissemination of this information at various levels. They should also utilize mass media for dissemination of information, apart from conducting intensive publicity campaigns.

Data Requirements and Suggested Areas of Research

80. The existing information on women's employment is inadequate. Nor it is available on a regular basis. Therefore, it is necessary to improve the coverage, flow and analysis of existing statistical data. There is a need to have particularly better coverage of the unorganized sector which employs large numbers of women. It is also vital to take a fresh look at the concept and definition of 'work'. Often, statisticians and planners have ignored the 'invisible'

contribution of women to the family farm or business, and to domestic chores including collection of fuel, fodder and water. The jobs performed within the home or outside as an employee or as her own account should be included.

81. The Women's Cell in the Ministry of Labour should collect and collate available information on the employment situation of women and bring out a periodic report.

82. The annual employment review brought out of the direction of Employment and Training should furnish information of education levels, placement, and registration of women job seekers. (The survey conducted by the Directorate General of Employment and Training (DGE & T) in 1972 of graduates of 1968 gave useful information on women. There is a need to take up periodic surveys of this type.)

83. There is also the need to collate, collect and disseminate information on studies on issues concerning employment policies and programmes and their implications for women.

Information on the impact and benefits of development programming on women, in view of benefits envisaged, e.g., empowerment or employment opportunities or managerial skills should also be collected.

84. The implementation of the Equal Remuneration Act and of other labour and welfare legislation should be routinely evaluated and reported and the findings disseminated.

85. Some of the areas which require research and analysis and which could be carried out by Governmental or non-Governmental agencies are listed below:

(i) Re-examination of the concept of work, and methodologies of assessing the nature and extent of employment discrimination are essential.

(ii) Assessment of the extent of mechanization in selected women oriented industries and the impact of technological changes on female employment in various sectors, especially in the areas of post-harvest technology, fisheries, handlooms, sericulture and cottage industries.

(iii) Studies on the none rural employment sectors employing women.

(iv) Research at the macro and micro level on the impact on women must be conducted before the introduction of new technologies associated with modernization so that women displaced by it can be retrained or absorbed in other avenues of employment.

(v) The nature and type of work performed by women in the urban informal sector and its inter-linkages with the informal-formal sector continuum.

(vi) Modes and levels of wage payment for women workers with a view to identify the areas where further labour legislation should be needed and enforcement strengthened.

(vii) Assessment of the existing system of hiring in both agricultural and non-agricultural works with particular reference to extra economic obligations imposed on women as conditions of employment.

(viii) Evaluation of the impact of different kinds of occupations and sectors on women's economic independence, their access to employment information, their job satisfaction, and the impact of specific occupations on their health.

(ix) Identification of factors responsible for the decline in women's work participation rate in the urban areas.

(x) Evaluation of the impact and attitude of women working towards the family and the community.

(xi) Review of the existing criteria of selection for candidates for jobs in order to identify the inbuilt discriminatory clauses if any against them, such as, age limit, physical characteristics, marital status, etc.

(xii) Study of part-time employment to analyse whether women are engaged in full-time jobs for part-time wages.

(xiii) Study of the impact of supportive service, such as health, education, child care, maternity benefits, etc., on women's work both in the home and outside.

(xiv) Study of the feasibility of introducing low-cost gadgets for reducing household drudgery.

(xv) Identification of contradictions in law arising from

conflict among family law, constitutional guarantees of women's rights, and protection of workers through labour legislation.

(xvi) Investigative studies to identify the areas of decline in employment with a view to assess their nature and magnitude.

(xvii) Identification of new areas suitable for promotion of women's employment.

(xviii) The impact of national rural development programmes like SFDA, TRYSEM, EGS, Food for Work and other programmes on women's employment.

(xix) The effects of young women's employment on household relation and on fertility.

(xx) Development of curriculum for agricultural universities to take account of women's roles and needs in agriculture.

(xxi) Credit as a crucial input for promoting women's employment. Analysis of the flow of credit to women, especially to low income group women.

(xxii) Research studies should be promoted to analyse women's multifarious roles in agriculture from production to processing and marketing, and the impact of agricultural development on women.

(xxiii) An inventory of available technologies in agriculture should be made. Promotion of access of women to appropriate science and technology should be aimed and research should be directed to the development of women's needs for specific technologies.

(xxiv) A major area of research that has to be provided impetus, is the study of economic viability of projects, both ongoing and newly planned, particularly socio-economic benefits/costing.

(xxv) It is also essential to study the impact of macro-policy on women, particularly the impact of agricultural policy, industrial policy, taxation, urbanization, institutional money flow as well as impact of technology policies.

(xxvi) Research ought to be initiated on the impact of structural adjustment on women, i.e., analysing the relationship among women, market and the State. Particularly, attention has to be given to the impact on women of changes in incomes, price of consumers goods, levels and composition of public expenditure, and working conditions.

(xxvii) General specific statistical inputs on development programmes, e.g., number of beneficiaries, allocations, etc., also need to be collected and made available.

Nine

Supportive Services and Women's Issues

Issues involving women are closely related to supportive services. These refer to a gamut of services and amenities that make the women more functional and productive, while at the same time reduce the overburdening drudgery of the daily chores which she is expected to perform for the survival of her family. The major supportive services that require attention are fuel, fodder, water, creche and housing services. One of the major hurdles to women's development activities is the difficulty of providing economically viable means of releasing them from day to day drudgery and survival activities which are neither awarded an economic value nor are shared by men. Data indicates that women are unable to avail of tubectomy services in the absence of a substitute who can care for the children while the women is away. Similarly, the education of girls is impeded because they are invariably required to help the mother to look after younger children. It is well known that besides adult women, children are also expected to fetch fodder, fuel and water. Cooking also accounts for a large chunk of the women's time. The use of inefficient smoky *chulhas* affect their lungs, eyes and health in general. This also interferes with social interaction.

The factors affecting women's advancement are thus critically linked to the socio-cultural environment. In keeping, with her sex-stereotyped role as a housewife and homemaker, an Indian woman irrespective of clan, creed, region, religion, spends most of her time on household chores. Many women are subjected to the drudgery of a day to day subsistence, working up to 16-18 hours per day. Unfortunately, such 'shadow work' brings her no monetary returns nor does it enhance her prestige in the family or society which is necessary for her to participate in decision making. In addition, women are often left to fend for the household's basic needs and sanitation, especially in the rural context. The Seventh

Plan notes that women play an important role in agriculture, animal husbandry and other related activities such as storage, marketing of produce, food processing, etc. About 54 per cent of rural women and 26 per cent urban women are engaged in marginal occupations in order to supplement family income by collection of fodder, firewood, cowdung, maintenance of kitchen gardens, tailoring, weaving, teaching, etc. It is uneasy for a woman to take up employment, unless there are alternative ways to saving time at home and sufficient remuneration to justify her employment outside. Thus all programmes for women, be it education, health, family planning, nutrition, social welfare or legislation are necessarily interrelated support structures for reducing the household drudgery.

Since drinking water, fuel and fodder are the basic requirements especially in the rural areas, a major portion of women's time is spent on collecting these. Strategies which help overcome such problems by providing the necessary support services need to be carefully devised and effectively integrated in development strategies/plans for women.

In the previous plan periods, the emphasis was mainly on issues concerning education, employment and social aspects, without giving commensurate attention to supportive services. For example, the section dealing with the 'Infrastructure for Women's Participation in a Modernizing Economy', the Report on the Status of Women, touched only upon child care services. The National Plan of Action (1976) was also silent on the structuring of various supportive services. However, the Sixth Five-Year Plan recommended separate Science and Technology (S&T) inputs for women (Item 19.35) as a part of Science & Technology for Human Resource Development. The Plan suggested the setting up of special cells for promotion of Science and Technology for women under the aegis of different organizations such as the University Grants Commission (UGC), Council of Scientific and Industrial Research (CSIR), Indian Council for Agricultural Research (ICAR), Indian Council of Medical Research (ICMR), Department of Adult Education (DAE), etc. Although it was proposed to apply Science and Technology for the improvement of the living conditions and status of women, support services were not specifically discussed.

The Seventh Plan was more emphatic on women's development and had a separate section on 'Socio-Economic Programmes for Women'. It notes that in giving Science and Technology inputs for Women, special efforts have to be made to reduce their drudgery.

The interlinkages between various sectoral and support services have to be fully understood so that an integrated purposeful view is taken of women's development. The programmes have to be planned on the basis of a detailed analysis both at micro and macro levels. The analysis should identify critical factors including resource availability, appropriate technologies, skill constraints, public awareness, and organizational, institutional and policy supports.

Fuel and Fodder

Fuel and fodder are best taken up together since they are biomass based and often, the same plant provides both. This system also integrates with food which, in turn, is linked to fuel through cooking. Hence the discussion here also touches upon forestry and wasteland utilization for growing a variety of biomass in the broader perspective.

Women participate in fodder production as a part of their activities in agriculture and in cutting and fetching fodder for feeding the animals. Generally, green fodder is raised as one of the crops or in grasslands and is gathered from the fields as and when required. Alternately a variety of straws and other agricultural residues are collected and stored as fodder or converted into silage or hay. Often women also have to visit the nearby forests to cut fodder from trees and bushes. This is generally done along with fuel collection. The harder biomass like twigs and firewood are used as fuel and the palatable leaves, as fodder. As for fuels, as indicated by a number of studies, cowdung and agricultural residues and firewood form the major fuels for cooking and are gathered and stored mainly by women. The act of making and storing cowdung cakes has developed into an art, with *bitodas* (cowdung storage structures) prominently standing out in the rural landscape. Cowdung cakes are preferred for slow cooking on low fires or heating milk, while firewood and agricultural residues serve to produce more intensive heat. Depending on resource availability, the utilization pattern varies with cowdung being more prominent in the northern regions. The major portion of total energy consumed is through such 'non-conventional' sources which, in rural areas, accounts for 90 per cent of the domestic energy expenditure.

The three recent plans (Fifth, Sixth and Seventh) have generally discussed the fodder under 'Animal Husbandry', fuel under 'Energy', and biomass under 'Forestry'. The Fifth Plan observed that the 'forestry' development has assumed a significant dimension as a source of timber and fuel and for the maintenance of the natural ecological system. Special plantations have been given high priority. Under the section 'Energy' it has been proposed to adopt a multipronged approach to develop biogas technology and tap new sources such as solar energy, tidal and wind power. The Sixth Plan noted that feed and fodder constitute 60 to 70 per cent of the cost of production of various livestock products and that the area under fodder crops has remained more or less static during the last two decades. It also stated that emphasis will continue to be placed on the promotion of fodder production as an integral part of crop husbandry through a mixed farming system, particularly, on the small landholdings. Effective farmer-oriented extension programmes will be taken up by the Government for evolving and popularizing high yielding varieties of fodder crops, and introduction of leguminous fodders in existing crop rotations. Production and distribution of high quality fodder seeds will also receive priority attention. Accordingly, a Central Fodder Seed Production Farm and Centres for Forage Production and Demonstration were set up during this plan. The development of extensive grasslands and creation of grass reserves were taken up by the State Forest Department. Under the social forestry programmes marginal and degraded forests were allocated for cultivation of fodder trees.

As for fuel, the Sixth Plan (item 9.248 under social forestry) proposed: (i) Mixed plantation of wasteland; (ii) Reforestation of degraded forests and raising of shelter belts. In the districts where shortage of fuel wood was particularly acute, new centrally sponsored schemes of social forestry including Rural Fuel Wood Plantation and Farm Forestry were introduced in selected areas.

New thrusts in the form of Tree for Every Child Programme, Economic Development Force, Eco-development Camps and Agro Forestry Programmes were devised during the Sixth Plan. The concept of organic recycling (Item 9.36) and the propagation of biogas technology (Items 9.40, 9.41) were also envisaged. Further, this plan dealt with the new and renewable energy sources and suggested that energy forestry, biogas and biomass conversion technologies have to be taken up along with solar and wind energy and a variety of other technologies. For example, item 15.95 on 'Energy Forestry' notes that firewood is the most important traditional fuel accounting for two-thirds of the total energy contribution from non-commercial sources and is becoming scarce. In view of the pressure on land, all available unutilized pockets of land could be used for energy plantations. Considering that rural communities will continue to depend heavily on such resources, it was proposed to decentralize energy production and distribution as a part of an Integrated Rural Energy System (item 15.105) which considers all energy resources in a given area.

In the Seventh Plan also, emphasis has been given to social forestry, agro-forestry and various renewable energy technologies and the necessity of creating awareness among people through mass media. The Plan notes that a proper implementation of some components of forestry programmes may be entrusted to local and voluntary bodies (NGOs). Concepts like 'social fencing' may be tested. In fact the revised 20-Point Programme (1986) has advocated a "New Strategy for Forestry".

In recognition of the importance of renewable resources, a Department of Non-conventional Energy Sources have been set up. Also a National Wasteland Development Board was created with objective of bringing 5 million hectares of land every year under fuelwood and fodder plantation.

In many of the above programmes the role of women in the production, collection and utilization of fuel and fodder and the related problems are not adequately emphasized. However, it is heartening to note that the Department of Science and Technology set up a cell on "Science and Technology for Women" in 1982. This cell divided the various technologies required for women into the following four areas: Technologies for Drudgery Reduction;

Employment Generation Technologies; Health and Sanitation Technologies; and Technologies for Minimizing Occupational Hazards.

Under the first category, the problems of fuel, fodder and drinking water were perceived from the point of view of women. Besides a number of projects funded through individual institutions, an 'All India Coordinated Project' was also undertaken on 'Fuel and Cooking Aspects' through the Science and Technology Department. More than 20 institutions from all over the country participated, analysing the data based on micro level surveys. The local specific and general problems of women in dealing with fuels were identified and the viability of a variety of technologies were field tested. Similarly, some of the selected technologies like the improved *chulha*, biogas solar cooking, biogas based technologies, etc., are being taken to the people through the Department of Non-Conventional Energy Sources. Apart from various governmental institutions like Department of Science and Technology (DST), Indian Council of Agricultural Research (ICAR), Council for Scientific and Industrial Research (CSIR) and Department of Non-Conventional Energy Sources, a number of relevant State departments are also taking up the implementation of such projects. Some reports analysing the reasons for the success as well as failures of experiments undertaken are available.

It is encouraging to know that recently a number of NGOs have taken up programmes with funding support from the various Government bodies noted above. A Bio-energy Society of India has also been established with a view to promote research and development as well as public awareness. Bio-energy education dealing with the production, conversion and utilization of biomass with special emphasis on fuel aspects is being given prominence. People's participations being promoted through social forestry and other programmes. However, the linking of women with these activities is still weak. A few movements like 'Chipko' stand out, emphasizing that much can be achieved by organizing women at the local levels.

The agricultural universities, dairy development institutions and forest institutes undertake research in fodder and fuel production and have a network of extension centres such as Krishi

Vigyan Kendras for taking these technologies from the lab to land. While agriculture provides fodder crops, special attention is also paid to trees and plant species like *sibabool* which can cater to both fuel and fodder needs. Researchers on social forestry and agro-foresty all over the country now recognize the need for integrating the food, fodder, fuel, fertilizer, fibre and other biomass based production and utilization aspects.

The various technologies developed are being complied into suitable directories for dissemination, e.g., the Science and Technology Women's Cell has listed a number of technologies for women. Council for Advancement of People's Action and Rural Technology (CAPART) has undertaken the publication of several volumes of National Directory of Rural Technologies, the first volume titled 'Post-Harvest Technologies' has already been printed.

However, the scope exists for designing and developing more technologies appropriate to women taking into consideration the agronomy, ease of handling, economics, etc. A special mention must be made of Agricultural Tool Research Centre at Bardoli, which has tried to make efficient agricultural tools especially suited for women.

Drinking Water

Although India is one of the wettest countries in the world with an average annual rainfall of 1170 mm, it still faces and is expected to face in future the threat of actual water shortage. Among the various usages of water in rural areas, drinking water followed by irrigation, sanitation and agriculture are of importance for the overall developmental process.

Water resources are generally dealt with as a part of irrigation in agriculture. In addition to this, the Sixth Plan laid special stress on rural water supply as a part of the 'Minimum Needs Programme'. As in the Sixth Plan, the Seventh Plan also highlights the importance of drinking water. The supply of drinking water to all problem villages features at Point 7 of the Twenty-Point Programme (1986). A 'Technology Mission on Drinking Water in Villages and Related Water Management' was established in 1986-87 under the Department of Rural Development, Ministry of Agriculture, Government of India. The collaborating agencies identified were Council of Scientific and Industrial Research, Ministry of Science and Technology, Department of Environment and Forests, Department of Defence Research and Development, Ministry of Health and Family Welfare, Ministry of Water Resources and State Governments. The 'problem' villages were identified as those with:

(i) No source of water;
(ii) Water sources more than 1.6 km distance, 15 km depth, and 100 metres elevation difference;
(iii) Biological contamination (guinea worm, cholera, typhoid); and
(iv) Chemical contamination (fluoride, brackishness, iron).

The number of such problem villages amounts to 39 per cent of the total villages (2.27 lakh out of 5.57 lakh). In respect of these problem villages, some basic targets envisaged are:

Eradication of guineaworm	9,920 villages by 1989
Control of fluorosis	8,700 villages by 1988
Control of brackishness	17,500 villages by 1988
Removal of excess iron	2,900 villages by 1988

Apart from these, the strategy has focused on 50 project areas (Minimization) to evolve new, cost effective science and technology techniques, to apply and replicate these techniques in the rest of the problem villages and to implement an integrated approach to water conservation.

A booklet outlining the project objectives, background, strategy, management structure, targets, methodology, milestones, accomplishment, resources and policy needs, has been brought out by the Ministry of Agriculture. Already this mission has started working with the States Departments concerned. In addition, universities, research institutions and voluntary organizations are also being involved. A first Regional Seminar to focus on these issues for Southern States and Union Territories was held at Gandhigram in Tamil Nadu in July 1987.

Most of the above efforts, however, are not directly addressed to women. Although in the Sixth Plan, special mention has been made about assuring the weaker sections of their due share of water, only a few organizations like the Science and Technology Women's Cell have looked at this problem from the women's development angle. In addition to sanctioning some institutional level projects on various aspects of potable water, an "All India Coordinated Project on Drinking Water" has also been proposed by this department.

Ideally, as in the case of urban services, the Government should be in a position to supply potable water to all households through pipelines and taps right at the doorsteps. However, considering the current constraints of finance and non-availability of suitable water sources, problem terrains, etc., this may not be feasible in the near future. Hence constructing and maintaining smaller water sources like wells, water tanks, hand pumps, etc., are to be given due consideration.

As with the implementation of any project, there is always the problem of ensuring people's participation in both maintenance and the distribution systems. Merely installing different kinds of units and equipment do not lead to sustained water supply. Thus organizing women to adopt different technologies is a key issue. In this context, a successful experiment by a voluntary agency in Rajasthan could be considered as a model for replication. In this case, the people were involved in identifying the locations for tubewells. A few persons were then trained in their actual construction and maintenance. The system of giving due remuneration for subsequent management to these trained personnel was also evolved. This ensured sustained working of the pumps/ tubewells and equitable distribution of water. Other case-studies worthy of note are the "Water Harvesting Systems" employed at Banwasi Sewa Ashram and the "Water Sharing System" evolved at Sukhamajari.

Although a number of technologies are available, only a few have reached the villages. More research and development are needed on issues like devices for carrying water in hilly terrain, water purification techniques suitable for different problem areas, storage at home levels, and rapid methods of water testing.

A list of available technologies have been compiled in a volume brought out by the Cell on Science and Technology for Women. The CAPART has also brought out publications on drinking water and the third volume of its National Directory of Rural Technologies will be on Drinking Water. The Technology

Mission on Drinking Water has brought out two publications entitled Sub-Mission on Desalination of Water and Sub-Mission on Eradication of Guineaworm. Table 9.1 gives the distribution of time of rural women in hours/day.

TABLE - 9.1
WORK-TIME DISTRIBUTION OF RURAL WOMEN IN HRS/DAY
[SRIVASTAVA, 1982]

Sl. No.	*Work*	*Landless Agricultural Labour*	*Small & Marginal Farmer*	*Average Farmer*	*Land Holder*
1.	Sweeping and cleaning	1.0	1.5	1.5	2.0
2.	Drawing and fetching water	1.5	1.5	1.5	1.0
3.	Washing clothes	1.5	1.5	1.5	1.0
4.	Cooking & serving	2.0	2.0	3.0	4.0
5.	Collecting fuel and making dung cakes	2.5	2.0	1.0	-
6.	Work for cattle	-	1.0	2.0	-
7.	Repair and maintenance of house (Average of year)	0.5	1.0	2.0	1.0
8.	Caring for children & looking after household chores	0.5	2.0	2.0	3.0
9.	Marketing food	-	3.0	2.00**	3.00**
10.	Work in the field/farm	8.0	2.0	*	*

* Stands for seasonal jobs of sowing, transplanting, harvesting and threshing.

** Covers cleaning, drying and storing food grains, making milk products, curd and butter and selling.

Creche/Daycare

With the advent of industrialization and modernization, and with the gradual disappearance of the traditional joint family and with its inbuilt security system, the problem of working mothers has become increasingly serious. Although it is mainly an urban phenomenon, rural India is beginning to experience it too. With increasing economic pressures more and more women have to take 'out of home' jobs. The situation is serious because the majority of women who need day care for their children are from the economically backward strata of society.

Working mother of low-income groups need day care most as they cannot afford to hire or pay for labour-saving devices. Thus, in addition to the general need for child care for all working mother's, there is also a more specific and strong need for child care for those belonging to the poorest sections of the society.

Rural mothers struggle hard not only in the fields but also to collect fuel, fodder and water. Thus their time "out of home" is much more and the majority of them are forced to either take their infants along or to leave them under the `supervision' of elder children who stay at home, or even alone. This situation not only keeps older children away from the educational system, but endangers the health of infants and small children. The need for child care services had already been accepted, both legal provision exists only for women in the organized sector, which comprise approximately 10 per cent of the working women.

After the submission of the CSWI report (1974), and the International Women's Year, child care has been recognized as an important and essential support service in women's development. The CSWI report has stated that despite the laws and ILO Convention, maternity and child care benefits are available only to 3-5 per cent of Indian women workers in the organized sector. The other 3-5 per cent of the organized sector (mainly in services) do not get creche facilities because they are not covered by labour laws. To the 90 per cent of women workers who are in the informal sector, these facilities have so far never been provided as highlighted in the report of the National Commission on Self-Employed Women and Women in the Informal Sector.

In 1950, creches were run by four national level voluntary organizations — the Indian Council for Child Welfare, Bhartiya Grameen Mahila Sangh, Bhartiya Adimjati Sevak Sangh and Harijan Sevak Sangh. The then Ministry of Social Welfare launched a scheme of creches/day-care centres for children of working and ailing mothers in February 1975. The aim of the scheme was to promote healthy all round development of such children. The scheme caters to the basic needs of young children of poor working and ailing women in the unorganized sector. The services under the scheme include health care, supplementary nutrition, sleeping facilities, immunization, entertainment and nursery school facilities for children, Starting in 1974-75 with 247 creches to cover 6,175 beneficiaries, the scheme has been considerably expanded since then. In the year 1987-88 there were 3137 agencies running 10,210 creches in the country which included both permanent and mobile units. The Department of Women & Child Development which now deals with the scheme plans that by the end of 1988-89, 12,000 creches would cover 2,82,800 children. The training of creche workers under this programme has commenced from September, 1986. Grants-in-aid to certain all-India level institutions are being released for conducting training courses. In the statutory sector, around 55,000 children are taken care of in creches/day-care centres.

The Balwadi Nutrition Programme is another programme being implemented since 1970-71 which looks after the social and emotional development of children in age group of 3-5 years, apart from providing supplementary nutrition to them. About 5045 Balwadi centres are functioning in the country covering about 2.29 lakh children.

The Integrated Child Development Services (ICDS) scheme launched by the government in 1975 is designed both as a preventive and developmental effort. It extends beyond the existing health and education systems to reach children below six years and their mothers in villages and slums and delivers to them an integrated package of services — non-formal pre-school education, immunization, health check ups, supplementary nutrition, medical referral services and nutrition and health education for women. As on 31 March, 1988 information received from 1455 ICDS projects indicate that 1,46,693 Anganwadis were providing supplementary nutrition to 96.10 lakh children. In these anganwadis, 18.40 lakh nursing mothers were receiving supplementary nutrition. Though focused on the all round development of the pre-school child, it is also the largest scheme providing part time creches facilities to children in rural and tribal areas and in slums. As an employment generation scheme for women, it employs nearly 2,00,000 women at the Anganwadi level.

The National Policy on Education, 1986 (NPE), for the first time took note of the growing awareness that the performance of household chores, specially care of younger siblings, is a major reason for the stagnation in enrolment of girls in school. At two places in the policy document, (vide para 5.2 in Early Childhood Care and Education (ECCE) and para 4.3 in Education for Women's

Equality), reference is made to the need for child care, attached to or near primary schools, as a support service to encourage and allow girls to attend school.

Housing

The rapid rate of urbanization in India, coupled with large-scale migration of people into the metropolitan cities, has created a tremendous pressure on the housing situation in the country. On the one hand, is the ever increasing shortage of housing which is estimated to be to the tune of 5.1 million dwelling units in urban areas alone (NBO 1981), and on the other, is the steep cost of urban housing and new construction which is unable to keep pace with the increasing demand and is beyond the reach of the urban dwellers.

In the successive Five-Year Plans, the Government of India has launched several social housing schemes for different income groups under which, loan/subsidy is given to the low income and economically weaker section families. The implementation of these schemes on a country-wide basis has created great awareness of the desirability of improving their housing and environmental conditions among all sections of the populations including women.

Several other measures which have been taken include providing house building advance, housing finance at low rates of interest through financial institutions, fiscal incentives, bulk acquisition and development of land and ceiling on land, use regulations, promotion of housing through cooperatives, setting up of Housing Boards and City Development Authorities and Slum Clearance Boards to augment the housing stock.

A Central Scheme of assistance for construction of hostel buildings for working women was initiated in 1972. The scope of the scheme was widened in 1980 by including a provision for day-care centres for children. Financial assistance is given to voluntary organizations for construction/expansion of hotel buildings for working women. Local bodies are also eligible for taking up these programmes. The total number of hostels sanctioned so far is 429 with a total capacity of 27,292 working women with day-care centre facilities for 2,920 children, since the inception of the scheme in 1972. It has been decided to reserve 5 per cent seats in the hostels for widows and other women in distress who are otherwise, eligible for hostel accommodation.

Under the Minimum Needs Programme to ameliorate housing and environmental conditions, the Government of India has been implementing various schemes viz., Slum Clearance Improvement Scheme, Scheme for Environmental Improvement in Slum Areas and the Scheme for Provision of House Sites to landless workers in rural areas and other social housing schemes for improving the living conditions of the urban and rural poor. The benefits of the schemes accrue to women also.

In the Twenty-Point Programme (1986) high priority has been accorded to provision of drinking water supply (Point No. 7), improvement of housing conditions for 14.6 million rural landless families (Point No. 14) and those living in slums and squatter settlements (Point No. 15).

Large-scale housing programmes have been taken up in different states under the National Rural Employment Programme (NREP) and Rural Landless Employment Guarantee Programme (RLEGP). Housing schemes with employment as the main feature have also been taken up in many States. For implementing the Indira Gandhi Grih Nirman Awas Yojna, an allocation of Rs 125 crore annually has been provided in the Seventh Five-Year Plan to build one million houses for Scheduled Caste and tribal families.

Improvement in the quality of life of people depends to a great extent on the quality of housing and related facilities which determine the physical environment. It is in recognition of this fact that the World Conference of the International Women's Year adopted a World Plan of Action in 1975 which included aspects related to housing amongst its recommendations. The Plan suggested that settlement planning and policies should be formulated keeping in view the trend to recognize women's role in the development process and should prioritize investments in infrastructure therein according to the needs of women. Subsequently, following the declaration of 1987 by the United Nations as the International Year of Shelter for the Homeless, the Ministry of Urban Development of the Government of India formulated a Draft National Housing Policy (March, 1987) with a view to ensuring every family, shelter of twentieth century.

Nowhere in its text, however, had the draft acknowledged that housing and women's needs required to be closely linked. Passing references to women were made only at page 12 para 13.4 of the draft wherein it stated that special efforts would be made to improve women's skills and working conditions in the housing sector.

For women, housing has a wider meaning. It implies their working and living environment to which they are confined for a greater portion of their lives, performing their multiple roles that of production which is often home based and therefore implies the use of the shelter and its environs as the working space; that of reproduction which is traditionally viewed as their primary role and includes child rearing activities linked to domestic chores; and that of management of resources and assets within the family unit which includes activities such as storage, managing domestic provisions, processing, etc.

Women's housing needs, arising from their multiple roles, have been listed as follows: as child bearers, they need access to sanitary facilities and a healthy living environment; as child rearers, they need space for child care and recreation within or outside the house; as managers of households, they need water, fuel, waste and garbage disposal, proper light and ventilation and space to perform domestic chores; and as producers, they need a working space as well as space for storage of raw materials and finished products, besides space for processing of materials. In addition, women also need privacy and security as well as facilities for education, recreation, production and training within the housing space. Housing thus, implies space beyond the confines of the immediate shelter.

An effective public distribution system for essential commodities like rations and cloth is a necessary support for women, especially women workers in the unorganized sector. Poor women are denied ration cards which forces them to purchase basis necessities from the open market at exorbitant prices. Even women with ration cards are often denied rations due to understocking or diversion of stocks.

Each of the above roles indicates that women's efficiency and effectiveness in performing the productive and reproductive tasks are linked to the quality of housing. Since they are in effect the primary users of housing, women must have a role to piay in decisions regarding housing as well as ensure that they have access to ownership of the same.

In planning for women's development, priority needs to be given to creating access to assets for single women and female headed households. An estimated 30-35 per cent of households in rural India are headed by women according to available micro studies. Women have hitherto had no rights to ownership or inheritance of property within the framework of customary law. Recent legislative provisions have tried to remedy this situation but ancestral property still remains inaccessible to women. By and large, the patriarchal patterns of land ownership and transfer have implied that land is transferred to males. This pattern has been adopted by the planners in formulation of housing programmes so that men are recognized as heads of households and land is distributed in their names. Although distribution of land deeds or *pattas* has been legally sanctioned for men and women jointly, in effect, women are not given land titles. Where women are able to gain access to land or assets, they are often required to have a man stand surety for the same, as also for loans and credit.

Within the patriarchal norm, women may not customarily claim ownership of the matrimonial home. This has often denied women access to shelter in times of crisis. In cases where women have been deserted and are destitute, they have not had any legal right to claim access to shelter, housing or any such assets. Only recently have policy makers and legislators realized that, it is imperative to accord priority to the provision of housing for single and women headed households.

Various strategies have been evolved to augment the housing stock in the country by urban planners and specialists especially for economically weaker sections. The target groups have however seldom been involved in planning for such housing. The norms applied to make such houses affordable for the identified target groups have ignored women's needs for space in the dwelling unit. It is necessary to scrutinize established standards and develop norms in housing especially for economically weaker sections, and to determine their adequacy for women. There must also be visible participation of women in the planning and execution of housing programmes in order to ensure that women's needs are adequately considered in the housing designs.

Women have had no traditional access to capital assets or to institutional finance and credit for housing. They have had to resort to borrowing from traditional credit sources at exorbitant rates of interest. Institutional sources of credit such as banks have not recognized women as credit worthy individuals in their own right so that they may borrow through existing schemes at differential rates of interest. Various agencies have tried to play an intermediary role in creating access for women to institutional credit but their outreach has been limited. It is essential, therefore, that institutions such as HDFC and HUDCO recognize women in their individual capacities as beneficiaries for housing credit and finance.

The housing market also offers a vast potential for employment, especially in the rural areas. Expanding construction activity in housing would ensure that greater opportunities for employment are created, while also creating shelter for the rural populace.

Recommendations

Fuel, Fodder, Water

1. Problems specific to women have to be highlighted in considering issues like fodder, fuel and drinking water. Since these directly concern women, their involvement in all programmes related to such issues must be given prominence. The interlinkages among fuel, fodder and drinking water with other aspects of the development of women such as education, employment, food and nutrition, health and sanitation must be recognized and integrated programmes worked out on a holistic basis for optimal utilization of personnel and financial inputs.

2. As has been stressed by the Seventh Plan, the government must ensure public participation and draw upon the resources of voluntary agencies educational (especially Science and Technology) institutions, industries and financial organizations in implementing various programmes for the development of women. Various

funding agencies may consider sponsoring All India or regional projects on a coordinated basis wherein, Science and Technology experts could collaborate with the NGOs and the people in designing and implementing programmes based on micro-level surveys.

3. Women must be specifically organized by involving the NGOs wherever necessary to participate in the implementation of social forestry programmes, water sharing projects and in the maintenance of various gadgets and devices. The necessary formal and non-formal education has to be appropriately matched with their time schedules, seasonal occupations and socio-cultural constraints.

4. In training programmes, in addition to NGOs, educational institutions could play an important role. Agricultural extension centres, home science colleges, and youth forums like NSS should be purposefully involved. Science and Technology institutions can take up the task of training and provide the technical back up in technology transfer as well as monitoring and evaluation.

5. A data bank may be set up with such resource centres where information may be made available not only on technologies but also on manufacturing availability of training facilities, etc. These centres must have working models readily available for demonstrations and requisite resource persons. Interaction among the centres will enable them to serve as a national network.

6. Research must be undertaken both in improving and developing hardware and software systems. All the necessary technologies on collection, processing, storage and utilization of fodder, fuel and drinking water may be carefully analysed and gaps identified. Many issues are regional and location specific and tackled best at the micro level. For example, carrying water is more problematic in hills than in plains; fuel problem is more acute in arid zones. The choice of fuel and fodder generating plants would depend on the agroclimate and terrains. The type of improved *chulha* required depends on the food and cooking practices. Perhaps an area based approach can be taken combining locations with similar type of problems into groups or clusters.

7. The necessary industrial support in the manufacturing of various small equipments should be created, e.g., manufacture of

small water storage systems, forage harvesting systems, etc. Women and small entrepreneurs should be involved in such ventures with suitable subsidies.

8. The decision makers both at the bureaucratic and political levels should be sensitized to the importance of programmes specifically targeted for women in the context of national development.

9. The socio-cultural and traditional practices must be suitably modified for conservation of various resources and more efficient utilization of time, energy and capital. For example, cooking recipies which require more fuel and time in cooking have to be pointed out and corrected. Where possible, community kitchens should be encouraged. Especially in the periphery of towns, the food prepared in neighbouring areas can be brought in packages. This would reduce the load on fuel, provide employment to women in the surrounding areas while benefiting many working women.

10. Many of the local hardware and software problems especially with respect to fuel and drinking water are not easily solved at the household level. The right level of scaling has to be planned, keeping in view both the economic viability and the consumer's convenience. For instance, in a biogas system, a 80m^3 community biogas plant is more economical than a 2m^3 household plant but the former calls for a more elaborate management system. Perhaps a sub-community biogas plant of 15-20m^3 for 15-20 families could be a solution. Thus for each problem, a suitable community or sub-community system has to be worked out.

11. Some of the above recommendations have been noted both in the 'Country Report of 1985' presented at Nairobi and "Forward Looking Strategies for the Year 2000". However, at the level of implementation, the programmes of various governmental departments tend to get superimposed. Hence it is important to identify one of the Ministries as the 'Nodal Ministry' for coordination and keeping abreast of all programmes related to women. The Ministry of Human Resource Development could perhaps take this up so that a Master Table could be prepared of all action/projects having a bearing on women, noting the time schedules for implementation, and the agencies involved in planning and action at the central, state, regional local levels. This

"Nodal Ministry" for women may constitute sub-committee with members drawn not only from government but also from other participating agencies to discuss the various issues and evolve strategies.

Creche/Daycare

12. Creche services must be universally provided to all women, especially in the poverty sector. This would enable some of them to augment their family income and at the same time, ensure proper care of their children. The children's health, sanitation, nutrition and early stimulation would get attention. Increasing the number of creches would also generate more employment opportunities for women. In view of the above, it is recommended that in rural areas wherever ICDS infrastructure already exists creches should be opened attached to the *Anganwadis*. These creches should make provision for babies below 3 years age. The timing of *Anganwadis* which provide pre-school services for children of 3-6 years adjusted according to the working hours of rural women. These creches will help in containing morbidity and mortality rates and malnutrition of infants and small children. They will also relieve the children in the school going age group from child care responsibilities, and give an opportunity to them to utilize the ICDS pre-school services.

13. The existing law that stipulates provision of a creche for employment of thirty or more women should be changed to thirty persons (men and women). This would ensure that employers do not use loopholes in the law to their advantage and would extend creche facilities to children of men workers whose wives, if they are not in the organized sector do not otherwise have access to such facilities.

14. The Government of India, being an employer of large number of women, must provide creche facilities in or near all workplaces.

15. Creche service must follow an integrated approach to child care.

16. Creche workers should preferably be local women to whom appropriate skill-oriented on the job training should be imparted.

17. Technical institutions and home-science colleges should be utilized to train creche workers as also provide inputs for systematic monitoring and supervision of the creche programmes.

18. Organizations running creches should be given flexibility to adopt timings suitable to the needs of the working mothers.

19. Local women's groups and mothers of the children attending creches must be given training in preparation of toys, play materials out of low cost/no cost indigenous material. Employment for women can be generated by employing local women to prepare the mid-day meals, etc.

20. Action research projects, such as, a study of the impact of day-care services on the education of girls should be initiated.

Housing

Traditionally, women have had a significant role in resource management including housing management. It is important to recognize this role and provide for women's participation in development programmes, and for incorporating their needs in schemes for improvement of housing and environmental conditions in the following manner:

21. Identify the needs of women in relation to housing and community facilities and build them in an integrated manner into housing development programmes.

22. Integrate environmental factors into development planning for women and their requirements in settlement planning.

23. Involve women at all levels of decision making and bring about their participation in programme implementation so as to ensure that the benefits of housing, essential services, and community facilities are directed to women in general and to the poor and vulnerable among them in particular.

24. The special needs of women should be identified and adequately catered to while formulating minimum housing standards.

25. Necessary facilities in homes should be provided to lessen the burden and drudgery of women in performing productive and reproductive roles.

26. Priority investment in infrastructure such as water supply, sanitation, energy, transportation, working women's hostels, public

distribution of basic needs, etc., should take into consideration the needs of women.

27. Provision of housing for working and/or single women is recommended on priority basis. In addition, women in difficult circumstances such as widows, refugees, destitutes, victims of social oppression, seasonal migrant workers, victims of natural disasters, etc., must be provided shelter as part of an integrated rehabilitation programme.

28. The National Housing Policy which has been formulated, must pay adequate attention to the special needs and roles of women in the implementation of housing programme.

29. The social and economic constraints which come in the way of women's participation should be removed and their active involvement in housing should be promoted by:

- Alloting house-sites in the joint name of wife and husband;
- Mobilizing savings of women for housing;
- Organizing self-help in undertaking house construction work;
- Imparting training so that women could become skilled labour (including masons and other skilled labour); and
- Ensuring access for women to institutional credit at low rates of interest without collateral.

Appendices

Declaration of Mexico Plans of Action. World Conference of the International Women's Year, 19 June-2 July, 1975. United Nations, December, 1975

In order to eliminate all obstacles that stand in the way of enjoyment by women of equal status with men, the Mexico plans of Action decided to promulgate 30 principles on the equality of women and their contribution to national development and international peace. For implementation purposes, the objectives of the Mexico Plans of Action were divided into two categories—the World Plan of Action and the Regional Plans of Action. The main purpose was to stimulate national, international and regional action to solve the problems of underdevelopment and of the socio-economic structure which place women in an inferior position.

The major highlights of the Mexico Plans of Action were the 14 minimum objectives to be achieved by member countries by the end of the first five-year period (1975-80) of the UN Decade for Women. These objectives were:

1. Marked increase in literacy and civic education of women, especially rural areas;
2. The extension of co-educational, technical and vocational training in basic skills to women and men in the industrial and agricultural sectors;
3. Equal access at every level of education, compulsory primary school education and the measures necessary to prevent school drop-outs;
4. Increased employment opportunities for women, reduction of unemployment and increased efforts to eliminate discrimination in terms and conditions of employment;
5. The establishment and increase in the infrastructural services, required in both rural and urban areas;
6. The enactment of legislation on voting and eligibility for election on equal terms with men, equal opportunity and

conditions of employment including remuneration, and on equality in legal capacity and the exercise thereof;

7. Encouragement of a greater participation of women in policy making positions at the local, national and international levels;
8. Increased provision for comprehensive measures for health education and services, sanitation, nutrition, family education, family planning and other welfare services;
9. Provision for parity in the exercise of civil, social and political rights such as those pertaining to marriage, citizenship and commerce;
10. Recognition of the economic value of women's work in the home, in domestic food production and marketing of voluntary activities not remunerated;
11. The direction of formal, non-formal and life-long education towards the re-evaluation of the men and women, in order to ensure their full realization as individuals in the families and in society;
12. The promotion of women's organizations as an interim measure within workers' organizations and educational, economic and professional institutions;
13. The development of modern and rural technology, cottage industry, pre-school day centres, time-and-energy-saving devices so as to help reduce the heavy work load of women, particularly those living in rural sectors and for the urban poor and thus facilitate the full participation of women in community, national and international affairs;
14. The establishment of interdisciplinary and multisectoral machinery within the government for accelerating the achievement of equal opportunities for women and their full integration into national life.

Convention on the Elimination of all Forms of Discrimination against Women — United Nations 1975

The 30 Article Convention calls for equal rights for women, regardless of their marital status, in all fields, political, economic, social, cultural and civil. It calls for national legislation to ban discrimination; recommends temporary special measure to speed equality between men and women; and action to modify social and cultural patterns that perpetuate discrimination.

Other measures provide for equal rights for women in political and public life; equal access to education and same choice of curricula; non-discrimination in employment and pay; and guarantee of job security in the event of marriage and maternity. The convention underlines the equal responsibilities of men and women in the context of family life. It also stresses the social services needed—especially child care facilities, for combining family obligations with work responsibilities and participation in public life. The Committee on the Elimination of Discrimination Against Women (CEDAW) monitors progress made in implementation of the Convention.

By 31 May, 1987, 93 countries had consented to be bound by the provisions of the Convention, either through ratification or accession. India has signed the convention but has not ratified it.

Programme of Action for the Second Half of the United Nations Decade for Women: Equality, Development and Peace. World Conference, Copenhagen 14-30 July 1980, Government of India, Ministry of Social Welfare, Women's Welfare and Development Bureau, New Delhi

The General Assembly resolution of 1975 decided that in 1980, at the midpoint of the Decade, a world conference of the UN Decade for Women would be convened. The purpose was twofold: (i) to review and evaluate progress made by member countries in implementing the recommendations of the World Conference of the International Women's Year held in 1975, and (ii) to readjust programmes for the second half of the Decade in the light of new data and research. This report, prepared by the Government of India, consists of three parts.

Part one outlines the historical background and conceptual framework of the Programme of Action. Part two consists of Programme of Action at the national level. These include national strategies for accelerating the full participation of women in economic and social development; objectives and priority areas for action taken in connection with the subtheme of the World conference. Part three consists of the Programmes of Action at the International and Regional levels.

Some priority areas requiring special attention were identified. These included food production, problems of rural women, provision of child care services, problems of migrant women, unemployed women, young women and women who alone are responsible for their families.

India-A Status Paper, World Conference of the UN Decade for Women 14-30 July, 1980. Government of India, Ministry of Social Welfare, 1980

Para 46 of the World Plan of Action adopted by the World Conference of the International Women's Year outlined 14 minimum objectives to be achieved by the end of the first half of the UN Decade for Women, i.e., 1975-80. This paper was prepared in 1980 by the Ministry of Social Welfare, Government of India in an attempt to review India's progress in attaining those minimum objectives. Various initiatives undertaken by the Government of India were highlighted.

The review also indicated the constraints and problems faced in promoting participation of women in development and in improving their status. The document pointed to the fact it had been possible to provide for *de jure* equality, services and facilities for education, health care and training of women. But due to the effect of traditional constraints and attitudes increasing affirmative action was required in favour of women to convert *de jure* equality into *de facto* equality.

Report of the Regional Intergovernmental Preparatory Meeting for the World Conference to Review and Appraise the Achievements of the United Nations Decade for Women: Equality, Development and Peace United Nations Economics and Social Commission for Asia and the Pacific, Tokyo, 26-30 March, 1984

Representatives from member countries and various organizations met in 1984 to review and appraise the achievements of the subtheme of United Nations Decade for Women: Equality, Development and Peace. It was noted that due to a growing recognition of the critical importance of integrating women into national socio-economic policies and plans, there had been some progress. But due to compartmentalization of women's issues the progress has been unsatisfactory—being unequally distributed, isolated and fragmentary in nature. Impediments to effective planning and plan implementation included the lack of an adequate resource base in terms of trained personnel, finance and inappropriate data. Forward looking strategies were designed. It was suggested that these strategies, should address these continuing concerns in a more effective manner so that women are recognized as productive contributions to development and its beneficiaries. To achieve these goals, it was also suggested to mobilize national and legislative machineries as well as promote a high degree of public awareness of women's contribution to national development. The other major obstacle highlighted was pervasiveness of social attitudes deep-rooted in tradition and history.

New Delhi Document on Women in Development. Conference of Non-Aligned and other Developing Countries on the Role of Women in Development, New Delhi, 10-11 April, 1985

The delegates examined in depth the role of women in developing countries, areas of cooperation exchange of expertise and shared experiences, in light of preparations for the World Conference. The intention was to approach the World Conference with full knowledge of their achievements and failures, and to evolve a strategy to tackle the problems confronting the world.

The current status of women was reviewed and appraised in the context of various sectors such as agriculture, food production, rural development, industrialization, education, mass media, science and technology, population, housing and environmental issues. Problem areas and obstacles in attaining the objectives of the UN Decade for Women were identified. One of the basic obstacles in achieving women's equality was the non-recognition of women's pivotal role in society. Lack of concerted and determined efforts to remove gender-bias was recognized as the second important obstacle. Thirdly project planning seemed to pay scant attention to the linkages between women's productive and reproductive work. Usually, programmes or projects focused on only one or the other aspect. Hence the need for a more "holistic" view of women's work and contribution was emphasized. New approaches and forward looking strategies to achieve the objectives of the UN Decade were designed.

Forward Looking Strategies for the Advancement of Women. The World Conference to Review and Appraise the Achievements of the UN Decade for Women: Equality, Development and Peace. Nairobi (Kenya), 15-26 July, 1985. Government of India, Ministry of Human Resource Development, Department of Women's Welfare, New Delhi.

The Forward Looking Strategies (FLS) for the Advancement of Women from 1986 to the year 2000 was adopted at the UN Decade for Women World Conference held in Nairobi, Kenya, in July 1985. They were built on the earlier world conference on women, on the work of the UN Commission on the status of women and on the activities and ideas of the worldwide women's movement. These strategies were designed to serve as guidelines for creating a new world order based on equality, development and peace. Some of the measures were intended to affect women directly. Others were designed to make the societal context less obstructive and more supportive of their progress such as the elimination of socio-economic-based stereotypes.

Women in India, Country Paper 1985. Government of India, Ministry of Social and Women's Welfare, New Delhi.

At the end of the UN Decade for Women, a country paper was prepared by the Ministry of Social Welfare, Government of India. The purpose was to identify areas in which work has been done to improve the status of women. The paper highlighted the developments with regard to demography, law, employment, health, education, political participation, family, science and technology and institutional arrangements. It also outlined the obstacles and bottlenecks in each area and suggested modifications and strategies to improve the situation.

Women in Development: Report of SAARC Ministerial Meeting, Shillong, May 6-8, 1986. Government of India, Ministry of Human Resource Development, Department of Women and Child Development, New Delhi.

In pursuance of the decision taken at the first Summit of the Heads of State or Government of the South Asian Association for

Regional Cooperation held at Dhaka in December, 1985, two meetings took place. The first Ministerial meeting on Women in Development was held at Shillong on May 6-8, 1986 at the invitation of the Government of India. The second official level meeting on Women in Development was held in New Delhi on April 8-10, 1986. The basic objectives were to promote the welfare of the people of South Asia and to improve their quality of life. This meeting reflected their conviction that no meaningful progress could be achieved without the active participation of women and the enhancement of the status of women who form half the population in this region.

At the Ministerial Meeting the ministers reviewed the overall situation of women in the South Asian countries and noted that considerable progress has been achieved in several social sectors affecting women. However, greater attention was still required to be focused on critical areas. Some of these were the low level of literacy, poor enrolment in schools coupled with high drop out rates; lack of vocational and technical training, marketing and credit facilities; the low level of political participation and involvement in policy making and its implementation. It was felt that special efforts were also required to disseminate appropriate technologies to eliminate drudgery and thus improve the quality of life of women particularly in the rural areas.

At the Official Level Meeting, delegates from each member country presented General Statements on the issues pertaining to Women in Development and highlighted major achievements as also major problems being faced by them. The basic categories included women's access to basic needs, women and environment, family welfare, access to employment, their participation in the development process and cooperation among NGOs. It was suggested that the exchange of training and consultancy services and personnel in the countries of the region be initiated. Basic information, data and documentation on women's issues in the countries of the region was found to be inadequate and steps were needed to compile such information.

NATIONAL DOCUMENTS

Towards Equality: Report of the Committee on the Status of Women in India, December 1974, Government of India, Ministry of Education and Social Welfare, Department of Social Welfare, New Delhi

The Committee on the Status of Women in India (CSWI) was appointed by the Government of India in 1971 (i) to evaluate the changes that had taken place in the status of women as a result of the constitutional, legal and administrative measures adopted since independence, (ii) to examine the impact of the complex process of social change on various sections of Indian women, and (iii) to suggest measures which would enable women to play their full and proper role in building up the nation.

The Committee set up six Task Forces and two Study Groups to examine the changes in the field of social life, law, economic, participation, educational development, political status, and women's welfare and development. The summary of recommendations of the CSWI was as follows:

Summary of recommendations

Chapter III-The Socio-Cultural Setting of Women's Status

The review of the disabilities and constraints on women, which stem from socio-cultural institutions, indicates that the majority of women are still very far from enjoying the rights and opportunities guaranteed to them by the Constitution. Society has not yet succeeded in framing the required norms of institutions to enable women to fulfil the multiple roles that they are expected to play in India today. On the other hand, the increasing incidence of practices like dowry indicate a further lowering of the status of women. They also indicate a process of regression from some of the norms developed during the freedom movement. We have been perturbed by the finding of the content analysis of periodicals in the regional languages, that concern for women and their problems, which received an impetus during the freedom movement, has suffered a decline in the last two decades. The social laws, that sought to mitigate the problems of women in their family life, have remained unknown to a large mass of women in this country, who are as ignorant of their legal rights today as they were before independence.

1. We realize that changes in social latitudes and institutions cannot be brought about very rapidly. It is, however, necessary to accelerate this process of change by deliberate and planned efforts. Responsibility for this acceleration has to be shared by the State and the Community, particularly that section of the community which believes in the equality of women. We, therefore, urge that community organizations, particularly women's organizations should mobilize public opinion and strengthen social efforts against oppressive institutions like polygamy, dowry, ostentatious expenditure on wedding and child marriage, and mount a campaign for the dissemination of information about the legal rights of women to increase their awareness. This is a joint responsibility which has to be shared by community organizations, legislators who have helped to frame these laws and the government which is responsible for implementing them.

Chapter IV-Women and the law

Eradication of Polygamy in Muslim Law

Full equality of sexes can hardly be possible in a legal system which permits polygamy and a social system which tolerates it (4.13). The only personal law, which has remained impervious to the changing trend from polygamy to monogamy is Muslim Law (4.14).

The solution of standard contracts fails to provide substantive relief to the first wife with children. As the second marriage is not invalidated, the position of the husband is not prejudicially affected but for the financial implications arising out of the step. The deterrence of the criminal sanction when a person intends to contract a second marriage is absent. Further, it is ineffective in cases of fake conversions to Islam from other religions, to circumvent the prohibition against bigamy. The remedy is out of step with the position in other personal laws in India and should be rejected (4.20).

While the desirability of reform in Muslim Law is generally acknowledged, the Government has taken no steps towards changing the law for over two decades on the view that public opinion in the Muslim community did not favour a change. This view cannot be reconciled with the declaration of equality and social justice. We are of the opinion that ignoring the interest of Muslim women is a denial of social justice. The right of equality, like the right of free speech, is an individual right (4.26).

2. We are of the firm view that there can be no compromise on the basic policy of monogamy being the rule for all communities in India. Any compromise in this regard will only perpetuate the existing inequalities in the status of women (4.30).

Enforcement of Provision Against Bigamy under Hindu Marriage Act

(a) In our opinion the right to initiate prosecution for bigamy should be extended to persons other than girl's family with prior permission of the Court to prevent the current widespread violation of a most salutary provision of the law which very clearly lays down the social policy of the country (4.33.34).

(b) We recommend that the word 'solemnized' should be replaced by the words "goes through a form of marriage". Further an explanation should be added to Section 17 of the Hindu Marriage Act that an omission to perform some of the essential ceremonies by parties shall not be construed to mean that the offence of bigamy was not committed, if such a ceremony of marriage gives rise to a de facto relationship of husband and wife (4.39).

(c) We recommend that a provision be introduced in Section 6 of the Hindu Marriage Act to the effect that nothing contained in the Hindu Marriage Act shall prevent a court from granting an injunction against a proposed bigamous marriage under the Act or under the provisions of the specific Relief Act, 1963.

Reform of Marriage Laws Prevalent in Former French and Portuguese Territories

In our opinion continuation of such diverse laws (permitting polygamy), contradictory to our social policy, in these territories is totally unjustified. We recommend the immediate replacement of these laws by the Hindu Marriage Act, 1965 (4.51).

Restraint of Child Marriages

(a) When the legal age of marriage in case of a female is below the age of discretion she cannot be expected to form an intelligent opinion about her partner in life. The policy of law which permits the marriage of a girl before she is physically and mentally mature is open to serious question. Child marriage is one of the significant factors leading to the high incidence of suicide among young married women in India. Therefore, increasing the marriage age of girls to eighteen years is desirable (4.61).

(b) An anachronism in Muslim law governs some sects. After puberty, a Muslim male in all sects and a Muslim female belonging to the Hanafi and Ithana Ashari sects can marry without a guardian. But a Malik, Shafi or Daudi or Sulayamani Bohra virgin cannot marry without a guardian and her only remedy is to change over to the Hanafi School and marry according to its tenets (4.62).

In our opinion a change in the law to remove the existing disability in these sub-schools, to bring them in conformity with the Hanafi law is necessary (4.63).

(c) There are large scale violations of the Child Marriage Restraint Act, particularly in the rural areas. The State of Gujarat has made it a cognizable offence with provisions for appointment of a Child Marriage Prevention Officer.

We recommend that all offences under the Child Marriage Restraint Act should be made cognizable and special officers appointed to enforce the law (4.65).

(d) The right to repudiate a child marriage by a girl on attaining majority is provided under Muslim Law if the following facts are established:

(i) that she was given in marriage by her father or other guardian before she attained the age of 15;

(ii) that she repudiated the marriage before she attained the age of 18;

(iii) that the marriage was not consummated (4.67).

In our view the right to repudiate the marriage on attaining majority should be made available to girls in all communities whether the marriage was consummated or not (4.68).

(e) The Parsee Marriage and Divorce Act provides that "no suit shall be brought in any court to enforce any marriage between Parsees or any contract connected with or arising out of any such marriage, if, at the date of the institution of the suit the husband shall not have completed the age of 16 years or the wife shall not have completed the age of 14 years."

We recommend legislation prohibiting courts from granting any relief in respect of a marriage solemnized in violation of the age requirements prescribed by law, unless both the parties have completed the age of 18 years (4.69).

Registration of Marriages

Compulsory registration of marriages as recommended by the UN will be an effective check on child and bigamous marriages, offer reliable proof of marriages and ensure legitimacy and inheritance rights of children (4.70-4.72).

We recommend that registration should be made compulsory for all marriages (4.73).

Prevention of Dowry

The Dowry Prohibition Act 1961 has signally failed to achieve its purpose. In spite of the persistent growth of this practice there are practically no cases reported under the Act (4.75). There is hardly any evidence of social conscience in this regard in the country today (4.77). The educated youth is grossly indifferent to the evil and unashamedly contributed to its perpetuation. Stringent enforcement of the policy and purpose of the Act may serve to educate public opinion better.

(a) A very small but significant step could be taken by the Government by declaring the taking and giving of dowry to be against the Government Servants' Conduct Rules. Such a lead was given earlier to prevent bigamous marriages and giving or taking of dowry should be similarly dealt with (4.78).

(b) The policy of making the offence non-cognizable nullifies the purpose of the Act. We recommend that the offences under the Dowry Act should be made cognizable (4.80).

(c) One of the major loop-holes in the existing legislation is that anything is allowed in the name of gifts and presents. Therefore, any gifts made to the bridegroom or his parents in excess of Rs 500 or which can be so used as to reduce his own financial liability should be made punishable (4.81).

(d) The practice of displaying the Dowry tends to perpetuate the practice as others follow suit. To curb the evil of dowry we recommend legislation on the lines of the West Pakistan Dowry

(Prohibition of Display) Act 1967 which penalized display of gifts made at the time or immediately before or after marriage (4.82).

(e) An evaluation of the impact of the amended Dowry Prohibition Act should be made after 5 years. The next step should be to set a ceiling even on the gifts that may be made to the bride (4.83).

Improvement of Laws of Divorce

The concept of 'union for life' or the sacramental nature of marriage which renders the marriage indissoluble has gradually been eroded and through legislation the right on divorce has been introduced in all legal systems in India, but the same variations and unequal treatment of sexes characterizes this branch of law also (4.84).

We recommend the following changes:

Hindu Law

(a) difference in the place of work should not be regarded as a ground for a case of desertion or restitution of conjugal rights (4.94).

(b) cruelty and desertion should be added as grounds for divorce in the Hindu Marriage Act so that persons are not compelled to follow the present circuitous route and undergo the expense of going to court twice (4.95).

Muslim Law

(c) We recommend that the right of the wife to divorce on the failure of the husband to maintain her, irrespective of her conduct which may be the main or contributory cause, should be clearly spelt out (4.100).

(d) We recommend immediate legislation to eliminate the unilateral right of divorce, and to introduce parity of rights for both partners regarding grounds for seeking dissolution of a marriage (4.103).

Christian Law

(e) We regret that the reforms in Christian Marriage laws as recommended by the Law Commission and incorporated in the Christian Marriage Matrimonial Causes Bill 1960 have not yet been enacted and recommend that no further time be lost to reform and amend this law (4.104 - 4.106).

Jewish Law

(f) We recommend that reform and codification on the Jewish law be undertaken and the principle of monogamy as well as the normal grounds for divorce as provided in the Special Marriage Act be adopted for this community also (4.108).

General

(g) In our opinion conversion should not be a ground for divorce as it offers an easy way of avoiding matrimonial obligations (4.111).

(h) We recommend that mutual consent as a ground for divorce should be recognized in all the personal laws so that two adults whose marriage has, in fact, broken down can get it dissolved honourably (4.112).

(i) The provision in the Parsee Marriage and Divorce Act which enable the wife to obtain a divorce if her husband has compelled her to prostitution should be included in all other personal laws (4.113).

(j) As a general principle, we recommend parity of rights regarding grounds for divorce for both husband and wife (4.114).

Adoption

(a) We recommend that the right of adoption should be equal for husband and wife, with the consent of the other spouse (4.125).

(b) We welcome the step taken by the Government in introducing a uniform and secular law of adoption, the adoption of Children Bill, 1972, and recommend an early enactment of the Bill as it will extend the right of adoption, equally to men and women of all communities, and will be a step towards a uniform secular law (4.129).

Guardianship

We recommend:

(a) that the control over the person and poverty of minor cannot be separated and should vest in the same person;

(b) that the question of guardianship should be determined entirely from the point of view of the child's interest and not the prior right of either parent;

(c) that the parent who does not have guardianship should have access to the child;

(d) that whatever the decision taken earlier, the child's choice of guardian should be obtained when the child reaches the age of 12(4.143).

(e) We support the recommendations of the UN Commission on the Status of Women as follows:

(i) Women shall have equal right and duties with men in respect to guardianship of their minor children and the exercise of parental authority over them, including care, custody, education and maintenance;

(ii) Both spouses shall have equal rights and duties with regard to the administration of the property of their minor children, with the legal limitations necessary to ensure as far as possible that it is administered in the interest of the children;

(iii) The interest of the children shall be the paramount consideration in proceedings custody of children in the event of divorce, annulment of marriages or judicial separation;

(iv) No discrimination shall be made between men and women with regard to decisions regarding custody of children and guardianship or other parental rights in the event of divorce, annulment of marriage or judicial separation (4.144).

Maintenance

The provision for maintenance in the Criminal procedure Code continues to reflect the old attitude to women. With some modifications like extending the rights to demand maintenance to indigent parents and to divorced wives, the obligation to maintain continues to be that of the man. There are today women economically independent who cannot only look after themselves but also their husband and children (4.147).

(a) As we believe in the equal status of husband and wife, and of son and daughter, we recommend amendment of the law of maintenance to provide for the obligation of the economically independent women:

(i) to maintain her dependent husband;
(ii) to share with him the duty to maintain their children;
(iii) to share with her brothers the duty to maintain their indigent parents (4.148).

(b) The underlying principle for the inclusion of the right of maintenance in the Criminal Procedure Code is to prevent starvation and vagrancy. The ceiling of Rs 500 on the total amount of maintenance for all dependent persons seems unjustified (4.148).

In extending the right of maintenance to those divorced wives who have received a sum of money payable under customary or personal law. This exclusion of all divorced Muslim women defeats the purpose of the section to provide a speedy remedy to indigent women (4.149).

We therefore recommend that the ceiling placed on the maximum amount payable as maintenance should be removed and the term 'wife to include divorced wife be made applicable to all women without any exception' (4.150).

(c) Under Muslim law the wife's right to maintenance lasts only as long as she remains a wife. If she is divorced, she loses her right and is only entitled to maintenance for 3 months. This has created a discrimination between the Muslim and other Indian women. We recommend the removal of this discrimination and extension of right of maintenance of divorced wives (4.155).

(d) In order to minimize the hardship caused by non-payment of maintenance, and to ensure certainty of payment, we recommend that all maintenance orders should be deducted at the source by the employer as done in the case of income tax. Where it is not possible to deduct at the source, as in the case of a business man or a self-employed person, the arrears of maintenance should be recovered as 'arrears of land revenue or by distress' (4.159).

(e) An additional mode of execution of the maintenance degree may be to adopt the same procedure as is done in the case of fines under the Criminal Procedure Code (4.160).

Inheritance

(a) The Indian Succession Act confers no restrictions on the power of a person to will away his property. Therefore, the protection enjoyed by a Muslim widow to a share of the estate and by a Hindu widow to be maintained is denied to other widows under this law. There is a need to incorporate some restriction on the right of testation, similar to that prevailing under Muslim law to prevent a widow from being left completely destitute (4.165).

(b) A characteristic feature of the Travancore and Cochin Christian Succession Laws is the discrimination against women (4.167). We recommend that immediate legislative measures be taken to bring Christian women of Kerala under the Indian Succession Act as a first step to unify the law (4.173).

(c) According to the law prevailing in Goa, the widow is relegated to the fourth position and is entitled to only the fruits and agricultural commodities. This needs to be remedied immediately (4.177). Similar anomalies prevail in the succession laws governing Christians of Pondicherry which relegate a woman to an inferior position and do not regard her as full owner even in the few cases where she can inherit property (4.178). We recommend the extension of the Indian Succession Act to Goa and Pondicherry (4.178).

(d) The one major factor which helps to continue the inequality between sons and daughters under the Hindu law is the retention of the Mitakshara co-parcenary, the membership of which is confined only to male members. A number of decisions and legislation in the 20th century have made inroads in the concept of the co-parcenary, but the suggestion regarding its abolition received opposition at the time of Hindu Law reform. The compromise arrived at provides limited inheritance rights to the nearest class I female heirs of a co-parcenary but perpetuate unequal treatment between brother and sister. The right of a co-parcenar to renounce his share in the co-parcenary deprives the female heirs of any share. Secondly, the right to transform self-acquired into joint family property is frequently used to reduce the share of a female heir (4.189-4.193).

We recommend the abolition of the right by birth and the conversion of the Mitakshara co-parcenary into Dayabhaga (4.194).

(e) Section 4(2) of the Hindu Succession Act, excludes the devolution of tenancy rights under State laws from the scope of the Act. This had led to the elimination of the beneficial effects of the Hindu Succession Act under the land legislation in many

States (4.195-200). In order to achieve the social equality of women as also in the interests of uniformity, we recommend the abolition of the exception provided in section 4(2) of the Hindu Succession Act relating to devolution of tenancies (4.201).

(f) Section 23 of the Hindu Succession Act relating to the right of inheritance to a dwelling house has also resulted in some discrimination between unmarried, widowed and married daughters. The main object of the section is unexceptionable as it asserts the primacy of the rights of the family as against the right of an individual and therefore the restriction against partition which is against the family interest should be retained. But nothing justifies the invidious distinction between married and other daughters (4.204 and 4.205). We recommend the removal of the discrimination between married and unmarried daughters regarding the right over a dwelling house (Sec.23 Hindu Succession Act).

(g) The unrestricted right of testation often results in depriving female heirs of their rights of inheritance (4.206). We recommend that the right of testation should be limited under the Hindu Succession Act, so as not to deprive legal heirs completely (4.207).

(h) We recommend legislation in Muslim Law to give an equal share to the widow and the daughter along with sons as has been done in Turkey (4.218).

(i) The medley of laws which govern the right of inheritance, not only to female heirs of different communities; but even of female heirs of the same community require immediate measures. Broad principles like equal rights of sons, daughters and widows, a restriction on the right of testation, so that dependent members are not left completely destitute are needed immediately (4.129).

General Recommendations

Matrimonial Property

In the socio-economic situation prevailing in our country the contribution of the wife to the family's economy is not recognized. A large number of them participate in the family's effort to earn a livelihood as unpaid family workers. Even when they do not do so the economic value of their effort in running the house, assuming all domestic responsibilities, thus freeing the husband for his avocation is not accepted in law either directly or indirectly. Married women who do not have independent source of income or give up employment after marriage to devote their full time in family obligations are economically dependent on their husbands. In majority of cases, movable and immovable property acquired during marriage are legally owned by the husband, since they are paid for out of his earnings. The principle of determining ownership on the basis of financial contribution works inequitably against women. In case of divorce or separation, women without any earnings or savings of their own are deprived of all property which they acquire jointly. Even property received by them at the time of marriage from the husband or his family is denied to the women in some communities. The fear of financial and social insecurity prevents them from resorting to separation or divorce even when the marriages are unhappy. It is necessary to give legal recognition to the economic value of the contribution made by the wife through house work for purposes of determining ownership of matrimonial property, instead of continuing the archaic test of actual financial contribution (4.222-4.225).

We, therefore, recommend that on divorce or separation, the wife should be entitled to at least 1/3 of the assets acquired at the time of and during the marriage (4.226).

Family Courts

The statutory law in all matrimonial matters follows the adversary principle for giving relief, i.e., the petitioner seeking relief alleges certain facts and the respondent refutes them. In addition, most of the grounds in these statutes are based on the 'fault principle' instead of the breakdown theory. As a result, strong advocacy rather than family welfare is often the determining factor in these cases. The absence of distinction between matrimonial causes and other civil suits leads to unusual delay which stands in the ways of conciliation and further embitters the relationship of the parties. Conciliation, which needs to be the main consideration in all family matters is not the guiding principle in the statutes dealing with them (4.227 4.228).

We strongly recommend the abandonment of the established adversary system for settlement of family problems, and establishment of Family Courts which will adopt conciliatory methods and informal procedure, aiming to achieve socially desirable results (4.233).

Uniform Civil Code

The absence of a uniform civil code 27 years after independence is an incongruity which cannot be justified with all the emphasis that is placed on secularism, science and modernization. The continuance of various personal laws which discriminate between men and women violates the Fundamental Rights and the Preamble to the Constitution which promises equality of status to all citizens. It is also against the spirit of national integration and secularism (4.236).

Our recommendations regarding amendments of existing laws are only indicators of the direction in which uniformity has to be achieved. We recommend expeditious implementation of the constitutional directive of Article 44 by the adoption of a uniform Civil Code (4.237).

Needed Reforms in Criminal Law

Consent to sexual intercourse

While consent to sexual intercourse is strictly interpreted and excludes consent given by the woman under duress or fraud, no provision is made for consent obtained by putting someone else in fear in the presence of the woman. We welcome the recommendation of the law commission in this regard (4.242).

In our view consent to have sexual intercourse requires more maturity than to have an abortion. The same age-limit should be applied in both cases. We recommend that the age of consent below which a girl's consent to sexual intercourse is not legal should be 18, permitting some degree of flexibility to the court in border-line cases to decide whether the girl is mature enough (4.243).

Bigamy

The present law restricts jurisdiction of the court to the place where the bigamous marriage was performed or where the husband and wife last resided. This causes difficulties to the wife who may have to move on after being abandoned by her husband.

We recommend that in addition to the two jurisdictions under the Criminal Procedure Code, provision be made for inquiry and trial for bigamy in a court within whose jurisdiction the wife is residing (4.246).

Adultery

Adultery in our opinion should be regarded only as a matrimonial offence, the remedy for which may be sought in divorce or separation. Retention of this as a criminal offence brings out clearly the value of the last century which regarded the wife as the husband's property. It also prevents lawyers and other from giving necessary help to an oppressed wife. We recommend that continuing to regard adultery as a criminal offence is against the dignity of an individual and should be removed from the Penal Code (4.248).

Nationality

(a) In the absence of any provision dealing with the case of Indian women marrying foreigners in the Citizenship Act, many of them have become stateless. We recommend that the Citizenship Act be amended to provide a special rule for Indian women marrying aliens, stating that she will in no case lose her Indian nationality as a result of her marriage to a foreigner (4 256).

(b) The present rule prevents the children of such Indian women from being considered as Indian citizens. Where the father and mother are separated and the mother is the guardian, there is no justification for the rule that the child's nationality will be transmitted through the father. We, therefore, recommend the amendment of section 4(1) of the Citizenship Act to read as follows:

> "A person born outside India on or after the 26th January, 1950, shall be a citizen of India by descent if his father or mother is a citizen of India at the time of his birth" (4.257).

Chapter V-Roles, Rights and Opportunities for Economic Participation

The Indian Constitution guarantees equality of opportunity in matters relating to employment and directs the State to secure equal rights to an adequate means of livelihood, equal pay for equal work and just and humane conditions of work. The impact of transition to a modern economy has meant the exclusion of an increasing number and proportion of women from active participation in the productive process. A considerable number continue to participate for no return and no recognition. The majority of those who do participate fully or on sufferance, without equal treatment, security of employment or humane conditions of work, a very large number of them are subject to exploitation of various kinds with no protection from society or the State. Legislative and executive actions initiated in this direction have made some impact in the organized sector, where only 6 per cent of working women are employed, but in the vast unorganized sector, which engages 94 per cent of working women in this country no impact of these measures have been felt on conditions of work, wages or opportunities.

Estimates of employment and underemployment clearly indicate that the position is worse for women. Measures to remove women's disability and handicaps in the field of economic participation have proved extremely inadequate. While several factors have handicapped and prevented women's integration into the process of development, the lack of a well-defined policy, indicating areas where they require special assistance and protection, leaves them without access to knowledge, skills and employment.

Prejudices regarding women's efficiency, productivity, capacity for skills and suitability debar them from employment in many areas, and result in wage discrimination. The criteria for determining their unsuitability for particular types of jobs are not clear or uniform. Recasting the employment policy for women requires re-examination of existing theories regarding their suitability for different types of work on scientific lines, and deliberate efforts to promote equality of opportunity by special attention to women's disability and handicaps. Our recommendations aim to make the Constitutional guarantees meaningful and arrest the trend towards gradual exclusion of women from their rights to a fuller participation in the economic process.

We therefore recommend the adoption of a well-defined

policy to fulfil the Constitutional directives and Government's long-term objective of total involvement of women in national development. Such a policy should be framed by a Government Resolution. This policy will need to be implemented carefully to avoid evasion by direct or indirect methods. Apart from specific occupations from which women are debarred by law, employers should not be permitted to exclude them from any occupation unless the basis for unsuitability is clearly specified.

19. The creation of a cell within the Ministry of Labour and Employment at both Central and State levels under the direction of a Senior Officer to deal with problems of women (5.323).

We further recommend the following changes in the existing laws:

Maternity Benefits Act 1961

(i) This Act should be extended to all industries not covered by the Act at present and the provision of maternity relief ensured by the creation of a Central Fund levying contributions from employers. The administration of the Fund should follow the pattern already established by the Employees State Insurance Corporation.

(ii) The Act should also cover agricultural labourers in the same manner as suggested for other industries. To facilitate its implementation, the Central Fund should also include a levy on Agricultural Holdings Tax by the Committee on Taxation of Agricultural Wealth and Income.

(iii) The anti-retrenchment clause already included in the Employees State Insurance Act 1948 should be incorporated in the Maternity Benefits Act.

(iv) For women retrenched for short periods and re-employed on the same jobs, the period of unemployment should not be treated as discontinuation of service for their eligibility for this benefit. For casual labour, a minimum of 3 months of service should be considered as qualifying them for this benefit.

(v) As decided by the Supreme Court in the case of bidi workers, the provision of maternity benefits should be extended to home workers in all other industries.

(vi) In order to eliminate unjust denial of maternity benefits, scrutiny of applications should be done by a Committee of the management and trade union representatives. The latter should preferably include a woman. This will provide greater incentive to women workers to participate in trade union activities.

(vii) The penalties for evasion of this law should be made more stringent.

(viii) The system of paying cash benefits in a lump-sum sometimes gives rise to inadequate attention to the nutritional needs of the mother and the child. Payment of maternity benefits should be made periodically (5.324).

Provision of Creches

(i) The present limit of 50 women workers for the application of this provision under the Factories Act should be reduced to 20.

(ii) Women employed as casual labour or as contract labour should be entitled to share this benefit.

(iii) Wherever there is a demand, a room should be provided for keeping small children for other group of women workers, e.g., workers in offices, hospitals, shops and commercial establishments.

(iv) As far as possible, creches should be established near the residence of women workers rather than the place of work. The ideal arrangements, in our view, would be neighbourhood creches (5.325).

Working Time

Permission to work up to 10.00 pm should be granted, provided arrangements for transport and security are made.

We further recommend effective implementation of the Maternity Benefits Act in all States, and the extension of the Employees State Insurance Scheme to those areas which are not covered by it at present (5.326).

Equalization of Wages

We recommend legislative enactment of Article 39(d) of the Constitution — equal pay for equal work — to add the weight of legal sanction to what is only a policy at present.

We further recommend incorporation of this principle in Minimum Wages Act (5.327).

Integrated Development of Training and Employment

(i) We recommend reservation of a definite quota for women for training within the industry in order to arrest their retrenchment as a consequence of modernization.

(ii) A similar quota should be reserved for women for training of apprentices under the National Apprentices Act.

(iii) We further recommend development programme of vocational training in close relationship with industries and resources located in the area. Links with possible employing agencies have to be developed from the beginning so that the training does not end in futility.

(iv) As recommended by the Committee of the All India Council for Technical Education, Polytechnics for Women should include a production centre with assistance from the Small-Scale Industries Departments of the State concerned.

(v) Training programmes in production and market organization to develop self-employment should be developed.

(vi) Special efforts have to be made to develop vocational training for both illiterate and semi-literate women workers.

(vii) We further recommend development of training-cum-production centres in small scale or cottage industries in both rural and urban areas to provide employment to women near their homes (5.328).

Part-time Employment

We recommend specific provision for part-time employment of women by suitable revisions in recruitment rules and service conditions. We also recommend detailed investigation of areas where part-time employment could be generated by agencies like the Directorate General of Employment and Training, the Institute of Applied Manpower Research, the National Council of Applied Economic Research, etc. Such studies should include examination of existing avenues for part-time employment, viz., In the unorganized industries and occupations (5.329).

Employment Information

We recommend expansion of the national employment service, particularly in rural areas and the development of a women's cadre in the service to provide employment information and assistance to women (5.330).

Provision for Re-entry

We recommend that provision for special leave without pay, subject to a maximum of 5 years during service, should be made in all occupations, in order to enable women to devote full-time for the care of their family. Their lien should be protected (5.331).

Enforcement of Laws Protecting Women Workers

We recommend increase in the number of women on the inspectorate, different labour departments as well as provision for women welfare officers wherever women are employed (5.332).

We Further Recommend

(i) Steps to organize labour unions in the field of agriculture, and other industries where such organizations do not exist at present.

(ii) Formation of Women's Wings in all trade unions, to look after the problems of women workers and to improve women's participation in trade union activities (5.333).

Chapter VI-Educational Development

Our investigation of the progress of women's education in India reveals that while there has been a tremendous increase in the number of girls receiving formal education in the period after Independence the gap between the enrolment of boys and girls has continued to increase at all levels and the proportion of girls in the relevant age groups covered by the school system still remains far below the constitutional target of universal education up to the age of 14. Social attitude to the education of girls ranges from acceptance of the need to one of absolute indifference. The reasons for the variation in social attitude and the consequent slow progress of women's education are both social and economic, which are intensified by inadequate facilities and the ambivalent attitude regarding the purpose of educating girls.

In spite of the expansion, the formal system of education now covers only 10 per cent of the total female population. Less than 7 per cent of the 15 to 25 age group and less than 2 per cent of the 25 and above group have received any formal education. The number of illiterate women has increased from 61 million in 1950-51 to 215 million in 1970-71.

The challenge of the widening illiteracy gap will have to be borne in mind in determining priorities in educational development in the years to come. The claims of the formal educational system which can cater to the need of only a minority for a long time will have to be balanced against the claims of eradication of illiteracy. This stand out as the most important and imperative need to raise the status of women who are already adults and constitute the largest group (6.53). While the constitutional directive of universal education up to the age of 14 must receive the highest priority in the formal system ... an alternative system has to be designed to provide basic education to adult women, particularly in the 15-25 age group (6.55).

Imbalances in women's education and literacy are the consequences of great disparity of educational progress between rural and urban areas, between different sections of the population and between regions, which reflect, to a great extent, variations in regional attitudes to women (6.57). The influence of these and other sociological factors, which, for instance, influence the low educational development among Muslim women or women of Scheduled Castes and Tribes ... make the use of national or state averages in assessing progress of education or literacy rather meaningless (6.61-63).

In our opinion, any plan for educational development of women which does not take these imbalances into account will contribute to the increase of inequalities between different sections of the population. Removal of these imbalances will require special attention from public authorities based on careful identification of factors responsible for them. Special programmes will need to be designed for their removal if equality of educational opportunities is to be brought within the access of the majority of women in this country (6.64).

Recommendations Regarding the Formal System

Co-education

In our opinion, the considerations of efficiency, economy as well as equal opportunity require the acceptance of co-education as a long term policy. In view of the divergent social attitudes, however, we recommend:

(i) Co-education should be adopted as the general policy at the primary level;

(ii) At the middle and secondary stages separate schools may be provided in areas where there is a great demand for them. But the effort to pursue co-education as a general policy at these stages should continue side-by-side;

(iii) At the university level co-education should be the general policy and opening of new colleges exclusively for girls should be discouraged;

(iv) There should be no ban on admission of girls to boys' institutions;

(v) Wherever separate schools/colleges for girls are provided, it has to be ensured that they maintain required standards in regard to the quality of staff, provision of facilities, relevant courses and co-curricular activities;

(vi) Acceptance of the principle of mixed staff should be made a condition of recognition for mixed schools. There is a misgiving, however, that this provision may lead to exclusion of girls from some schools. Therefore, it is suggested that this measure may be reviewed for a few years after it is implemented;

(vii) Wherever there are mixed schools, separate toilet facilities and retiring rooms for girls should be provided (6.72).

Curricula: We Recommend

(i) There should be a common course of general education for both sexes till the end of class X, all courses being open to boys and girls.

(ii) At the primary stage, simple needle craft, music and dancing should be taught to both sexes.

(iii) From the middle stage, differences may be permitted under work experience.

(iv) In classes XI-XII girls should have full opportunity to choose vocational and technical courses according to local conditions, need and aptitudes.

(v) At the university stage there is a need to introduce more relevant and useful courses for all students (6.81).

Pre-School Education: We Recommend:

(i) The provision of three years pre-school education for all children by making a special effort to increase the number of 'balwadis' in the rural areas and in urban slums.

(ii) In order to enable them to fulfil the social functions discussed above, an effort should be made to locate them as near as possible to the primary and middle schools of the locality (6.85).

Universalisation of Education for the Age-Group 6-14: We Recommend:

(i) Provision of primary schools within walking distance from the home of every child within the next 5 years.

(ii) Establishment of ashram or residential schools to serve clusters of villages scattered in difficult terrains. Where this is not immediately possible, preparatory schools may be provided for the time being.

(iii) Provision of mobile schools for children of nomadic tribes, migrant labour and construction workers.

(iv) Sustained propaganda by all types of persons preferably women-officials, social and political workers, to bring every girl into school in Class I preferably at the age of 6. They should visit local schools and involve parents and community leaders in order to promote the schooling of girls, particularly in backward areas.

(v) Provision of incentives to drop-outs. Since poverty is the major cause of drop-outs the most effective incentive, in our opinion is the provision of mid-day meals. The rate of children passing the primary level has definitely gone up in States which have introduced mid-day meals. In Kerala, which has the highest literacy rate among women, this provision is one of the major factors for the enrolment and retention of children in schools today. In reply to our questionnaire, the majority has given highest priority to this incentive. The other important incentives which require to be provided to needy children are free school uniforms, scholarships or stipends and free supply of books and other study material. For girls particularly, the lack of adequate clothing is a great deterrent to attending schools. For schools which do not prescribe any uniform, some provision of clothing is necessary.

(vi) Special incentives for areas where enrolment of girl is low. This will need to be worked out according to local conditions. We suggest special awards or recognition to the community, teachers, students, etc.

(vii) At least 50 per cent of teachers at this stage should be women.

(viii) Provision of at least two teachers in all schools, and conversion of the existing single teacher ones as early as possible.

(ix) Developing a system of part-time education for girls who cannot attend school on a full-time basis. This system should provide education to girls at a time convenient to them.

(x) Adoption of the multiple entry system for girls who could not attend school earlier or had to leave before becoming functionally literate.

(xi) Provision of additional space in schools so that girls can bring their younger brothers and sisters to be looked after, either by the girls themselves in turn, or by some local women (6.87).

(xii) Opening of schools and greater flexibility in admission procedure in middle schools (multiple only), to help girls to complete their schooling (6.88).

Sex Education: We Recommend:

(i) Introduction of sex education from middle school.

(ii) Appointment of an expert group by the Ministry of Education to prepare graded teaching material on the subject. The group should include some experts on mass media, to advise on the use of films and other mass media for this purpose.

(iii) This material may be used for both formal and non-formal education (6.89).

Secondary Education: We Recommend:

(i) Free education for all girls up to the end of the secondary stage.

(ii) Improving the quality of teaching and provision of

facilities for important subjects like science, mathematics and commerce.

(iii) Introduction of job-oriented work experience, keeping in view, the needs, the resources and the employment potential of the region, e.g., courses leading to training as ANM, typing and commercial practice, programmes oriented to industry and simple technology, agriculture and animal husbandry (6.92).

General Recommendations

(i) Provision of mixed staff in all mixed schools. This should be made a condition of recognition.

(ii) Adequate provision of common-rooms and separate toilet facilities for girls in all schools.

(iii) Adequate arrangements for co-curricular activities for girls in all schools.

(iv) Provision of more need-cum-merit scholarships and hostel facilities for girls (6.93).

Higher Education: We Recommend:

(i) Development of more employment opportunities, particularly of a part-time nature, to enable women to participate more in productive activities.

(ii) Development of employment information and guidance services for women entering higher education. Many of them suffer from lack of information regarding job opportunities and regret their choice of subjects when faced by difficulties in obtaining employment (6.96).

Non-formal Education

As stated earlier, the greatest problem in women's education today is to provide some basic education to the overwhelming majority who have remained outside the reach of the formal system because of their age and social responsibilities as well as the literacy gap. For the sake of national plans for development, it is imperative to increase the social effectiveness of women in the 15-25 age group even if we cannot do so for the still older groups. Ad hoc approaches through the adult literacy, functional literacy and other programmes of the government have proved inadequate.

They also draw a sharp distinction between men and women in the content of the training. These distinctions, in our view, are out of date. Changes in family life, food habits, family planning, all require joint efforts of men and women and continuing this kind of artificial division between the sexes may defeat the purpose of these programmes. As for vocational and occupational skills, the needs of women are greater than those of men. While we do not deny the value of crafts, women's need for vocational training cannot be limited to them. The skills differ according to the industrial and market potentials of regions and it is imperative to relate the training to local needs, resources and employment possibilities instead of adopting an artificial sex-selective approach. Ad hoc approaches through a multiplicity of programmes by various governmental agencies will lead to overlapping, lack of coordination and wastage of resources. The problem is an integrated one and cannot be solved by short term programmes. What is needed is a continuous process (6.97-6.101).

No attempt to professionalize this system will lead to development of the limiting, selective and a rigid approach with fixed curricula and classroom procedures. The prohibitive cost of such professionalization would inevitably limit its operation to a few selected centres. The teachers in a non-formal system must have other skills of direct relevance to the problems of the community. Without this kind of community involvement, such programmes will lack stability and continuity (6.104).

The object of the system should be to provide access to information and use of information for better participation in social life with literacy as the core of the package. Though primarily meant for adolescents, the system should not exclude the young, particularly those who have been denied any formal education. Some of the latter may use it as a stepping stone to enter the formal system if our recommendation regarding multiple entry is accepted (6.105-6.106).

The system will have to be organized through community groups. The Panchayats and the Women's Panchayats recommended in Chapter VII would appear to be the ideal bodies for this purpose. Government's role should be limited to providing technical guidance and advice and enabling Government functionaries at the local level to participate in the programme apart from supportive assistance in the form of literature and reading material. Development of basic libraries in village and the slum areas of towns is an imperative necessity for this purpose. We therefore recommend concentration of governmental effort on providing this infrastructure (6.107).

Equality of Sexes as a Major Value to be Inculcated Through the Educational Process

The educational system is the only institution which can counteract traditional belief in inequality of sexes. The educational system today has not even attempted to undertake this responsibility. The schools reflect and strengthen the traditional prejudices through their curricula, classification of subjects on the basis of sex and the unwritten code of conduct enforced on their pupils. This is one area where a major change is needed in the content and organization of education. Educators must admit their responsibility and bring about this much needed change in the values of the younger generation (6.108-111).

Chapter VII-Political Status

Though women's participation in the political process has increased, both in elections and in their readiness to express their views on issues directly concerning their day-to-day life, their ability to produce impact on the political process has been negligible because of the inadequate attention paid to their political status, education and mobilization by both political parties and women's organizations. Parties have tended to see women voters as appendages of the males. Among women, the leadership has become diffused and diverse-with sharp contradictions in their regard and concern for the inequalities that affect the status of women in every sphere-social, economic and political. The revolution in status of women for which constitutional equality was to be only the instrument, still remains a very distant objective. While the position of some groups have changed for the better, the large masses of women continue to lack spokesmen in the representative bodies of the State. Though women do not constitute a minority numerically, they are acquiring the features of one by the inequality of class, status and political power. In this sense the new rights have proved to be only confessional. Our recommendations aim to make women's political rights more functional as required by the needs of a democratic system (7.95-101).

In order to provide greater opportunities to women to actively participate in the decision making process, it is imperative to recognize the true nature of the social inequalities and disabilities that hamper them. This can best be achieved by providing them with special opportunities for participation in the representative structure of local government. The present form of associating women in these bodies, through cooption or nomination has become a kind of tokenism. The time has come to move out of this token provision to a more meaningful association of women in local administration, and to counteract the general apathy and indifference of the local bodies to women's development and change of status (7.115-6).

Women's Panchayats

We therefore recommend the establishment of Statutory Women's Panchayats at the village level with autonomy and resources of their own for the management and administration of welfare and development programmes for women and children, as a transitional measure, to break through the traditional attitudes that inhibit most women from articulating their problems. Women are participating actively in the existing local bodies. They should be directly elected by the women of the village and have the right to send representatives to the Panchayat Samities and/or Zila Parishads. A viable relationship with the Gram Panchayats should be maintained by making the Chairman and Secretary of both bodies ex-officio members of the other.

Reservation on Municipalities

At the level of municipalities, the principle of reservation of seats for women is already prevalent in certain States. We therefore, recommend that this should be adopted by all States as a transitional measure. We also recommend the Constitution of permanent committees in municipalities, to initiate and supervise programmes for women's welfare and development.

Policy for Political Parties

We recommend that political parties should adopt as definite policy regarding the percentage of women candidates to be sponsored by them for elections to Parliament and State Assemblies. While they may initially start with 15 per cent this should be gradually increased so that in time to come the representation of women in the legislative bodies has some relationship to their position in the total population of the country or the State.

Association in Important Bodies

We further recommend the inclusion of women in all important communities, commissions or delegations that are appointed to examine socio-economic problems.

Chapter VIII - Policies and Programmes for Women's Welfare and Development

Health and Family Planning

Demographic indicators, viz., female, maternal and infant mortality rates, and indicators of access to medical care, both reveal an increase in the neglect of female lives as an expendable asset. This is the only reasonable explanation for the declining sex ratio observed to persist over several decades. In our opinion, the neglect of maternity and child health services and general public health services through overconcentration on efforts for family planning have contributed to this trend as well as defeated the ultimate objective of the family planning programme. We are entirely in agreement with the draft Fifth Five-Year Plan that integration of family planning with more positive health services like maternal and child health, and nutrition and improvement in the life expectancy of children and mothers will provide a far greater incentive to the adoption of family planning measures than the hitherto adopted negative approach. While welcoming this proposed integration, we wish to offer certain suggestions with regard to its organization at different levels so that the objective of integration is not defeated by organizational separatism (8.117).

We recommend that:

(a) The rank of the Chief Executive for the integrated maternity and child health services, including family planning, should be upgraded to at least additional Commissioner, so that this service does not again become subordinate to family planning. This procedure should be adopted at all levels of the administration at the Centre and the States.

(b) A separate budget head for maternity and child health services should be created, drawing on the provisions now made for family planning and the general health services. It is important to increase the provision for these services to avoid their being neglected as has been the trend so far. Since programmes for immunization and nutrition of infants yield better results when they form a part of general maternity and child health services, we see no difficulty in increasing the allocation for these services.

(c) At the level of the primary health centres, the maternity and child health services should be separated for purposes of administrative provision, medical personnel and budget. While they may share the same buildings and equipment, a separation of the administrative structure required for maternity and child health services will ensure greater priority of treatment. Facilities in the way of maternity beds, equipment for immunisation of children and family planning for women could be allocated to the MCH Unit. The PHC could be made responsible for sterilization operations for men along with other general health services.

The MCH Unit could coordinate the nutrition and immunization measures which form a basic component of the integrated child development programme. It could also collect and maintain fertility and morbidity statistics for women and children for better research and evaluation in these fields.

We recommend that each MCH centre should collect this data which should be studied and evaluated at the district level by persons of required competence. This will call for a health statistics Section at the district level.

(d) We recommend the abolition of the present practice of providing financial incentives to promoters of family planning. Incentives to women who accept family planning should be in the shape of a token or certificate to ensure them greater priority in health care facilities for both the mothers and their children. Such a step will promote greater acceptance of family planning and correct social attitudes towards these practices. Compensation for loss of wages during sterilization operations should however be paid to daily wage labourers. Others should be given paid leave for this purpose.

(e) The qualifications prescribed for recruitment of personnel for these services in rural areas need to be gradually raised. Until women of requisite higher qualifications are available, the present requirements may continue, but they should be reviewed and progressively increased after three years. Attempts should also be made to obtain the services of older and mature women for these services in the rural areas.

(f) We further recommend the promotion of research in the field of female disorders, e.g., puerperal psychosis and effects of family planning methods.

(g) We disapprove the denial of maternity benefits to women in government service after three children as adopted by some State Governments and recommend rescinding of such orders.

(h) We also recommend that mass campaigns for family planning should also aim to correct prevailing social attitudes regarding fertility and metabolic hereditary disorders and the sex of the child for which the women are generally blamed. Correct information in these matters would go a long way to improve the status of women (8.177).

Changes Needed in the Medical Termination of Pregnancy Act

(a) According to Section 4(a) of the Act, consent of a minor girl is not required for this operation while in other surgical operations of children above 12 such consent is necessary. In our view this distinction is uncalled for and may lead to guardians compelling young girls to undergo this operation even when they do not want it. The consent of the patient should be essential. In the case of a minor girl nearing majority, if the doctor and the patient are in agreement, the consent of the guardian may be dispensed with. In all such cases, greater discretion should be permitted to the doctor (8.85).

(b) Section 8 of the Act provides an overriding precaution to the doctor for any damage caused by the operation. Since no such protection is given for other operations, this seems an unnecessary clause and may lead to negligence. It may, therefore, be dropped (8.85).

(c) While we appreciate the ethical considerations which make many doctors reluctant to perform this operation, we feel that it is a woman's right to have control over the size of her family. At the same time it is important that doctors should have the authority to discourage such operations when they pose definite risk to the health of a patient. The condition being imposed in many hospitals that abortion will only be performed if the patient agrees to sterilization, should not be compulsive. It would be far better to adopt methods of persuasion through expert counselling (8.80-81).

(d) The procedure and paperwork involved in these operations need to be simplified. It is also necessary to extend facilities for authorized termination of pregnancies, particularly in the rural areas (8.83).

(e) Many hospitals continue to insist on the husband's consent before performing these operations though this is not required by the law. A special effort needs to be made to convince the medical profession of the social value of this law from the point of view of both individuals and society (8.83).

(f) Most doctors are reluctant to perform these operations in the case of unmarried girls. It is necessary to clarify the point that rape is not the only ground to justify termination in case of unmarried girls, nor is there any legal obligation on the doctor to inform the police of an operation done in a rape case (8.84).

Welfare and Development

49. In order to prevent any ambiguity in the understanding of what constitutes women's welfare and to prevent the development of policies that sometimes go against the basic objectives, we recommend that the Government of India should evolve a national policy on women's development in the light of the constitutional directives and pledges made to the women of this country and to the international community from time to time (8.178).

In view of the need to maintain links among governmental, voluntary and community effort for promotion of women's welfare and to assist the process of Government planning with actual knowledge and experience of the problems and needs of women at different levels.

We recommend:

(a) Reorganization of the Central Social Welfare Board as a statutory and autonomous specialized agency for planning; coordination and management of welfare and development programmes for women and children.

(b) Reorganization of the State Social Welfare Advisory Boards as statutory autonomous agencies at the State level with similar functions. In addition, the State Boards may also serve as links among the Central agency, the State Government and the local bodies.

Need for Agencies for Coordination, Communication and Implementation of Measures to Improve the Status of Women (Note After Chapter IX):

The UN Commission on the Status of Women in its 25th Report has recommended establishment of a National Commission or similar bodies "with a mandate to review, evaluate and recommend measures and priorities to ensure equality between men and women and the full integration of women in all sectors of national life". We accordingly recommend the Constitution of statutory autonomous Commissions at the Centre and the State with the following functions:

(a) Collection of information on different matters, e.g., education, employment, health, welfare, political participation, impact of social legislation, etc., with its right to call for information on different matters from the concerned agencies of the Government and to suggest improved methods for collection of data in different fields.

(b) Evaluation of existing policies, programmes and laws that have a bearing on status of women with the following powers:

(i) To ensure non-implementation of these measures;

(ii) To point out lacunae or deficiencies in such measures and suggest amendments.

The Commission's criticisms and suggestion made after due consultation with relevant Ministries or Departments of Government should be placed before Parliament or the State Legislatures. They would be answered by the Government within a stated period with explanation or assurances.

(c) Recommendations of new laws, policies or programmes aiming to implement the Directive Principles of State Policy and the objectives of the UN Resolutions and Conventions regarding the status of women. These should be made to Parliament or the State Legislatures and Government will be statutorily responsible to consider such recommendations for action or to explain why they cannot be accepted.

(d) Redressal of grievances in cases of actual violation of existing laws.

The Commissions may be empowered to take effective steps to redress the grievances of effected parties.

Composition of the Commission

The composition of these Commissions should be broadbased, one category being selected for their representative status from different bodies like leading women's organizations, trade unions, legislatures, employers, etc., and the other group consisting of experts from the field of law, health, education, social research planning and administration. The Chairmen and the majority of the members of all the Commissions should be women. The Chairmen should be non-officials, but on a full time basis.

52. We further recommend the establishment of special Tribunals for all violations of human rights, discrimination against women, violation or evasion of existing laws and policies for the protection of women and their rights in society.

Index